CBSE Term II
2022

English Language & Literature

Class X

Chapterwise Summary in All Sections Reading, Writing & Grammar, Literature

Extract Based Questions

Short/ Long Answer Questions

3 Practice Papers

Author
Dolly Jain

ARIHANT PRAKASHAN (School Division Series)

ARIHANT PRAKASHAN (School Division Series)

ॐ **Administrative & Production Offices**

Regd. Office
'Ramchhaya' 4577/15, Agarwal Road, Darya Ganj, New Delhi -110002
Tele: 011- 47630600, 43518550

ॐ **Head Office**
Kalindi, TP Nagar, Meerut (UP) - 250002, Tel: 0121-7156203, 7156204

ॐ **Sales & Support Offices**
Agra, Ahmedabad, Bengaluru, Bareilly, Chennai, Delhi, Guwahati, Hyderabad, Jaipur, Jhansi, Kolkata, Lucknow, Nagpur & Pune.

ॐ **ISBN :** 978-93-25796-65-2

ॐ **PRICE :** ₹200.00

PO No : TXT-XX-XXXXXXX-X-XX

Published by Arihant Publications (India) Ltd.

For further information about the books published by Arihant, log on to www.arihantbooks.com or e-mail at info@arihantbooks.com

Follow us on   

Contents

Watch Free Learning Videos

Subscribe **arihant** You**Tube** Channel

- ☑ Video Solutions of CBSE Sample Papers
- ☑ Chapterwise Important MCQs
- ☑ CBSE Updates

Syllabus

READING

Question based on the following kinds of unseen passages to assess inference, evaluation, vocabulary, analysis and interpretation:

1. Discursive passage (400-450 words)
2. Case based Factual passage (with visual input/ statistical data/ chart etc. 300-350 words)

WRITING SKILL

1. Formal letter based on a given situation
   ☒ Letter of Order
   ☒ Letter of Enquiry
2. Analytical Paragraph (based on outline/chart/cue/map/report etc.)

GRAMMAR

1. Tenses
2. Modals
3. Subject Verb Concord
4. Determiner
5. Reported Speech
6. Commands and Requests
7. Statements
8. Questions

LITERATURE

Questions based on extracts / texts to assess interpretation, inference, extrapolation beyond the text and across the texts.

FIRST FLIGHT

1. Glimpses of India
2. Madam Rides the Bus
3. The Sermon at Benares
4. The Proposal (Play)

POEMS

1. Amanda
2. Animals
3. The Tale of Custard the Dragon

FOOTPRINTS WITHOUT FEET

1. The Making of a Scientist
2. The Necklace
3. The Hack Driver
4. Bholi

CHAPTER 01

Reading Comprehension

In this Chapter...

- Discursive Passages
- Case Based Factual Passages

Reading comprehension or reading the passage is the ability of making meaning from text. The main objective to read the passages is to gain an overall understanding of what is described in the text.

In Class 10th Term 2 examination, two types of passages will be given

(i) **Discursive Passage** (400–450 words) A discursive passage may include the opinion of a person which are generally argumentative, persuasive and interpretative. It allows students to arrive at a conclusion through reasoning and understanding rather than intuition. It presents a balanced and objective approach towards the subject being discussed.

(ii) **Case Based Factual Passage** (300–350 words) A case based factual passage is composed of information in a direct manner about a particular subject. It also contain visual and verbal inputs such as graphs, charts, pie-charts, etc. These passages focus completely on details or facts. It may include instructions, a report or a description. It helps the reader to develop a complete idea of a specific person, place, object or thing.

Steps to Attempt Reading Comprehension Questions

- Read each and every line of the passage carefully. Reading the passage twice is always helpful, as it helps in better understanding and makes it easier for the students to find answers.
- If the title of the passage is given, read it first, as it gives the central idea of the passage.
- Underline the difficult words while reading the passage.
- Always give emphasis on the beginning and end of the passage. These parts often hold the most important information of the passage.
- While answering, be sure that you've clearly understood the question. Answer must be relevant to the question.

Chapter Practice

• Discursive Passages

Read the passages given below carefully.

Passage 1

India 2020
By Dr. APJ Abdul Kalam

1. Nations are built by the imagination and untiring enthusiastic efforts of generations. One generation transfers the fruits of its toil to another, which then takes forward the mission. As the coming generation also has its dreams and aspirations for the nation's future, it therefore adds something from its side to the national vision; which the next generation strives hard to achieve. This process goes on and the nation climbs steps of glory and gains higher strength. The first vision: Freedom of India

2. Any organisation, society or even a nation without a vision is like a ship cruising on the high seas without any aim or direction. It is the clarity of national vision which constantly drives the people towards the goal.

3. Our last generation, the glorious generation of freedom fighters, led by Mahatma Gandhi and many others set for the nation a vision of free India. This was the first vision, set by the people for the nation. It therefore went deep into the minds and the hearts of the masses and soon became the great inspiring and driving force for the people to collectively plunge into the struggle for freedom movement. The unified dedicated efforts of the people from every walk of life won freedom for the country. The second vision: Developed India

4. The next generation (to which I also belong) has put India strongly on the path of economic, agricultural and technological development. But India has stood too long in the line of developing nations. Let us, collectively, set the second national vision of Developed India. I am confident that it is very much possible and can materialise in 15 – 20 years' time. Developed status

5. What does the developed nation status mean for the common man? It means the major transformation of our national economy to make it one of the largest economies in the world, where the countrymen live well above the poverty line, their education and health is of high standard, national security is reasonably assured, and the core competence in certain major areas gets enhanced significantly so that the production of quality goods, including exports, is rising and thereby bringing all-round prosperity for the countrymen.

6. What is the common link needed to realise these sub-goals? It is the technological strength of the nation, which is the key to reach this developed status. Build around our strength

7. The next question that comes to the mind is, how can it be made possible? We have to build and strengthen our national infrastructure in an all-round manner, in a big way. Therefore, we should build around our existing strengths including the vast pool of talented scientists and technologists and our abundant natural resources. The manpower resource should be optimally utilised to harness health care, services sectors and engineering goods sectors.

(410 words)

Questions

Based on your understanding of the passage, answer **any five** out of the seven questions by choosing the correct option.

(i) According to the author, what, from the following, a nation without a vision is?
(a) Futuristic
(b) Prudent
(c) Desultory
(d) Belligerent

(ii) Select the option that suitably completes the dialogue with reference to the above passage.

John: The diversity of India is a gift, wouldn't you agree? I think it adds to the glory of our nation and makes it unique in its existence.

Matt: I do agree. In fact, I think ....
(a) If everyone stays isolated, that would nurture the nation's strength
(b) Unity in diversity is what will make our nation great
(c) Generalisation of every citizen as a part of one single community is very integral to the growth of the nation
(d) It separates our nation and makes India superior than all others

(iii) Choose the option that best conveys the message in – "It therefore went deep into the minds and the hearts of the masses and soon became the great inspiring and driving force…"
(a) A person is a coward because they think they are.
(b) A person is brave because their family and friends support them.
(c) A person's happiness depends upon a healthy relationship with the society.
(d) A person's valour is determined by their contribution to the world.

(iv) What qualities do the writer of the above passage displays when they talk about the necessary steps to build our nation's strength? Choose one option from the following.
(a) Ambitious and alertness
(b) Tendency to help everyone in need
(c) Visionary and confident
(d) Leading people by trying to do everything in their own way

(v) Select the option with the underlined words that can suitably replace 'driving'.
(a) He was the acting force behind the new ballet company.
(b) You should never take chance while swiftly drunk riding a car.
(c) Covered in engine, dragging forcefully the 31-foot propeller shaft for the 2 propellers.
(d) During the first year of the war, he was active in exerting force out and maltreating Union men.

(vi) What does the author advise, in paragraph 7?
(a) To strengthen the nation's technological strength.
(b) To strengthen the nation's defensive strength.
(c) To strengthen the nation's nuclear strength.
(d) To strengthen the nation's educational strength.

(vii) Choose the option that lists the quote best expressing the central idea of the passage.
(a) Not merely a nation, but a nation of nations. (Lyndon B Johnson)
(b) To survive in peace and harmony united and strong, we must have one people, one nation, one flag. (Pauline Hanson)
(c) After climbing a great hill, one only finds that there are many more hills to climb. (Nelson Manela)
(d) In the truest sense, freedom cannot be bestowed; it must be achieved. (F. D. Roosevelt)

Passage 2

1. Archaeology as a profession faces two major problems.

   First, it is the poorest of the poor. Only paltry sums are available for excavating and even less is available for publishing the results and preserving the sites once excavated. Yet archaeologists deal with priceless objects every day.

   Second, there is the problem of illegal excavation, resulting in museum-quality pieces being sold to the highest bidder.

2. I would like to make an outrageous suggestion that would at one stroke provide funds for archaeology and reduce the amount of illegal digging. I would propose that scientific archeological expeditions and governmental authorities sell excavated artifacts on the open market. Such sales would provide substantial funds for the excavation and preservation of archaeological sites and the publication of results. At the same time, they would break the illegal excavator's grip on the market, thereby decreasing the inducement to engage in illegal activities.

3. You might object that professionals excavate to acquire knowledge, not money. Moreover, ancient artifacts are part of our global cultural heritage, which should be available for all to appreciate, not sold to the highest

bidder. I agree. Sell nothing that has unique artistic merit or scientific value. But, you might reply, everything that comes out of the ground has scientific value. Here we part company. Theoretically, you may be correct in claiming that every artifact has potential scientific value. Practically, you are wrong.

4. I refer to the thousands of pottery vessels and ancient lamps that are essentially duplicates of one another. In one small excavation in Cyprus, archaeologists recently uncovered 2,000 virtually indistinguishable small jugs in a single courtyard, even precious royal seal impressions known as 'melekh handles' have been found in abundance — more than 4,000 examples so far.

5. The basement of museums is simply not large enough to store the artifacts that are likely to be discovered in the future. There is not enough money even to catalogue the finds; as a result, they cannot be found again and become as inaccessible as if they had never been discovered. Indeed, with the help of a computer, sold artifacts could be more accessible than are the pieces stored in bulging museum basements. Prior to sale, each could be photographed and the list of the purchasers could be maintained on the computer. A purchaser could even be required to agree to return the piece if it should become needed for scientific purposes. It would be unrealistic to suggest that illegal digging would stop if artifacts were sold in the open market. But the demand for the clandestine product would be substantially reduced. Who would want an unmarked pot when another was available whose provenance was known, and that was dated stratigraphically by the professional archaeologist who excavated it?

(454 words)

Questions

Based on your understanding of the passage, answer **any five** out of the seven questions by choosing the correct option.

(i) According to the author, what, from the following, is the lesson taught by the process of excavation?
   (a) Archaeology is the most important branch of studies.
   (b) Finding and preserving artifacts is integral to knowing more about our cultural past.
   (c) Earth has many valuable objects hidden which must be found and sold.
   (d) Nothing should remain hidden for a very long time.

(ii) Select the option that suitably completes the dialogue with reference to the above passage.

   Dev: I think in order to save the ancient findings from being sold illegally, we should sell them in open markets.

   Prachi: I agree but ....
   (a) Only the artifacts that are not of import and are excavated in multiple quantity
   (b) Not the artifacts that are of scientific or historic importance
   (c) It is not our decision or concern should we should not discuss it
   (d) Both (a) and (b)

(iii) Choose the option that best conveys the message in – 'Practically, you are wrong.'
   (a) One must leave everything on God and have faith that all will be right.
   (b) One must strive to do better in life, every step of the way.
   (c) One must not despair in life and try their best to make things better.
   (d) Money and success are the most important things in life.

(iv) Which of the following can be said about the people in the profession of archaeology?
   (a) Collectors of artifacts
   (b) Seekers of knowledge
   (c) Smugglers of knowledge
   (d) Acquire of knowledge for business purposes

(v) Select the option with the underlined words that can suitably replace 'clandestine'. (Paragraph 5)
   (a) The result of weeks of <u>public planning</u> now sat hidden inside the bedside cupboard.
   (b) The proceeds went to fund its <u>justifiably correct</u> war against the Russians.
   (c) There had been some sort of <u>secretly conducted</u> liaison between the lady and Darrel for sometime.
   (d) Gagan became much more <u>open and frank</u> when asked about the lyrical contents of his songs.

(vi) Which of the following words means "a study of human activity through recovery and analysis of material culture"?
   (a) Stratigraphically   (b) Archaeologist
   (c) Archaeology   (d) Excavation

(vii) Select the qualities that the author seems to exhibit, on the basis of your reading of the passage.
   (1) Conniving   (2) Business-minded
   (3) Shrewd   (4) Sharp
   (5) Clever
   (a) 1 and 3   (b) 2, 4 and 5
   (c) 1, 3 and 4   (d) 2 and 5

Passage 3

1. Do children really need such long summer breaks, was a question posed by some experts recently. Apparently, such a long break disrupts their development and comes in the way of their learning process. Let's get the takes back to their books, is perhaps the expert view, if not in so many words. One would have thought the children are doing too much during their vacations and not too little, given the plethora of course, classes, camps and workshop involving swimming, art, personality development, music, computers and the like that seem to cram their calendar. Even the trips taken in the name of holidays seem laden with exotic destinations and customised experience packed into a short period of time. We can go Europe in 10 days and Australia in a week and come back armed with digital memories and overflowing suitcase. Holidays are, in some ways, no longer a break but an intensified search for experience not normally encountered in everyday life.

2. It is a far cry from summer holidays one experienced while growing up. For holidays every year meant one thing and one thing alone—you went back to your native place, logging in with emotional headquarters of your extended family and spent two months with a gaggle of uncles, aunts and first and second cousins. The happiest memories of the childhood of a whole generation seem to be centered around this annual ritual of homecoming and of affirmation. We tendered tacit apologies for the separateness entailed in being individuals even as we scurried back into the cauldron of community and continuity represented by family. Summer vacation was a time sticky with oneness, as who we were and what we owned oozed out from our individual selves into a collective pot.

3. Summer was not really a break, but a joint. It was the bridge used to re-affirm one's connectedness with one's larger community. One did not travel, one returned. It was not an attempt to experience the new and the extraordinary but one that emphatically underlined the power of the old and the ordinary. As times change, what we seek from our summer breaks too has changed in fundamental ways. Today, we are attached much more to the work and summer helps us temporarily detach from this new source of identity. Summer breaks have become like working vacations, especially for the children. We refuel our individual selves now and do so with much more material than we did in the past. But for those who grew up in different times, summer vacation was the best time of their lives.

(429 words)

Questions

Based on your understanding of the passage, answer **any five** out of the seven questions by choosing the correct option.

(i) According to the passage, what, from the following, is the lesson being taught by the author's nostalgic mention of the summer holidays of the older times?

(a) It was a time when everyone looked for adventure and new experiences.

(b) It was a time when everyone went back to their homes and relaxed.

(c) It was a time when everyone apologised to their loved ones.

(d) It was a time of mending broken relationships and building new ones.

(ii) Select the option that suitably completes the dialogue with reference to the above passage.

Jai: Vacations are starting from next week. Let's get together to decide where we want to go on a tour. What do you think?

Prateek: No, I can't come with you. My parents ....

(a) Are taking me and my siblings to our grandparents' village to meet our relatives

(b) Want me to stay home and work on my studies

(c) Are going to visit my grandparents and have asked me to stay back at home

(d) Want me to work during the vacations

(iii) Choose the option that best conveys the message in – 'Summer was not really a break, but a joint.'

(a) It was a time to get away from one's hectic life to have some relaxation time.

(b) Friends met in summer break to enjoy some time together.

(c) It was a time to build one's professional career.

(d) People got the chance to connect with their families.

(iv) What qualities do children of today's world display during their summer vacations, as highlighted by the author in the first paragraph? Choose one option from the following.

(a) Talented yet distracted

(b) Observational and alert

(c) Laid back and relaxed

(d) Hard working and determined

(v) Select the option with the underlined words that can suitably replace 'scurried' (paragraph 2).

(a) The agent <u>stayed away</u> and Denton immediately turned on <u>her</u>.

(b) Delivery people <u>made haste</u> about situating floral arrangements and dry ice.

(c) Dayton angrily followed her as she <u>hid secretly</u> in the room upstairs.

(d) He was <u>keenly observing</u> to observe how far from the parent <u>rock any pebbles</u> could be found.

(vi) An Oxymoron is a figure of speech in which apparently contradictory terms appear in conjunction.

From the options given below, select an Oxymoron that appears in the above passage.

(a) Summer break
(b) Annual ritual
(c) Working vacation
(d) Customised experience

(vii) Select the qualities, from the passage, that the author wants us to imbibe during summer vacations.

(1) Anti-social
(2) Acceptive
(3) Emotional
(4) Isolated
(5) Forgiving

(a) 2, 4 and 5
(b) 2 and 5
(c) 1, 3 and 4
(d) 1, 2 and 3

Passage 4

1. Over the last few days, Delhi residents have been protesting against the government's approval for felling over 14,000 trees in South Delhi. Faced with severe criticism, the National Buildings Construction Corporation, tasked with redeveloping half a dozen South Delhi colonies, on Monday assured the Delhi High Court that no trees would be cut for the project till July 4, which is transitory relief. Many of the trees proposed to be felled are mature, local, fruit-bearing ones that provide clean air, shade and water recharge to humans and are homes to many birds. These areas of Delhi have served as the 'lungs' of the city. However, the project reports overlook these qualities.

2. Large constructions have been difficult to manage in India. The sector has systematically lobbied to be excluded from the environmental norms of the country and has been successful in carving out special privileges for itself in the environment clearance process. From 2006, most construction projects have been approved based on an application form instead of detailed assessment reports. In 2014, schools, colleges and hostels for educational institutions were exempted from taking environment clearances as long as they followed specific sustainability parameters. In 2016, projects with areas of less than 20,000 sq m were permitted to proceed as long as they submitted a self-declaration ensuring adherence to environmental norms. As a result of these privileges, construction projects contribute significantly to urban air and noise pollution and high water consumption in cities. Compensatory afforestation taken up in lieu of trees felled by projects is a failure due to poor survival rates of saplings and no monitoring.

3. Yet all regulatory bodies treat large constructions with kid gloves. The Minister for Urban Development has stated that this public campaign is 'misinformed'. But that is far from the truth. In a literate, urban society that has high access to the Internet, the lack of official information on urban development and its impacts can only be understood as an indirect form of public silencing. There are no public hearings held for urban construction projects and governments assume that citizens have nothing to say about them. Since Delhi is ruled by so many agencies, you can run from pillar to post and still not have a clue about who is in charge of what. The residents are now appealing to the government to embrace inclusive ways of redesigning the city. The governments could join hands by committing to review these projects.

4. One of the severe side effects of constantly lessening number of trees in the city is the increase in air pollution, which is only adding to the already existing gigantic issue of smog that ails the city in winters. *(444 words)*

Questions

Based on your understanding of the passage, answer **any five** out of the seven questions by choosing the correct option.

(i) According to the author, what, from the following, is the greatest lesson to be learnt from the above passage?

(a) Steps must be taken to ensure that no government can do as they wish and harm anyone in the process.
(b) Steps must be taken to ensure that any construction that happens follows the environmental norms.
(c) Steps must be taken to ensure that trees are grown in large numbers around the city.
(d) Steps must be taken by the general public to hinder any such construction that may have adverse affect on the environment.

(ii) Select the option that suitably completes the dialogue with reference to the above passage.

Kajal: Many trees have been cut down to make space for the new apartments near our society. It is very unfair. The birds have already left. Don't you agree?

Vaibhav: ....

(a) No, I don't. We need more homes to live

(b) Yes, I do. But it's not too bad. They are going to use the wood in making the houses

(c) No, I don't. It is not of our concern

(d) Yes, I do. It is very bad for nature and for all living beings

(iii) Choose the option that best conveys the message in – "These areas of Delhi have served as the 'lungs' of the city."

(a) Due to presence of many trees, the Ministry for Urban Development provides oxygen for most of the city.

(b) Due to presence of many trees, the urban society provides oxygen for most of the city.

(c) Due to presence of many trees, the South Delhi area provides oxygen for most of the city.

(d) Due to presence of many trees, the Delhi uses most of the oxygen from the city.

(iv) What qualities do the large construction companies display when extract special privileges for them in environment clearance process? Choose one option from the following.

(a) Shrewd and self-serving

(b) Philanthropist and ameliorating

(c) Sadistic behaviour toward the destitute

(d) Malignant and hostile

(v) A Portmanteau [words like brunch (breakfast + lunch)] is a blend of words in which parts of multiple words are combined to form a new word. From the options given below, select a Portmanteau word that appears in the above passage.

(a) Sapling   (b) Felled

(c) Smog   (d) Recharge

(vi) Select the qualities that are being discussed in the line – "However, the project reports overlook these qualities".

(1) The benefits that the presence of trees provide to all living beings.

(2) The enthusiasm of people to save their environment.

(3) The importance of trees in the environment.

(4) The laidback approach of the Judiciary.

(5) The destruction and noise pollution accompanying the projects.

(a) 1 and 3   (b) 2, 3 and 5

(c) 1, 4 and 5   (d) 2 and 4

(vii) Choose the option that contains the correct meaning of the given idiom, as used in the third paragraph.

Treat/handle with kid gloves

(a) To upset someone by treating them like a child.

(b) To equate someone with a child.

(c) To deal gently and tactfully with someone.

(d) To say that someone is very childish.

Passage 5

1. Every event a person sees and every noise he hears is part of a life that has been created for him as a unit. Whether major or insignificant, no event in the universe happens by coincidence. No flower blooms or fades by chance. No man comes into existence or dies out of pure coincidence. No man becomes sick by mistake and neither does his sickness develop in an uncontrolled manner. In each case these occurrences are especially predestined by God, from the very moment they were created.

2. Destiny is something that you have been creating unconsciously. You can also create it consciously. You can rewrite it; all that we do in the form of a spiritual process is just that. If you can touch the core within you, if you can experience that the source of creation is within you and then shift your whole focus on yourself, you can rewrite your own destiny. This is true as far as I know.

3. All the time your focus is scattered because what you consider as 'me' is your house, your car, your wife, your children, your education, your position and your other identities. If I strip you of all these things, including your body and mind, which are just accumulations, you will feel like a nobody.

4. Once you become a true individual, your destiny is yours. Individual comes from 'indivisible' – it cannot be divided any more. It cannot be here and there. Why people in the spiritual process, who are in a hurry for spiritual growth, are not getting into marriage, children and relationships, is because the moment you have a wife or a husband, you fall into a trap. 'Me' gets identified with the others. The significance of Sanyasi and Brahmacharya is to just shift your focus on you. When I say 'you', it is just 'you', not your body or mind.

5. If you are unable to be like that, you just choose one identity. When you say 'you', make it you and your Guru. You attach yourself to the Guru without any hesitation because you can get as entangled as you want with him but he is not going to get entangled. The moment you are 'ripe' you can drop the attachment. With other relationships, it is never so. Even if you want to get free, the others will not let you go. So, just create a longing to grow, to dissolve, to know. What has to happen will happen. Once you become an individual, your destiny becomes yours. Once your destiny is happening in awareness, the next step will happen by itself, because life within you has the intelligence to choose freedom.

(444 words)

Questions

Based on your understanding of the passage, answer **any five** out of the seven questions by choosing the correct option.

(i) According to the passage, what, from the following, is the greatest lesson being taught by the author?
   (a) Destiny can be changed and re-written if one focuses on one's surroundings.
   (b) Destiny can never be changed by selfish people like Sanyasis and Brahmacharyas.
   (c) Every person creates their own destiny.
   (d) Every person's destiny is already set in stone by God.

(ii) Select the option that suitably completes the dialogue with reference to the above passage.

   Maya: I have decided to become a Sanyasi and follow the path of spiritualism. Please join me.

   Atharva: ....
   (a) Yes, after all it's the path to self-discovery.
   (b) Yes. What is left in the world anyway?
   (c) No. It's a hoax and cannot teach anyone anything.
   (d) No. Individual thinking that spiritualism promotes is very selfish and harmful to the society.

(iii) Which of the following sentences from the above passage is not an example of 'happenstance'?
   (a) "This is true as far as I know."
   (b) "Once you become a true individual, your destiny is yours."
   (c) "What has to happen will happen."
   (d) "No man becomes sick by mistake and neither does his sickness develop in an uncontrolled manner."

(iv) What qualities do the Sanyasis and Brahmacharyas imbibe on their quest of spiritual growth? Choose one option from the following.

(a) Self-assessment and devotion
(b) Selfless assistance of others
(c) Emphasis on the complete disregard for others
(d) Self-doubt and depreciation

(v) Select the option with the underlined words that can suitably replace 'entangle' (paragraph 5).
   (a) He became <u>extremely angry</u> in what can only be called two intrigues.
   (b) An <u>overly enlarged</u> whale can survive for a long time if its <u>feeding ability</u> is not impaired, according to Straley.
   (c) But the bear hadn't killed the bull until it <u>became hidden</u> in the brush.
   (d) We managed to <u>twist together</u> the string of lights into a hopeless mess of wires.

(vi) Select the qualities from the passage, that the author wants us to imbibe.
   (1) Atheist   (2) Anti-social
   (3) Individualistic (4) Introspective
   (5) Confining
   (a) 1, 3 and 4   (b) 1, 3 and 5
   (c) 2, 4 and 5   (d) 3 and 4

(vii) Choose the option that lists the quote best expressing the central idea of the passage.
   (a) When you connect to the silence within you, that is when you can make sense of the disturbance going on around you. (Stephen Richards)
   (b) To the mind that is still, the whole universe surrenders. (Lao Tzu)
   (c) It is not until you come to a spiritual understanding of who you are, not necessarily a religious feeling, but deep down, the spirit within, that you can begin to take control. (Oprah Winfrey)
   (d) You have to grow from the inside out. None can teach you, none can make you spiritual. There is no other teacher, but your own soul. (Swami Vivekananda)

Passage 6

1. Right from the early Vedic period people have been celebrating the birth of a son, but in those days daughters born into a family were not neglected but were educated properly. This changed during the later Vedic Age and daughters were considered a social burden. Only girls belonging to upper class families enjoyed the right of education and got proper nourishment.

2. In the medieval period the conditions deteriorated for the females and, even in royal families, girls could not get the same status as boys. In Muslim households they were taught at their homes while Hindu girls were privileged by getting primary education in nearby schools.

3. From thereon, the condition of the females in the society only worsened. However, in the nineteenth century, many social reformers like Raja Ram Mohan Roy, Sir Syed Ahmed Khan, Annie Besant, MG Ranade, Jyotiba Phule, Swami Dayanand Saraswati, etc came forward for the emancipation of women in India. In fact, Raja Ram Mohan Roy fervently advocated female education.

4. Since then, there has been a tremendous progress in every field but unfortunately girls are still neglected. In most of the families birth of a girl child is not desired, and even when accepted, they are considered as inferior to boys and their education is not considered important because it seems like wastage of money to most of the parents. They think it unreasonable because afterwards they would be compelled to spend a heavy amount of money on their dowry. So, the female literacy rate has grown unsatisfactory and has a direct impact upon the overall development and growth of the nation.

5. If India wants to be a developed nation, it must concentrate on female education. The old African proverb – "If you educate a man, you educate an individual, but if you educate a woman, you educate an entire family (nation) focuses on the fact that the root cause of all the problems women are facing is the lack of education. If women are educated, then all problems like female infanticide, dowry, female suicides, domestic battering, malnutrition of women, child marriage and other related atrocities would vanish from India. Education provides an essential qualification to fulfill certain economic, political and cultural functions and improves women's socio-economic status. It brings reduction in inequalities. If their standard of living is improved, it will indirectly uplift the society. If they are financially strong, they will be able to take proper care of their children and provide them with good education. *(411 words)*

Questions

Based on your understanding of the passage, answer **any five** out of the seven questions by choosing the correct option.

(i) According to the author, what, from the following, is the greatest lesson being taught by the Vedic period?
(a) Girls are burden to their families.
(b) Equal treatment of boys and girls.
(c) Only upper class girls deserve proper education.
(d) The birth of a boy should be celebrated lavishly.

(ii) Select the option that suitably completes the dialogue with reference to the above passage.

Shruti: Now that school is over, what are your plans for the future?

Kaira: I want to study at Yale, but my parents ....
(a) sent my brother there
(b) won't allow me because it is too far
(c) don't want me to study any further
(d) want me to study there as well

(iii) What does the author mean by the phrase 'emancipation of women'?
(a) Liberating women from their previous deteriorating condition.
(b) Worsening the condition of women in society.
(c) Abasement of men in the society.
(d) Enslavement of men in order to liberate women.

(iv) What qualities do social reformers like Raja Ram Mohan Roy display? Choose one from the following.
(a) Selfish assistance to help other people.
(b) A dauntless attitude towards life.
(c) Determination to help and protect others.
(d) Fearful for people who are suffering.

(v) Select the option with the underlined words that can suitably replace 'fervently' (paragraph 2).
(a) He was incorrigibly frivolous, idle and unconcerned; his father had given.
(b) He spoke with passionate intensity of the opportunity which offered itself to those who loved the freedom of Greece.
(c) I ask all in favor to stop being so typically aggressive and voice your opinion.
(d) Left to himself, Louis might have been too violently revolutionary for resistance.

(vi) Select the option that lists the social evils that will be cured by the education of women.
(1) child marriage
(2) domestic violence
(3) caste distinction
(4) female foeticide
(5) xenophobia
(a) 1, 2 and 3   (b) 2, 4 and 5
(c) 2, 3 and 4   (d) 1, 2 and 4

(vii) Choose the option that lists the quote best expressing the central idea of the passage.
(a) All I want is education and I am afraid of no one. (Malala Yousafzai)
(b) Education, leading to financial independence, has surely made women empowered. (Sudha Murty)
(c) When girls are educated, their countries become stronger and more prosperous. (Michelle Obama)
(d) Men and Women must be educated, in a great degree, by the opinions and manners of the society they live in. (Mary Wollstonecraft)

Passage 7

1. Everybody wants to succeed in life. For some, success means achieving whatever they desire or dream. For many it is the name, fame and social position. Whatever be the meaning of success, it is success which makes a man popular.

2. All great men have been successful. They are remembered for their great achievements. But it is certain that success comes to those who are sincere, hardworking, loyal and committed to their goals. Success has been man's greatest motivation. It is very important for all. Success has a great effect on life. It brings pleasure and pride. It gives a sense of fulfillment. It means all-around development. Everybody hopes to be successful in life. But success smiles on those who have a proper approach, planning, vision and stamina. A proper and timely application of all these things is bound to bear fruit. One cannot be successful without cultivating these certain basic things in life. It is very difficult to set out on a journey without knowing one's goals and purposes. Clarity of the objective is a must to succeed in life. A focused approach with proper planning is certain to bring success. Indecision and insincerity are big obstacles on the path to success.

3. One should have the capability, capacity and resources to turn one's dreams into reality. Mere desire cannot bring you success. The desire should be weighed against factors like capability and resources.

   This is the basic requirement of success. The next important thing is the eagerness, seriousness and the urge to be successful. It is the driving force which decides the success. It is the first step on the ladder of success.

4. One needs to pursue one's goals with sincerity and passion. One should always be in high spirit. Lack of such spirit leads to an inferiority complex which is a big obstruction on the path to success. Time is also a deciding factor. Only the punctual and committed have succeeded in life. Lives of great men are examples of this. They had all these qualities in plenty which helped them rise to the peak of success.

5. Hard labour is also one of the basic requirements of success. There is no substitute for hard labour. It alone can take one to the peak of success. Every success has a ratio of five percent inspiration and ninety-five percent perspiration. It is the patience, persistence and perseverance which play a decisive role in achieving success. Failures are the pillars of success as they are our stepping-stones and we must get up and start again and be motivated.

(426 words)

Questions

Based on your understanding of the passage, answer **any five** out of the seven questions by choosing the correct option.

(i) According to the author, what, from the following, is first and foremost step on the journey to achieve success?
  (a) Keenness and urge to be successful
  (b) Indecisive behaviour and sincerity
  (c) To be very inspired
  (d) Punctuality and divided commitment

(ii) Select the option that suitably completes the dialogue with reference to the above passage.

   Jiya: One day I'll be very successful, like my grandfather, father and brother. It is in my genetics to become successful. It doesn't matter what I do or how I do it, I know I am sure to be successful.

   Ruhi: You mustn't think like that. Success ....
  (a) Only comes to those fail a lot
  (b) Is not for spoiled-brats like you
  (c) Is only ever going to bless people like me
  (d) Only comes to those who work hard to achieve it

(iii) Choose the option that best conveys the message in – 'It gives a sense of fulfillment'.
  (a) Failure makes you understand success.
  (b) Achieving success feels like a person's life's purpose is fulfilled.
  (c) Hard work never goes unrewarded.
  (d) Success means achieving everything you want.

(iv) Select the option with the underlined words that can suitably replace 'persistence' (paragraph 5).
  (a) He admired her dogged <u>continuing effort</u> in pursuing the job.
  (b) By the time the rebel troops arrived, the village had already been <u>cast aside</u>.
  (c) The son was reluctant to <u>turn over</u> involvement in the company.
  (d) This illness induced a spiritual change, and he resolved to <u>sign away</u> whatever kept him back from God.

(v) A Metaphor is a figure of speech in which a word or phrase is applied to an object or action to which it is not literally applicable.

   From the options given below, select a phrase from the above passage that can be an example of metaphor.

(a) "…labour is also one of the basic requirements…"
(b) "… they are our stepping-stones…"
(c) "It is the first step on the ladder of success."
(d) Both (b) and (c)

(vi) Which of the following shows the correct meaning of the phrase – "Whatever be the meaning of success"?
(a) Success means to become powerful, rich and famous.
(b) Success can mean different thing to different people.
(c) Success is the acquiring of money through whichever method possible.

(d) Success is the acquiring of knowledge through whichever method possible.

(vii) Choose the option that lists the quote best expressing the central idea of the passage.
(a) Success is not the key to happiness. Happiness is the key to success. (Albert Schweitzer)
(b) A successful man is one who can lay a firm foundation with the bricks others have thrown at him. (David Brinkley)
(c) The successful warrior is the average man, with laser-like focus. (Bruce Lee)
(d) Success is the result of perfection, hard work, learning from failure, loyalty, and persistence. (Colin Powell)

Passage 8

1. In the days gone by, heroes emerged when wars broke out and messiahs appeared when decadence overtook societies. Through the centuries, adversities have inspired people to rise to the occasion and display special skills which have earned them the label of a leader.

2. The driving force behind a leader's actions and behaviour is his instinct. It guides silently, telling him what to do, which way to go and how to develop skills that can enable him to overcome any challenge that life proposes. Abraham Lincoln failed in almost all his endeavours through his life. And yet his instinct urged him to keep trying, finally culminating in earning him the highest seat of political leadership in America.

3. So what is instinct? Is it genetic, or is it cultivated? Instinct is what drives a newborn into sensing that he is hungry or cold, making him cry for help.

4. It can be best described as a compass of objective observation, although born with it, we tend to lose touch with our instinct as we grow older.

5. If everybody is born with this sense, why is it that some people become leaders and others don't? Firstly, external circumstances greatly dictate our evolution. All people who are deprived of opportunities to develop their latent abilities fail to grow into leaders.

6. The second reason relates to internal attitude. There are many people who, despite being blessed with all the right opportunities, still fail. This is because they are insensitive to their own instincts, ignoring all the signals that can enable them to act appropriately. Listening is a critical skill that needs to be evolved over time. While our earlier experiences enable us to list and put evaluated choices, it is eventually our instinct that helps us in determining which one to go for. At such times, people who are tuned in to their instincts are more likely to make the right decisions than those who are not. Instinct is like a psychomotor. When a leader gives his team an emotionally charged speech in the attempt to motivate them into action, he can invariably tell even before he has completed it, whether or not he has succeeded. In fact, right through the process of speaking, he is constantly modulating his behaviour.

7. Leadership is a quest for doing the right things, a quest that is initiated not for fulfilling one's own selfish needs but for the greater good of all concerned.

(409 words)

Questions

Based on your understanding of the passage, answer **any five** out of the seven questions by choosing the correct option.

(i) According to the author, what, from the following, is the greatest lesson being learnt about instincts?
(a) If cultivated properly, instincts can help a person become a great leader.
(b) If cultivated properly, instincts can help a person make proper observation.
(c) If cultivated properly, instincts can help a person be very successful.
(d) If cultivated properly, instincts can help a person modulate their behaviour.

(ii) Select the option that suitably completes the dialogue with reference to the above passage.

Jyoti: I didn't get many opportunities in life to help develop my leadership skills. Thus, my father's entire business went to my younger sister.

Uday: I am sorry to hear that. I myself was .... failed to become a leader.

(a) Full of self doubt which is why I

(b) Tried very hard to improve my skills and as a result,

(c) Filled with courage and determination but

(d) In a different boat as you and

(iii) Choose the option that best conveys the message in – '…reason relates to internal attitude'.

    (a) A person's behaviour towards their instincts is not really important.

    (b) A person's behaviour towards their instincts is equally important.

    (c) A person's behaviour towards their surroundings is equally important.

    (d) A person's behaviour towards the opportunities is not really important.

(iv) What qualities do Abraham Lincoln display that eventually made him the president of the USA? Choose one option from the following:

    (a) Hard work

    (b) Determination to help other

    (c) Self-sacrificing attitude towards life

    (d) Never give up trying

(v) Select the option with the underlined words that can suitably replace 'latent' (paragraph 5).

    (a) The <u>obviously active</u> heat of vaporisation of mercury was found by Marignac to be 103 to 106.

    (b) Being at high risk is a <u>second-to-last</u> stage of coronary heart disease.

    (c) When the builders dug into the ground, they discovered a <u>quite dormant</u> source of oil.

    (d) The <u>plainly palpable</u> opposition was aroused by the Vatican decrees.

(vi) Which of the following is shown by the example of Abraham Lincoln?

    (a) That he was a great man.

    (b) That he was a President of the USA.

    (c) That he trusted his instincts and acted accordingly.

    (d) That he was calculative and never did a thing without thinking.

(vii) Choose the option that lists the quote best expressing the central idea of the passage.

    (a) Trust your own instinct. Your mistakes might as well be your own, instead of someone else's. (Billy Wilder)

    (b) There is no instinct like that of the heart. (Lord Byron)

    (c) Women have a wonderful instinct about things. They can discover everything except the obvious. (Oscar Wilde)

    (d) I would rather trust a woman's instinct than a man's reason. (Stanley Baldwin)

Passage 9

1. The therapeutic value and healing powers of plants were demonstrated to me when I was a boy of about ten. I had developed an acute persistent abdominal pain that did not respond readily to hospital medication. My mother had taken me to the city's central hospital on several occasions, where different drugs were tried on me. In total desperation, she took me to Egya Mensa, a well-known herbalist in my hometown in the Western province of Ghana.

2. After a brief interview, he went out to the field. He returned with several leaves and the bark of a tree and one of his attendants immediately prepared a decoction. I was given a glass of this preparation, it tasted extremely bitter, but within an hour or so I began to feel relieved. Within about three days, the frequent abdominal pain stopped and I recall gaining a good appetite. I have appreciated the healing powers of medicinal plants ever since.

3. In fact, demographic studies by various national governments and inter-governmental organisations such as the World Health Organisation (WHO) indicate that for 75 to 90 per cent of the rural populations of the world, the herbalist is the only person who handles their medical problems.

4. In African culture, traditional medical practitioners are always considered to be influential, spiritual leaders as well, using magic and religion along with medicines. Illness is handled with the individual's hidden spiritual powers and with application of plants that have been found especially to contain healing powers.

5. Over the years I have come to distinguish three types of medicinal practitioners in African societies and to classify the extent to which each uses medicinal plants. The first is the herbalist, who generally enjoys the prestige and reputation of being the real traditional medical professional. The second group represents the divine healers. They are fetish priests whose practice depends upon their purported supernatural powers of diagnosis. Thirdly, the witch doctor, the practitioner who is credited with the ability to intercept the evil deeds of a witch.

6. From the drugstores in New Delhi, I picked up some well-packaged bark and roots of Rauwolfia Serpentina, a plant that was very well known in ancient Asiatic medicine. The storekeeper said that it cures hypertension.

7. For health, social and economic reasons, it seems clear that developing countries should begin an extensive programme aimed at an examination and research into the properties of the most important medicinal plants. In most countries, the information on such plants is dispersed and unorganised. Much of it is in the heads of aging herbalists, who represent a dying breed.

(Adapted from Edward S. Ayensu-Worldwide Role of the Healing Power of Plants)   *(446 words)*

Questions

Based on your understanding of the passage, answer **any five** out of the seven questions by choosing the correct option.

(i) According to the author, what, from the following, is the greatest lesson to be learnt from the story of how Egya Mensa helped the author?
- (a) Healing powers of medicinal plants should not be exaggerated.
- (b) Healing powers of medicinal plants should be questioned.
- (c) Healing powers of medicinal plants should not be underestimated.
- (d) Only allopathic medicines should be trusted with severe cases.

(ii) Select the option that suitably completes the dialogue with reference to the above passage.

Akshat: I can only trust modern medicines with any kind of disease. They have a proper and trustworthy method of treatment, unlike herbal medicine which can never truly cure anything.

Rhea: I don't agree with you. I've heard of instance where ....
- (a) Herbal medicine has saved lives when drugs couldn't
- (b) Herbal medicine has taken lives
- (c) Herbal medicine has accelerated the affliction
- (d) None of the above

(iii) Select the option with the underlined words that can suitably replace 'purported' (paragraph 5).
- (a) The range includes products that are dyed using a natural water based dye that is completely <u>confirmed</u> not to fade.
- (b) However, since its introduction, its <u>without proof</u> advantages have been widely known.
- (c) Doing so may render invalid any <u>illegally acquired</u> acceptance of the Offer.
- (d) In spring 2008, a controversy erupted regarding the <u>mystical dangers</u> of consuming too much soy.

(iv) A Compound Noun is a word which if made up of two or more existing words.

From the options given below, select a compound noun that appears in the above passage.
- (a) Unorganised
- (b) Illness
- (c) Drugstore
- (d) Decoction

(v) Select the qualities that a 'divine healer' would display based on the author's description.
- (1) Fake   (2) Helping
- (3) Fraudulent   (4) Manipulative
- (5) Guileless
- (a) 2 and 5   (b) 1, 4 and 5
- (c) 2 and 3   (d) 1, 3 and 4

(vi) What does the writer advise the developing countries to do?
- (a) Maintain the information on medicinal plants in an unorganised manner.
- (b) Research the properties of the medicinal plants.
- (c) Disperse the information on medicinal plants.
- (d) All of the above

(vii) Choose the option that lists the quote best expressing the central idea of the passage.
- (a) Nature itself is the best physician. (Hippocrates)
- (b) The plants have enough vision to transform our limited vision. (Rosemary Gladstar)
- (c) It can accurately be said that plants created, and continue to create, the world we live in. (David Crow)
- (d) Often, people take herbal medicines for physical response, but what they find is that the body also responds in an emotional way to the plant medicine that they're taking. (Karen Rose)

Passage 10

1. Frankness may be among the most overrated of virtues! And here's why. Because unrestricted and unfiltered frankness is a recipe for breaking relationships, even the closest ones. Such frankness is understandable, acceptable and even 'cute' only in children under the age of five.

2. Thinking before one speaks and using restraint are hallmarks of growing maturity and preparation for life. Learning to put a filter between thought and spoken word (and, even more importantly, written word) is an important life skill. Think is a popular acronym for Trúe, Helpful, Inspiring, Necessary and Kind. This would do wonderfully well as a filter in our minds.

3. It is good to speak what's true, but only along with the other attributes in the acronym, particularly the last one, kindness. In the righteous glow of speaking what we see as the truth, we often forget to be kind. We blurt out 'truths' even when it is totally unhelpful and unnecessary to do so, let alone inspiring! Too often, such truth–telling is destructive rather than noble. Only those who do not care about the consequences can afford the luxury of 'speaking their minds' whenever and wherever they please. When relationships are at stake, it is essential to choose the time, place and words appropriately when imparting unpleasant truths. And even then, only when absolutely necessary and with the utmost kindness.

4. Speaking without forethought can be even more dangerous in other circumstances, for example, when someone has entrusted us with a secret. A sign of maturity is the ability to keep a secret. Very young children are incapable of understanding the concept of a secret. To them, every piece of information is interesting, new and meant to be shared. As we grow older, we all learn how to keep a secret, but too often we keep only our own secrets and not those that others confide in us. We may blurt out something a friend told us in confidence, perhaps carelessly but often to appear important in other people's estimation. It gives us a sense of power to know something that our friends don't, and it requires conscious effort to keep the information to ourselves.

5. But this is the real test of an important life skill: self–restraint. Revealing a friend's secret is betrayal of the friendship. It may lead to gossip spreading like a wildfire, destroying peace of mind and even lives. Words thoughtlessly spoken can bring the end of the world.

6. Of course it is important to communicate. But it is far more important to be considerate and compassionate. Speaking well is a skill: speaking kindly is a life skill.

(442 words)

Questions

Based on your understanding of the passage, answer **any five** out of the seven questions by choosing the correct option.

(i) According to the author, what, from the following, is the greatest lesson being taught by the acronym 'think'?
 (a) Necessary truths must be shared.
 (b) Truth must always be shared with others.
 (c) Only necessary truths should be shared and with kindness.
 (d) People should always keep their friends' secrets.

(ii) Select the option that suitably completes the dialogue with reference to the above passage.

 Prachi: I should just tell my sister about our parents' divorce, don't you think? She is going to find out about it in a few days anyway.

 Anita: No, you shouldn't tell her. It is not your place as it is not your secret. ....
 (a) Let your parents suffer her temper tantrum after telling her
 (b) Let your parents tell her. They will be able to explain better
 (c) She should find it from me, her best friend
 (d) She knows they fight all the time. I'm sure she might've already guessed

(iii) Choose the option that best conveys the message in – 'spreading like a wildfire'.
 (a) Taking time and slowly affecting everyone.
 (b) Become known very quickly.
 (c) Destroy everything in the path.
 (d) Cause the demise of everyone who knows about the secret.

(iv) Which of the following is the writer warning against in paragraph 4?
 (a) Exercising power that our friends don't possess
 (b) Concealing a friend's secret
 (c) Learning other people's secret
 (d) Disclosing a friend's secret to others

(v) Select the option with the underlined words that can suitably replace 'hallmark' (paragraph 2).
 (a) No doubt they will show the stoical fortitude that is the <u>failed example</u> of their state and carry on eating.
 (b) Clarity, freshness and taut rhythms were the <u>notorious specimens</u> of Beethoven.
 (c) Neutral colors and simple, luxurious bathroom decorations are a <u>distinctive feature</u> of this style.
 (d) <u>Complimenting ideas</u> have been in the greeting card business for a century.

(vi) Hyperbole is a figure of speech in which words are exaggerated in order to impress the readers.

 From the options given below, select a phrase/sentence from the above passage that can be an example of hyperbole.
 (a) "Frankness may be among the most overrated of virtues"
 (b) "Speaking kindly is a life skill"
 (c) "Words thoughtlessly spoken can bring the end of the world."
 (d) "Gossip spreading like a wildfire"

(vii) Choose the option that lists the quote best expressing the central idea of the passage.
  (a) Kind words can be short and easy to speak but their echoes are truly endless. (Mother Teresa)
  (b) Love and kindness are never wasted. They always make a difference. They bless the one who receives them, and they bless you, the giver. (Barbara de Angelis)
  (c) One thing I do know for a fact is that the nicer we are to our fellow human beings, the nicer the universe is to us. (Joe Rogan)
  (d) Kindness is more than deeds. It is in attitude, an expression, a look, a touch. It is anything that lifts another person. (Plato)

Answers and Explanations

PASSAGE 1

(i) (c) 'Desultory' means lacking of a definite plan or aimless.

The passage suggests that a nation without a vision is 'aimless', like a ship cruising without direction.

(ii) (b) The passage talks about the unified efforts of diversified people which will make India a great nation. Hence, option (b) is the correct answer.

(iii) (a) "A person is a coward because they think they are"–gives the correct meaning of the given sentence.

(iv) (c) 'Visionary' and 'confident' are the qualities that the author displays while talking about taking the necessary steps to build our nation's strength.

(v) (d) 'Driving' means exerting force or motivating force. Hence, the sentence in option (d) contains the words that can replace 'driving'.

(vi) (a) According to the paragraph 7, the author advises to strengthen the nation's technological strength.

(vii) (c) The quote in option (c) best expresses the central idea of the passage.

PASSAGE 2

(i) (b) Finding and preserving artifacts is integral to knowing more about our cultural past is the lesson taught by excavations.

(ii) (d) According to given passage, both options (a) and (b) are appropriate to complete the dialogue.

(iii) (a) The sentence in option (a) gives the same meaning as the sentence in the question.

(iv) (b) The people in the profession of archaeology can be said to be seekers of knowledge.

(v) (c) 'Clandestine' means secret or secretly conducted. Hence, the sentence in option (c) contains the words that can suitably replace 'clandestine'.

(vi) (c) ' Archaeology' means a study of human activity through recovery and analysis of material culture.

(vii) (b) The author seems to be business-minded, sharp and clever.

PASSAGE 3

(i) (b) The lesson being taught by the author's mention of the summer holidays of the older times is that it was a time when everyone went back to their homes and relaxed.

(ii) (a) According to the given passage, option (a) is the correct answer.

(iii) (d) "People got the chance to connect with their families"–gives the correct meaning of the sentence in the question.

(iv) (d) 'Hard working' and 'determined' are the qualities children of today's world display during their summer vacations.

(v) (b) 'Scurry' means to make haste. Hence, the sentence in option (b) contains the words that can suitably replace 'scurried'.

(vi) (c) 'Working vacation' is an oxymoron.

(vii) (b) During the summer vacations, the author wants us to be 'acceptive' and 'forgiving'.

PASSAGE 4

(i) (b) The greatest lesson to be learnt from the given passage is that appropriate steps must be taken to ensure that any construction that happens follows the environmental norms.

(ii) (d) According to the given passage, option (d) is suitable to complete the dialogue.

(iii) (c) "Due to presence of many trees, the South Delhi area provides oxygen for most of the city"–is the correct meaning of the sentence in the question.

(iv) (a) 'Shrewd' and 'self-serving' are the qualities talked about in the question.

(v) (a) 'Smog' is portmanteav of smoke and fog.

(vi) (a) (1) and (3) gives the qualities mentioned in the line in the question.

(vii) (c) The idiom 'treat/handle' with kid gloves means to deal gently and tactfully with someone.

PASSAGE 5

(i) (c) The greatest lesson being taught by the author is that every person creates their own destiny.

(ii) (a) According to the passage, option (a) is the correct answer.

(iii) (d) Happenstance refers to a situation of coincidence. Hence, only option (d) is not an example of such a situation.

(iv) (a) 'self assessment' and 'devotion' are the qualities the sanyasis and Brahmacharyas imbibe on their quest of spiritual growth.

(v) (d) 'Entangle' means twisted together. Hence, the sentence in option (d) contains the words that can replace 'entangle'.

(vi) (d) 'Individualistic' and 'Introspective' are the qualities that the author want us to imbibe.

(vii) (c) The quote in option (c) best expresses the central idea of the passage.

PASSAGE 6

(i) (b) The greatest lesson being taught by the Vedic period is that girls and boys should be treated equally.

(ii) (c) According to the passage option (c) "don't want me to study any further" is appropriate to complete the dialogue.

(iii) (a) By the phrase 'emancipation of women', the author means the liberation of women from their previous deteriorating condition.

(iv) (c) The social reformers were determined to help and protect others.

(v) (b) 'Fervently's means passionately. Hence, the sentence in option (b) contains the words appropriate to replace 'fervently'.

(vi) (d) 'Child marriage', 'domestic violence' and 'female foeticide' will be cured by the education of women.

(vii) (c) The quote in option (c) best expresses the central idea of the given passage.

PASSAGE 7

(i) (a) Keenness and the urge to be successful are the first steps in on the journey to achieve success.

(ii) (d) The phrase given in option (d) appropriately completes the dialogue.

(iii) (b) "Achieving success feels like a person's life's purpose is fulfiled"–gives the meaning of the sentence in the question.

(iv) (a) 'Persistance' means continual effort to achieve something. Hence, option (a) contains the sentence that uses the words appropriately.

(v) (d) The figure of speech metaphor is used in both the phrases in option (b) and (c). Hence, option (d) is the correct answer.

(vi) (b) "Success can means different thing to different people"–is the correct meaning of the phrase given in the question.

(vii) (d) The quote given in option (d) but expresses the central idea of the passage.

PASSAGE 8

(i) (a) The greatest lesson being learnt about instincts is that if cultivated properly, they can help a person become a great leader.

(ii) (c) "Filled with courage and determination but" is appropriate to complete the dialogue.

(iii) (b) "A person's behaviour towards their instincts is equally important" is the correct meaning of the phrase given in the question.

(iv) (d) The 'never-giving-up' and trying attitude was displayed by Abraham Lincoln that eventually made him the President of the USA.

(v) (c) 'Latent' means 'quite dormant'. Hence, the sentence in option (c) contains the words appropriate to replace 'latent'.

(vi) (c) By the example of Abraham Lincoln, it is being shown that he trusted his instincts and acted accordingly.

(vii) (a) The quote in option (a) best expresses the central idea of the passage.

PASSAGE 9

(i) (c) The greatest lesson to be learnt from the story of Egya Mensa and the author is that the healing powers of medicinal plants should not be underestimated.

(ii) (a) "Herbal medicine has saved lives when drugs couldn't" is appropriate to complete the dialogue.

(iii) (b) 'Purported' means allegedly true or a claim; without proof. Hence, the sentence in option (b) contains the words appropriate to replace 'purported'.

(iv) (c) 'Drugstore', formed from two nouns 'drug' and 'store', is a compound noun.

(v) (d) A 'divine healer' would display the qualities of fakeness, fraudulence and manipulation, according to the author's description.

(vi) (b) The author advises to the developing countries to research the properties of medicinal plants.

(vii) (a) The quote in option (a) best expresses the central idea of the passage.

PASSAGE 10

(i) (c) The greatest lesson being taught by the acronym 'think' is that only necessary truths should be shared and that too, with kindness.

(ii) (b) 'Let your parents tell her'. They will be able to explain better' is appropriate to complete the dialogue.

(iii) (b) 'To become known very quickly' best expresses the message in 'spreading like a wildfire'.

(iv) (d) The writer is warning against disclosing a friend's secret to others, in paragraph 4.

(v) (c) 'Hallmark' means a distinctive feature. Hence, the sentence in option (c) contains the appropriate words to replace 'hallmark'.

(vi) (c) The sentence in option (c) uses the figure of speech hyperbole.

(vii) (a) The quote in option (a) best expresses the central idea of the passage.

• Case Based Factual Passages

Read the passages given below carefully.

Passage 1

1. India's population is expected to grow by 25%, with reference to 2011, to 1.52 billion by 2036, according to the final report of the technical group on population projections dated July 2020. The group was constituted by the National Commission on Population (NCP) under the Ministry of Health and Family Welfare with the mandate to provide population projections for the period 2011 to 2036.

2. India's population growth rate is expected to decline to its lowest since the Independence in the 2011-2021 decade, with a decadal growth rate of 12.5%. It will decline further to 8.4% in the 2021-2031 decade, as per the report, which The Wire has seen. According to these projections, India will overtake China as the world's most populous country around 2031 – almost a decade later than the United Nations projection of 2022.

India's population is projected to increase to 1.52 billion by 2036.

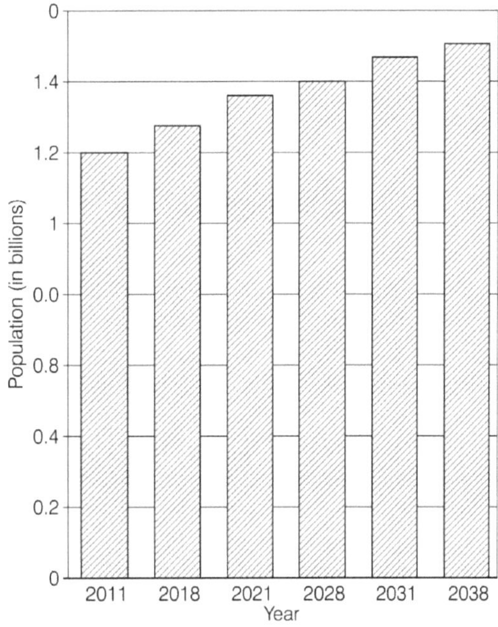

Source: Report of the technical group on population projections

3. The projections have been delayed quite significantly. "Ideally, they should have come by 2016. But there were delays in setting up the committee and then more delays at the government's end even after we submitted the report. We had submitted our report in November 2019," said a member of the committee wishing to remain anonymous. This was confirmed by two other members as well.

4. India's population was 1.21 billion as per the Census of 2011 and the projections now estimate that the population will grow by 311 million by 2036.

5. The report projects that as much as 70% of this increase will be in urban areas. India's urban population will increase from 377 million in 2011 to 594 million in 2036 – a growth of 57%. So, while 31% of Indians were living in urban India in 2011,that will grow to 39% by 2036.

6. Consequently, the proportion of the rural population will decline from 69% to 61% as the urban population is projected to increase more than twice the projected increase in the rural population.   (321 Words)

Questions

Based on your understanding of the passage, answer **any five** out of the seven questions by choosing the correct option.

(i) The purpose of the above report was to give ....
Choose the correct option.

(a) Population projections for 2036
(b) Population projections for 2011
(c) Population projections for 2011-2036
(d) Population projections for 2031

(ii) Select the option that is true for the two statements given below.
   (1) India will become the most populous country in the world by 2031.
   (2) China's population will diminish owing to increasing deaths due to the COVID-19 pandemic.
   (a) (1) is the result of (2)
   (b) (1) is the reason for (2)
   (c) (1) is independent of (2)
   (d) (1) is true (2) is false

(iii) Select the option that gives the correct meaning of the following statement.

   "It will decline further to 8.4% in the 2021-2031 decade…"
   (a) India's population growth rate is expected to decline drastically.
   (b) India's mortality rate is expected to decline drastically.
   (c) India's infancy rate is expected to decline drastically.
   (d) India's population is expected to decline drastically.

(iv) According to the research, rural population will ....
   (a) Decline as compared to the urban population's growth
   (b) Increase as compared to the urban population's growth
   (c) Remain the same as at present
   (d) None of the above

(v) Select the option which gives the number by which the population of India is estimated to grow by 2036.
   (a) 377 million   (b) 311 million
   (c) 594 million   (d) 1.21 billion

(vi) Why did the projections come in July of 2020?
   (a) Delay in setting up the committee
   (b) Delay by the government
   (c) Delay by the committee
   (d) Both (a) and (b)

(vii) This passage contains the decadal growth rate for the decade 2011-2021, which is .... Select the correct option.
   (a) 8.4%   (b) 12.5%   (c) 57%   (d) 25%

Passage 2

1. Schizophrenia is a chronic and severe mental disorder affecting more than 21 million people worldwide which is characterised by distortions in thinking, perception, emotions, language, sense of self and behaviour. Common experiences include hallucinations and delusions which involve having fixed, false beliefs.

2. Since schizophrenia is a chronic illness that influences virtually all aspects of life of affected persons, treatment planning has three goals which are to reduce or eliminate symptoms, to maximise quality of life and adaptive functioning and to promote and maintain recovery from the debilitating effects of illness to the maximum extent possible. Medications are invaluable in the management of patients with mental illnesses. Pharmacists are therefore indispensable in improving the quality of service rendered to patients with mental illnesses such as schizophrenia which contributes to reduction of the numerous problems associated with and faced by patients with mental disorders.

3. Management of patients with conditions such as schizophrenia is generally a collaborative effort which encompasses incorporation of skills of a myriad of health care professionals involved in patient care. Clinical pharmacists have been instrumental in several roles such as being educators, consultants and providers for over 30 years. Since pharmacists are authorities in pharmaceutical care, they also apply their complementary skills and knowledge in managing patients with mental illnesses together with other health care professionals in the multidisciplinary team. Clinical pharmacists as such contribute to patient care by playing a vital role in the detection, resolution and prevention of medication-related problems. In ensuring the safe and efficacious use of medications, clinical pharmacists are also pivotal. In addition, pharmacists are available to provide comprehensive drug information to patients with mental illnesses such as schizophrenia, the patient's relatives and other health care professionals involved in patient management. Pharmacists spearhead medication adherence and are involved in education on primary prevention of mental illnesses, health promotion and lifestyle modification.

(307 Words)

Questions

Based on your understanding of the passage, answer **any five** out of the seven questions by choosing the correct option.

(i) The purpose of this passage was to study the .... Choose the correct option.
   (a) Schizophrenia and its benefits
   (b) Schizophrenia and its treatment
   (c) Schizophrenia and its cure
   (d) Schizophrenic people and their behaviour

(ii) Select the option that is true for the two statements given below.
   (1) People face distortions in thinking, lose the sense of self and start seeing things that are not really there.
   (2) Schizophrenia is a mental illness that is affecting more than 21 million people in the world.

(a) (1) is the result of (2).

(b) (1) is the reason for (2).

(c) (1) is independent of (2).

(d) (1) is true (2) is false.

(iii) Complete the sentence to give correct meaning of the following phrase.

"Common experiences include hallucinations and delusions…"

As a result of schizophrenia, people ....
(a) Start feeling the sudden urge to kill someone
(b) Start behaving erratically and irrationally
(c) Start seeing and hearing things and have mistaken beliefs
(d) Start feeling unreasonably jovial and ecstatic

(iv) According to the research, managing the suffering patients requires a ....
(a) Single-handed effort by incorporating skills.
(b) Joint effort of health care professionals.
(c) Educational degree in psychology.
(d) Sympathetic treatment by surrounding people.

(v) Select the option listing the objectives of treatment of schizophrenia.
(1) Reduce symptoms
(2) To set suffering mind straight
(3) Stop hallucinations
(4) To increase the quality of life
(5) To promote recovery
(6) To fix a person's thinking
(a) 2, 4 and 6
(b) 1, 2 and 6
(c) 1, 4 and 5
(d) 2, 3 and 5

(vi) What are the clinical pharmacists involved in besides making sure that medication is strictly followed?
(a) Education on preventing the mental illness
(b) Promoting a healthy life
(c) Modifying lifestyle in accordance with the treatment
(d) All of the above

(vii) This passage suggests that clinical pharmacists provide .... to patients suffering from mental illness.

Select the correct option.
(a) Comprehensive drug information
(b) A complete booklet of information
(c) Professionally administered syringes with drugs
(d) Step-by-step procedure of cure

Passage 3

1. On the eve of International Youth Day, which is observed globally every year on 12th August, experts and policy commentators in India have called for more steps by the government to create employment opportunities.

2. According to a 2011 Census, people aged 15-24 comprise one-fifth or 19% of India's total population. Multiple reports, however, indicate that the number of unemployed youth in the South Asian country is rising.

3. The Centre for Monitoring Indian Economy, a think tank, said India's labor participation rate in May was 40%, with 15 million jobs lost in the month. "May 2021 is also the fourth consecutive month of a fall in employment. The cumulative fall in employment since January 2021 is 25.3 million. Employment in January 2021 was 400.7 million. This has dropped to 375.5 million," said the report published in June.

4. Similarly, The Financial Express, a leading business daily, recently reported that according to the International Labour Organisation's database, India's unemployment rate rose to 7.11% in 2020 – the highest in at least three decades.

5. "High rates of unemployment are dangerous. If you have so many unemployed people, it means they are neither saving nor consuming. This has a direct impact on economic growth and the country's economic potential," Rajrishi Singhal, a policy consultant who has also worked at the country's top financial newspapers, told Anadolu Agency.

Ritu Dewan, vice president of the Indian Society of Labour Economics, said the situation has further worsened due to COVID-19.

6. "Unemployment was there even before the pandemic, but now the situation has turned from bad to worse," Dewan, who is also a former director of the Department of Economics at the University of Mumbai, told Anadolu Agency.

She said that several reports of late have pointed out that unemployment among both men and women is very high in the country and "we need to take steps urgently."

7. The government has acknowledged that virus lockdowns have affected economies across the globe, including that of India. Earlier this month, Prime Minister Narendra Modi asked industry representatives to look at ways to increase exports, a move that could help boost employment.

(346 Words)

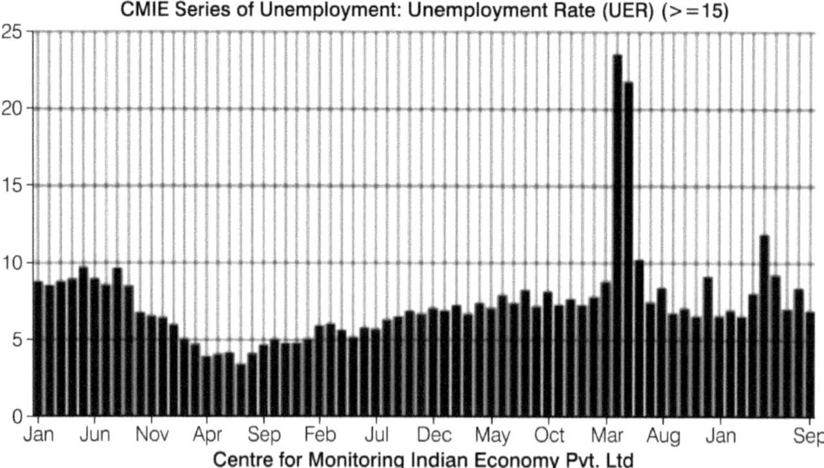

Questions

Based on your understanding of the passage, answer **any five** out of the seven questions by choosing the correct option.

(i) The purpose of above passage is to focus on .... Choose the correct option.
   (a) The decreasing problem of youth unemployment in India
   (b) The increasing problem of youth employment in India
   (c) The increasing problem of youth unemployment in India
   (d) The decreasing problem of youth employment in India

(ii) Select the option that is true for the two statements given below.
   (1) COVID-19 lockdown contributed to the already worsening situation.
   (2) The unemployment rate in India has risen over the past year.
   (a) (1) is the result of (2)
   (b) (1) is the reason for (2)
   (c) (1) is independent of (2)
   (d) (1) contradicts (2)

(iii) Select the option that gives the correct meaning of the following statement.

   "This has a direct impact on economic growth and the country's economic potential."
   (a) Employed people have a harmful effect on the country's economic potential.
   (b) Unemployed people have a harmful effect on the country's economic potential.
   (c) Unemployed people have a positive effect on the country's economic potential.
   (d) Employed people have a harmful yet positive effect on the country's economic potential.

(iv) According to the ILO report, India's unemployment rate ....
   (a) Fell to the lowest in the last 30 years
   (b) Rose to the highest in the last 3 years
   (c) Rose to the highest in the last 30 years
   (d) Fell to the lowest in the last 3 years

(v) Select the option listing the organisations/people who commented on the problem of youth unemployment, according to the passage.
   (1) Department of Economics
   (2) ILO
   (3) The Financial Express
   (4) Anadolu Agency
   (5) Ritu Diwan
   (a) 2, 3 and 5   (b) 1, 4 and 5
   (c) 2, 3 and 4   (d) 1, 2 and 4

(vi) What did PM Modi ask the industry representatives to do?
   (a) To boost employment   (b) To hire more people
   (c) To increase exports   (d) To educate the youth

(vii) The passage mentions that the unemployment rate in India rose to .... in 2020. Select the correct option.
   (a) 19%   (b) 40%
   (c) 7.11%   (d) 25.3%

Passage 4

1. Sprouts relatively contain the largest amount of nutrients per unit of any food known to man. Sprouts produce a fountain of power for chemical changes. Enzymes are produced, starch gets converted into glucose, protein is transformed into amino acids and vitamin value increases. In fact, a new explosion of life force takes place. According to Dr Bailey of the University of Minnesota, USA, the vitamin C value of wheat increases 600% in the early sprouting period. Dr CR Shaw of the University of Texas Cancer Centre found that cancer was inhibited upto 90% when healthy bacteria were exposed to a cancer causing substance in the presence of a juice made from wheat sprouts.

2. Enzymes, which initiate and control almost every chemical reaction in our bodies, are greatly activated in the sprouting process. Enzymes spark the entire digestive system to synthesise the nutrients in our food into blood. They are the key to longevity.

3. Sprouts are enjoyed more when they are fresh. Mix sprouts with other foods and dressing according to your taste and enjoy eating them. But you must eat them every day you will soon realise that making sprouts a part of your diet has a dramatic effect on your health. With this live food, all the cells of your body will become active and agile.

4. The nourishment which develops as the sprouts grow is very stable and can be frozen or dried for future. Sprouted potato or tomato seeds are likely to be poisonous. Alfalfa and moong bean sprouts are excellent soft food. They are almost predigested and can be easily assimilated even by the children and the elderly. They contain every known vitamin in perfect balance necessary for the human body.

Health Benefits of Sprouts

- Aid in digestion
- Boost immune system
- Aid in weight management
- Protect body against cancer
- Improve blood circulation in body
- Help to reduce risk of heart ailments
- Help in growth and development of body
- Reduce risk of neural tube defects in infants
- Help to prevent cataracts and mascular degeneration
- Inhibit growth of cold sores and reduce effect of allergic reactions and asthma

Caution : Wash well before use to prevent any type of microbial infection

Questions

Based on your understanding of the passage, answer **any five** out of the seven questions by choosing the correct option.

(i) Which element initiates chemical reaction in our body?
  (a) Enzymes   (b) Sprouts
  (c) Bacteria   (d) Vitamins

(ii) According to Dr CR Shaw, cancer was inhibited upto ...... with the help of sprouts.
  (a) 80%   (b) 90%
  (c) 20%   (d) 95%

(iii) As per the passage eating sprouts is good for
  (a) children
  (b) adults
  (c) the elderly
  (d) All of these

(iv) The qualities of sprouts as mentioned in the last para of the passage are
  I. excellent soft food
  II. predigested
  III. can be easily assimilated
  IV. contain poisonous element
  Codes
  (a) I and II
  (b) I, II and III
  (c) III and IV
  (d) I, III and IV

(v) The word .... from the passage means absorb of 'digest'.
  (a) assimilated
  (b) predigest
  (c) dried
  (d) soft

(vi) Choose the option that lists the statement that is NOT TRUE.
  (a) Sprouts contain hard proteins that are not easily digested.
  (b) The perfect balance of the vitamins in the body can be obtained from sprouts.
  (c) In the sprouting process, enzymes are greatly activated.
  (d) All of the above

(vii) Which of the following is not a step in the sprouting process?
  (a) Production of enzymes.
  (b) Conversion of starch into glucose.
  (c) Release of essential vitamins.
  (d) Transformation of protein into amino acids.

Passage 5

1. Worsening air pollution has been amongst India's most pressing problems in recent years. Toxic air is not only a massive health and environmental concern, but also takes a huge economic toll: it impedes development and affects people's welfare. According to the Health Effects Institute, in 2015, over 1.1 million premature deaths in India were caused by air pollution. In 2019, air pollution led to about 18 per cent of all deaths in the country. In the same year, it resulted in an economic loss of approximately 1.4 per cent of GDP. Studies have identified the severely negative impacts of air pollution across a multitude of sectors, including labour productivity and crop yields.

2. Indeed, India's air quality has deteriorated exponentially in the past few decades, due to various reasons including rapid urbanisation, industrialisation and population growth. According to IQAir, in 2020, India ranked third amongst all countries in the world with the worst air quality. The Northern regions alone are home to no less than 13 of the 15 most polluted cities in the world.

3. Governments have initiated policy initiatives and created regulatory agencies and other institutions all meant to combat air pollution; they are highly inadequate. The current scenario shows a need for better and more effective ways of improving air quality across the country, especially in the densest and most populated urban spaces. One imperative is to ramp up the role of technology and encourage the private sector to engage in partnerships between each other, and with the government, to tackle air pollution. It is equally important to involve the grassroots, especially the most vulnerable populations, through community-based initiatives.

4. Any effort, however, must begin with accurate and timely information on air pollution. This will ensure that awareness is heightened about the magnitude of the crisis and its manifold impacts. Disseminating proper, adequate information should also seek to inspire individual action, and a collective commitment to a future where there is clean air for all.

(323 Words)

Questions

Based on your understanding of the passage, answer **any five** out of the seven questions by choosing the correct option.

(i) The purpose of the above passage is to .... Choose the correct option.
  (a) Improve the air quality in India
  (b) Highlight the issue of bad quality of air in India
  (c) Suggest necessary steps to be taken to improve the bad air quality in India
  (d) Show the harmful effects of air pollution

(ii) Select the option that is true for the two statements given below.
  (1) The Government of India has taken several steps and measures to deal with the problem of air pollution.
  (2) Finally, the initiatives have shown positive results and the air quality has become much better.
  (a) (1) is the result of (2)
  (b) (1) is the reason for (2)
  (c) (1) is independent of (2)
  (d) (1) is true (2) is false

(iii) Which of the following is true about the toxicity of air?
  (a) It causes increase in labour and crop yields.
  (b) It doesn't have any effect on the economic growth of the country.
  (c) It causes decrease in labour and crop yields.
  (d) It resulted in an increase in GDP by 1.4 per cent.

(iv) According to the research, ... in India owing to air pollution.
  (a) More than 1.1 million people died timely deaths
  (b) Almost 1.1 million people died untimely deaths
  (c) More than 1.1 million people died untimely deaths
  (d) Almost than 1.1 million people died timely deaths

(v) Select the option listing severe effects of unclean and toxic air.
  (1) It is an obstacle in development.
  (2) It kills people with the help of harmful gases.
  (3) It causes numerous health problems.
  (4) It badly affects the economy of a country.
  (5) It destructs any and all government initiatives.
  (a) 1, 2 and 4
  (b) 1, 3 and 4
  (c) 2, 3 and 5
  (d) 2, 4 and 1

(vi) How can the problem of air pollution be dealt with?
  (a) By encouraging private sectors to come together and use technology to deal with it.
  (b) By encouraging private sector to come together with the government and use technology to tackle with the problem.
  (c) By involving people from the ground level.
  (d) All of the above

(vii) Choose the correct option to answer the following.

According to paragraph 4, at which level actions should be taken against the increasing crisis of air toxicity?
  (a) At individual level with a collaborative commitment.
  (b) At ground level with an individual effort and commitment.
  (c) At authoritative level with better initiatives and policy.
  (d) At scientific level with creation of a antidote.

Passage 6

1. India is home to an estimated 10% of the global Snow Leopard population spread across five Himalayan states of Jammu and Kashmir, Himachal Pradesh, Uttarakhand, Sikkim and Arunachal Pradesh which is only 5% of the available global habitat for the animal.

2. Project Snow Leopard was introduced in India by the Project Snow Leopard Committee instituted by the Ministry of Environment and Forests, Government of India, in the year 2009 to safeguard and conserve India's unique natural heritage of high altitude wildlife populations and their habitats by promoting conservation through participatory policies and actions.

3. Project Tiger and Project Elephant is prevalent in India with the former introduced in 1973 garnering worldwide attention.

4. The Snow Leopard usually occurs at an altitude of >2700m above sea level and is the apex predator in the Himalayan Region along with the Tibetan Wolf. The project is not only to protect the Snow Leopard, but as with Project Tiger, it is considered an umbrella species and with its protection, comes the protection of other species and the habitat which they are all a part of.

5. Top 3 National Parks in India where the Snow Leopard can likely be seen

  (i) Kibber Wildlife Sanctuary – Himachal Pradesh   (ii) Ulley Valley – Ladakh

(iii) Hemis National Park – Himachal Pradesh

The reasons for introduction of Project Snow Leopard are as follows

  (i) High altitudes of India > 3000m including the Himalayan & Trans-himalayan biogeographic zones support a unique wildlife assemblage of global conservation.

  (ii) There has been relatively less attention on the region from the viewpoint of wildlife conservation.

(iii) The region represents a vast rangeland system supporting important traditional pastoral economies and lifestyles.

(iv) The region provides essential ecosystem services and harbours river systems vital for the nation's food security.

(v) India has ratified international agreements promoting the conservation of high altitude wildlife species such as the snow leopard.

(vi) The region is important for the country's national security as well as international relations.

(vii) The high altitude wildlife in India today faces a variety of threats.

(viii) The existing high altitude protected areas in India require considerable strengthening.

(ix) Wildlife Management in the region needs to be made participatory. *(360 Words)*

Questions

Based on your understanding of the passage, answer **any five** out of the seven questions by choosing the correct option.

(i) The purpose of above study is to show that snow leopards are .... Choose the correct option
 (a) Near threatened species that can be protected
 (b) Vulnerable species and must be protected
 (c) Least concerned species that need no protection
 (d) Species that live in the Himalayas

(ii) Select the option that is true for the two statements given below.
 (1) Project Snow Leopard was introduced in India in 2009 to conserve unique high altitude wildlife like snow leopards.
 (2) Project Tiger was introduced in India in 1973 to conserve the endangered Bengal tigers and save them from extinction.
 (a) (1) is the result of (2). (b) (1) is the cause of (2).
 (c) (1) is independent of (2). (d) (1) contradicts (2).

(iii) Select the option that gives the correct meaning of the following phrase.
 "Snow Leopard… is considered an umbrella species…"
 (a) Other species will also be protected by protecting Snow Leopards.
 (b) It consists of many other species.
 (c) It is the most important species in the region.
 (d) None of the above

(iv) According to the above passage, high altitude regions should be protected because they ....
 (a) Support unique wildlife of global significance
 (b) Support endangered wildlife that must be protected
 (c) Consist of very insignificant ecosystems and organisms
 (d) Are rich in minerals and natural resources

(v) According to the passage, which other species can be found in the Himalayan Region besides the Snow Leopard?
 (a) Asian Elephants (b) Endangered Tiger
 (c) Tibetan Wolf (d) Both (a) and (c)

(vi) Which of the following is integral to the nation's food security?
 (a) Wildlife management (b) Vast rangeland system
 (c) Aquatic ecosystems (d) River systems

(vii) The passage concludes that promotion of conservation of high altitude wildlife species by India requires it to ....
 Select the correct option
 (a) Keep the region neat and tidy
 (b) Protect the region as well
 (c) Donate money to the human inhabitants of the region
 (d) Hold such species captive in order to protect them

Passage 7

1. India has already commissioned two nuclear power stations, one at Tarapur and the other at Rana Pratap Sagar. Each one has the installed capacity of producing 420 M. W. of electricity. Two other stations, one at Narora and the other at Kalpakkam, are operational. This energy will be able to meet the power shortage throughout the country. If industries work at their full capacity, production will be higher and so per capita income will increase and inflation will be neutralised.

2. With the help of controlled nuclear explosions, artificial dams can be made. In fact for building a dam there should be two huge mountain walls enclosing a deep valley just near the course of a river. These conditions are not available at all the places. So with the help of controlled nuclear explosions mountains can be blown up. This can also help in laying roads in the mountainous areas. In fact, some of the borders of India have mountainous terrain and the movement of the army is quite difficult. So even for the sake of national security it is necessary to have roads in those areas.

3. With the help of radiation the shelf life of vegetables and fruits can be increased. In the tropical countries like India, it is necessary that the perishable fruit stuffs are preserved for a long time. Radiation can check the sprouting of onions and potatoes which are much in demand in foreign countries.

Similarly fruits like bananas and mangoes which have much export potential can be preserved for a very long time. The texture and taste of the fruit do not undergo any change.

4. Nuclear technology can also be harnessed for medical purposes. It is said that radioactive iodine is used for detecting the disease of the thyroid glands. Similarly, India has been able to prepare, with the help of UN experts, radiated vaccine which can immunise sheep from lungworm disease, which used to take a heavy toll of sheep every year.

5. Properly processed nuclear fuel is also used for artificial satellites in space. Weather satellites can predict cyclones and the rainfall with extreme accuracy. Communication satellites can help in conveying the message to very long distances. In a huge country like India, communication satellites are necessary.

6. Radiation is also used for preparing the mutant seeds. Many varieties of rice and some cereals have been prepared at Tarapur laboratory. This will increase our agricultural production and help India to become economically better off. So for India it is necessary to make peaceful uses of nuclear energy.

(335 Words)

Questions

Based on your understanding of the passage, answer **any five** out of the seven questions by choosing the correct option.

(i) India is building nuclear power stations to ....
   (a) become rich
   (b) become self-reliant
   (c) increase industrial production
   (d) help the poor

(ii) Controlled nuclear explosions can be used to blow up ....
   (a) roads   (b) dams   (c) mountains   (d) seas

(iii) In the line, "…has already commissioned", the word 'Commissioned' DOES NOT refer to
   (a) be opened or established
   (b) create something new
   (c) a rank conferred by a commission
   (d) bring (something newly produced) into working condition.

(iv) Based on your understanding of the passage, choose the option that lists the uses of nuclear energy.
   1. Creation of artificial dams   2. Development of space theories
   3. Increasing shelf life of food   4. Mutation of different flowers
   5. Medical facilities   6. Weather predictions

   (a) 1,3 and 6   (b) 2,4 and 5
   (c) 1,3,5 and 6   (d) Only 5

(v) Select the option that is true for the two statements given below.
   1. With the help of controlled nuclear explosions, artificial doms can be made.
   2. With the help of radiation the shelf life of vegetables and fruits can be increased.
   (a) (1) is the result of (2)
   (b) (1) is the reason for (2)
   (c) (1) is independent of (2)
   (d) (1) is true (2) is false

(vi) Radiation is helpful in ....
   (a) growing vegetables
   (b) growing fruits
   (c) growing onions
   (d) preserving fruits

(vii) Which of the following is the use of weather satellite?
   (a) Predicting average temperature
   (b) Predicting rainfall and cyclones with accuracy
   (c) Predicting heat waves
   (d) Predicting ozone gaps

Passage 8

1. The term 'child labour' is often defined as work that deprives children of their childhood, their potential and their dignity and that is harmful to physical and mental development. It refers to work that:

   - is mentally, physically, socially or morally dangerous and harmful to children; and/or

   - interferes with a child's ability to attend and participate in school fully by obliging them to leave school prematurely or requiring them to attempt to combine school attendance with excessively long and heavy work.

2. There are many inter-linked factors contributing to the prevalence of child labour. Child labour is both a cause and consequence of poverty. Household poverty forces children into the labour market to earn money. Some perform child labour to supplement family income while many also are in it for survival. They miss out on an opportunity to gain an education, further perpetuating household poverty across generations, slowing the economic growth and social development. Child labour impedes children from gaining the skills and education they need to have opportunities of decent work as an adult. Inequality, lack of educational opportunities, slow demographic transition, traditions and cultural expectations all contribute to the persistence of child labour in India. Age, sex, ethnicity, caste and deprivation affect the type and intensity of work that children perform.

3. Child labour remains a persistent problem in the world today. The latest global estimates indicate that 160 million children – 63 million girls and 97 million boys – were in child labour globally at the beginning of 2020, accounting for almost 1 in 10 of all children worldwide. Seventy-nine million children – nearly half of all those in child labour – were in hazardous work that directly endangers their health, safety and moral development.

4. Global progress against child labour has stagnated since 2016. The percentage of children in child labour remained unchanged over the four-year period while the absolute number of children in child labour increased by over 8 million. Similarly, the percentage of children in hazardous work was almost unchanged but rose in absolute terms by 6.5 million children.

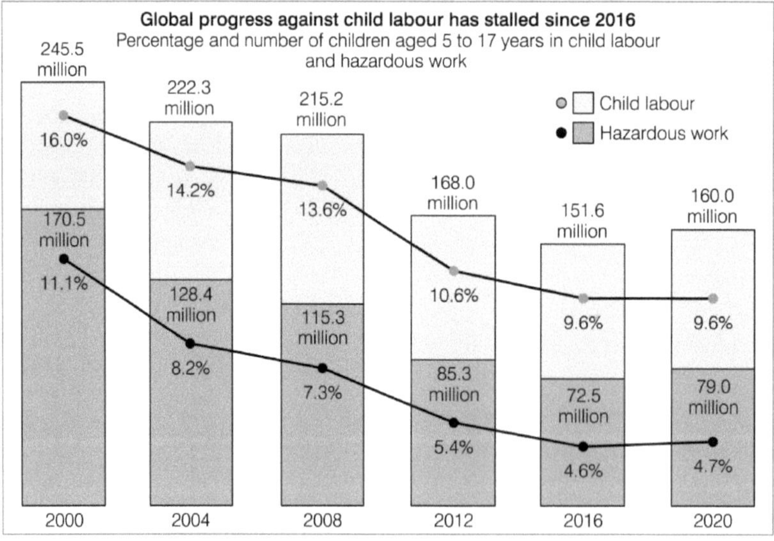

(339 Words)

Questions

Based on your understanding of the passage, answer **any five** out of the seven questions by choosing the correct option.

(i) The purpose of the passage is to highlight .... Choose the correct option.
   (a) The issue of child labour
   (b) The reasons behind child labour
   (c) The increase in the number of child labourers in the past four years
   (d) The decrease in the number of child labourers in the past four years

(ii) Select the option that is true for the two statements given below.
   (1) Poverty forces children into the labour market.
   (2) Child labour perpetuates poverty across generations.
   (a) (1) is the result of (2)   (b) (1) is the reason for (2)
   (c) (1) is independent of (2)   (d) (1) contradicts (2)

(iii) Select the option that gives the correct meaning of the following statement.

"Global progress against child labour has stagnated since 2016."

(a) The fight against the evil of child labour has increased.

(b) The fight against the evil of child labour has decreased.

(c) The fight against the evil of child labour has stopped altogether.

(d) None of the above

(iv) According to the data provided in the above passage, ... engaged in labour are in hazardous work.

(a) Almost half of all children

(b) Almost all of children

(c) 10% of all children

(d) None of the above

(v) Select the option listing the severe effects of child labour.

(1) Impedes their education

(2) Inequality

(3) Poverty

(4) Slow demographic transition

(5) Hinders skill development

(a) 1, 4 and 5

(b) 2, 3 and 4

(c) 1 and 5

(d) All of these

(vi) What does child labour do to a young minds?

(a) It makes them retarded.

(b) It hinders them from participating in school.

(c) It causes mental illness in children.

(d) It makes them violent and aggressive.

(vii) This passage gives the definition of 'child labour' suggesting that it deprives children of their childhood and affects their ....

Select the correct option.

(a) Potential and their dignity

(b) Harmful physical and mental growth

(c) Hard work and thus, market value

(d) Mental concentration for any future jobs

Passage 9

1. As the virus began to spread around the world, some Indians began to return home, to relative safety. When Kerala registered India's first COVID-19 case on 30th January, 2020 (IDFC Institute, 2020), the state was prepared. Four days before registering its first case, Government of Kerala (GoK) had already released novel corona virus-specific guidelines that established case definitions, screening and sampling protocol, hospital preparedness and surveillance.

2. Over the weeks that followed, a series of comprehensive measures were rolled out. The rapid screening and quarantining of patients and isolation of their contacts delayed the transmission from imported cases for up to 40 days, until Kerala witnessed its first cluster outbreak in the district of Pathanamthitta. A total of 14 confirmed cases were registered over the two days that followed.

3. Given the early spread of the virus in Kerala, it is commendable that the state had two consecutive days of zero new cases over the 100- day period from the day it registered the first case of COVID-19. Given its relatively efficient public health care systems, backed by strong socio-economic foundation and the experience of previously handling the Nipah virus in 2018, the State was able to act swiftly. Kerala prepared itself to address the pandemic as early as January. The State followed the time-tested strategy of case identification, isolation, contact tracing and vulnerability mapping in containing the virus.

4. Kerala's public healthcare system is decentralized with facilities at the state, district, sub-district, panchayat, and ward level. The field-level staff including health inspectors, ASHA (Accredited Social Health Activists) workers.

5. Coordination at the middle level was largely done by the District Collectors who worked in close coordination with the District Medical Officers and the district-level heads of the police. One of the flagship measures adopted by the State was the development of COVID First Line Treatment Centers and COVID-19 Care Centers.

6. Local testing labs, district-wise allocations and, later, walk-in sample kiosks, allowed Kerala to quickly scale up testing capacities and, over time, conduct mass screenings and serological tests.

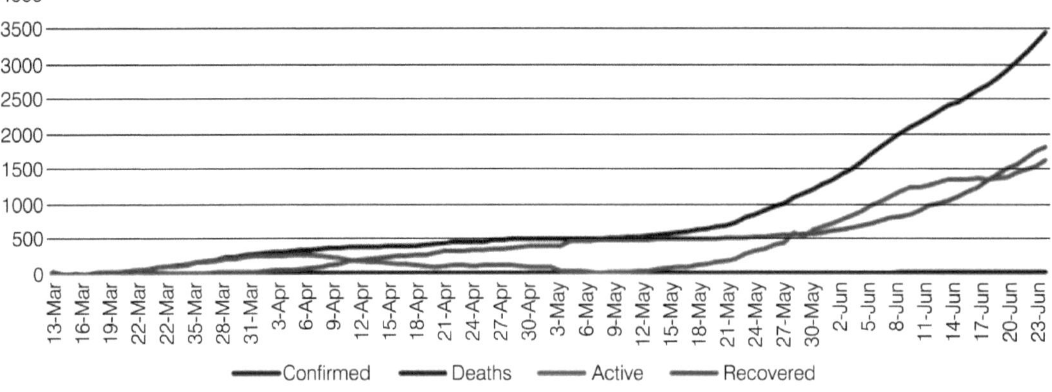

COVID-19 Kerala Graph, June 2020

(334 Words)

Questions

Based on your understanding of the passage, answer **any five** out of the seven questions by choosing the correct option.

(i) The purpose of the above passage is to show that the .... Choose the correct option.
 (a) Spread of any virus can be controlled with proper preventive measures
 (b) State of Kerala has always been the best at handling virus outbreaks
 (c) Handling of any epidemic is almost impossible, regardless of any measures
 (d) State of Kerala was the only state to have been affected by the COVID-19 pandemic

(ii) Select the option that is true for the two statements given below.
 (1) When faced with the problem of the COVID-19 pandemic, Kerala was quick to act.
 (2) Kerala's experience with similar virus outbreak had the state prepared.
 (a) (1) is the result of (2)
 (b) (1) is the reason for (2)
 (c) (1) is independent of (2)
 (d) (1) contradicts (2)

(iii) Select the option that gives the correct meaning of the following statement.

 "Kerala's public healthcare system is decentralised with facilities at the state, district, sub-district, panchayat and ward level."
 (a) It's not just the state that is responsible but every level.
 (b) The state is solely responsible for the healthcare system.

(c) The Centre is solely responsible for the healthcare system.
(d) None of the above

(iv) According to the passage, for how many days there was no case of corona virus in Kerala after the first case was registered?
 (a) For 100 days
 (b) For two days
 (c) For two weeks
 (d) For 40 days

(v) Select the option listing the steps taken by the Kerala Government to contain the spread of the virus.
 (1) Rapid screening of the patients
 (2) Sending away the infected people
 (3) Quarantining the patients
 (4) Isolation of the patients
 (5) Immediate elimination of the infected people
 (a) 1, 2 and 5
 (b) 2 and 4
 (c) 2, 3 and 5
 (d) 1, 3 and 4

(vi) Who did the District Collectors work with in coordination?
 (a) Other District Collectors
 (b) ASHA Workers
 (c) District Medical Officers
 (d) Health Inspectors

(vii) The passage suggests that .... allowed Kerala to conduct mass screenings and tests. Select the correct option.
 (a) Local testing labs
 (b) District-wise allocations
 (c) Walk-in simple kiosks
 (d) All of the above

Passage 10

1. Nuclear power in India delivers a total capacity of 6.7GW, contributing to just under 2% of the country's electricity supply. India's nuclear plants are controlled by Nuclear Power Corporation of India (NPCIL), a state-owned corporation which was founded in 1987. India boasts a fleet of seven nuclear power plants, as of November 2020.

2. Kudankulan Nuclear Power Plant, located in Tamil Nadu, is the highest-capacity nuclear plant in India, with a total of 2,000MW currently installed with a further 2,000MW under construction. It is the only nuclear plant in India that uses Pressurised Water Reactors (PWR) rather than Boiling Water Reactors (BHWR) or Pressurised Heavy-Water Reactors (PHWR).

3. Presently, India has 22 operating nuclear power reactors, with an installed capacity of 6780 MegaWatt electric (MWe). Among these eighteen reactors are Pressurised Heavy Water Reactors (PHWRs) and four are Light Water Reactors (LWRs).

4. The nuclear energy programme in India was launched around the time of independence under the leadership of Homi J Bhabha.

   Prototype Fast Breeder Reactor (PFBR) is being manufactured by the Bharatiya Nabhikiya Vidyut Nigam Limited (BHAVINI), a wholly owned Enterprise of the Government of India under the administrative control of the Department of Atomic Energy (DAE).

5. The Government of India is further set to increase the country's nuclear power generation capacity with plans to commission more nuclear plants.

6. The move will help India substantially increase its share of non-fossil fuel in total energy mix in sync with its pledges under the Paris Agreement. Though India's share of installed capacity of non-fossil fuel-based electricity generation has already reached nearly 39% of its total power generation capacity against its existing target of 40% by 2030, the step towards nuclear energy would help it upgrade its climate action goal.

7. The government has granted for ten new reactors, as well as an administrative approval and financial sanction for ten Pressurised Heavy Water Reactors (PHWRS).

8. The new reactors are expected to increase India's nuclear power generation capacity to 22,480MW by 2031.

   Highest priority will be given to safety in all aspects of nuclear plant development, including sitting, design, construction, commissioning and operation.

   The government also plans to build more nuclear power plants in the future. *(310 Words)*

Questions

Based on your understanding of the passage, answer **any five** out of the seven questions by choosing the correct option.

(i) The purpose of increasing India's nuclear power generation capacity is to .... Choose the correct option.
(a) Generate more fossil fuel energy
(b) Decrease the amount of non-fossil fuel energy
(c) Generate more clean energy
(d) Build nuclear weapons at a faster speed

(ii) Select the option that is true for the two statements given below.
(1) India's climate action goal can be upgraded by its steps towards clear energy.
(2) India has reached nearly 39% of its total power generation capacity.
(a) (1) is the result of (2)   (b) (1) is the reason for (2)
(c) (1) is independent of (2)   (d) (1) contradicts (2)

(iii) According to given passage, what is the current capacity of the highest-capacity nuclear plant in India?
(a) 4000 MW   (b) 2000 MW
(c) 6780 MW   (d) 22480 MW

(iv) According to the research, Prototype Fast Breeder Reactor is being constructed by ....
(a) The UN
(b) The Union Minister for Atomic Energy
(c) NPCIL
(d) BHAVINI

(v) Select the option listing the aspects of development that will be given highest priority.
(1) sitting   (2) designing
(3) constructing   (4) commissioning
(5) operating
(a) 1, 3 and 4   (b) 2, 4 and 5
(c) 1, 2 and 4   (d) All of these

(vi) The nuclear energy programme in India was launched by
(a) The Government of India
(b) Dr. Jitendra Singh
(c) Homi J Bhabha
(d) Department of Atomic Energy

(vii) Choose the correct option to answer the following.

According to the above passage, how much does nuclear power contribute to the country's electricity supply?
(a) About half of the supply.
(b) All of the country's electricity supply comes from nuclear power.
(c) About 2% of the supply.
(d) None of the above

Answers and Explanations

PASSAGE 1

(i) (c) The purpose of the given report was to give population projections for '2011-2036'.

(ii) (d) The statement (2) is not apparent from the given paragraph and hence, is false. Hence, option (d) is the correct answer.

(iii) (a) "India's population growth rate is expected to decline drastically"–gives the correct meaning of the statement in the question.

(iv) (a) Rural population will decline as compared to the growth of urban population.

(v) (b) India's population is expected to grow by 311 million by 2036, according to the given passage.

(vi) (d) The projections came in July of 2020 because of delay in setting up of the committee and delay on the government's part.

(vii) (b) The decadal growth for the decade 2011-2021, according to the passage, is 12.5%.

PASSAGE 2

(i) (b) The purpose of the passage was to study schizophrenia and its treatment.

(ii) (a) According to the passage, schizophrenia is a mental illness in which people face thinking distortions, lose the sense of self and start hallucinating. Hence, option (a) is the correct answer.

(iii) (c) A result of schizophrenia is hallucination people see and hear things which are not really there and have mistaken beliefs. This is the correct meaning of the phrase in the question.

(iv) (b) The management of people, ailed with schizophrenia required joint effort of health care professionals.

(v) (c) The objectives of treatment of schizophrenia include to reduce symptoms, to increase the quality of life and to promote recovery.

(vi) (d) The clinical pharmacists are involved in educating on prevention of the mental illness, promoting a healthy life and modifying lifestyle in accordance with the treatment. Hence, option (d) is the correct answer.

(vii) (a) 'Comprehensive drug information' is appropriate to fill the blank in order to answer the question.

PASSAGE 3

(i) (c) "The increasing problem of youth unemployment in India" is the focus of the given passage.

(ii) (b) It is true that the unemployment rate in India has risen over the past year because of the nationwide lockdown imposed due to the COVID-19 pandemic.

(iii) (b) "Unemployment and unemployed people have a harmful effect on the country's economic potential" is the correct meaning of the statement in the question.

(iv) (c) According to the given passage and the ILO's report, India's unemployment rate rose to the highest in the last 30 years.

(v) (a) The ILO, The Financial Express and Ritu Diwan spoke on the problem of youth unemployment along with Rajrishi Singhal and the centre for monitoring Indian Economy, according to the passage.

(vi) (c) PM Modi asked the industry representatives to increase exports.

(vii) (c) In 2020, the unemployment rate in India rose to 7.11%.

PASSAGE 4

(i) (a) Enzymes initiates chemical reaction in our body.

(ii) (b) According to Dr. CR Shaw, cancer was inhibited upto 90% with the help of sprouts.

(iii) (d) As per due passage eating sprouts is good for children, adults and elderly.

(iv) (b) In the last para of the passage, sprouts are excellent soft food, predigested and can be easily assimilated.

(v) (a) The word assimilated means absord of 'digest'.

(vi) (a) The statement (a) is not correct according to the passage.

(vii) (c) Releasing of essential vitamins is not a step in the sprouting process.

PASSAGE 5

(i) (b) The passage focuses to highlight the issue of bad quality of air in India.

(ii) (d) The statement (2) is false as the passage doesn't state any positive impacts or results. Hence, option (d) is the correct answer.

 (iii) (c) It is true that the toxicity of air causes decrease in labour and crop yields.

 (iv) (c) Owing to air pollution, more than 1.1 million people died untimely deaths.

 (v) (b) The severe effects of unclean and toxic air includes it being an obstacle in development, it causing numerous health problems and the bad effects on the economy of a country.

 (vi) (d) All of the given options are correct.

 (vii) (a) According to paragraph 4, action against the increasing crisis of air toxicity should be taken at individual level and with a collaborative commitment.

PASSAGE 6

 (i) (b) The purpose of the passage is to show that snow leopards are vulnerable species and must be protected.

 (ii) (c) Both statements give information of two projects introduced to conserve the concerned endangered species but they are not dependent on each other.

Hence, option (c) is the correct answer.

 (iii) (a) 'Umbrella species' refers to such species whose protection will ensure the protection of other species. Hence, option (a) is the correct answer.

 (iv) (a) High altitude regions should be protected as they support unique wildlife of global significance.

 (v) (c) Along with the snow leopards, 'Tibetan Wolf' is also found in the Himalayan region.

 (vi) (d) River systems are integral to the nation's food security.

 (vii) (b) 'Protect the region as well' is appropriate to fill the blank to complete the sentence.

PASSAGE 7

 (i) (c) India is building nuclear power stations to increase industrial production.

 (ii) (c) Controlled nuclear exposions can be used to blow up mountains.

 (iii) (b) The word commissioned does not refer to 'creating something new'.

 (iv) (c) 'Creation of artificial dams, increasing self life of food, medical facilities and weather predictions are uses of nuclear energy.

 (v) (c) Statement (1) is independent of statement (2).

 (vi) (d) Radiation is helpful in preserving fruits.

 (vii) (b) Weather satellite is use for predicting rainfall and cyclones with accuracy.

PASSAGE 8

 (i) (a) The purpose of the passage is to highlight the issue of child labour.

 (ii) (b) The connection between poverty and child labour is cyclic, as suggested in paragraph 2. Poverty forces children to work which eventually results in failure to acquire education and thus, remain poor. Hence, option (b) is the correct answer.

 (iii) (c) The given sentence means that the fight against the evil of child labour has come to a half.

 (iv) (a) The data provided in the passage suggests that 'almost half of all children', engaged in labour, are in hazardous work.

 (v) (d) The severe effects of child labour include obstacles in education, unequal opportunities, poverty, slow demographic transition and obstruction of skill development.

 (vi) (b) Child labour hinders young children from participating in school.

 (vii) (a) The passage suggests that child labour affects the 'potential and dignity' of young children.

PASSAGE 9

 (i) (a) The passage wishes to show that the spread of any virus can be controlled with proper preventive measures.

 (ii) (a) Statement (1) is the result of statement (2).

 (iii) (a) The given statement means that not only the state or Central Governments but the districts, sub-districts, panchayats, etc. are also responsible.

 (iv) (b) For two days, no corona case had been registered in Kerala after the first case was registered.

 (v) (d) In order to contain the spread of virus, the Kerala Government began rapid screening of the patients, quarantining them and isolating them.

 (vi) (c) The District Collectors worked with the District Medical Officers in coordination.

 (vii) (d) 'Local testing labs', 'district-wise allocations' and 'walk-in simple kiosks' allowed Kerala to conduct mass screenings and tests.

PASSAGE 10

 (i) (c) The purpose of increasing India's nuclear power generation capacity is to 'generate more clean energy'.

 (ii) (c) Both the statements are apparent from the given passage but are not dependent on each other.

 (iii) (b) The current capacity of the highest-capacity nuclear plant in India is 2000 MW, according to the passage.

 (iv) (d) Prototype Fast Breeder Reactor is being constructed by 'BHAVINI'.

 (v) (d) The aspects of development that will be given highest priority include sitting, designing, constructing, commissioning and operating.

 (vi) (c) The nuclear energy programme in India was launched by 'Homi J Bhabha'.

 (vii) (c) Nuclear power's contribution to the country's electricity is around 2%.

Chapter Test

• Discursive Passages

1. Read the passage given below.

1. In life we sometimes have disagreements with people. When this happens, the important thing is to try not to let a calm discussion turn into a heated argument. But of course this is easier said than done.

2. The way you begin the conversation is very important. Imagine you are a student sharing a flat with another student who you think isn't doing her share of housework. If you say, 'Look, you never do your share of the housework', the discussion will very soon turn into an argument. It's much more constructive to say something like, 'I think we'd better have another look about how we divide up the housework.'

3. If you're the person who is the wrong, just admit it! This is the easiest and best way to avoid an argument just apologise and move on. The other person will have more respect for you in the future if you do that.

4. Don't exaggerate. Try not to say things like 'You always come home late when my mother comes to dinner' when perhaps this has only happened twice. This will just make the other person think you're being unreasonable, and will probably make him or her stop listening to your arguments.

5. Sometimes we just can't avoid a discussion turning into an argument. But if you do start arguing with someone, it is important to keep things under control.

6. Don't raise your voice. Raising your voice will just make the other person lose their temper too. If you find yourself raising your voice, stop for a moment and take a deep breath. If you can talk calmly and quietly, you'll find your partner will be more ready to think about what you are saying.

7. It is also very important to stick to the point. Try to keep to the topic you are talking about. Don't bring up old arguments, or try to bring in other' issues. Just concentrate on solving the one problem, and leave the other things for another time.

8. If necessary call 'Time out'. If you think that an argument is getting out of control, then you must say, 'Listen, I'd rather talk about this tomorrow when we've both calmed down'. You can then continue the discussion the next day when both of you are less tense and angry.

That way there is much more chance that you will be able to reach an agreement. You'll also probably find that the problem is much easier to solve.

9. Some people think that arguing is always bad. This is not true. Conflict is a normal part of life, and dealing with conflict is an important part of any relationship. If you don't learn to argue properly, then when a real problem comes along, you won't be prepared to face it together. Think of the smaller arguments as training sessions. Learn how to argue cleanly and fairly. It will help your relationship become stronger and last longer.

On the basis of your reading answer any eight out of the following questions.

(i) According to author what is easy to suggest but quite difficult to do?
   (a) To have disagreements with people.
   (b) Not to let a peaceful discussion change into a heated argument.
   (c) Never raise your voice
   (d) To have heated argument with friends.

(ii) Which of the following steps should one follow to stop arguing, according to the passage?
   1. Keeping calm   2. Leaving the room
   3. Stop talking   4. Don't raise your voice
   5. Stick to your point 6. Time out
   (a) 1,2 and 3
   (b) 4,5 and 6
   (c) 1,3 and 5
   (d) 2,4 and 6

(iii) Which of the following will be the most appropriate title for the passage?
   (a) How Not to Argue?
   (b) Discussion Vs Argument
   (c) Stopping an Argument
   (d) How to Control Arguments?

(iv) What happens if a complaint is exaggerated?
   (a) The other person thinks you are unreasonable
   (b) The other person think that you are overbearing
   (c) The other person finds you stupid
   (d) The other person stops paying any attention to you

(v) Select the option that makes the correct use of 'agreement' as used in the passage, to fill in the blank space.
   (a) This .... was proposed to the General Assembly in 1870.
   (b) Dean was beginning to have serious .... about the trip.
   (c) It is a willing .... to a set of values and procedures and a standard of conduct.
   (d) In discussing nutrition, there is often .... on the nature of the problems.

(vi) Select the option that suitably completes the dialogue with reference to the above passage.

Max : Making mistake is a part of human nature sometimes you get stuck in ugly situations.

Jack : We can just apologise person ..... and the other.

    (a) will argue
    (b) will have more respect for you
    (c) will fight
    (d) will complain against you

(vii) The second paragraph suggests that
    (a) we must share our workload
    (b) how we start a discussion is very important
    (c) our words can hurt people
    (d) we must use words that do not presuppose an argument

Read the passage given below.

1. We live in an age of wonders and miracles. It has been called the 'Age of Science', and different aspects of our life that have changed in the preceding centuries have been attributed to science. This is completely true, but it is only one side of the coin. The flip side is that as we have advanced more and more, something fundamental to humanity has been left behind. Values such as empathy and concern for our fellow-human beings are gradually being eroded due to the onslaught of our ever-evolving lifestyles, aided by the marvels of technological advancement.

2. Take the example of the Internet. On the one hand, access to information and knowledge at the click of a button is a boon to everyone making our lives much simpler. On the other, it has severely limited actual contact with teachers, friends and elders. Thus, the learning that a person gains is incomplete as he or she cannot easily take the advice that another person can give on the basis of knowledge and practical experience that is at his or her disposal.

3. Today, a small child can access and navigate the Internet with ease that still astounds those from the older generation. But what is even more astounding is the neglect of the basic human traits of friendship, society, relationships and family values. Owing to all the technological advancements and the gadgets available today, children often miss out on the most enriching of childhood experiences such as playing outdoor games with friends, which apart from being immensely enjoyable and physically exhilarating, also develops traits such as teamwork and discipline from an early age.

4. But now when the concept of friends is gradually being limited to virtual friends, one shudders to think of the implications for the personality development of a child because the time spent with computers or mobile phones for entertainment can never really substitute for the holistic benefits of outdoor play.

5. As for me I think this age of rapid development has created at least as many problems as it has solved. The reason is that the basic goal of life, the pursuit of happiness, has now been replaced by the pursuit of money. Money and happiness are considered analogous in our present society, but actually are not so. In this mindless pursuit of money, nobody has time now to appreciate the beauty of life, which consists of a simple act of kindness to someone in a time of need.

6. So there is an urgent need to stop for a moment and think about where we are actually heading- is it development or destruction? Do we have to wait until people have grown so much apart from each other that we cannot see the suffering of our own species due to our mindless greed, or can we still mend our ways?

On the basis of your reading answer any ten of the following questions.

(i) According to passage it is like one side of the coin to say that life has changed owing to science as
    (a) age of science has brought wonders and miracles.
    (b) different aspects of life have changed due to science.
    (c) there is another side of the coin to look at.
    (d) this side of coin is true and sufficient to look at.

(ii) Choose the option that best captures the central idea of the passage from the given quotes.
    (a) "The most important journey of our lives is doing good for the world, especially working for the upliftment of human conditions, human values, human dignity and human rights."? – Amit Ray
    (b) "It is impossible to escape the impression that people commonly use false standards of measurement — that they seek power, success and wealth for themselves and admire them in others and that they underestimate what is of true value in life."? –Sigmund Freud
    (c) "The saddest aspect of life right now is that science gathers knowledge faster than society gathers wisdom."? – Isaac Asimov
    (d) "Rather than love, than money, than fame, give me truth.? – Henry David Thoreau

(iii) Internet hampers the holistic growth of a child by
    (a) encouraging human traits of friendship, society and family.
    (b) enriching childhood experiences of outdoor games.
    (c) providing virtual friends and gadgets.
    (d) developing teamwork and discipline.

(iv) Which of the following lists the values that humans have lost with advancement?

1. Materialism	2. Kindness
3. Concern	4. Empathy
5. Respect	6. Equality

    (a) 1 and 3   (b) 5 and 6
    (c) 1,5 and 6   (d) 2,3 and 4

(v) Which of the following will be the most appropriate title for the passage?
(a) Understanding Society
(b) Technological Advancement- The Flip Side
(c) Not All is Good
(d) Is this Development?

(vi) Select the option that makes the correct use of 'navigate' as used in the passage, to fill in the space.
(a) You can .... this site by subject or by alphabet.
(b) Andrew had been his confidante and mentor whose guidance had helped him .... his role properly.
(c) The improvement of the Missouri is far more difficult to .... than the Mississippi-was begun by Congress in 1832.
(d) She was more comfortable on the ground crawling than trying to .... the shaking earth on her feet.

(vii) What does older generation wonder about?
(a) How to access internet and the gadgets.
(b) How can small children easily navigate through internet.
(c) Where have they lost the morals and virtues.
(d) How to inculcate morals and virtues in the younger generations.

• Case Based Factual Passages

Read the passage given below.

1. Data released by India's food quality regulator, the Food Safety and Standards Authority of India (FSSAI) earlier, shows that nearly 25% samples of edible goods it tested this year were found to be adulterated or in violation of prescribed standards.

2. The samples included milk and dairy products, spices, cereals as well as branded food products. A total of 85,729 samples were sent, so far. FSSAI carried out the testing following a spike in complaints from consumers over quality and adulteration, said an agency official.

3. According to the data, 20,390 samples of the 85,729 sent to the agency were found to be non-confirming to prescribed standards. While agency officials maintain that Food Safety Officers in each state regularly test samples to check for compliance and also take recourse in cases of violations according to the Food Safety and Standards Act, 2006, experts claim that poor enforcement on the ground and a lack of awareness plague the process.

4. Consumer activist Bijon Mishra said the lengthy legal procedure involved in penalizing violators provides an opportunity to the accused to keep doing business. "Law enforcement is very poor. It takes years to finalise a case and by that time, sellers keep on making profits. Moreover, people are also not aware. Hardly anybody complains about adulteration," he added.

5. Umesh Sharma, an advocate, said enforcement of rules is very poor on the ground. "The issue is directly related to public health and the government should take serious initiatives to implement food safety rules," he said. Data from the agency shows an abysmal conviction rate.

6. In 2017, the Law Commission had issued a set of recommendations regarding the issue. The panel had recommended that IPC Sections 272 (dealing with adulteration of food and drinks) and 273 (dealing with the sale of noxious food and drinks) be amended to make adulteration a serious crime. It was also recommended that depending on the gravity of the offence, punishment can include life imprisonment and the minimum sentence should be six months' jail term.

7. The panel, headed by former Supreme Court judge BS Chauhan, also wanted amendments to Section 357 of the Criminal Procedure Code so that courts can order compensation for victims.

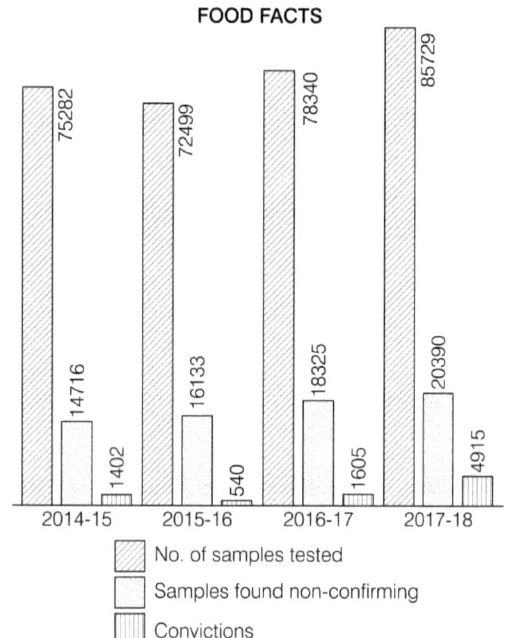

On the basis of your reading answer any ten of the following questions.

(i) What did the data revealed by FSSAI show?
(a) Branded food contains cancer causing adulterants
(b) Food items consumed violate the food quality standards
(c) With food adulteration, food quality checks have increased
(d) Food adulteration has grown exponentially over the years

(ii) Based on your understanding of the passage, choose the option that lists the punishments set for offenders.
1. Life imprisonment   2. Fine
3. Sentence of 6 months   4. Death sentences
5. Public shaming
(a) 1,2 and 3   (b) 1,4 and 5
(c) 1,3 and 4   (d) 2,3 and 5

(iii) What was the reason behind the survey?
(a) The increasing number of complaints regarding quality and adulteration
(b) Increasing mortality rate
(c) For consumer awareness
(d) Increasing malnutrition

(iv) What do the experts claim regarding the data?
(a) Quality of food is as per the Food Safety and Standards Act, 2006
(b) The poor enforcement on the ground and a lack of awareness results in adulteration
(c) The procedure of penalization is very lengthy
(d) The officials are corrupted to the core allowing the penalized to escape

(v) .... allows the penalised to continue their business.
(a) Poor law enforcement
(b) Higher connections
(c) Lengthy process
(d) The scope of the business

(vi) Select the option that is true for the two statements given below.
1. Adulteration became a serious crime.
2. Depending on the gravity of the offence, punishment can include life imprisonment.
(a) (1) is the result of (2)
(b) (2) is the result for (1)
(c) (1) is independent of (2)
(d) (1) contradicts (2)

(vii) The panel head also called for
(a) checking of the food safety officers
(b) video data of all safety tests
(c) compensation for the victims
(d) Both (a) and (c)

Read the passage given below.

1. If you went only by the number of shopping malls in the country, you would think the brick-and-mortar retail space in India is booming. By the end of this year, India will have more than 87 million square feet of shopping space in its malls. The country already has 570 functional malls, with this number having doubled over the last five years.

2. There is, however, one problem: buyers are no longer doing their shopping at malls. What looked like India's great retail growth story is turning out to be a tale of empty shopping complexes and stalled projects, with developers giving up midway instead of trying to make these projects profitable. The culprit, data suggests, could be online shopping.

3. A report by The Associated Chambers of Commerce and Industry of India pegs the growth rate of e-commerce in India at 40-50% in the next five years. Physical stores are the ones bearing the brunt of massive discounts and comfort that e-commerce has brought to the desks and palms of the youngsters who no longer feel it necessary to visit a retail outlet to buy something.

According to the report, 80-85% of the space in the new malls is lying vacant. This problem is being faced by mall owners across the board, starting with metropolitan cities like Delhi, Mumbai and Chennai, followed by Ahmedabad and Hyderabad. In each of these cities, mall rentals fell by more than 40% owing to fewer footfalls.

4. At the same time, online shopping grew by over 350% in just one year, the report adds. "Apart from convenience, rising fuel price, security reasons, online discounts and availability with abundance of choices are keeping consumers indoors," said DS Rawat, Secretary General of ASSOCHAM.

5. Even then, revenues continue to come in for some of the malls. The reason: anchor stores. Anchor stores are those specialised stores that offer exclusive products generally not available online. Brands like Zara, H&M and even Starbucks are acting as anchor stores for mall owners, who are rushing to sign them, at times with revenue sharing models and larger exclusive spaces.

6. Evidently, the surge of online retail has also forced mall owners to set their priorities straight, as watching movies and dining out remains among the last few things that people cannot get delivered to their doorstep. "The arrival of the mall syndrome has accelerated the growth of cineplexes as multiplexes are the anchor tenants in most of these malls," Shravan Shroff, managing director, Shringar Cinemas.

Only 17% of Indians are online as of now, a low number compared to other countries. However, these numbers are soon set to swell up exponentially as India hits the mark of 300 million people online before the year ends, leaving mall owners as well as retailers with the mammoth task of luring people away from their computers and phones to physical stores at a time when developers are slowing down on projects.

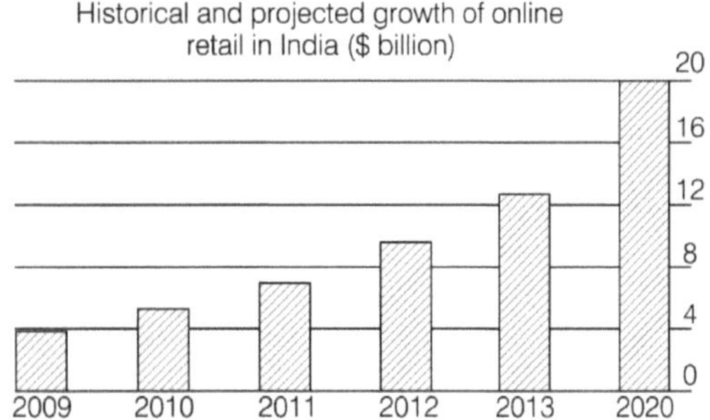

On the basis of your reading of the passage, answer any ten of the following questions.

(i) What does the given passage highlight?
 (a) Increasing number of mall in India.
 (b) Growth of online retail in India.
 (c) Impact of online retail on malls.
 (d) The strategies that malls must utilise to increase footfall.

(ii) In the line, "... a tale of empty", the word "Tale" DOES NOT refer to
 (a) a story   (b) a situation
 (c) a report   (d) an account

(iii) How does online retail growth affect the shopping malls?
 (a) They are empty.
 (b) Mall projects are stalled.
 (c) No focus on making business profitable.
 (d) Both (a) and (b)

(iv) Based on your understanding of the passage, Choose the option that lists the ways in which the e-commerce industry had taken over malls.
 1. Discounts   2. Offers   3.Travelling
 4. Security   5. Choices   6. Convenience

 (a) 1,2 and 3
 (b) 4,5 and 6
 (c) 1,2 and 5
 (d) All of these

(v) Choose the option that lists the statement that is not true according to the given graph.
 (a) Between the year 2013 and 2020, online shopping has seen exponential growth.
 (b) Online shopping became a part of the Indian shopping market in 2009.
 (c) Online shopping saw consistency between 2009-2012.
 (d) Online shopping drastically changed the shopping scenario after 2012.

(vi) What are Anchor stores?
 (a) Stores that sell customised products.
 (b) Stores that provide all kinds of stuff at one place.
 (c) Stores that sell product that is not available online.
 (d) Stores that offer various options of a product.

(vii) What depicts that the growing retail story of India is problematic?
 (a) Reduction in footfall.
 (b) Dependence on anchor stores.
 (c) Malls remaining empty.
 (d) Difficulty faced by mall owners in paying rent.

ANSWERS

Discursive Passages

1. (i) (b)   (ii) (b)   (iii) (d)   (iv) (a)   (v) (c)   (vi) (b)   (vii) (b)
2. (i) (b)   (ii) (b)   (iii) (c)   (iv) (d)   (v) (b)   (vi) (a)   (vii) (b)

Case Based Factual Passages

1. (i) (b)   (ii) (a)   (iii) (a)   (iv) (b)   (v) (c)   (vi) (b)   (vii) (d)
2. (i) (c)   (ii) (a)   (iii) (d)   (iv) (d)   (v) (b)   (vi) (c)   (vii) (b)

CHAPTER 01

Formal Letters

In this Chapter...

Letter is the most common and convenient method of expressing our thoughts and opinions. It is an important mode of communication. There are two types of letters:

1. **Formal Letters** These letters are written in formal, simple and polite language. These follows a certain format. Such letters are written for official purposes to authorities, colleagues, seniors, etc.

2. **Informal Letters** These include letters written to parents, friends, relatives, etc. They are written in easy and conversational language. These are mainly used for personal communication.

Types of Formal Letters

Formal letters can be broadly classified into four types. These are

1. Complaint letters   2. Enquiry letters

3. Letters of order (Placing/Cancelling an order)

4. Letter to the Editor, etc.

In CBSE Class 10th term II syllabus, Letters of order (Placing / cancelling an order) and Letters of Enquiry will be discussed.

Letters of Order

These are business letters which include placing or cancelling an order for products/services from another company or organisation. They are written in a very well formatted and formal manner.

While placing an order, the writer has to be very careful about giving accurate information. Any inaccuracies may result in delayed/wrong deliveries with serious financial implications. Such letters should mention the following

- Specifications (with quantities) of the products/services to be supplied.
- Reference number of the quotation/price list against which the order has been placed.
- Payment terms/credit terms (as applicable).
- Required date of delivery.
- Mode of transport of goods (if required).
- All taxes/delivery charges.
- Any other terms and conditions.

Letters of Enquiry

A letter of enquiry is written when we want to get some specific information from someone. It could be about a product or a service. It is also written in response to advertisements.

The letter includes the following

- A brief introduction about yourself and/or your organisation.
- Details of the product or service required.
- Clearly mention the details you want to know.
- If there is a time limit within which you need the information, specify it in the letter.

Points to be Kept in Mind

- The subject line should match with what is asked in the question. It should be short and to the point.
- Get right to the purpose of the letter in polite and formal language. Do not give unnecessary details.
- Be clear, concise and to the point. Stick to the word limit mentioned in the question paper.
- Use simple language so that the letter is easy to understand. Do not use long-winded sentences.
- Review your finished letter for clarity from the reader's viewpoint.

Parts of a Formal Letter

An effective formal letter is one which has the following parts

1. Sender's Address

It is the address of the writer. It is written at the top left hand corner of the page. If the address consists of several parts, each part should be written in a separate line.

Example 2334/31, Mangal Pandey Nagar
Ekta Park
Meerut–250002

Note You must not put a comma at the end of each line.

2. Date

Either of the given formats can be used to write the date

20th January, 20XX,   January 20th, 20XX

Note Do not use abbreviation like Jan, Feb, etc., and do not write 19 instead of 2019.

3. Receiver's Address

All official letters are addressed to the authority/post of the person concerned. Hence, we write receiver's address after addressing the official.

Example The Editor
The Times of India
Daryaganj
Delhi–110002

4. Subject

It expresses the main theme or objective of the letter clearly. It must be as brief as possible.

5. Salutation

It is the greeting to the person to whom the letter is addressed. In official letters we use

Sir/Madam, or

Dear Sir/Dear Madam.

Note When writing the salutation, we have to keep in mind the gender of the receiver, if specified in the question.

6. Body of the Letter

It contains all the information that the writer wants to convey. The body includes three main parts.

(i) **Introductory Paragraph/Sentence** It states the purpose of writing the letter.

(ii) **Informative Paragraph** Gives details of the problem, its causes, effects, possible solutions, etc.

(iii) **Concluding Paragraph/Sentence** It states your hopes, comments, requests, suggestions, etc.

7. Complimentary Close

It's a courteous way of ending the letter. We can write

- Yours sincerely   • Yours faithfully   • Yours truly

Note 1 The first letter of second word (here 's', 'f', 't') is never written in capital.

Note 2 Do not use Your's instead of Yours.

8. Signature

This is the sender's name. If applicable, the sender's designation may be added below the name.

Format of Formal Letter

You are Rama/Ramesh of D-105, Lajpat Nagar, New Delhi. You want information about German Language Courses at German Embassy, Chanakya Puri, New Delhi. Write a letter to the Director enquiring about the same.

D-105, Lajpat Nagar New Delhi 1100XX	Sender's Address
12th August, 20XX	Date
The Director German Embassy Chankya Puri New Delhi 1100XX	Receiver's Official Capacity and Address
Subject Enquiry regarding German courses	Subject
Sir/Madam	Salutation
I wish to make certain enquiries about the German language courses offered by your institution.	Introductory Sentence
I have just completed class X and want to pursue my career in German. I would like to know the duration of the course, the fee structure and the transport facilities available. I have always had a flair for language and have wanted to be a multilingual. Hence, the desire to learn the German language. I will be grateful if you could send me the brochure along with the enrolment form enabling me to register myself for the course at the earliest. Also, please find enclosed with the letter a draft of Rs. 200/- for the brochure. Any balance money shall be paid on receipt of the same.	Body of the Letter
I hope to hear from you soon.	Concluding Sentence
Yours faithfully Rama	Complimentary close Signature

Chapter Practice

• Letter for Placing/ Cancelling an Order

Objective Questions

1. Which of the following comes after the Sender's Address in a formal letter?
(a) Receiver's Address   (b) Date
(c) Subject   (d) Salutation

Ans. (*b*)

2. Which of the following is a proper complimentary close in letters for placing / cancelling an order?
(a) Yours faithfully   (b) Yours lovingly
(c) Yours sincerely
(d) With all my love and respect

Ans. (*a*)

3. Which of the following gives the correct format of the Date in a formal letter of placement/cancellation of an order?
(a) Aug 20XX   (b) January 20th
(c) 14th November 20XX   (d) Both (a) and (c)

Ans. (*c*)

Directions (Q. Nos 4 and 5) The letter given below is incomplete. Choose the correct options to complete the letter.

New Age Computer Shop

Ganesh Nagar

Delhi 1100xx

24th April, 20xx

The Incharge

Enfotech

Preet Vihar

Delhi 1100xx

   Subject : ....(4).......

Sir / Madam

Please refer to your quotation dated 2nd April, 20xx along with item list. I am please to place an order for the following items as per terms and rates mentioned in the quotations.

Needles to say that all the ordered items should reach us in good condition. Any damage during the transportation will be your responsibility.

Name of the Items and Brands	Ram	No. of Items
Dell	8GB	50
HP	4GB	60
Lenovo	4GB	30
Asus	8GB	20

The payment will be made on delivery as per the agreement. ...(5)... the above mentioned products at the earliest.

Yours faithfully

Nidhi Das

Manager, New Age Computer

4. (a) Cancelling an order for computers
(b) Placing on order for laptops
(c) Enquiry about laptops
(d) Send us the laptops mentioned below

Ans. (*b*)

5. (a) I demand that you send me the
(b) I expect you to send me pictures of
(c) I request you to send me
(d) I implore you to send me details of

Ans. (*c*)

Directions (Q. Nos. 6-8) Answer the questions given, with reference to the context below.

6. You are store–incharge in ABC Senior Secondary School, Kolkata. Write a letter to the Manager, Pioneer Traders & Co., Kolkata, placing an order of stationery articles for your school store. You are Naveen.

(i) Which of the following aspects are required to be mentioned in the letter by Naveen?
  1. Details of order
  2. Date on which letter is to be written

3. Expected date of reply
4. Expected date of delivery
5. Receiver's home address

(a) 1, 2 and 5   (b) 2, 3 and 4
(c) 1, 2 and 4   (d) 3, 4 and 5

Ans. (*c*)

(ii) Choose the correct subject for the letter.
    (a) Supply of stationery articles
    (b) Stationery articles
    (c) Supply
    (d) Supply our order

Ans. (*a*)

(iii) Choose the correct opening line for the letter.
    (a) Three days ago we had discussed about the different stationery articles at your store.
    (b) This is in reference with our telephonic conversation about the different stationery articles at your store.
    (c) This is with reference to our telephonic conversation three days ago wherein we had discussed about the different stationery articles at your store.
    (d) This is to refer to your telephonic conversation three days ago.

Ans. (*c*)

(iv) Choose the option which has the correct list of order

(a)

S. No.	Articles	Qty
1.	White Paper (17" x 27")	10 reams
2.	Stencil Paper	10 boxes
3.	White Chalk Stick	12 gross
4.	Footballs	12

(b)

S. No.	Articles	Qty
1.	White Paper (17" x 27")	10 reams
2.	Stencil Paper	10 boxes
3.	White Chalk Stick	12 gross
4.	Carbon Paper (Black)	12 boxes
5.	School bags	20

(c)

S. No.	Articles	Qty
1.	White Paper (17" x 27")	10 reams
2.	Stencil Paper	10 boxes
3.	Slates	5

(d)

S. No.	Articles	Qty
1.	White Paper (17" x 27")	10 reams
2.	Stencil Paper	10 boxes
3.	White Chalk Stick	12 gross
4.	Carbon Paper (Black)	12 boxes

Ans. (*d*)

(v) Choose the option that provides a suitable concluding portion for the letter.
    (1) We would, therefore, request you to deliver the above articles latest by 10th June. The payment shall be done digitally after receiving the order.
    (2) Deliver the above articles latest by 10th June. The order will be sent back after the said date. The payment shall be done digitally after receiving the order.

    (a) No to option (1) because of use of informal language
    (b) Yes to option (1) because of use of polite tone
    (c) Yes to option (2) because of use of authoritative tone
    (d) No to option (2) because of use of formal language

Ans. (*b*)

(vi) Choose the correct complementary closing for the above letter.
    (a) Yours faithfully
    Naveen
    Store–incharge
    ABC Senior Secondary School
    Kolkata
    (b) Yours faithfully
    Naveen
    Kolkata
    (c) Yours lovingly
    Naveen
    Store–incharge
    (d) Yours obediently
    Naveen
    Store–incharge
    ABC Senior Secondary School
    Kolkata

Ans. (*a*)

7. You are the librarian of Amla Public School. You had placed an order for textbooks with Dhanpati and Sons. Since the books did not arrive on time, you have decided to cancel the order. Write a letter to the Manager, Dhanpati and Sons, Chennai, cancelling the order.

(i) Which of the following aspects are required to be mentioned in the letter by the librarian?
    1. Photocopy of the Invoice
    2. Date on which letter is to be written
    3. Expected date of reply
    4. Expected date of delivery
    5. Receiver's address

    (a) 1, 2 and 5
    (b) 2, 3 and 4
    (c) 1, 2, 4 and 5
    (d) 3, 4 and 5

Ans. (*c*)

(ii) Which of the following options is correct for Sender's Address, Date and Receiver's Address? Answer in reference to the letter.

    (a) Manager
        Dhanpati and Son
        Chennai
        15th September, 20XX
        Librarian
        Amla Public School
        Bangalore

    (b) Amla Public School
        15th of September 20XX.
        Manager, Dhanpati and Sons
        Chennai

    (c) Amla Public School
        Bangalore
        15th September, 20XX
        Manager
        Dhanpati and Sons
        Chennai

    (d) Dhanpati and Sons Chennai
        September 15th, 20XX
        Librarian
        Amla Public School
        Bangalore

Ans. (c)

(iii) Choose the correct subject for the letter.

    (a) Supply of books   (b) Cancellation of order
    (c) Supply   (d) Supply our order

Ans. (b)

(iv) Choose the correct opening line for the letter.

    (a) I hope that you are in possession of receipt of our order No. A/27/2/04 dated 20th December 20XX for the supply of 200 copies of MA Kalam's Accounting, by 10th January 20XX.

    (b) I hope that you are in possession of receipt of your order No. A/27/2/04 dated 20th December 20XX by 10th January 20XX.

    (c) You are in possession of receipt of your order No. A/27/2/04 dated 20th December 20XX for the supply of 200 copies of MA Kalam's Accounting.

    (d) I think that you are in possession of receipt of our order No. A/27/2/04 dated 20th December 20XX for the supply of 200 copies of MA Kalam's Accounting, by 10th January 20XX.

Ans. (a)

(v) Complete the following to give the reason for cancellation of the order.

I regret to inform you that the (i) .... We have no option but to cancel the order. We request you to (ii) ....

    (i) (a) delivery was to be till 19 January
        (b) delivery is made till 19 January
        (c) delivery had not been made till 19th January
        (d) delivery has not been made till 19th January

Ans. (d)

    (ii) (a) treat the cancelled order
        (b) kindly treat the order
        (c) kindly treat the order as cancelled
        (d) order as cancelled

Ans. (c)

(vi) Choose the correct concluding line of the letter.

    (a) I expect a written confirmation of this cancellation from you and a full refund within 7 to 10 days.

    (b) I expect a written confirmation of this cancellation from you and a full refund within 7 to 10 days. Please find enclosed a copy of the invoice.

    (c) I expect full refund within 7 to 10 days.

    (d) I expect a written confirmation of this cancellation. Please find enclosed a copy of invoice.

Ans. (b)

PART 2
Subjective Questions

1. You are Vaibhavi Sinha, examination incharge, Goodway Public School, Aurobindo Road, Indore. You require 4 reams of white paper, 2 packets of carbon paper, one dozen registers, blue and red ball point pens (50 each). Place an order with Sunrise Stationery Mart, 12 Mall Road, Indore mentioning terms of payment, discount asked by you and delivery date.   **CBSE 2020**

Ans. Goodway Public School
Aurobindo Road, Indore

5th March, 20XX

Sunrise Stationery Mart
12 Mall Road, Indore

Subject Placing an order for Stationery

Sir/Ma'am

We would like to place a bulk order of stationery items for the academic session 2020-2021. The particulars of the products and the quantity to be supplied are given below.

S.No	Product	Quantity
1.	White Paper	4 reams
2.	Carbon Paper	2 packets
3.	Registers	1 dozen
4.	Blue Ballpoint pens	50 units
5.	Red Ballpoint Pens	50 units

Please send us fresh supplies by 4th July. Any delivery after that would be returned. Also, please send the bill at the time of delivery. As always, we will first check the supplies and then transfer the payment digitally.

We hope that we will get additional discount given that we are your regular customers.

Yours truly
Vaibhavi Sinha
Examination Incharge
Goodway Public School

2. As the head of the music department of your school, write a letter to Mysore Music Associations, placing an order for some instruments such as flute, casio, sitar, harmonium, etc. You are Nandini/Namit of Army School, Safdarjung, Enclave, Delhi.

Ans. Army School
Safdarjung Enclave
Delhi

12th April, 20XX

The Proprietor
Mysore Music Associations
Delhi

Subject Order for Musical Instruments

Sir/Ma'am

This is to inform you that our school's management has decided to order music instruments from your company. The prices mentioned in your quotation no. 12/49/17/82 dated 8 April 20XX have been approved. The list of the instruments required is given below:

S.No.	Name of Instruments	Quantity
1.	Flutes	20
2.	Casio	5
3.	Sitar	3
4.	Harmonium	5
5.	Drums	2

Kindly ensure that the delivery is made within 15 days between 10 AM and 2 PM. We are sure that proper packing of the instruments will be taken care of. Any damage caused during transportation will be your responsibility.

The payment will be made only after the quality of the instruments has been checked and approved by the school management.

For any enquiry, feel free to contact the undersigned.

Yours sincerely
Nandini/Namit
(Head-Department of Music)
Mobile No. 97604XXXXX

3. Write a letter to Lightways Sports, Amrapalli, Thane, placing an order for sports articles (minimum 4 items) to be supplied to your school, ABC Matriculation School, Civil Lines, Pune. Sign as Ravi/Raveena, Sports Secretary.

Ans. ABC Matriculation School
Civil Lines,
Pune

11th August, 20XX

Lightways Sports
Amrapalli,
Thane

Subject Purchase Order for Sports Articles

Sir/Ma'am

This is to inform you that we require the following sports articles for our school's sports room.

S.No.	Item Description	Brand	Quantity
1	Football with bladder	Nivea	4
2	Cricket bats	SVG	6
3	Cricket balls	SVG	6
4	Batting Gloves (pairs)	SVG	8

Please send these items at the price mentioned in your quotation no, 15A/23/17-18 dated 4 August 20XX. The delivery can be made to the school on any weekday between 8 AM and 2 PM.

Payment will be made after the consignment is received and checked by the school's games department. Please ensure that the quality of products matches the standard of the samples shown. If defects are found in the goods, the whole consignment will be returned without any payment.

Yours sincerely
Ravi/Raveena
Sports Secretary

4. You are Ambika/Mohit, Librarian, High Scope Public School, Hauz Khas, Delhi. Write a letter to Jindal Publishers, Pratap Vihar, Delhi to place an order for English to Hindi dictionaries, illustrated children's encyclopedia, fiction books, etc. for your school library. Request them for a catalogue, discount offered, mode of payment and time taken for delivery.   **CBSE 2019**

Ans. High Scope Public School
Hauz Khas
Delhi

23rd October, 20XX

Jindal Publishers
Pratap Vihar, Delhi

Subject Purchase Order for Books

Sir/Ma'am

This is with reference to our telephonic conversation on 15 October 20XX regarding an enquiry about certain books for school children. Based on your verbal quotation, we would like to place an order for the following books.

S. No.	Name	Quantity
1	English to Hindi Dictionary	20
2	Illustrated Children's Encyclopedia	25
3	Panchatantra	15
4	Nancy Drew : Compiled Mysteries	15
5	Arabian Nights	15

Please make sure that the latest editions of these books are delivered in proper condition. We will be pleased if you give us a suitable discount and send us a catalogue too. Also, let us know the mode of payment and time taken to deliver.

Your sincerely
Ambika/Mohit
Librarian

5. You are Vidushi/Vishal, Hostel Warden, Zenith Public School, Kosi Kalan. Write a letter to the Sales Manager, Bharat Electricals and Domestic Appliances Limited, Delhi, placing an order for fans, microwaves ovens, geysers and tubelights that you wish to purchase for the hostel. Also ask for the discount permissible on the purchase.

Ans. Zenith Public School
Kosi Kalan

11th March, 20XX

Sales Manager
Bharat Electricals and Domestic Appliances Limited
Delhi

Subject Purchase Order for Electrical Goods

Sir/Ma'am

This is to inform you that we are placing an order for the following electrical goods at the prices mentioned in your price list no. BE DA/43 dated 1 January 20XX.

S. No.	Item	Brand	Quantity
1.	Ceiling Fans 36"	Usha	10
2.	Table Fans 12"	Usha	10
3.	Microwave Ovens	Thompson	2
4.	Geysers 2.5 KW	Thompson	5
5.	Tubelight Fixtures	Philips	20

Please deliver the goods to school hostel on any week day between 9 AM and 1 PM. We also request you to provide some discount on this purchase. Payment will be made after the consignment is received and checked by the Hostel Committee of the school.

If any defect is found in the products, the whole consignment will be returned without any payment. If you have any query, feel free to contact the undersigned.

Yours sincerely
Vishal/Vidushi
(Hostel Warden)
(Mobile No 99680XXXXX)

6. You are Madan/ Shama, Purchasing Manager of Electra Trading Concern, North Avenue, New Delhi. Draft a suitable letter canceling the order you have placed with your supplier, Sales Manager, Proton Electronics, Airport Road, New Delhi, because of the unusual delay in the delivery of goods.

Ans. Electra Trading Concern
North Avenue
New Delhi

5th February, 20XX

Sales Manager
Proton Electronics
Airport Road
New Delhi

Subject Cancellation of Order No: 01/33/04 dated 15 January 20XX

Sir/ Ma'am

We hope that you have received our order No. 01/33/04 dated 15th January 20XX for the supply of thirty Sony Televisions to be supplied to us on or before 1st February 20XX.

We regret to inform you that you have neither executed the order within the agreed date nor informed us of your inability to execute the order. We have to suffer much for the no delivery of Sony Television within the time.

We have, thus, decided to cancel the order for your failure to execute the order in time as time was of prime importance in this respect.

We, therefore, request you to kindly treat our order as canceled. Please note that we shall refuse the goods, if delivered, because of the cancellation of the order.

Yours faithfully
Madan/ Shama
Purchasing Officer
Electra Trading Concern

7. You are Priya/ Prem, Vice Principal of ABC School, Park Street, Bengaluru. You have ordered some textbooks from GenX Books Pvt Ltd., Bengaluru. Write a letter to cancel the order since you no longer needed them.

Ans. ABC School
Park Street
Bengaluru

23rd May, 20XX

Manager
GenX Books Pvt Ltd.
Bengaluru

Subject Cancellation of an order numbered 15246

Sir/ Ma'am

I am writing this letter to inform you that I would like to cancel the order of 13 physics textbooks and 15 Social Science textbooks which was placed earlier this week. The order number is 15246. The school has decided to provide books by themselves, and hence we won't need them.

Please send the refund amount to the account number given below. I am incredibly sorry for all the trouble and inconvenience caused. Kindly send me the confirmation for the cancellation of the order.

Bank Name – XYZ Bank, Park Street Branch
Account No. – 6532XXXXXX
Contact no. – 785XXXXXXX

Yours sincerely
Priya/Prem
Vice Principal
ABC School

8. You are Vaibhav/Vaibhavi, Incharge, Readers Club of Alpha Public School, Ajmer. The club has been established recently which requires a number of books. Write a letter to the Manager (Marketing), National Book Trust, A-5, Green Park, New Delhi placing an order for some books for the Readers Club.

Ans. Alpha Public School,
Ajmer

10th June 20XX

The Marketing Manager
National Book Trust
A-5, Green Park,
New Delhi

Subject Placing an order for books

Sir/Madam

I would like to place a bulk order for a number of books required for the Reading Club of Alpha Public School, Ajmer. The reading club has been recently established; therefore we require the following books :

Title of the book	Number of copies
Panchtantra (English)	20
Panchtantra (Hindi)	20
Children's Illustrated Encyclopedia	15
Nancy Drew: Compiled Mysteries	25
Arabian Nights	20
English to Hindi dictionary	10

Please send us new copies of the above mentioned books by 16th June, 20XX. Any delivery after that would be returned back. Also, send the bill at the time of delivery. As always, we will first check the supplies and then transfer the payment digitally. We hope that we will get an additional discount since we are your regular customers.

Thanking you
Yours truly
Vaibhav/ Vaibhavi
Incharge,
Readers Club, Alpha School

• Letter of Enquiry

PART 1

Objective Questions

1. Which of the following comes first and is mentioned on the top left corner of a formal letter?
(a) Sender's address   (b) Date
(c) Receiver's address   (d) Both (b) and (c)

Ans. (*a*)

2. Which of the following options mentions an appropriate concluding sentence in a letter of enquiry?
(a) Call the undersigned with any doubt
(b) Call the concerned authority if you have any doubt
(c) I hope to hear from you soon
(d) Please write a reply as soon as you get this letter

Ans. (*c*)

Directions (Q. Nos. 4 and 5) Answer any five out of the six questions given, with reference to the context below.

3. You are Anshika, a student of class XII and resident of 56 D, Ring Road, ITO, New Delhi, and wants to be a choreographer. Write a letter to the director, National Institute of Choreography, Noida, seeking information about their course, admission procedure, eligibility criteria and other necessary details.

(i) Which of the following options mentions the receiver's address?

    (a) 56 D, Ring Road
        ITO
        New Delhi

    (b) The Director
        National Institute of Choreography
        Sector 16, Noida

    (c) 56 D, Ring Road, ITO

    (d) National Institute of Choreography
        Sector 16, Noida

Ans. (*b*)

(ii) Pick the correct subject for the letter.

    (a) Enquiry course in choreography
    (b) A course in choreography
    (c) Enquiry in choreography
    (d) Enquiry regarding course in choreography

Ans. (*d*)

(iii) Select the correct opening line for the letter.

    (a) I came across your advertisement in The Times of India. I would like to know in detail about the course offered by your institute.

    (b) I came across your advertisement dated 11 July 20XX. I would like to know in detail about the choreography course.

    (c) I came across your advertisement in The Times of India dated 11 July 20XX. I would like to know in detail about the choreography course offered by your institute.

    (d) I came across your advertisement in The Times of India dated 11 July 20XX. I would like to know in detail about all the courses offered by your institute.

Ans. (*c*)

(iv) Complete the following to give your introduction and reason of enquiry about the course.

I am currently in XII class and preparing for my final exams. I am very much interested in dancing and (i) .... I am also given to understand that this institute is (ii) .... so far as choreography is concerned and I would very much like to be part of it.

    (i) (a) want it as a career
        (b) as a career
        (c) want to take it as a career
        (d) want to take it

Ans. (*c*)

    (ii) (a) by far the best
         (b) the best
         (c) by and far the best
         (d) by and large the best

Ans. (*a*)

(v) Choose the option that shows the correct list of information to be mentioned in the letter.

    (a)
    - The department and programme faculty
    - Funding opportunities
    - Scholarships available
    - Admission procedure
    - Eligibility criteria

    (b)
    - The department and programme faculty
    - Admission procedure
    - Eligibility criteria

    (c)
    - Funding opportunities
    - Scholarships available
    - Hostel facilities

    (d)
    - Funding opportunities
    - Scholarships available
    - Admission procedure
    - Courses offered

Ans. (*a*)

(vi) Choose the correct concluding line for the letter.

    (a) Send me the brochure along with the enrolment form at the earliest so that I could register myself for the course.

    (b) Kindly send me the brochure along with the enrolment form at the earliest so that I could register myself for the course.

    (c) Kindly send me the brochure along with the enrolment form to get me registered for the course.

    (d) Kindly send the brochure at the earliest so that I could register myself for the course.

Ans. (*d*)

4. You are David/Ronny of 305, B–block, New Ashok Nagar, Delhi. You need an accommodation at a hotel in Shimla. Write a letter to the Manager of the hotel enquiring about booking an accommodation.

(i) Arrange the following to give format of the enquiry letter.

    1. Receiver's address   2. Subject
    3. Sender's address   4. Content
    5. Salutation   6. Complementary close

    (a) 312546   (b) 625134   (c) 251436   (d) 165423

Ans. (*a*)

(ii) Choose the correct subject for the letter.

    (a) Enquiry about your hotel
    (b) Accommodation at your hotel
    (c) Accommodation needed
    (d) Enquiry about the accommodation

Ans. (*d*)

(iii) Choose the opening line for the letter.

    (a) I have read a lot about your hotel on internet and ratings are also very good. Your hotel is famous for the excellent arrangements, the pick–ups, the food, etc.

    (b) Your hotel is famous for the excellent arrangements, the pick–ups, the food, etc.

    (c) I have read a lot about your hotel on internet and ratings are also very good.

    (d) I have read a lot about your hotel on internet and the excellent arrangements, the pick–ups, the food, etc.

Ans. (*a*)

(iv) Complete the following to give the travel details for the letter.

So, I am writing this letter to you as I am going to visit Shimla with my family next month, (i) .... I need (ii) .... for 6 days.

    (i) (a) from 14 October 20XX to 21 October 20XX

       (b) from 4 October 20XX to 15 October 20XX

       (c) from 4 October 20XX to 8 October 20XX

       (d) from 4 October 20XX to 10 October 20XX

Ans. (*d*)

    (ii) (a) one double bedrooms with attached bathrooms

        (b) two double bedrooms with attached bathrooms

        (c) two double bedrooms

        (d) two attached bathrooms

Ans. (*b*)

(v) Choose the option which shows the correct list of information to be mentioned in the letter.

(a)
- Availability of accommodation for 10 days
- Tariffs for the rooms
- Payment procedure
- Pick-up and drop facility from railway station
- Sight-seeing arrangements
- Other terms and conditions

(b)
- Availability of accommodation for 6 days
- Tariffs for the rooms
- Payment procedure
- Pick-up and drop facility
- Sight-seeing arrangements
- Other terms and conditions

(c)
- Availability of accommodation for 10 days
- Tariffs for the rooms
- Payment procedure
- Pick-up and drop facility from railway station
- Sight-seeing arrangements
- Other terms and conditions

(d)
- Availability of accommodation for 10 days
- Tariffs for the rooms
- Payment procedure

Ans. (*c*)

(vi) Choose the option that mentions the correct concluding line for the letter.

    (1) On hearing from you, I shall remit you for advance booking and finalise my travel programme. Hope to hear from you soon!

    (2) I want to hear from you soon so that I shall remit you for advance booking and finalise my travel programme.

    (a) No to option (1) because of use of informal language

    (b) Yes to option (1) because of use of polite tone

    (c) Yes to option (2) because of use of authoritative tone

    (d) No to option (2) because of use of formal language

Ans. (*b*)

PART 2
Subjective Questions

1. You are interested to join a swimming club of repute in your town. Write a letter to the Secretary, College Square Swimming Club, Kolkata, enquiring about the details about membership and other terms and conditions of the club. You are Monalisa of 143, Palm Avenue, Kolkata.

Ans. 143, Palm Avenue

Kolkata

25th June, 20XX

The Secretary
College Square Swimming Club
Kolkata 700XXX

Subject Enquiry about membership

Sir/ Ma'am

I came across your advertisement in the Daily Times dated 24th June 20XX. I would like to know the details about the membership of your club. I have heard very good reports about the hygiene part of the pool and the swimming coaches who are extremely well–trained. All this has made me more determined to join your swimming club. I am studying in Class X and wish to pursue swimming under a good coach. Kindly send me the following details

- Availability of swimming coaches
- Monthly charges
- Duration of training
- Other terms and conditions

I would be grateful if you provide me the details as soon as possible so that I can get myself registered at your swimming club.

Yours faithfully

Monalisa

2. As of the current IT scenario, you are interested to pursue a short–term BPO/KPO training course after your 12th exam. Write a letter to the Director, Virtue Training Center, Noida, enquiring about their short–term courses and all other necessary details. You are Rahul/Rajiv.

Ans. 54, Tagore Park

New Delhi

30th June, 20XX

The Director
Virtue Training Center
Noida, UP

Subject Enquiry about BPO/KPO training course

Sir/ Ma'am

I came across your advertisement in The Hindu dated 29 June 20XX. I would like to know in detail about the courses offered by your institute. I am of the opinion that these courses will help me in the selection of my future career course too.

A short–term course in BPO / KPO will be the threshold for the other business management courses. I am in Class 12th. I wish to pursue BPO/KPO training course after the exam.

Kindly send me all the necessary details, including fees, duration of training and its prospects, etc. at the above address.

Thanking you

Yours faithfully

Rahul

3. You have lost your original certificates of Class X and XII. You want to get their duplicates issued but you do not know the procedure.Write a letter to the Chairman, CBSE, Preet Vihar enquiring about the fee to be deposited, mode of payment, time taken by the board for issuing duplicate certificates and any other formalities. You are Tarun/Taruna, 7/9, Kunj Apartments, Shimla.

CBSE 2019

Ans. 7/9, Kunj Apartments

Shimla

10th December, 20XX

The Chairman
CBSE, Preet Vihar
New Delhi

Subject Procedure to get Duplicate Certificates

Sir

This is to inform you that I, Tarun/Taruna, passed Class X (Roll no. 90XXXXX) in the year 2016 and Class XII (Roll no. 105XXXX) in the year 2018 from CBSE Board. Unfortunately, I have lost my original certificates of Class

X and Class XII as the bag containing those certificates has been stolen. Now, I urgently need the duplicates of those certificates.

Therefore, please let me know the following details

* Procedures to get the duplicate certificates
* The amount of fee to be deposited
* Mode of payment
* Time taken by the board to issue the certificates

Also, if there is any other formality to be completed, please do let me know. I would be much obliged.

Thanking you

Yours sincerely

Tarun/Taruna

4. Your are Sudhir/Sita, the Head Boy/Girl of ABC Public School, Jayanagar, Bengaluru. Your school has planned an overnight excursion of students and teachers to Mysuru and nearby areas. Write a letter to the Secretary, Ace Youth Hostel, Mysuru requesting him to send you a quotation for the costs of providing accommodation for 15 girls, 20 boys and two teachers for two days next month. Specify the dates when you want the accommodation and any other terms and conditions.

Ans. ABC Public School

Jayanagar
Bengaluru

23rd October, 20XX

The Secretary
Ace Youth Hostel
Mysuru

Subject Cost of Accommodation for a Group of Students for Two Days

Sir

This is to inform you that our school has planned an overnight excursion of students and teachers to Mysuru and nearby areas on 10 and 11 November 20XX.

There would be 15 girls, 20 boys and two teachers in the group. They would need the overnight accommodation on the night of 10th November in Mysuru.

The group will reach at 11 am on 10th and will depart by 5 pm on 11th November. Therefore, two dormitories for students (one for girls and one for boys) and two single rooms for teachers would be required.

Kindly let us know that cost of accommodation at the earliest. Further, if you need any more information, you may contact the undersigned.

Yours sincerely

Sudhir/Sita
(Head Boy/Head Girl)
Contact No. 97546XXXXX

5. You are the Head of Housekeeping Department in a three star hotel. Write a letter to the Manager, Herbal Bath Care, Ajmal Khan Road, Indore, making an enquiry about some towels, rugs and other bathroom products for the hotel.

Ans. Golden Star Hotel
GT Road, Indore

20th May, 20XX

The Manager
Herbal Bath Care
Ajmal Khan Road, Indore

Subject Enquiry about some Bath Care Products

Sir
We are an established chain of hotels in Indore. We need bathroom rugs, mats, towels, napkins and shower caps for our hotel at GT Road. Please provide us a copy of your brochure along with the price list. Also, let us know if you would be willing to provide a special discount of 25% on the bulk order.

If the quality of your products, their prices and your terms suit us, we would like to place the order. I look forward to your quick response.

Yours sincerely
Mahendra Nagpal
(Head–Housekeeping)

6.

> **Advertisement**
> Institute of Hospitality Management F-5, Junk Road, New Delhi
> A few seats available in Housekeeping course, contact immediately for further details.

You are Ramesh Kumar/Radhika Kumari, 12A, Fort Road, Agra. You read the above advertisement in a local daily. You want to pursue the course in housekeeping. Write a letter to the Director of the Institute enquiring about the duration of the course, fees and other details.   **CBSE 2019**

Ans. 12A, Fort Road
Agra

14th March, 20XX

The Director
Institute of Hospitality Management
F-5, Junk Road
New Delhi

Subject Enquiry about the Housekeeping Course

Sir
With reference to your advertisement in Agra Patrika dated 11 March 20XX, I would like to know the details of the Housekeeping Course offered by your reputed institute.

I am a Commerce graduate and wish to make a career in the Hospitality industry.
So, kindly provide me the following information
- The course details
- Amount of fees to be paid
- Mode of payment
- Accommodation facilities
- Job prospects via you institution
- Any other information regarding the course

I would be grateful if you provide me the details as soon as possible so that I can take the decision of enrolling myself in the course.

Yours sincerely
Ramesh Kumar/Radhika Kumari

7. You are Vipul/Apoorva, living at D-424, Island Avenue, Ernakulam. You have seen an advertisement about a diploma course in French language soon to be organized by Maxwell Institute of Languages, Fort Road, Kochi. Write a letter to the advertiser seeking all the relevant information like admission procedure, fee structure, duration of the course, timing of the class, transport facilities etc.   **CBSE 2020**

Ans. D-424, Island Avenue,
Ernakulam

9th December, 20XX

The Director
Maxwell Institute of Languages
Fort Road
Kochi

Subject Enquiry about a diploma course in French Language

Sir/Madam,
With reference to your advertisement in daily newspaper dated 7th December, 20XX, I would like to know the details of the diploma course in French language offered by your reputed institute.

I am a Commerce graduate and wish to learn a new language which can help me in my career. So, kindly provide me the following information :
Admission procedure
Fee structure
Duration of the course
Timing of the class
Transport facilities
Any other relevant information regarding the course
I would be grateful if you provide me the details as soon as possible so that I can take the decision of enrolling myself in the course.

Yours Sincerely
Vipul/Apporva

8. As a health conscious person, you have noticed an advertisement in a newspaper on yoga classes in your neighbourhood. Write a letter to the Organiser, Yoga for Public, R.K. Puram, New Delhi requesting him/her to send you information about the duration of the course and other relevant details. You are Shweta/Srikar of 15, R.K. Puram, New Delhi.   **CBSE 2019**

Ans. 15, R.K. Puram

New Delhi

26th December, 20XX

Organizer
Yoga for Public
R.K. Puram
New Delhi

Subject Enquiry regarding yoga course

Sir/Madam

This is with reference to your advertisement of Yoga classes in R.K. Puram. I would like to appreciate the efforts put by you for the benefit of people. Yoga is a very good exercise for all age groups. It helps to connect mind and body and helps to relax.

As a health conscious person myself, I practice yoga everyday. It makes me energetic and refreshed the whole day. I would like to join the yoga course at your institute and would like to have the following details

- Date of commencement of the course
- Duration of the course
- Timings of the classes
- Fee structure
- Any other relevant detail about the course

I would be thankful if you send the details as soon as possible.

Thanking you

Your sincerely
Shweta/Srikar

Analytical Paragraph

In this Chapter...

- Format of Analytical Writing
- Chapter Practice

An analytical paragraph is a written text based on the analysis of a data. It explain your research or argument with the help of data, chart, outline, clues or table. In other words, an analytical paragraph does not only describe the data but also points out some specific parts from it to justify your statement. For writing an analytical paragraph, following points to be kept in mind

- Read the data carefully
- Understand the topic on which the analytical paragraph is to be written
- Carefully study the trends, figures and information given for analysis
- Use the trends as an evidence to support your statement
- Give a clear introduction and conclusion
- Try to avoid repetition of information

Elements of An Analytical Paragraph

- **Claim or Topic Statement** Make a clear statement or give a title to your paragraph about what you want to communicate based on the given data.
- **Evidence** Use the figures or the textual information to justify your argument.
- **Explanation** Explain your analysis and understanding of the data in detail.
- **Conclusion** End the paragraph with rewriting your argument in a new way.

Format of Analytical Paragraph

Given alongside is a graph that pertains to the percentage of the population living below the poverty line across different states of India in two years, 1973-74 and 1999-2000. Use the information provided to write a paragraph on the age-old problem of poverty in India. Mention the regional trends and the way the scenario has changed over the years.

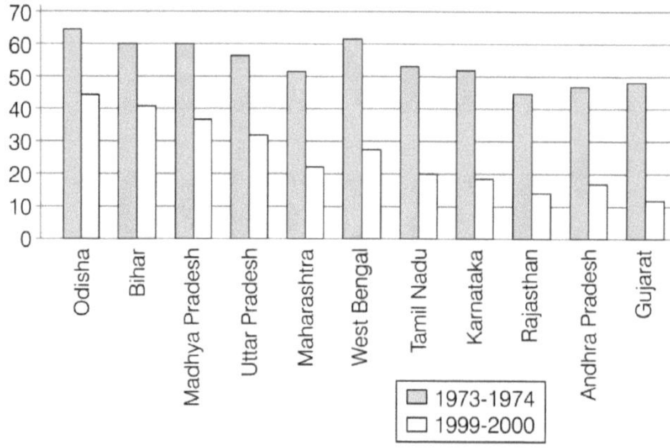

Title

Poverty : A Perrenial Problem in India

Introduction
(This paragraph contains the topic statement, the claim or the central argument of the analysis)

Poverty in India has manifested itself in many ways. It has become one of the major ever-continuous problems that our country faces today. Be it landless laborers, street cobblers, rag pickers, vendors or beggars, all of them fall under the category of "poor". Even though there has been a decrease in the population of people living below the poverty line, the problem still persists.

Overview
(This paragraph contains the main points of the analysis. It contains the evidences and the explanations that justify your argument)

The given bar graph compares the percentage of the population living below the poverty line across different states of India in two years, 1973-74 and 1999-2000.The decrease of the poor population is very evident in all of the states. It comes as an encouraging note that in two of the states the decline has been drastic. Gujarat has seen a decrease of 27% of the poor population from 48% to 15% in the space of about 26 years. A similar decrease of 36% is seen in West Bengal from 63 % to 27% within the same time gap. At the same time, many states including Uttar Pradesh, Bihar, Madhya Pradesh and Odisha show a slow decline. They account for 70% of the poor stratum of the society in 1999-2000.

Conclusion
(The last paragraph reinstates the main argument of the whole paragraph.)

Thus, a lot need to be done to completely eradicate this social evil from the country.

Chapter Practice

Objective Questions

I. Answer any five out of the six questions given, with reference to the context below.

The graph below gives information from a 2008 report about consumption of energy in France since 1980 to present. Based on the graph write an analytical report in 150-200 words.

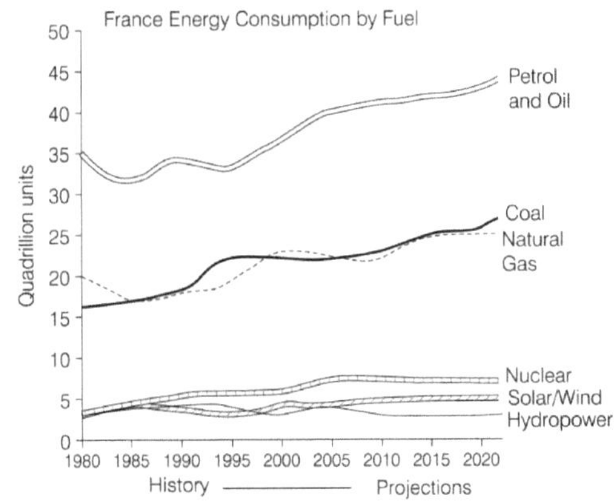

(i) Select a suitable topic for the paragraph.
   (a) France Energy Usage
   (b) Consumption of Energy in France
   (c) Fuel used in France
   (d) Consumption of Fuels

Ans. (*b*) Consumption of Energy in France

(ii) Which type of fuel shows the highest consumption among the people of France?
   (a) Nuclear power   (b) Wind hydropower
   (c) Petrol and oil   (d) Coal and natural gas

Ans. (*c*) Petrol and oil

(iii) Which type of fuel shows the least consumption among the people of France?
   (a) Nuclear power   (b) Wind hydropower
   (c) Solar power   (d) All of these

Ans. (*d*) All of these

(iv) Which year shows an increase in the consumption of coal?
   (a) 1995-2005   (b) 1995-2000
   (c) 2015-2020   (d) 1985-1990

Ans. (*d*) 1985-1990

(v) The main trend to be observed is that
   (a) The consumption of renewable energy resources, i.e., nuclear/ solar/ wind hydropower has increased over the time.
   (b) Coal and natural gas consumption is a better and economical option.
   (c) Consumption of non-renewable energy resources is continuously increasing.
   (d) None of the above

Ans. (*c*) Consumption of non-renewable energy resources is continuously increasing.

(vi) The increase in nuclear power is from ....
   (a) 4 quadrillion units to 7 quadrillion units
   (b) 2 quadrillion units to 8 quadrillion units
   (c) 3 quadrillion units to 11 quadrillion units
   (d) 4 quadrillion units to 10 quadrillion units

Ans. (*a*) 4 quadrillion units to 7 quadrillion units

II. Answer any five out of the six questions given, with reference to the context below.

The graph given below shows estimated sales of gold in Dubai in 2019.

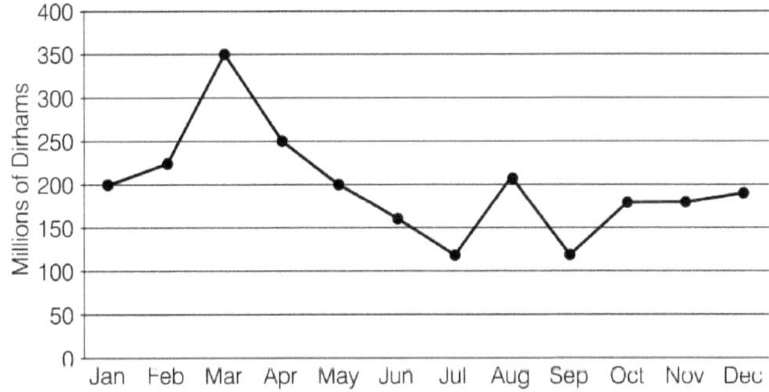

(i) Select a suitable topic for the paragraph.
   (a) Dubai Gold 2019   (b) Dubai Gold Sales in 2019
   (c) Gold Sales 2019   (d) Dubai Gold in 2019

Ans. (*b*) Dubai Gold Sales in 2019

(ii) The graph covers a period of ....
     (a) 12 months   (b) 2 years
     (c) 3 years   (d) last 5 years

Ans. (*a*) 12 months

(iii) Which month has the highest sales?
     (a) August
     (b) February
     (c) March
     (d) April

Ans. (*c*) March

(iv) Which months have the lowest sales?
     (a) January and December
     (b) October and November
     (c) July and September
     (d) June and December

Ans. (*c*) July and September

(v) Where did the sales plateau in the months of October and November?
     (a) 140 millions of Dirhams
     (b) 180 millions of Dirhams
     (c) 150 millions of Dirhams
     (d) 200 millions of Dirhams

Ans. (*b*) 180 millions of Dirhams

(vi) The sales at the end of the year were ....
     (a) quite lower than the starting of the year
     (b) almost same as the starting of the year
     (c) higher than the starting of the year
     (d) None of the above

Ans. (*b*) almost same as the starting of the year

III. Answer any five out of the six questions given, with reference to the context below.

The pie chart shows the proportion of people from different households living in poverty in the UK in 2017.

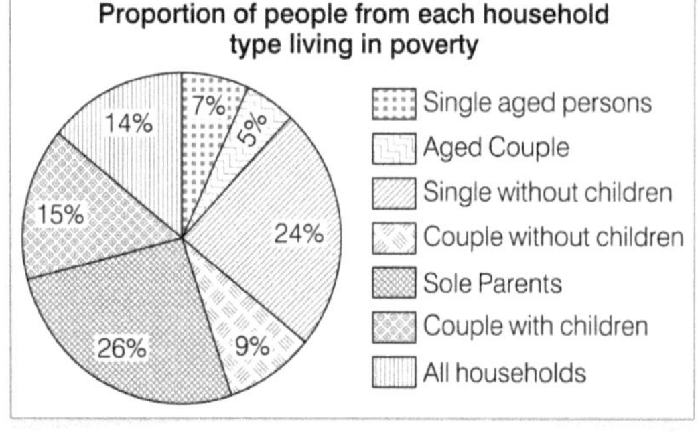

(i) Which type of household shows the highest percentage of poverty?
     (a) All households
     (b) Couples without children
     (c) Couples with children
     (d) Sole parents

Ans. (*d*) Sole parents

(ii) How much aged people account, for poverty?
     (a) 7%   (b) 5%
     (c) 12%   (d) 24%

Ans. (*c*) 12%

(iii) The main concluding point of the above data is that
     (a) The younger generation is poorer than their aged counterparts.
     (b) The aged generation is poorer than their younger counterparts.
     (c) Couples without children have a better economic condition.
     (d) Single without children have far better economic condition.

Ans. (*a*) The younger generation is poorer than their aged counterparts.

(iv) The second highest proportion of poverty is shown by ....
     (a) Couples without children
     (b) Single without children
     (c) Couples with children
     (d) All households

Ans. (*c*) Couples with children

(v) Choose a suitable title for the paragraph.
     (a) Poverty in the UK
     (b) Poor Households in the UK
     (c) Proportion of Poverty in the UK
     (d) None of the above

Ans. (*d*) None of the above

(vi) What are the main parts of an analytical paragraph?
     1. Title
     2. Body with analysis of given data
     3. Date
     4. Introduction
     5. Format
     6. Conclusion
     (a) 1, 2, 4 and 6   (b) 1, 3 and 5
     (c) 2, 3, 5 and 6   (d) 4, 5 and 6

Ans. (*a*) 1, 2, 4 and 6

IV. Answer any five out of the six questions given, with reference to the context below.

The following pie charts show the main reasons for migration to and from the UK in 2018.

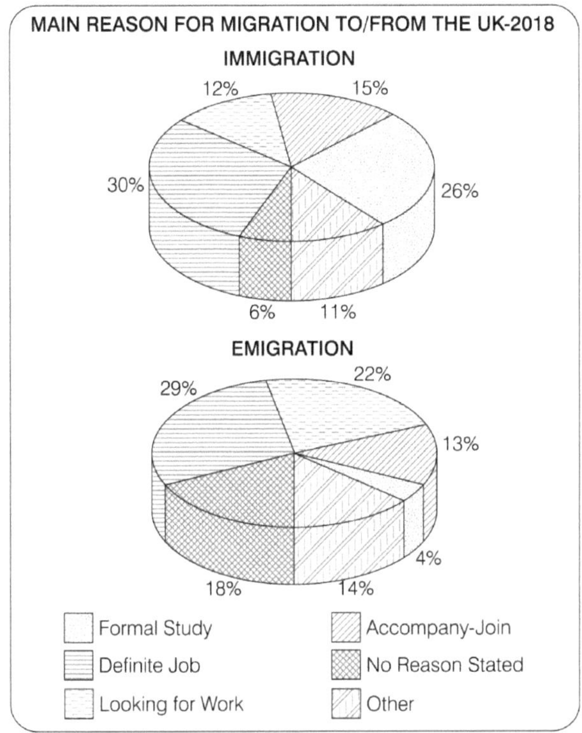

(i) What is the main reason for immigration and emigration?

(a) Employment opportunities, i.e., either definite job or searching for jobs

(b) Accompanying relative or family member

(c) Formal study

(d) All of the above

Ans. (*a*) Employment opportunities, i.e., either definite job or searching for jobs

(ii) Which reason has the least percentage of emigration from the UK?

(a) No reason stated (b) Other reasons

(c) Formal study (d) Definite job

Ans. (*c*) Formal study

(iii) How much percentage of people gave either other reason or no reason for leaving the UK?

(a) 17% (b) 32% (c) 6% (d) 14%

Ans. (*b*) 32%

(iv) Choose a suitable title for the paragraph.

(a) Migration in the UK

(b) Reasons for Migration

(c) Migration

(d) Migration to and from the UK

Ans. (*d*) Migration to and from the UK

(v) How much percentage of people immigrated to the UK for formal study?

(a) Over a quarter of people

(b) Less than a quarter of people

(c) Quarter of people

(d) More than half of people

Ans. (*a*) Over a quarter of people

(vi) Which of the following had almost similar percentages of immigration and emigration?

(a) Job opportunities (b) Accompany-join

(c) No reason stated (d) Both (a) and (b)

Ans. (*d*) Both (a) and (b)

PART 2
Subjective Questions

1. The maps given below show the changes that have taken place in Meadowside Village and Fonton, a neighbouring town, since 1962. Analyse the changes that had taken place over the years and write an analytical paragraph.

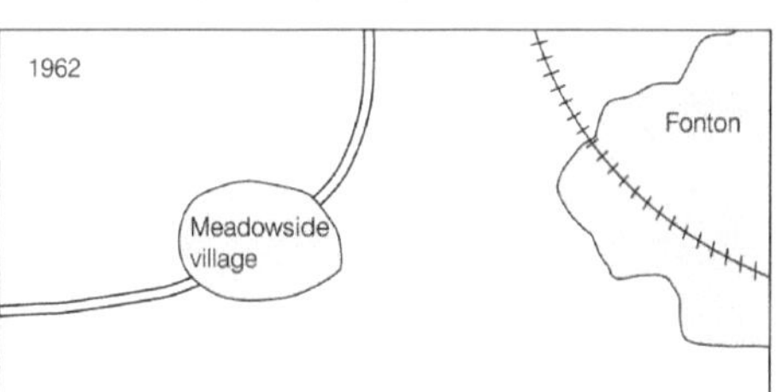

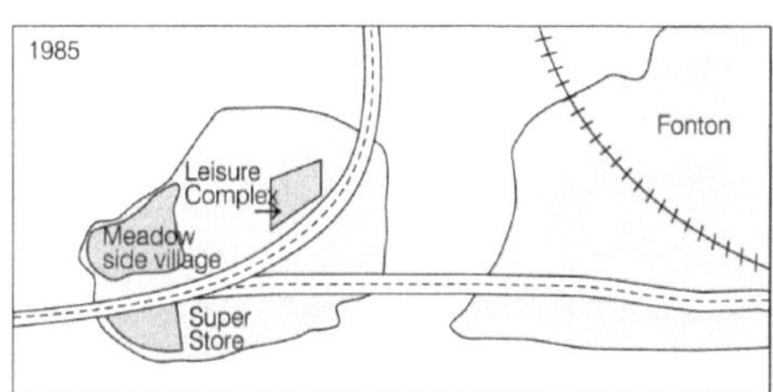

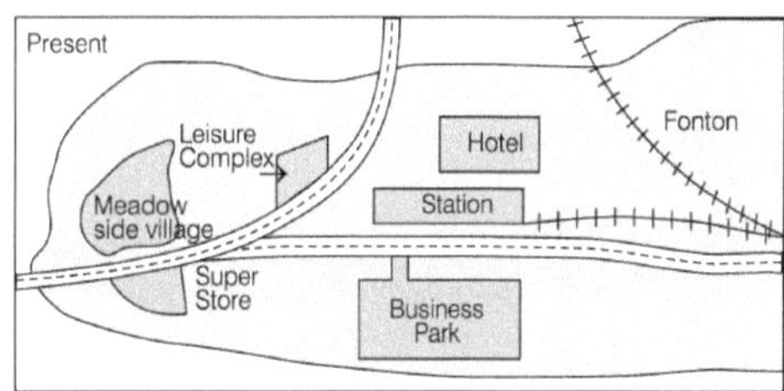

Ans. **The Growth and Development of the Region**

The maps given illustrate how the Meadowside village and Fonton, the neighbouring town has changed and developed over the years. It depicts the map of both the locations for the years 1962, 1985 and the present respectively. It is pretty evident from the maps that the size of both the village and the town increased over the years to have finally merged together as one.

In 1962, the village and town were separate entities with a different infrastructures, housing and other line facilities. There were no roads or rails to connect the village with the town. While there was a railways other line going through Fonton and a road from Meadowside village, they went in completely different directions. By 1985, both the locations not only grew in size but were also connected by another road that extended to the West. The growth and development of the region was unstoppable. Soon, the village and the town merged into a new area housing many luxurious facilities. A new railway line has also been introduced in the area, alongwith a railway station to board from.

Presently, the area even has a hotel and a business park that vouches for the great development of the region.

2. The following table gives statistics showing the aspects of quality of life in five countries. Write an analytical paragraph on the given information by selecting and reporting the main features and make comparisons wherever relevant.

County	GNP Per Head (1982 : US dollars)	Daily Calorie Supply Per Head	Life Expectancy at Birth (years)	Infant Mortality (per 1000 live births)
Bangladesh	140	1877	40	132
Bolivia	570	2086	50	124
Egypt	690	2950	56	97
Indonesia	580	2296	49	87
USA	13160	3653	74	12

Ans. **Quality of Life**

The given table shows the aspects of quality of life of five countries. Using the four economic indicators it shows the standard of living in these countries in the year 1982. From the data available to us, we can surely say that the standard of living in the USA was the highest among the five.

To begin with, the USA which is a developed country, has a GNP of 13,160 dollars per head. It has a relatively higher daily calorie intake rate and a high life expectancy rate at the time of birth. Infant mortality rate is also very low in the country. In comparison to the USA, these factors for other countries are at a much lower level. The range of the indicators depicted show a similar trend for the countries Egypt, Indonesia and Bolivia. Out of the three, Egypt seems to have the highest standard of living.

Within the same category, Egypt also shows a higher Infant Mortality Rate standing at 97 deaths per 1000 infants.

Out of the five countries, Bangladesh has the lowest quality of life with its GNP being a hundred times less than that of the USA. It has a significantly higher Infant Mortality Rate, and its daily calories intake as well as Life Expectancy is half of that of the USA. Given that, we can rank the countries as such- USA, Egypt, Indonesia, Bolivia and Bangladesh.

3. Read the following report and write an analytical paragraph based on the data provided in it.

> Recent studies have shown a rapid conversion of impaired glucose tolerance to diabetes in the Southern states of India, where the prevalence of diabetes among adults has reached approximately 20% in urban populations and approximately 10% in rural populations. Because of the considerable disparity in the availability and affordability of diabetes care, as well as low awareness of the disease, the glycemic outcome treated patients is far from idea.

Ans. **The Indian Diabetic Burden**

India, a country experiencing rapid socio-economic progress and urbanisation, carries a considerable share of the global diabetes burden. Studies in different parts of India have demonstrated an escalating prevalence of diabetes not only in urban populations, but also in rural populations as a result of the urbanisation of lifestyle parameters.

The prevalence of prediabetes is also high. Recent studies have shown rapid conversion of impaired glucose tolerance to diabetes in the Southern states of India where the prevalence of diabetes among adults has reached approximately 20% in urban populations and approximately 10% in rural populations.

Due to the considerable disparity in the availability and affordability of diabetes care, as well as awareness of the disease, the glycemic outcome in treated patients is far from ideal. Lower age at onset and a lack of good glycemic control are likely to increase occurrence of vascular complications.

The economic burden of treating diabetes and its complications is considerable. It is appropriate that the Indian Government has initiated a national programme for the management and prevention of diabetes and related metabolic disorders. Lifestyle modification is an effective tool for the primary prevention of diabetes in India.

4. Gautam was alarmed to see the graph that tracked the rising levels of Carbon dioxide in the air of his city, Nagpur. He decided to write a paragraph on the data to show his alarm and painted the present picture in order to caution people against environmental pollution. Write an analytical paragraph for Gautam.

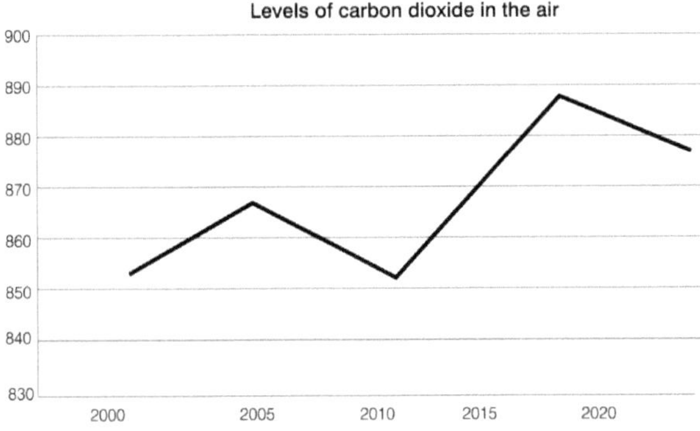

Ans.
Air Pollution- The Deadly Air

Air pollution is a serious issue affecting our planet today, yet many people continue to turn a blind eye thinking that it's not that serious. The given graph shows how alarming the issue of air pollution is specifically in Nagpur.

The graph shows a significant increase in the air pollution levels of the city. No doubt, people of Nagpur have been suffering from many respiratory diseases. While in 2000, the air pollution levels were not very low, the quality of air then was way better than the air the subsequent generations inhaled and are inhaling.

The years after 2005 leading to 2010 saw a decrease in the levels of Carbon Dioxide in the air which might be amounted to the raising of awareness regarding the issue. But this factor also falls short when suddenly after 2010, there was drastic change.

The quality of air was constantly declining and the percentage of carbon dioxide was ever on increase. The level of the gas reached from about 855 to 890.

Since then, many government policies, programmes and awareness sessions have been launched to aware people about it and to figure out a solution.

Therefore, the level of carbon dioxide has seen a slow decline. This decline indicates that there is still a lot of changes that needs to be implemented to make our environment pollution free.

5. Below is the graph that illustrates tiger population in India. Referring to the same, write an analytical Paragraph in 150-200 words.

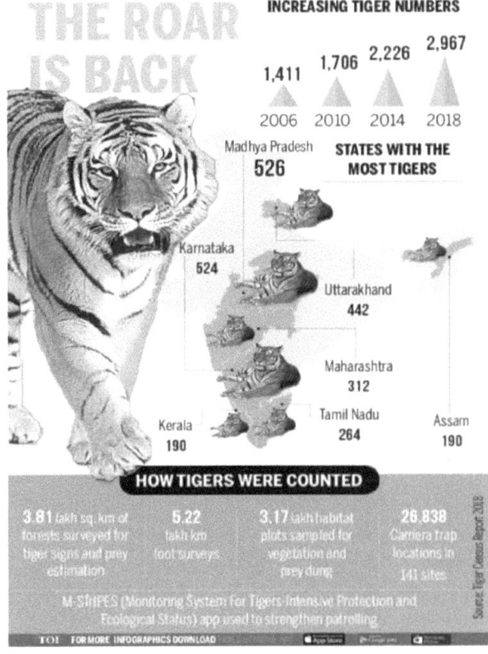

Ans.
The Roar Is Back

The tiger is an iconic species whose dwindling population is a concern for our whole country. To conserve the population of this mysterious animal, many programs and project were initiated by the country and it seems that the projects had worked well. The given graph shows the increasing number of the tiger in the country.

Poaching, one of the greatest dangers resulting in the decline, was the first thing addressed. Cameras were set at different locations where there was an abundance of tigers. Apart from the cameras, forest areas were converted into reserved regions where no poaching was allowed. To do so, approximately 5.22km of foot surveys were made to make sure that the area could remain a habitat for the species. As a result, the declining number started rising. The population of the tigers increased from 1411 in 2006 to 1706 in 2010 and then to 2226, 2967 in 2014 and 2018 respectively. The regions that saw the growth includes Madhya Pradesh where the tiger populations in 2018 was 526. The other states with high number of tigers are Karnataka, Uttarakhand, Maharashtra, Tamil Nadu, Kerala, and Assam with 524, 442, 312, 284, 190, and 190 respectively.

The given data suggests that, the tiger conservation projects and programmes have been quite successful in preventing the animal from becoming extinct and also in preserving their natural habitat.

6. The following data shows rise in number deaths due to violence which has considerably increased during recent years. Using this data, write an analytical paragraph focusing on how the educated youth can play a major role in establishing peace in the society.

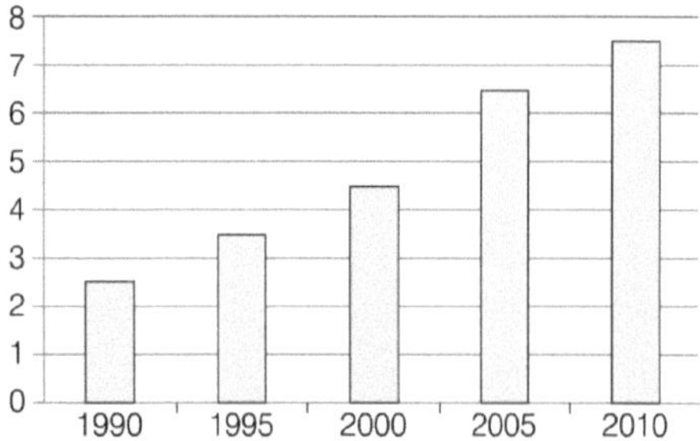

Ans.

Youth and Peace

Youth and peace are interlinked in society. Youth can play an important role in establishing peace in society. The above given graph depicts the data found in a survey presenting the decline of peace and the growth of violence in our society.

In the survey conducted, it was found that number of deaths due to violence has increased enormously since the nineties. The numbers presented in the data is quite alarming. There is absolutely no decline but a significant exponential growth in the death rate due to violence. In the year 1990, the death rate was 2.5 which increased to 3.5 in 1995.

This ever continuous growth is more visible in between the years 2000-2005 wherein the rate went up from 4.5 to 6.5. In 2010, it has increased to 7.5 and in the present does not really seem to stop. This condition is really very sad and needs an immediate action.

Our youth can play a major role in controlling this crime graph. They can contribute towards establishing peace in many ways. They can awaken the people towards the necessity of peace. They can help the police in catching the criminals. The youth of today holds the capacity to make the world a serene and a peaceful place to live.

7. Read the following report and write an analytical paragraph on the basis of the data provided.

> Single-use plastic water bottles cause dangerous substances to 'leach' into the soil and water. The bottles typically don't begin to break down for one hundred years or can take even longer. Their decomposition may be speeded up by extreme weather conditions, e.g. very hot or very cold temperatures.

> As they break down, they release dangerous chemicals like Bisphenol-A (BPA) into the soil. Bisphenol-A is an endocrine disruptor, i.e., it can affect the level of hormones within the human body, creating scope for diseases. In addition, BPA is known to be carcinogenic (cancer-causing) to humans.

> All these chemicals accumulate in the soil and eventually sink into the water table, thus contami- nating the water. Making these threats to health even more frightening is the fact that there is currently no known technology for removing BPA or any other leachates from the soil and water once they are there.

Ans.

Hazards of Using Plastics

The millions of tons of plastic found in the ocean beds and even in the animal stomach has garnered a whole lot of media attention recently. The issue of the harmful effects of plastics on the environment has always been an issue of discussion. However, in the recent times, the harmful effects that the plastics have on the human body has come into limelight.

It is not a hidden fact that only a tiny portion of the plastic used daily is recycled and reused. Most of the everyday plastics fill the landfills or the water bodies where it takes thousands of years to decompose. Within these years, the plastics drains out in the soil and the water. Researches across the world are warning against such mircroplastics that are a part of the land and water that we use.

They have a long-term negative effect on the ecosystem and adversely affect human health. Over the years, the leaching of the plastic reaches the water table and contaminates the water with toxic substances. The water reaches our food chain and makes us prone to many diseases. One such substance found by the researchers is Bisphenol-A which has shown to affect human health negatively.

Given that not much research has been successful within the field, we need to understand that plastic is dangerous for all. Instead of making it a part of our ecosystem, we should try to reduce its usage in our daily life.

8. The diagrams given below shows the changes that have taken place at Mount Mary School, Goa since its construction in 1950. Comparing the maps, write an analytical paragraph.

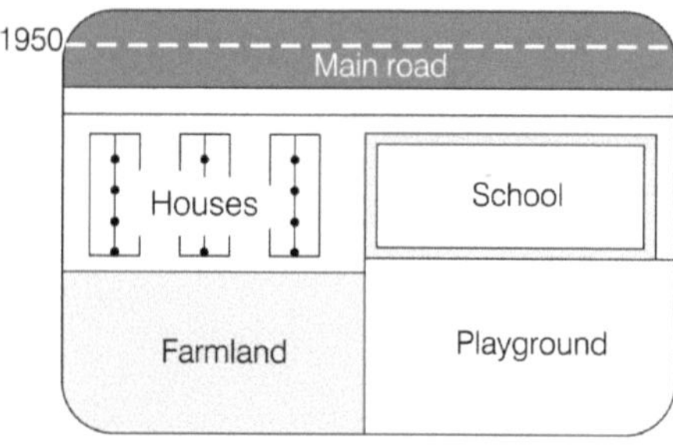

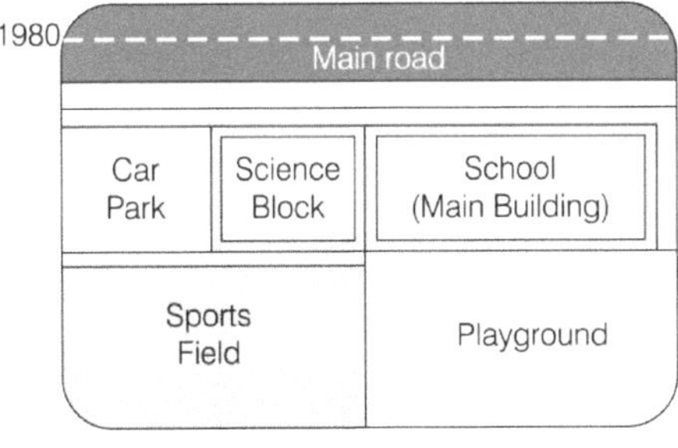

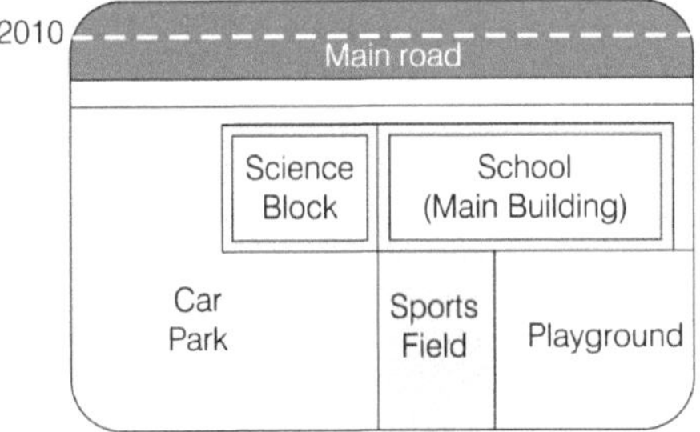

Ans.   **Changes in the Mount Mary School's
Infrastructure**

The given diagrams show how the Mount Mary School located in Goa has undergone change and development since the time it had been constructed in 1950.

It is very clear from the diagrams that overall, the main building of the school did not change throughout the years. But, all the other parts of the school were replaced by the needs of the time.

The time frame that the diagrams cover is of three years, that is, 1950 when it was constructed, 1980 and 2010. In 1950, the school had a playground behind it, a farmland in the South-West and houses in the Western part of its complex.

By the 1980s, the houses and the farmland were replaced. The houses were removed to make space for car parking and a science block was added to the school. The farmland was converted into a sports field.

The latest additions were made in 2010 when the complex and its various parts were resized. While the science building remained the same, the areas of the playground and the sports field were reduced to make more space for car parking.

Concluding, the main complex, that is, the school building is over 60 years old and very well accommodates the changing culture.

9. The chart given below shows how frequently people in the USA ate in the fast food restaurants between 2003 and 2013. Using the given data, write an analytical paragraph.

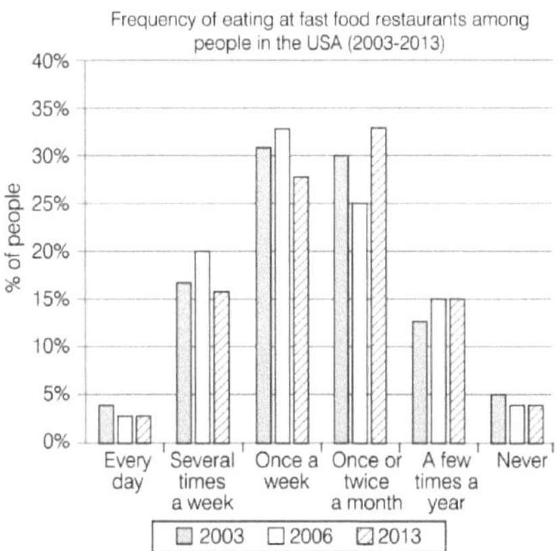

Ans.   **Dependence on Fast Food**

With the changing lifestyle, it is becoming difficult for us to cook meals at home every day. We prefer going out to our favourite fast food restaurant at least once in week or a month.

This tendency of eating fast food is clearly evident in the above graph which shows the frequency of eating at a fast food restaurant among the people of the USA. Overall, most people of the USA preferred going to a fast food restaurant either once in a week or once or twice in a month throughout the timeframe. At the same time, there were only a few people who went to the fast food chains every day or did not go at all.

The number seem to change almost negligently. For all the three years, i.e. 2003, 2006, 2013, the Americans preferred fast food only once or twice in a month or a week resting somewhere around to 30-35%. The Americans who either ate fast food everyday or never at all always remained below 5%.

Among the Americans, there were people who would eat at fast food chains several times a week and some also ate at fast food chains only a few times a year. Given that the data did not change much, we can say that the love for fast food remains the same.

10. The graph below shows how people buy music. Analyse the given data and write an analytical paragraph.

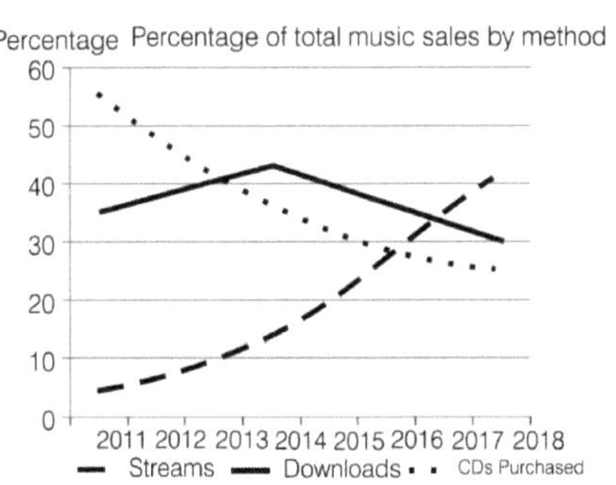

Ans. **Trends in Buying Music**

In this busy and crowded world, music has become an agency for us to be happy and relaxed. Its importance is very well depicted by the new music and new applications for music streaming being introduced every day. The given graph focuses on this increasing popularity and illustrates the trends in music buying habits between the years 2011 and 2018.

The data presents three different methods of buying music: streaming, downloading and buying CDs. Overall, both downloads and physical sales of music have steadily declined. The latter has slumped since 2011, while the downturn for the former began in 2014. However, there has been a sharp rise in people streaming music since 2013.

In 2011, the majority of music sales were of CDs, at approximately 55% of all sales. In contrast, streaming was not common at all as it was at only 5%. Although people had started to download music, it only represented 35% of sales. As sales of CDs began to fall, the era of downloads began. Downloading rose steadily and soon overtook physical sales in mid-2013. During the same period, with newer technology streaming doubled to 10% and started to grow more dramatically.

Downloads peaked in between 2013 and 2014 at about 43% of sales but fell to 30% by 2018. This was slightly higher than physical sales, which reduced to 25%. Streaming, on the other hand, overtook both of them and accounted for just over 40% of sales in 2018.

11. Study the following chart that presents the year wise percentage of attendance in secondary schools of India and write an analytical paragraph based on it.

Types of School in India	% of Attendance	% of Attendance	% of Attendance	% of Attendance
Year	2000	2005	2010	2015
Government Schools (In City)	62%	68%	70%	78%
Government Schools (In Villages)	24%	28%	32%	44%
General English Medium Schools	52%	49%	54%	59%
Convent-Run Schools	80.5%	82%	84%	89%

Ans. **Year wise Percentage of Attendance in Senior Secondary Schools of India**

The given graph shows that the percentage of attendance is recorded with a gap of 5 years. The given table gives information from the year 2000 to 2015. During the 15 years, there is a steady and healthy increase in the percentage of attendance in all the four types of schools. The increase in Convent-Run Schools is much higher compared to that in the other three types of schools. Initially, the Government Schools in village show a noticeably poor percentage in attendance and the General English Medium Schools show a lesser percentage of attendance compared that in to the Convent-Run Schools. All in all, the continuously higher percentage indicates that the relevant authorities are learned about improving the education of the country.

The disappointing percentage of attendance in the Government Schools in village in 2010 takes a big leap in 2015. This shows that the government took proper measures and initiatives to ensure the betterment of education in the villages. Noteworthy increase in the attendance indicates solid infrastructure and focuses towards the healthy growth of the corresponding authorities.

12. The chart below displays data about the number of digital devices purchased in Rishunagar across the years 2015-2019. Write a paragraph analysing the given data.

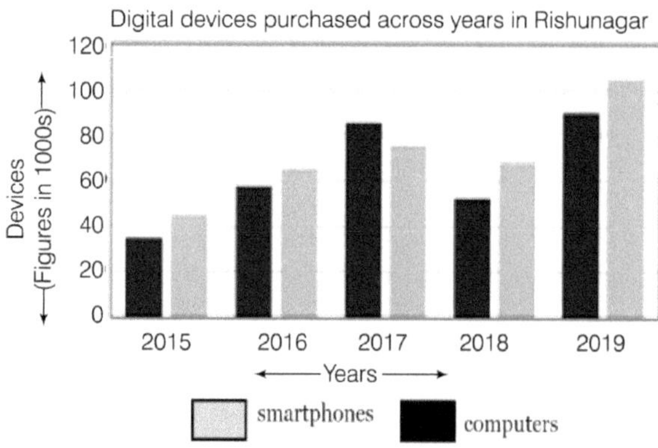

Ans. The given data displays data regarding the numbers of digital devices purchased in Rishunagar across the years 2015-2019. According to the given data, the purchase of the common digital devices such as smartphones and computers has seen an increase between the years 2015 and 2019. With the increasing functionality of smartphones, the sales of computers has decreased, except for the year 2017 wherein more computers were purchased. Both computers and smartphones were becoming central to the lives of people, especially working people. As a result, more and more people were purchasing both these items. The sales of these digital devices increased considerably from 2015 to 2017. However, the year 2018 saw a very large reduction in their sales and purchase. In comparison to 2017, the year 2018 saw a market where more smartphone were purchased by relatively low population. This trend was limited to the year 2018 as again in 2019, the sales of digital devices increased exponentially. While many reasons contribute to these fluctuations, one can definitely say that the digital age had taken its force in Rishunagar.

• Letter Writing

1. As a health conscious person, you noticed an advertisement in the newspaper on Yoga classes, in your neighbourhood. Write a letter to the organisers of yoga for public, R K Puram, New Delhi requesting him/her to send you information about the duration of the course and other relevant details. You are Shweta/Srikar of 15, R K Puram, New Delhi.

2. You are Salim/ Sarika, Administrative Officer of M/s Sanjeev Security Agencies, Saharanpur. You are opening your new office in the city for which you require suitable office furniture for an office with two rooms and a hall. Draft an enquiry letter to M/s Office Suppliers, Saharanpur, asking for a quotation for the items required. Specify the number required to each item and ask for credit in payment.

3. You are Garima/Girish, Manager, Sindhu Enterprises, Ranchi. You need various furniture items for your newly constructed head office. Write a letter of M/s Office Equipment Corporation, Ranchi, placing a bulk order for various items of office furniture (minimum 4), giving necessary details. Ask for discount on bulk purchase and base your order on the supplier's quotation no OEC/34/17-18.

4. Write a letter to M/S Laxmi Stationary Mart, Chawri Bazar Delhi placing an order for essential stationary products (minimum 4). You are RK Mittal, Office Superintendent, Bundelkhand Public School, Jhansi.

5. You are Chandan/Chandni. Write a letter to a bookseller cancelling your order due to delay in its execution.

• Analytical Paragraph

1. Study the following chart and write an analytical paragraph based on it in 150-200 words.

Year-Wise Percentage of Attendance in Secondary Schools of India

Types of Schools in India	Percentage of Attendance	Percentage of Attendance	Percentage of Attendance	Percentage of Attendance
Year	2000	2005	2010	2015
Government Schools (In City)	62%	68%	70%	78%
Government Schools (In Village)	24%	28%	32%	44%
General English Medium Schools	52%	49%	54%	59%
Convent-Run Schools	80.5%	82%	84%	89%

2. Study the chart given below. The chart is a result of a survey conducted by the Ministry of education in public and government schools of Vadodara. The chart depicts the types of activities that teenagers like to get involved in during their free time. Write an analytical paragraph based on the chart in 150-200 words.

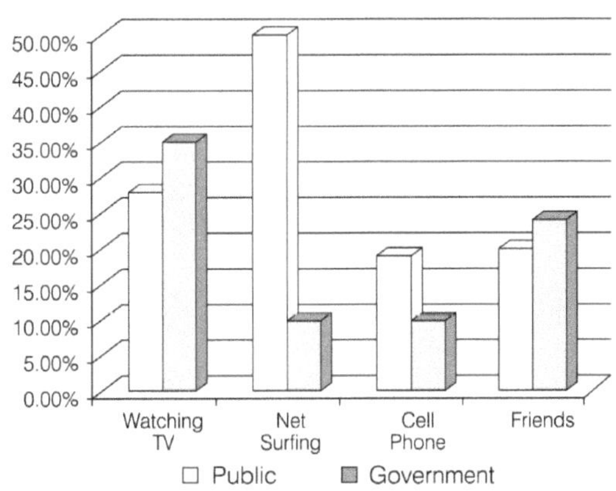

CHAPTER 01

Tenses

In this Chapter...

- Classification of Tenses
- Chapter Practice

Tense is defined as the form of verb that gives the relation between **Time** and **Action**. Time is the duration of work and action is the work done. Tense gives the time when the action is done.

There are three phases of time

(i) **present** (time that is now)

(ii) **past** (time that has passed)

(iii) **future** (time that is yet to come)

Let's consider the sentences given below

(i) Hari eats a mango. (Present)

(ii) Hari ate a mango. (Past)

(iii) Hari will eat a mango. (Future)

We can observe that each sentence given above has a different meaning. The reason is that each sentence has a different form of verb. These different forms of verbs are called tenses. The tense of a verb shows the time of an action or the state of being.

Classification of Tenses

There are three tenses

(i) Present Tense   (ii) Past Tense   (iii) Future Tense

Each tense is further divided into four forms. Study the chart given below to understand more about all tenses and their forms.

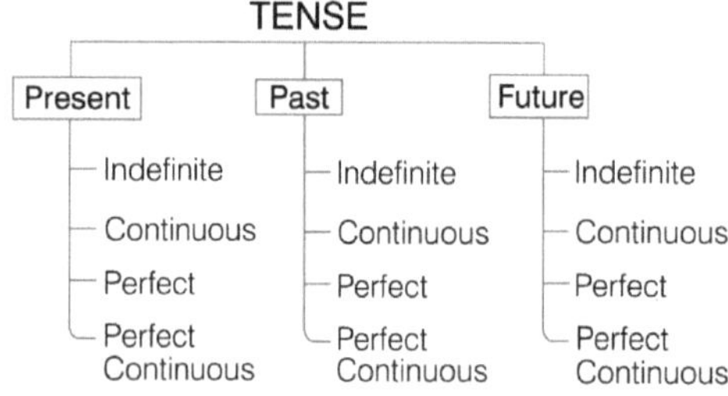

Present Tense (Present Indefinite Tense)

This tense is also called simple present tense.

This tense is used in the following ways

(i) To express habitual action, habit or custom.
e.g. She gets up every morning at 6 o'clock.

(ii) To talk about a general or universal truth.
e.g. The Earth revolves around the Sun.

(iii) To indicate a future event which is part of a plan or arrangement.
e.g. The school reopens next week.

(iv) To introduce quotes with the verb 'says'.
e.g. Newton says, "Every action has an equal and an opposite reaction."

(v) Exclamatory sentences that begin with here or there.
e.g. (a) Here you go!   (b) There he goes!

Rules for Affirmative Sentences

- Singular subject + first form of verb + s/es + ...
- Plural subject + first form of verb + ...

  e.g. (a) They play cricket in the ground.
  - (b) She cooks food in the evening.
  - (c) Water boils at 100°C.
  - (d) We study in ABC institution.
  - (e) She advises me not to smoke.

Rules for Negative Sentences

- Singular subject + does not + first form of verb + ...
- Plural subject + do not + first form of verb + ...

  e.g. (a) Reena does not watch television.
  - (b) We do not smoke.
  - (c) She does not write a letter to her friend.
  - (d) They do not like to swim.

Rules for Interrogative Sentences

- Do/does + subject + first form of verb + ...?
- Question word + do/does + subject + first form of verb + ...?

  e.g. (a) Do you play cricket?
  - (b) Does she wash clothes?
  - (c) Does he not go to school daily?
  - (d) Why do you weep now?
  - (e) Whose book do you read?
  - (f) Whom do you teach?
  - (g) Which subject does Garima not want to study?
  - (h) Who teaches you English?
  - (i) Why do you not complete your homework?

Present Continuous Tense

This tense is used in the following ways

(i) To describe an action in progress and the continuity of the action.
  e.g. The passengers are wandering to and for.

(ii) An action that is not happening at the time of speaking but is in progress.
  e.g. He is working in an MNC.

(iii) An action that has been pre-arranged to take place in the near future.
  e.g. The wedding is going to take place on Sunday.

(iv) Persistent and undesirable habit, especially with adverbs like *always, continually, constantly* etc.
  e.g. (a) You are always running me down.
  - (b) He is constantly gazing at me.

Rules for Affirmative Sentences

- Singular subject + is/am + first form of verb + ing +.......
- Plural subject + are + first form of verb + ing +.......

  e.g. (a) I am playing a game.

  - (b) She is reading a book.
  - (c) We are going to Shimla.

Rules for Negative Sentences

- Singular subject + is/am + not + first form of verb + ing +.......
- Plural subject + are + not + first form of verb + ing +.......

  e.g. (a) Ram is not surfing the internet.
  - (b) They are not watching a movie.
  - (c) I am not swimming in the water.

Rules for Interrogative Sentences

- Is/are/am + subject + first form of verb + ing + ...?
- Question word + is/are/am + subject + first form of verb + ing + ... ?

  e.g. (a) Is Reena cooking the food?
  - (b) Are you not writing a letter?
  - (c) What is Raveena doing here?
  - (d) Which newspaper are you buying?
  - (e) Why was the camel not drinking water?

Present Perfect Tense

This tense is used in the following ways

(i) To express an action that has recently been completed.
  e.g. She has just taken tea.

(ii) To describe an action, the time of which is not given.
  e.g. Have you done M. Sc in Maths?

(iii) To describe past events, the effect of which still exists.
  e.g. I have finished my work and now I am free.

(iv) To describe actions that started in the past and are continuing until now and will possibly continue into the future.
  e.g. I have already used this brand of soap.

(v) To show how a past situation relates to the present.
  e.g. I've done my homework, so I can help you with yours now.

Rules for Affirmative Sentences

- Singular subject + has + third form of verb + ...
- Plural subject + have + third form of verb + ...

  e.g. (a) She has gone to the market.
  - (b) I have met her.
  - (c) They have bathed.
  - (d) It has become dark now.

Rules for Negative Sentences

- Singular subject + has + not + third form of verb + ...
- Plural subject + have + not + third form of verb + ...

  e.g. (a) I have not called him.
  - (b) The train has not gone.

Rules for Interrogative Sentences

- Has/have + subject + third form of verb +.....?
- Question word + has/have + subject + third form of verb + ... ?

e.g. (a) Has she gone to Delhi?

    (b) Have they not seen the Taj Mahal yet?

    (c) What have they eaten today?

    (d) Why has the peon not come yet?

Present Perfect Continuous Tense

This tense is also called present perfect progressive tense.

This tense is used in the following ways

(i) To describe an action that began in the past and is still continuing.

    e.g. They have been staying in the village for a long time.

(ii) To express an action already completed, but whose effect is still continuing.

    e.g. I have been running around for the job all day and am now tired.

Rules for Affirmative Sentences

- Singular subject + has + been + first form of verb + ing + ... + for/since +......
- Plural subject + have + been + first form of verb + ing + ... + for/since +......

    e.g. (a) Arpit has been sleeping since 6 o'clock.

        (b) They have been running for three hours.

Rules for Negative Sentences

- Singular subject + has + not + been + first form of verb + ing + ... + for/since +......
- Plural subject + have + not + been + first form of verb + ing + ... + for/since +......

    e.g. (a) You have not been suffering from fever for one week.

        (b) Reena has not been going to music class for 2 months.

Rules for Interrogative Sentences

- Has/Have + subject + been + first form of verb + ing + ... + since/for +.....?
- Question word + has/have + subject + been + first form of verb + ing + ...+ since/for + ...?

    e.g. (a) Have you been sleeping since 8 o' clock?

        (b) Has he not been living in this house for a long time?

        (c) Why have they been playing football since morning?

Past Tense (Past Indefinite Tense)

This tense is also called simple past tense.

This tense is used in the following ways

(i) To indicate an action that happened in the past and to report completed actions. It is used often in recounts and narratives.

    e.g. I visited the Taj Mahal three months ago.

(ii) To indicate past habits or repeated events that are now over.

    e.g. In those days, my mother gave me some pocket money every day.

(iii) The habitual past can also be expressed by using 'used to'.

    e.g. My grandfather used to read a few chapters of the Gita every day.

(iv) Sometimes this tense is used without an adverb of time. In such cases, the time may be either implied or indicated by the context.

    e.g. I learnt Punjabi in Chandigarh.

(v) To indicate another action which happened in the middle of a longer action.

    e.g. The light went out while I was watching my favourite TV serial.

Rule for Affirmative Sentences

- Subject + second form of verb +......

    e.g. (a) I played football in the ground.

        (b) She sang a song in the party.

Rule for Negative Sentences

- Subject + did not + first form of verb +......

    e.g. (a) I did not attend the function.

        (b) They did not watch television.

Rules for Interrogative Sentences

- Did + subject + first form of verb + ... ?
- Question word + did + subject + first form of verb +........?

    e.g. (a) Did you play a game?

        (b) Why did she abuse her friends?

        (c) When did father go to office?

        (d) Why did Supriya not speak the truth?

Past Continuous Tense

This tense is used in the following ways

(i) To indicate an action that was happening at some time in the past. The time of action may or may not be indicated.

    e.g. We were watching TV the whole evening.

(ii) Used with always, continually, etc for persistent habits in the past.

    e.g. He was always sulking.

(iii) The past continuous is also used for an action that was going on during a given period or at a period of time in the past.

    e.g. While Rohan was filling in the hole, his dog was digging another.

Rules for Affirmative Sentences

- Singular subject + was + first form of verb + ing +.....
- Plural subject + were + first form of verb + ing +.....

    e.g. (a) She was driving her car.

        (b) They were making a noise.

Rules for Negative Sentences

- Singular subject + was + not + first form of verb + ing +.....
- Plural subject + were + not + first form of verb + ing +.....

    e.g. (a) She was not singing a song.

        (b) They were not eating mangoes.

Rules for Interrogative Sentences

- Was/were + subject + first form of verb + ing +......?
- Question word + was/were + subject + first form of verb + ing +.....?

  e.g. (a) Were you eating a mango?

  (b) When was the milkman milking the cow?

  (c) Why was the blind boy crying?

Past Perfect Tense

This tense is used in the following ways

(i) To indicate an action that was completed before a definite time or before another action that took place in the past.

  e.g. The patient had died before the doctor reached the hospital.

(ii) It indicates desires in the past that have not been fulfilled.

  e.g. I wish I had not wasted my time.

(iii) It expresses those conditions of the past that were impossible to fulfil.

  e.g. If you had questioned him earlier, things would have improved.

Rule for Affirmative Sentences

Subject + had + third form of verb + ...

  e.g. She had cooked the food.

Rule for Negative Sentences

Subject + had + not + third form of verb + ...

  e.g. They had not attended the function.

Rule for Interrogative Sentences

Had + subject + third form of verb + ... ?

Question word + had + subject + third form of verb +.........?

  e.g. (a) Had she watched a movie?

  (b) Why had you not gone to Delhi?

Past Perfect Continuous Tense

This tense is also called past perfect progressive tense.

This tense is used in the following way

It indicates an action which began in the past and continued up to a certain point of time in the past.

e.g. When we met in Lucknow, she had been studying in city college for 3 years.

Rule for Affirmative Sentences

- Subject + had been + first form of verb +ing + ... + since/for +.....

  e.g. (a) You had been suffering from fever since Tuesday.

  (b) I had been studying for three hours.

Rule for Negative Sentences

- Subject + had + not + been + first form of verb + ing + ... + since/for +......

  e.g. They had not been going to office since the 5th of July.

Rules for Interrogative Sentences

- Had + subject + been + first form of verb + ing + ... + since/for + ...?
- Question word + had + subject + been + first form of verb + ing + ...since/for+..... ?

  e.g. (a) Had you not been reading the book since morning?

  (b) Where had he been playing since morning?

Future Tense (Future Indefinite Tense)

This tense is also called simple future tense.

This tense is used in the following ways

(i) To say what we believe or think will happen in the future.

  e.g. I believe she will join the office tomorrow.

(ii) Things which we cannot control and are factual.

  e.g. The Sun will rise at 6:00 AM.

(iii) To indicate an instant decision.

  e.g. It is our first marriage anniversary. I shall give you a precious gift.

Rules for Affirmative Sentences

- You/He/She/It/They (Second and Third Person Pronouns) + will + first form of verb + ...
- I/We (First Person Pronouns) + shall + first form of verb + ...

  e.g. (a) He will sell his house.

  (b) I shall purchase a new car.

Rules for Negative Sentences

- You/He/She/It/They (Second and Third Person Pronouns) + will + not + first form of verb + ...
- I/We (First Person Pronouns) + shall + not + first form of verb + ...

  e.g. (a) My friend will not host dinner this evening.

  (b) We shall not skip the exams.

Rules for Interrogative Sentences

- Will/Shall+ subject + first form of verb +......?
- Question word + will/shall + subject + first form of verb + ...?

  e.g. (a) Will she not come in the party?

  (b) Who will help him?

  (c) Why will your friend not come here?

Future Continuous Tense

This tense is used in the following ways

(i) To indicate an action that will occur in the normal course.

  e.g. She will be cooking the food tomorrow.

(ii) To indicate an action that will be in progress at a given point of time in the future.

  e.g. At this time tomorrow, we shall be attending the party.

Rules for Affirmative Sentences

- You/He/She/It/They (Second and Third Person Pronouns) + will + be + first form of verb + ing + ...
- I/We (First Person Pronouns) + shall + be + first form of verb + ing + ...

  e.g. (a) Next year my teacher will be going to China.
  (b) I shall be teaching my students.

Rules for Negative Sentences

- You/He/She/It/They (Second and Third Person Pronouns) + will + not + be + first form of verb + ing + ...
- I/We (First Person Pronouns) + shall + not + be + first form of verb + ing + ...

  e.g. (a) They will not be studying in city college.
  (b) I shall not be bathing this evening.

Rules for Interrogative Sentences

- Will/shall + subject + be + first form of verb + ing + ...?
- Question word + will/shall + subject + be + first form of verb + ing +.....?

  e.g. (a) Will this boy be wandering in the forest?
  (b) How long will they be travelling?

Future Perfect Tense

This tense is used to describe an action which will be completed at some point of time in the future.

e.g. I shall have finished this work by tomorrow.

Rules for Affirmative Sentences

- You/He/She/It/They (Second and Third Person Pronouns) + will + have + third form of verb + ...
- I/We (First Person Pronouns) + shall + have + third form of verb + ...

  e.g. (a) Your examination will have been over by Tuesday.
  (b) We shall have cooked the food by the evening.

Rules for Negative Sentences

- You/He/She/It/They (Second and Third Person Pronouns) + will + not + have + third form of verb + ...
- I/We (First Person Pronouns) + shall + not + have + third form of verb + ...

  e.g. (a) The passengers will not have reached the station before the train starts.

  (b) Your brother will not have read this novel before next Saturday.
  (c) I shall not have written the letter by noon.

Rules for Interrogative Sentences

- Will/shall + subject + have + third form of verb +......?
- Question word + will/shall + subject + have + third form of verb ......?

  e.g. (a) Will he not have gone before I reach?
  (b) What will he have eaten before he sleeps?

Future Perfect Continuous Tense

This tense is also called future perfect progressive tense.

This tense is used in the following ways

It describes an action that will be in progress over a period of time that will end in the future.

e.g. At noon, Anuradha will have been singing songs for an hour.

Rules for Affirmative Sentences

- You/He/She/It/They (Second and Third Person Pronouns) + will + have + been + first form of verb + ing + ... + since/for + ...
- I/We (First Person Pronouns) + shall + have + been + first form of verb + ing + ... + since/for + ...

  e.g. By next April, we shall have been leaving for the USA.

Rules for Negative Sentences

- You/He/She/It/They (Second and Third Person Pronouns) + will + not + have + been + first form of verb + ing + ... + since/for + ...
- I/We (First Person Pronouns) + shall + not + have + been + first form of verb + ing + ... + since/for + ...

  e.g. (a) Mahima will not have been going to Kanpur for a long time.
  (b) I shall not have been writing for half an hour.

Rules for Interrogative Sentences

- Will/shall + subject + have + been + first form of verb + ing + ... + since/for + ... ?
- Question word + will/ shall + subject + have + been + first form of verb + ing + ... + since/for + ... ?

  e.g. (a) Will she have been playing for some time?
  (b) How long will you have been enjoying vacations on April 12th?

Chapter Practice

PART 1

Objective Questions

• Multiple Choice Questions

Choose the correct option to fill the blank with verbs of appropriate tenses.

1. This time tomorrow my friends .... to their home towns.
(a) will travel
(b) will travelling
(c) will be travelling
(d) will have travelling

Ans. (*c*)

2. Amin could not open the door because one of the other students .... it from inside.
(a) locked
(b) was locking
(c) has locked
(d) had locked

Ans. (*d*)

3. At this moment, ... an exercise to review the tenses.
(a) I do
(b) I doing
(c) I have done
(d) I'm doing

Ans. (*d*)

4. I .... working all afternoon and have just finished the assignment.
(a) have been (b) had been (c) shall be (d) am

Ans. (*b*)

5. Rohan .... the movie before he read the review.
(a) watches
(b) have watched
(c) had watched
(d) was watching

Ans. (*c*)

6. Every boy and girl .... in the class today.
(a) are present
(b) is present
(c) have present
(d) had present

Ans. (*b*)

7. When I .... at the headmaster's door, he was speaking to someone.
(a) am knocking
(b) has knocked
(c) knocked
(d) knocks

Ans. (*c*)

8. The boat .... before the rescue team arrived.
(a) will sink
(b) has sunk
(c) is sinking
(d) had sunk

Ans. (*d*)

9. Joseph .... by everyone after he won the competition.
(a) congratulate
(b) congratulated
(c) was congratulated
(d) shall be congratulated

Ans. (*c*)

10. She has decided to distribute the duties after everyone .... their work.
(a) completed
(b) complete
(c) completes
(d) will complete

Ans. (*c*)

11. By the time I .... , the registrations had been closed.
(a) was informed
(b) informed
(c) inform
(d) was informing

Ans. (*a*)

12. The crowd that .... due to the quarrel has dispersed now.
(a) have gathered
(b) had gathered
(c) has been gathered
(d) has been gathering

Ans. (*b*)

13. The children .... in the park throughout the evening.
(a) played
(b) playing
(c) plays
(d) has played

Ans. (*a*)

14. The Rajdhani Express .... food, cold drinks, water and blankets at night.
(a) provide
(b) provides
(c) provided
(d) Both (b) and (c)

Ans. (*b*)

15. It was Krishna who .... Arjun by giving him Upadesas of Gita.
(a) had inspired
(b) inspired
(c) inspires
(d) inspiring

Ans. (*b*)

PART 2
Subjective Questions

A. *Fill in the blanks with verbs of suitable tenses.*

1. Hardly had the minister finished the speech when the earthquake .... (shake) the stadium.

Ans. shook

2. Everybody will be at office at about 08:30 tomorrow as the meeting .... (start) at nine o'clock.

Ans. starts

3. While climbing onto the mountain top, I.......... (encounter) a strange animal which I had never seen before.

Ans. encountered

4. She .... (know) about their problem for years.

Ans. has known

5. Mother .... (work) in the garden for the whole day.

Ans. has been working

6. Most shops .... (close) at 6 p.m on Saturday.

Ans. close

7. When I .... (come) home this evening, my parents had gone out for a walk.

Ans. came

8. By the time the troops .... (arrive), the war will have ended.

Ans. arrive

9. By the year 2020, linguists .... (study) the Indo-European language family for more than 200 years.

Ans. will have been studying

10. By the time he was 14, Mozart .... (compose) an enviable number of musical pieces.

Ans. had composed

B. *Fill in the blanks with verbs of suitable tenses.*

1. We .... (visit) the seashore many times before but last summer we enjoyed ourselves more than ever.

Ans. had visited

2. By Saturday next week, I .... (work) on this painting for exactly one month.

Ans. will have been working

3. By the year 2030, the population of Delhi .... (grow) substantially.

Ans. will have grown

4. They were very tired in the evening because they .... (help) on the farm all day.

Ans. had been helping

5. Whey they .... (walk) through the park yesterday, they met their neighbours.

Ans. were walking

6. When I was a young boy, I .... (meet) Santa Claus.

Ans. met

7. I .... (see) this movie about a dozen times already.

Ans. have seen

8. We .... (sleep) all day yesterday.

Ans. slept

9. Rahul .... (study) for his maths test right now.

Ans. is studying

10. He finally .... (decide) to call her yesterday to know how she was.

Ans. decided

II. *Fill in the blanks using correct verb tenses.*

1. He lost his watch while he .... (see) the sights of the city.

Ans. was seeing

2. I was coming down the stairs when my friend .... (ring) the doorbell.

Ans. rang

3. A few years ago he .... (live) in Germany where he worked as a journalist.

Ans. lived

4. Jaya got a degree in 2006 after she .... (study) at the University for over 5 years.

Ans. had studied

5. The plane that you .... (look) at just now has taken off for Paris.

Ans. were looking

6. When we went to see them last night they were playing cards. They said they .... (play) cards since 6 o'clock.

Ans. had been playing

7. I am so sorry that I .... (have) to leave the party so early yesterday.

Ans. had

8. He usually .... (work) at the restaurant after school. After work he goes to the fitness centre twice a week.

Ans. works

Modals

In this Chapter...

- Nature of Modals
- Functions of Modals
- Chapter Practice

Modals is a class of helping verbs that expresses the degree of certainty of the action in the sentence or the attitude or opinion of the writer/speaker concerning the action. Can, could, will, would, shall, should, may, might, must, ought to, have to, has to and had to are modals. Need, dare and used to are called semi-modals.

Nature of Modals

- Modals are never used alone.

  e.g. (a) I *can* upon the harmonium.   *(Incorrect)*

  (b) I *can* play upon the harmonium.   *(Correct)*

  Modals always have a principal verb with them.

- Modals don't change according to the number or person of the subject.

  e.g. (a) I *can* play.   (b) He *can* play.

  (c) We *can* play.   (d) They *can* play.

- Modals don't have an infinitive form. We can't place 'to' with them in order to use them in a sentence.

  e.g. (a) We *must* to get there before time.   *(Incorrect)*

  (b) We *must* get there before time.   *(Correct)*

- Two modals can never be used together.
- We always use first form of verb with modals.

Functions of Modals

Will

(i) **To show promise, intention, willingness, determination with the first person** (I, we)

  e.g. (a) I *will* give you a gift of your choice. *(promise)*

  (b) We *will* help you. *(willingness)*

(ii) **To express request, invitation, insistence, assumption, characteristic or habit**

  e.g. (a) *Will* you please help me? *(request)*

  (b) She *will* be in the school during school hours. *(assumption)*

- **Negative Form of will : Will not/ Won't**

  e.g. (a) I *will not* spend my pocket money.

  (b) She *won't* eat unhygienic food.

Would (Past form of 'will')

(i) **It expresses the past form of 'will'**

  e.g. He informed me that he *would* dance at my marriage function.

(ii) **To express past habit**

  e.g. He *would* drink a cup of coffee in the morning.

(iii) **For request**

  e.g. *Would* you please give me your bike?

(iv) **To express wish**

e.g. I wish she *would* be healthy.

(v) **To express an imaginary condition**

e.g. I *would* have a big house if I earned ₹10 crore every year.

- **Negative Form of Would** : Would not / Wouldn't

e.g. She *would not* get up early in the morning.

Shall

(i) **To ask for suggestion, request, advice with the first person (I, We) in an interrogative sentence**

e.g. (a) *Shall* we start the class? *(advice)*

(b) *Shall* I have a cup of coffee from your shop? *(request)*

(ii) **In the second and third person to indicate threat, warning, command, promise, assurance and determination**

e.g. (a) If you sit with bad boys, you *shall* be punished. *(threat)*

(b) You *shall* go now. *(command)*

- **Negative Form of Shall** : Shall not/ Shan't

e.g. (a) She *shall not* sing tomorrow.

(b) They *shall not* win the match.

Should (Past form of 'shall')

(i) **To express duty or obligation**

e.g. (a) I *should* help my friends. *(duty)*

(b) You *should* not be lazy. *(obligation)*

(ii) **To express opinion**

e.g. They *should* be on the way to Jaipur.

(iii) **To give or take advice or suggestion**

e.g. (a) We *should* go to the temple.

(b) We *should* obey our elders.

(iv) **After 'lest' when someone expresses fear**

e.g. Walk carefully *lest* you should fall down.

- **Negative Form of Should** : Should not /Shouldn't

e.g. (a) You *should not* come to me daily.

(b) You *shouldn't* make a noise here.

Can

(i) **To express an ability, capability, capacity or power**

e.g. (a) I *can* lift 60 kg. *(Ability)*

(b) She *can* pass the MBA examination. *(Capability)*

(ii) **To show possibility**

e.g. (a) She *can* fall on the road.

(b) I *can* go there.

(iii) **To take or give permission**

e.g. (a) *Can* I sit here?

(b) You *can* park your scooter here.

- **Negative Form of Can** : Cannot /Can't

e.g. (a) They *cannot* climb the mountain.

(b) She *can't* run fast.

Could (Past form of 'can')

(i) **To express ability/talent in the past**

e.g. (a) They *could* win the game last month.

(b) She *could* sing beautifully.

(ii) **To express polite request**

e.g. (a) *Could* I have your pen?

(b) *Could* I ride on your bike?

- **Negative Form of Could** : Could not/ Couldn't

e.g. (a) *Could* you *not* smoke outside the house?

(b) She *couldn't* cook delicious food.

May

(i) **To show possibility or probability**

e.g. (a) The inspector *may* attend the school today.

(b) She *may* win the match.

(ii) **To give or take permission**

e.g. (a) *May* I come in ?

(b) Yes, you *may* come in.

(iii) **To wish or pray**

e.g. (a) *May* you get well soon!

(b) *May* God bless you with a child!

(iv) **To show a purpose**

e.g. (a) My friend is joining a new company so that he *may* achieve his target.

(b) He is working hard so that he *may* win.

- **Negative Form of May** : May not/ Mayn't

e.g. (a) It *may not* rain today.

(b) She *mayn't* attend the meeting.

Might (Past form of 'may')

(i) **To express less possibility**

e.g. (a) He *might* help us.

(b) She *might* be a winner in the competition.

(ii) **For permission**

e.g. (a) *Might* I begin to reveal the truth?

(b) *Might* this be the Key?

(iii) **To express a guess**

e.g. That *might* be Rohit.

- **Negative Form of Might** : Might not/ Mightn't

e.g. (a) It *might not* rain.

(b) She *mightn't* talk to me this evening.

Must

(i) **To express necessity or obligation**

e.g. (a) You *must* take part in the competition.

(b) We *must* love our motherland.

(ii) **To indicate assumption or conclusion**

e.g. (a) She *must* be here in the evening.

(b) Mr AK Gupta *must* be a good teacher.

(iii) In case of prohibition

e.g. You *must* not bunk school.

- **Negative Form of Must** : Must not/ Mustn't

e.g. (a) You *must not* play in sunlight.

(b) You *must not* write your name on the walls.

(c) You *mustn't* make a fuss over this.

Have to/ Has to/ Had to

(i) To **express obligation or compulsion (While talking about rules, laws)**

e.g. (a) I *have to* reach school early.

(b) She *has to* work late in the office.

(c) They *had to* follow the instructions.

- **Negative Form of Have to** : Don't have to

e.g. (a) I *don't have to* cook the food at home.

(b) She *doesn't have to* work till late in the office.

Ought to

(i) To **express moral obligation or duty**

e.g. (a) You *ought to* respect your parents.

(b) You *ought to* serve the nation.

(c) We *ought to* help our relatives.

(d) We *ought to* speak the truth.

(ii) To **give advice**

e.g. You *ought to* study hard to achieve success.

- **Negative Form of Ought to** : Ought not to/ Oughtn't to

e.g. (a) You *ought not to* hate your neighbours.

(b) You *oughtn't to* insult your elders.

Use of 'Need', 'Need to', 'Dare' and 'Used to'

Need and **dare** are considered semi-modals because they can be used either as modal auxiliaries or as main verbs.

Need/Need to

As a modal auxiliary verb in negative terms, it **indicates absence of obligation**. It expresses the **speaker's authority or advice** and is used for the present and the future.

e.g. You **needn't** type this letter.

(i) **The interrogative is formed by inversion.**

e.g. *Need* I speak to him?

(ii) Its past is **needed** to in the affirmative sentence, **need not have** in the negative and **need have** in the interrogative.

e.g. (a) *Need* I have gone to him? *(Interrogative in the past)*

(b) I *needed* to go to him. *(Affirmative in the past)*

Dare

As a modal auxiliary, **dare** refers to being bold and courageous. The negative is formed by **dare not** and the interrogative by inversion.

e.g. (a) *Dare* we talk to them?

(b) I *dare not* disturb them.

Used to

(i) A discontinued habit or a past situation which is no more in the present.

e.g. He *used to* drink daily. *(Now he does not drink)*

(ii) Something existing in the past

e.g. This *used to* be a dense jungle before.

Chapter Practice

Objective Questions

• Multiple Choice Questions

Choose the correct option to fill the blank with appropriate modals.

1. When he was young, he .... swim very well. He won medals and championships!

(a) may   (b) can   (c) could   (d) shall

Ans. (*c*) The given sentence talks about ability and is in the past tense, so 'could' is the correct word to fill the blank.

2. The company .... go bankrupt if they don't find a lot of money quickly!

(a) should   (b) shouldn't
(c) need   (d) might

Ans. (*d*) The given sentence talks about possibility, so 'might' is the correct word to fill the blank.

3. It's wet and windy outside today. You .... go out without an umbrella.

(a) shouldn't   (b) won't
(c) ought to   (d) must

Ans. (*a*) The given sentence talks about advise, so 'shouldn't' is the appropriate word here.

4. If you had let me know earlier, I .... have been able to come.

(a) will   (b) shall
(c) would   (d) must

Ans. (*c*) It is a conditional clause; the main clause is in past tense, so 'would' should be used here.

5. .... anybody attend the lecture or is it just for registered students?

(a) Will   (b) Can
(c) Must   (d) Should

Ans. (*b*) The given sentence talks about ability and is in the present tense, so 'can' is the correct word to fill the blank.

6. You .... have bothered coming. I've done it already.

(a) wouldn't   (b) mightn't
(c) needn't   (d) won't

Ans. (*c*) The given sentence talks about necessity, so 'needn't' is the correct word to fill the given blank.

7. If there is an age restriction then you .... go in as you are too young.

(a) should   (b) shouldn't
(c) shall not   (d) will not

Ans. (*b*)

8. The government .... vote on the issue tomorrow. It's scheduled for 10am.

(a) will   (b) may
(c) would   (d) could

Ans. (*a*) The given sentence is in future tense, so 'will' is used here.

9. You .... have worked so hard last week. You look so tired now.

(a) must not   (b) ought not
(c) can't   (d) won't

Ans. (*b*) The phrase 'ought to' is used for the advise, so 'ought not' is the appropriate word here.

10. I'm not really sure where the cat is, but I think she .... be playing in the kitchen.

(a) can   (b) must
(c) will   (d) had

Ans. (*b*) The given sentence talks about obligation, so 'must' is the correct word to fill the blank.

11. If I had left early like everyone else did, I .... be sitting here now listening to all this rubbish.

(a) may not   (b) wouldn't
(c) won't be   (d) can't

Ans. (*b*)

12. If I'd gone down to Bodrum like all my friends did, I, too, ... have taken scuba diving lessons.

(a) would   (b) will
(c) can   (d) may

Ans. (*a*)

13. You .... look at me when I am talking to you.

(a) could   (b) should
(c) would   (d) may

Ans. (*b*)

14. If you don't start working harder, you .... repeat the course next year.
  (a) could (b) must
  (c) will have to (d) ought to

Ans. (c) 'Have to' expresses compulsion and obligation. The sentence also refers to an action of future hence, 'will have to' is appropriate to fill the blank.

15. You .... forget your sun cream. It's going to be very hot!
  (a) couldn't (b) mustn't
  (c) needn't (d) dare not

Ans. (*b*)

PART 2
Subjective Questions

A. *Fill in the blanks with suitable modals*

1. Usha .... run a hundred yards in ten seconds.

Ans. can

2. .... his soul rest in peace!

Ans. May

3. The baby is crying, he .... be hungry.

Ans. must

4. .... you tell me the way to the post office, please?

Ans. Will

5. You .... keep your scooter locked.

Ans. should

6. .... I bring you a cup of coffee?

Ans. Shall

7. When I was a boy, I .... walk forty miles in a day.

Ans. could

8. I have come to ask if Geeta .... use your bicycle tomorrow.

Ans. may

B. 1. You .... have watered the flowers, for it is going to rain.

Ans. need not

2. If we had taken the other road, we .... have arrived earlier.

Ans. would

3. The bank closes at 2 PM, but the manager .... allow you to get in.

Ans. might

4. .... you please send me an application form?

Ans. Would

5. As Rahul was the last one to leave, it .... be he who left the door open.

Ans. might

6. You .... read his latest book.

Ans. should

7. She .... speak three languages even when she was twelve.

Ans. could

8. I .... see quite clearly what the children are doing in the garden.

Ans. can

9. He .... be at least sixty.

Ans. must

10. Your job .... be very demanding, but at least it isn't boring.

Ans. may

C. 1. It's not very important. You .... not do it now.

Ans. need

2. I have no time. I must leave now or I .... miss the bus.

Ans. will

3. .... we go out tonight, please? Yes, but you must not be late.

Ans. May

4. I haven't decided where I .... go to during my next holidays.

Ans. will

5. .... you water the plants while I am away?

Ans. Could

6. .... I buy the tickets for the concert?

Ans. Shall

7. .... you speak German?

Ans. Can

8. Jayati .... not play the violin when she was five but now she can play it very well.

Ans. could

9. You .... not be so nervous. I think it will be very easy.

Ans. should

10. He had been working for more than eleven hours. He .... be tired after such hard work.

Ans. must

CHAPTER 03

Subject-Verb Concord

In this Chapter...

- Rules Involved in Subject-Verb Agreement
- Subject and Verb in Person and Number
- Chapter Practice

We often need to write sentences which contain only a subject and a verb. The subject could be a noun, a proper noun (name of a person or place) or an abstract noun.

Rules Involved in Subject-Verb Agreement

- The most basic rule is Singular Subject → Singular Verb
  Plural Subject → Plural Verb
- When we make a sentence, we tell something about a person or a thing. The part of the sentence which states the person or thing in the sentence is called the **subject** of the sentence and the part which gives us more information about the subject is called the **predicate** of the sentence.

A subject can be

Singular	—	A book, an egg, a key
Plural	—	Women, boys, flowers
Uncountable	—	Sugar, water, air

Subject and Verb in Person and Number

The subject and verb must agree in person and number. If the subject is singular, the verb should also be singular. If the subject is plural, the verb should also be plural.

(i) Singular Subject → Singular Verb
  e.g. **I am** in the classroom.

(ii) Plural Subject → Plural Verb
  e.g. **They are** in the classroom.

(iii) When two or more singular subjects are joined together, plural verb is used.
  e.g. Mrs and Mr Gupta **are** going to the market.

(iv) When two subjects together express one idea, singular verb is used.
  e.g. Earning your bread and butter **is** essential for living. (Bread and butter is symbolic and expresses one idea, which is livelihood)

(v) Everybody, somebody, nobody, anybody and anyone take a singular verb.
  e.g. Nobody **is** perfect in this world.

(vi) Nouns joined by 'and' take a plural verb.
  e.g. Sita and Gita <u>are</u> going to Mumbai.

(vii) If subjects are joined by 'or', 'nor', 'either', 'neither', the verb agrees with the subject nearest to it.
  e.g. He or his friends **are** to be blamed.

(viii) The title of a book, play, story or a musical composition, even though plural, takes a singular verb.
  e.g. The Three Musketeers **is** a very good book.

(ix) When a plural noun comes between a singular subject and its verb, the verb agrees with the singular subject.

e.g. Each of the apples **is** juicy.

(x) If the words are joined to a singular subject by 'with', a singular verb is used.

e.g. The Prime Minister, **with** his cabinet colleagues, is supposed to be present.

(xi) If subjects are joined by 'as well as', the verb must agree with the first subject, irrespective of whether it is singular or plural.

e.g. My friends **as well as** my father **are** going abroad.

(xii) Two nouns qualified by each or every, even though connected by 'and', require a singular verb.

e.g. Every boy and every girl **was** given vaccination.

(xiii) *None* is singular but takes a plural/singular verb according to the sense involved in the sentence.

e.g. (a) None **were** given a chance to speak.

(b) I asked for a maid, but none **was** there.

(ivx) When the plural noun is a proper name for some single object or some collective unit, it must be followed by a singular verb.

e.g. The United Nations **is** not an effective body for world peace.

(xv) Nouns like glasses (spectacles), pants, trousers, shoes, people, police, scissors always take a plural verb. Also, descriptive nouns like the rich, the blind, the guilty are always plural.

e.g. (a) Your shoes **are** glossy.

But when used with 'a pair of', they become singular.

(b) A pair of branded shoes **is** quite expensive these days.

(xvi) Uncountable nouns like advice, news, media, stationery, weather, progress are singular and take a singular verb.

e.g. One must not offer **advice** unless asked.

(xvii) Nouns like news, physics, economics, measles, cards, aerobics are plural in form, but they are treated as singular.

e.g. Aerobics **is** a good exercise.

(xviii) A collective noun takes a singular verb when the collection is thought of as one whole. It takes a plural verb when the stress is on the individuals.

e.g. (a) The cartel of oil supplying countries **has** submitted its report.

(b) The cartel of oil supplying countries **are** divided over the issue.

(ixx) A singular verb is used when a plural noun denotes some specific quantity or amount.

e.g. (a) One-fifty rupees **is** too much for this bag.

(b) Two-thirds of the city **is** in ruins.

Chapter Practice

Objective Questions

• Multiple Choice Questions

Choose the option with the correct form of verb that agrees with the subject.

1. The regulations of the administration .... from the curriculum.
   (a) stem
   (b) stems
   (c) stemming
   (d) are stemmed

Ans. (*a*)

2. The children of the man who works with me .... broken the window this morning.
   (a) were   (b) have   (c) had   (d) has

Ans. (*b*)

3. One man among the crew .... into the water every week.
   (a) dive
   (b) had dived
   (c) is diving
   (d) dives

Ans. (*d*)

4. The men of the community .... not support the leader.
   (a) does   (b) have   (c) has   (d) do

Ans. (*d*)

5. Few students who .... playing football missed the class.
   (a) would be   (b) could be   (c) had   (d) were

Ans. (*d*)

6. The police .... to be careful since the criminal was dangerous.
   (a) were told
   (b) were telling
   (c) was telling
   (d) was saying

Ans. (*a*)

7. Students' minds .... about the order of structures.
   (a) has been confused
   (b) have been confused
   (c) had confused
   (d) have confused

Ans. (*b*)

8. The man whom I was talking with .... the Dean of our faculty.
   (a) were
   (b) are
   (c) is
   (d) was

Ans. (*d*)

9. Neither the man nor his son .... convinced of the idea.
   (a) had
   (b) has
   (c) was
   (d) have

Ans. (*c*)

10. Do you know the woman .... next to the window?
   (a) stands
   (b) is standing
   (c) stand
   (d) standing

Ans. (*d*)

11. He and I .... good friends but now we won't talk anymore.
   (a) have been
   (b) am
   (c) were
   (d) was

Ans. (*c*)

12. Although every student in my class .... the schedule, one of my students always comes late to the class.
   (a) knew
   (b) knowing
   (c) know
   (d) knows

Ans. (*d*)

13. After the meeting, he said a great deal of advice ....
   (a) were given
   (b) has been given
   (c) had been given
   (d) have been given

Ans. (*c*)

14. Only when each of the committee members .... reading the instructions can you take them to the hall.
   (a) would finish
   (b) is finishing
   (c) finish
   (d) finishes

Ans. (*d*)

15. Istanbul .... in 1453 by Sultan Mehmet, the Conqueror.

   (a) had been conquered   (b) conquered

   (c) was conquered   (d) would be conquered

Ans. (c)

PART 2
Subjective Questions

A. *Fill in the blanks with correct form of verb that agrees with the subject.*

1. Anita and her brothers .... at school.

Ans. are

2. Either my father or my mother .... coming to the meeting.

Ans. is

3. Ravi and Rahul .... want to see the play.

Ans. don't

4. He .... know the answer.

Ans. doesn't

5. One of my friends .... going to London on a trip.

Ans. is

6. The man with all the cats .... on my street.

Ans. lives

7. The movie, including all the previews, ... about two hours to watch.

Ans. takes

8. The players, as well as the captain, ... to win.

Ans. want

9. Either answer .... acceptable.

Ans. is

10. Everyone of those books .... fiction.

Ans. is

B. **1.** Nobody .... the problems I have faced.

Ans. knows

2. This is one of the best movies that .... been released this year.

Ans. have

3. Fifty rupees .... the fare from Patel Nagar to Shivaji Nagar.

Ans. is

4. There .... fifteen candles in that bag. Now there .... (is/are) only one left.

Ans. were, is

5. The committee .... these questions carefully.

Ans. debates

6. The committee members .... very different lives in private.

Ans. lead

7. All of the vases, even the cracked one, ... in this box.

Ans. are

8. Two-thirds of the city .... in ruins.

Ans. is

9. The formation of paragraphs .... very important.

Ans. is

10. No news .... good news.

Ans. is

II. *Complete the following lines with appropriate verb that agrees with the subject.*

1. When does next boat .... ?

Ans. leave

2. Why does the article .... famous singers?

Ans. mention

3. My mother loves to .... ancient temples.

Ans. see

4. Where .... they like to go on vacation?

Ans. do

5. Most of the milk .... gone bad.

Ans. has

6. A number of my friends .... (love/loves) riding bicycles, but neither my brother nor my sister own a bicycle.

Ans. love

7. The pair of shoes on the floor .... mine.

Ans. is

8. Finding a job where you can learn new skills .... a lot of effort.

Ans. takes

9. A photograph of two children .... on the desk.

Ans. sits

10. This website .... useful for studying English.

Ans. is

Determiners

In this Chapter...

- Characteristics of Determiners
- Classification of Determiners
- Articles–A, An, The
- Demonstrative Adjectives
- Quantifiers
- Possessives
- Chapter Practice

Determiners are words that modify nouns. In other words, determiners are words that can be used before nouns to determine or to modify their meaning. Determiners function like adjectives. They are also called 'fixing words'.

Characteristics of Determiners

Characteristics of determiners are as follows

- A determiner may determine or fix a place, person or thing.
- A determiner may identify two or more persons or things.
- A determiner may precede numerals or objects.
- A determiner may indicate a quantity or amount.

Classification of Determiners

Determiners can be classified into

1. **Articles** A, an, the.
2. **Demonstrative Adjectives** This, that, these, those.
3. **Quantifiers** A quantifier is a word or phrase which is used before a noun to indicate the amount or quantity. Types of quantifiers are as follows
    (i) **Definite** One, two, hundred, ..., first, second, both, etc.
    (ii) **Indefinite** Some, many, much, enough, few, a few, all, little, a little, several, most, etc.
    (iii) **Distributive** Each, every, all, either, neither.
    (iv) **Difference** Another, other.
    (v) **Comparative** More, less, fewer.
4. **Possessives** My, your, his, her, its, our, their, mine, hers, yours, ours, theirs, etc.

Determiners and Kinds of Nouns With Which They are Used

- **A, an, each, everyone, another** and **either** are used with singular countable nouns.
- **This** and **that** are used with uncountable nouns/singular countable nouns.
- **These** and **those** are used with uncountable nouns/plural countable nouns.
- **A little, a lot of, a great deal of, much** are used with uncountable nouns.
- **More, most, a lot of, enough, adequate, some** are used with uncountable nouns/plural countable nouns.
- **A few, several, many, both** are used with plural nouns.
- **The, some, any, my, her, your, our, their, its, which, whose, what** are used with any type of noun.

1. Articles— A, An, The

Use of Indefinite Articles : A/An

'A' is used before a noun beginning with a consonant sound.

e.g.　**a** woman, **a** horse, **a** university
　(*Here* woman, horse *and* university *are words beginning with a consonant sound.*)

'An' is used before a noun beginning with a vowel sound.

e.g. **an** orange, **an** egg, **an** elephant, **an** hour
　　　　　　　　(*Here* orange, egg, elephant *and* hour *are words beginning with a vowel sound.*)

Use 'A' and 'An'

- The use of 'a' and 'an' is determined by sound. The following words begin with a vowel, but not with a vowel sound. A unique thing, a one rupee coin, a European, a unicorn, a university, a useful thing, a union.
  So here 'a' is used.
- On the other hand, with the following words, 'an' is used although they begin with a consonant. An hour, an honest man, an heir to the throne, an MCA.
  The sound is the criterion to decide whether a/an will be used.

Use of Definite Article : The

'The' is used before singular countable nouns, plural countable nouns and uncountable nouns.

'The' is used

I. While talking about a particular person or thing or one already referred to (that is, when it is clear from the context which one do we mean).

　e.g.　**The** book you want is not available.

II. When a singular noun represents the whole group.

　e.g.　**The** dog is a faithful animal.

III. Before some proper names that denote physical features.

　(i) Oceans and seas e.g. **The** Pacific ocean, **The** Arabian Sea
　(ii) Rivers e.g. **The** Yamuna, **The** Thames
　(iii) Canals e.g. **The** Suez Canal
　(iv) Deserts e.g.　the Thar Desert, the Sahara Desert.
　(v) Group of islands e.g. the West Indies, the Netherlands
　(vi) Mountain ranges e.g. the Himalayas, the Satpura Ranges
　(vii) A few names of countries, which include words like States, Republic or Kingdom e.g. **The** People's Republic of China, the United Kingdom, the USA, the Republic of Korea, the Hague, etc.

IV. Before the names of religious or mythological books.
　e.g. the Vedas, the Puranas, the Mahabharata
　　　(*but we say Homer's Iliad, Valmiki's Ramayana*).

V. Before the names of things which are unique or one of their kind.
　e.g. **the** Sun, **the** Moon, **the** Pacific Ocean

VI. Before a proper noun, when it is qualified by an adjective or a defining adjectival clause.
　e.g.　**The** Great Caesar, **the** King of Rome
　　　　The Mr Verma whom you met last night is my boss.

VII. With superlative degrees.
　e.g. This is **the** worst performance I have ever seen.

VIII. With ordinals.
　e.g. He was **the** first man to walk on the Moon.

IX. Before musical instruments.
　e.g. He can play **the** tabla very well.

X. Before an adjective when the noun is understood.
　e.g. **The** rich always exploit **the** poor.
　　　(*Here the word 'people' is understood.*)

XI. As an adverb with comparatives.
　e.g. **The** more money we have, **the** more we want.

Omission of Article 'The'

- Before material, abstract and proper nouns used in a general sense.
　e.g.　(a) Honesty is the best policy.　　(*not The honesty....*)
　　　　(b) Sugar tastes sweet.　　　　　(*not The sugar....*)
　　　　(c) Paris is the capital of France.　(*not The Paris....*)
- Before plural countable nouns used in a general sense.
　e.g.　Children like toys.
- Before names of people.
　e.g.　Rohit
- Before names of continents, countries; cities etc
　e.g.　Europe, Pakistan, Nagpur.
- Before names of individual mountains
　e.g.　Mount Everest
- Before names of meals used in a general sense.
　e.g.　Dinner is ready.
- Before languages and words like school, college, university, church, hospital.
　e.g.　(a) I learn English at school.
　　　　(b) My uncle is still in hospital.

2. Demonstrative Adjectives
(This, That, These, Those)

I. **That** (in case of plural, **those**)
　(a) It refers to person(s) or thing(s) far from the speaker.
　　e.g.　• Get **that** dog out of here.
　　　　　• **Those** houses are for sale.
　(b) It is used to avoid the repetition of the preceding noun(s).

e.g. • My bat is better than **that** of my friend.
      • Our soldiers are better equipped than **those** of Pakistan.

II. **This** (in case of plural, **these**)

(a) It refers to person(s) or thing(s) near the speaker.

e.g. • **This** book is very interesting.
      • **These** flowers are very beautiful.

3. Quantifiers

'Some', 'many', 'a lot of' and 'a few' are examples of quantifiers. Quantifiers can be used in affirmative sentences, questions, requests or commands with both countable and uncountable nouns.

e.g. • There are **some** books on the desk.
      • He's got only **a few** dollars.
      • How **much** money have you got?

Some quantifiers can go only with countable nouns, some can go only with uncountable nouns while some can be used with both countable and uncountable nouns.

A few examples of quantifiers are given below

Only with Uncountable Nouns	With both Countable and Uncountable Nouns	Only with Countable Nouns
a little	no, none, not any	a few
a bit of	some, all	a number of
—	any	several
a great deal of	a lot of, lots of	a great number of
a large amount of	plenty of	a large number of

Usage of quantifiers is as follows

I. Use of **few/a few** and **little/a little**

(a) **Few, a few** and **the few**

Few emphasises the lack of something.

e.g. There are **few** sweets left in the jar.
      (We should be careful not to eat them too quickly because they are almost finished.)

A few emphasises that something still remains.

e.g. We still have **a few** minutes left before the class gets over. Do you have any questions?
      (We still have some time, so we should use it.)

The few means not many, but all of theose.

e.g. I ran back **the few** yards to where the figure had disappeared.

(b) **Little, a little** and **the little**

Little emphasises the lack of something.

e.g. We have **little** money right now; we should go out for dinner another day.
      (We should be careful and use the money wisely because we don't have much.)

A little emphasises that something still remains.

e.g. There's **a little** ice-cream left; who will eat it?

'The little' means-not much 'but' all that is. It also has positive meaning.

e.g. The cat has knocked over the little milk in the jug.

II. Use of **much** and **many**

(a) We use **much** with singular uncountable nouns and **many** with plural nouns.

e.g. • I haven't got **much** change; I've only got a hundred rupee note.
      • Are there **many** campsites near your place?

(b) We usually use **much** and **many** with interrogative sentences and negative sentences.

e.g. • Is there **much** unemployment in that area?
      • How **many** eggs have not been used in this cake?

III. Use of **more, less** and **fewer**

(comparative determiners)

(a) We use **more** or **less** before singular uncountable nouns by adding than after it, or for an additional or lesser quantity of something.

e.g. • I do **more** work than Suresh.
      • Please give me some **more** salad.

(b) We use **fewer** before plural countable nouns to refer to a group of things smaller than another.

e.g. • **Fewer** students succeeded in passing than last year.

IV. Use of **each** and **every** (distributive determiners)

(a) We use **each** for two or more than two items and **every** is always used for more than two items. Both of these are followed by singular countable nouns and singular verbs.

e.g. • **Each** of the two boys has won a prize.
      • **Every** student in the school is present today.

(b) We use **each** when the number in the group is limited or definite, but **every** is used when the number is indefinite or unknown.

e.g. • **Each** student in my class was promoted.
      • **Every** person in the world has a parent.

V. Use of **most, several** and **all**

(a) We usually use **most** with plural and uncountable nouns.

e.g. • **Most** of the people can be trusted.
      • **Most** of the time I am not at home.

(b) We usually use **several** with plural nouns, but it refers to a number which is not very large (i.e. less than **most**).

e.g. • **Several** people were crushed in the stampede.

(c) **All** requires a plural verb when used with a countable noun, but requires a singular verb with an uncountable noun.

e.g. • **All** are going to Delhi.
      • **All** that glitters is not gold.

VI. Use of **another** and **other**

We use **another** only with singular countable nouns, whereas **other** can be used with singular countable, plural countable or uncountable nouns.

e.g.
- Bring me **another** knife, as this one is blunt.
- I would prefer the **other** house.
- The **other** students went back home.
- He is a better human being than most **others**.

VII. Use of **either** and **neither**

(a) We use **either** to refer to two things, people, situations etc. It may mean one or the other of two or each of the two.

e.g. I don't agree with **either** Ram or Shyam.

(b) We use **neither** with only singular countable nouns and a singular verb. **Neither** is the negative of **either**.

It allows us to make a negative statement about two people or things at the same time.

e.g. Neither France nor Belgium won the 2021 Euro Cup.

4. Possessives

(My, Your, His, Her, Its, Our, Their etc)

Possessive determiners or possessive adjectives tell us who owns something. We use a possessive determiner before a noun to show who owns the noun we are talking about. They come in front of any other adjectives.

e.g.
- This is **your** book.
- That is **our** beautiful house.

We use different possessive determiners depending on who owns the thing we are talking about.

My, **her**, **his** and **its** are used with singular nouns, while **our** and **their** are used with plural nouns. **Your** can be used with either singular or plural nouns, depending on the sense.

e.g.
- This is **my** book.
- The dog licked **its** paw.
- Which is **their** car?
- All three of you, have you done **your** homework?

Chapter Practice

Objective Questions

• Multiple Choice Questions

Fill in the blank with appropriate determiners from the options.

1. Very .... people fly just because of terrorist activities.
  (a) little
  (b) much
  (c) many
  (d) few

Ans. (d)

2. Johnny is a keen player but unfortunately he has .... skills.
  (a) few
  (b) none
  (c) some
  (d) little

Ans. (a)

3. If we don't move faster, we'll miss our transfer to Munich. There isn't .... time to waste.
  (a) little (b) any (c) many (d) few

Ans. (b)

4. Unfortunately, I haven't got .... time for watching TV.
  (a) few (b) no (c) much (d) little

Ans. (c)

5. You can buy these maps at .... station. They all have them.
  (a) a lot of (b) several (c) some (d) any

Ans. (d)

6. If you have .... questions, I'm ready to answer.
  (a) little (b) any (c) much (d) plenty

Ans. (b)

7. I didn't have .... trouble getting the passports. I only had a problem with my photo because it was an old one.
  (a) much
  (b) any
  (c) no
  (d) several

Ans. (a)

8. There is .... water left, so drink only if you must.
  (a) some
  (b) little
  (c) few
  (d) much

Ans. (b)

9. There isn't .... point at all in getting upset about it.
  (a) few
  (b) several
  (c) any
  (d) many

Ans. (c)

10. .... coat will do. It doesn't need to be a raincoat.
  (a) Little
  (b) No
  (c) Any
  (d) Few

Ans. (c)

11. Despite the advances in technology, ... of the universe is yet to be discovered.
  (a) much
  (b) a quantity
  (c) several
  (d) an amount

Ans. (a)

12. She has gone to Turkey for .... months for her treatment.
  (a) much
  (b) several
  (c) whole
  (d) most

Ans. (b)

13. .... the sixteen teams in the cup were represented with their flags.
  (a) Plenty of
  (b) Much of
  (c) Many
  (d) All

Ans. (d)

14. Very .... people are travelling by train because of its slow movement.
  (a) few
  (b) plenty
  (c) little
  (d) some

Ans. (a)

15. There weren't .... people in the stadium because of the heavy rain.
  (a) many
  (b) much
  (c) each
  (d) plenty

Ans. (a)

PART 2
Subjective Questions

A. *Fill in the blanks with appropriate determiners.*

1. There are .... books in the library.

Ans. many

2. Have you ever had .... high fever?

Ans. a

3. .... National Health Service was set up in Britain in 1946.

Ans. The

4. In .... countries, you have to pay for medical treatment.

Ans. many

5. My brother is .... dentist.

Ans. a

6. Only .... houses were spared by the earthquake.

Ans. a few

7. You must learn .... English everyday to improve your language.

Ans. a little

8. There isn't .... bread in that tin.

Ans. any

9. Sometimes .... patience and advice help more than medicine.

Ans. a little

10. Could you bring me .... books I left in the garden?

Ans. those

B. **1.** She gave a cookie to .... child.

Ans. each

2. I've got to solve .... math problems before I go to sleep.

Ans. some

3. .... Cherries are delicious.

Ans. These

4. My mother doesn't drink .... coffee.

Ans. much

5. I always keep .... money in my wallet for emergencies.

Ans. some

6. They were bored because there was .... to do.

Ans. little

7. We invited .... friends over to our house for a party.

Ans. a few

8. .... of the cakes had been baked the day before.

Ans. most

9. .... the children went to their respective classes.

Ans. all

10. I invited Ram and Sheila to the party, but .... of them came.

Ans. neither

II. *Fill in the blanks with suitable determiners.*

1. I admit that I don't have .... knowledge of the subject.

Ans. much

2. May I taste .... of the soup that you cooked this morning?

Ans. a little

3. When Sapna realised that she still had a little time left, she gave me .... assistance with my work.

Ans. some

4. I took an apple from .... refrigerator and ate it.

Ans. the

5. The man complained that .... boys were stealing some of his mangoes.

Ans. a few

6. Are there .... sandwiches for you?

Ans. any

7. There are .... people at the theatre.

Ans. many

8. The children in the Kindergarten are given a cup of milk and .... biscuits during the break.

Ans. some

9. .... goats have wandered into the garden and damaged the plants.

Ans. Several

10. How .... tablets have you taken?

Ans. many

CHAPTER 05

Reported Speech

(Commands and Requests, Statements, Questions)

In this Chapter...

- Basic Rules of Speech and Conversion
- Chapter Practice

The act of reporting the words of a speaker is called **narration**. There are basically two ways in which the words of the speaker can be conveyed in writing.

(a) **Direct Speech** (*Direct Narration*) The reporting of the words of the speaker without making any changes to it is known as **Direct Speech**. Direct speech is written inside double quotation marks.

(b) **Indirect Speech** (*Indirect Narration*) The act of reporting the words of the speaker by making necessary changes to it is called **Indirect Speech**. In indirect speech, while narrating something, changes are made in the original words of the person. For example, tenses and pronouns are changed according to the reporting verb.

e.g.

(i) My mother told me, "You have to work harder at school." (Direct speech)

(ii) **My mother told me that I had to work harder at school.** (Indirect speech)

In sentence (i), we can notice that this is the speaker's direct narration as it is written inside double quotation marks, but in sentence (ii), tense and pronouns are changed and quotation marks are removed.

Observe the following changes carefully.

- He said, "I work in a factory." (Direct speech)
  He said that he worked in a factory. (Indirect speech)
- They said, "We are going to the cinema." (Direct speech)
  They said that they were going to the cinema. (Indirect speech)
- She said, "I am playing." (Direct speech)
  She said that she was playing. (Indirect speech)
- He said to me, "You have been a great help to me." (Direct speech)
  He told me that I had been a great help to him. (Indirect speech)
- Ashish said to me, "I will go to the market today." (Direct speech)
  Ashish told me that he would go to the market that day. (Indirect speech)

Basic Rules of Speech and Conversion

(a) **In Direct Speech**

(i) Put the words spoken by the speaker within " " (double quotes or double inverted commas).

(ii) Separate the reporting verb from the direct speech by a comma.

(iii) Begin the first word inside inverted commas with a capital letter.

(b) **In Indirect Speech**

(i) Change the reporting verb according to the sense conveyed by the speech.

(ii) Do not change the tense of the reporting verb.

(iii) Remove the comma separating the reporting verb from the direct speech.

(iv) Remove inverted commas.

(v) Introduce the indirect speech by some connector like *that, if, whether, what, where, how, why* etc depending

on whether you want to transform a statement, question or request, as the case may be.

(vi) Convert all kinds of sentences into assertive statements.

(vii) Make other necessary changes in person, verb forms, time, place and expressions.

Some changes to consider

(a) **1st person** (I, we etc) → change according to the subject of the reporting verb.

(b) **2nd person** (You, your etc) → change according to the object of the reporting verb.

(c) **3rd person** (He, she, it, they, his, her etc) → make no change.

(d) Change **1st person** into **3rd person** if the reporting verb has no object mentioned.

Rules for Changing Simple Direct Speech into Indirect Speech

Rules	Direct Speech	Indirect Speech
Remove separating comma, inverted commas and use the connector 'that' when there is no object in the sentence.	▪ He said, "I work in a shipyard."	▪ He said that he worked in a shipyard.
The reporting verb 'said' becomes 'told' along with the subject and the connector 'that' when it is followed by an object.	▪ Kamya said to me, "You have been a great help."	▪ Kamya told me that I had been a great help.

Changes into Reported Speech with Respect to the Tense Present Tense

Rules of Conversion	Direct Speech	Indirect Speech
Simple Present changes into Simple Past	▪ He said, "I do not like computers."	▪ He said that he did not like computers.
Present continuous changes into past continuous	▪ I said, "It is raining."	▪ I said that it was raining.
Present perfect changes into past perfect	▪ She said, "He has finished his work."	▪ She said that he had finished his work.
Present perfect continuous changes into past perfect continuous	▪ He said, "I have been studying since 3 o' clock."	▪ He said that he had been studying since 3 o' clock.

Past Tense

Rules of Conversion	Direct Speech	Indirect Speech
Simple past changes into past perfect	▪ My teacher said to me, "You answered correctly."	▪ My teacher told me that I had answered correctly.
Past continuous changes into past perfect continuous	▪ He said, "Mohit was listening to music."	▪ He said that Mohit had been listening to music.
Past perfect remains past perfect (tense does not change)	▪ He said, "I had started a business."	▪ He said that he had started a business.

Future Tense

Rules of Conversion	Direct Speech	Indirect Speech
Simple future: *will* changes into *would*	▪ He said, "I will study the book."	▪ He said that he would study the book.
Future continuous: *will be* changes into *would be*	▪ Shreya told him, "I will be waiting for you."	▪ Shreya told him that she would be waiting for him.
Future perfect: *will have* changes into *would have*	▪ He said, "I will have finished the work."	▪ He said that he would have finished the work.

Rules for Changing Interrogative Sentences into Indirect Speech
(The reporting verb 'said' becomes 'asked' and 'to' is removed)

Rules	Direct Speech	Indirect Speech
Use 'if' or 'whether' in place of 'that' as a connector.	• She said to me, "Do you like tea or coffee?"	• She asked me whether I liked tea or coffee.
Remove the question mark while forming an assertive sentence.	• She said to Shyam, "Do you have an extra copy?"	• She asked Shyam if he had an extra copy.
The questions starting with question words like **when**, **why**, **where**, do not use 'if' or 'whether'. The question words are retained to introduce the reported question.	• He said, "What is your problem?"	• He asked me what my problem was.

Rules for Changing Imperative Sentences into Indirect Speech
(Commands, Requests and Suggestions)

Rules	Direct Speech	Indirect Speech
Use conjunction 'to' instead of 'that'.	• I said to Hari, "Do not pluck the flowers."	• I ordered Hari not to pluck the flowers.
In sentences beginning with 'Let', the reporting verb is changed to 'proposed' or 'suggested'.	• He said, "Let us keep quiet in this matter."	• He suggested that we should keep quiet in this matter.

Rules for Changing Exclamatory Sentences into Indirect Speech

Rules	Direct Speech	Indirect Speech
Words such as 'Alas', 'Bravo', 'Oh', 'Wow', should be left out in indirect speech.	• Ram said, "Alas! I have been ruined."	• Ram exclaimed with sorrow that he had been ruined.
Forms of the verb 'wish' is used if the sentence conveys a wish.	• She said, "If I were a bird."	• She wished to be a bird./She wished that she were a bird.

Chapter Practice

Objective Questions

• Multiple Choice Questions

I. Choose the correct option to change the following sentences into direct/indirect speech.

1. The teacher said, "You are suspended!"
(a) The teacher exclaimed that I am suspended.
(b) The teacher exclaimed to me to suspend.
(c) The teacher informed me that I was suspended.
(d) The teacher exclaimed that I was suspended.

Ans. (c)

2. The guard asked, "Who are you?"
(a) The guard asked who he was.
(b) The guard asked me who he was.
(c) The guard asks me who he was.
(d) The guard asked who I was.

Ans. (d)

3. She said, "Bring a glass of water, please."
(a) She commands me to bring a glass of water.
(b) She requested me to bring a glass of water.
(c) She asked me to brought a glass of water.
(d) She ordered me to bring her a glass of water.

Ans. (b)

4. She said, "Shut the door!"
(a) She asked me whether I would shut the door.
(b) She ordered me to shut the door.
(c) She said that I should shut the door.
(d) She shouted and said to shut the door.

Ans. (b)

5. "Alas! It can't be this bad," he said.
(a) He exclaimed with sorrow that it couldn't be that bad.
(b) He grieved that it couldn't be that bad.
(c) He said that it was really that bad.
(d) He said with sorrow that was bad.

Ans. (a)

6. The policeman said, "Don't cross the speed limit."
(a) The policeman said not to cross the speed limit.
(b) The policeman asked if I would cross the speed limit.
(c) The policeman forbade me to cross the speed limit.
(d) The policeman asks if I had crossed the speed limit.

Ans. (c)

7. The secretary said, "Is Mr. Fisher in his office?"
(a) The secretary said that if Mr. Fisher was in his office.
(b) The secretary enquired if Mr. Fisher was in his office.
(c) The secretary enquired that if Mr. Fisher was in his office.
(d) The secretary asked if Mr. Fisher had been in his office.

Ans. (b)

8. The student said, "Ma'am, please extend the deadline."
(a) The student asked the teacher to extend the deadline.
(b) The student said if the teacher would extend the deadline.
(c) The student requested ma'am to extend the deadline.
(d) The student said that ma'am should extend the deadline.

Ans. (c)

9. The driver said, "Do you want to halt for a while?"
(a) The driver said if we wanted a halt for a while.
(b) The driver asked if we want to halt for a while.
(c) The driver asks if we wanted to halt for a while.
(d) The driver asked if we wanted to halt for a while.

Ans. (d)

10. He said that he would deposit the cheque the following day.
(a) He said, "I will deposit the cheque the next day."
(b) He said, "I would deposit the cheque soon."
(c) He said, "I will deposit the cheque tomorrow."
(d) He said, "I would deposit the cheque the following day."

Ans. (c)

II. Choose the correct option to change the following sentences into direct speech.

1. He asked me whether you were ready or he should wait.
(a) He said to me, "Is she ready or shall I wait?"
(b) He said, "Are you ready or should I wait?"

(c) He said to me, "Are you ready or shall I wait?"
(d) He said, "Are you ready or not?"

Ans. (*a*)

2. She exclaimed with joy that that was her birthday party.
(a) She said, "It is my birthday party."
(b) She said, "On! It is my birthday party."
(c) She said, "I have been waiting for my birthday party."
(d) She said, "Yay! It is my birthday party."

Ans. (*d*)

3. He asked where his belongings were.
(a) He said, "Where were my belongings?"
(b) He said, "Where my belongings had been?"
(c) He said, "Where are my belongings?"
(d) He said, "Where would my belongings be?"

Ans. (*c*)

4. He requested the audience to maintain silence.
(a) He said to the audience, "Maintain silence!"
(b) He said, "The audience must maintain silence."
(c) He said, "Will the audience maintain silence?"
(d) He said to the audience, "Please maintain silence."

Ans. (*d*)

5. The coach asked us if we had any doubts.
(a) The coach said, "Has anyone have doubts?"
(b) The coach said to us, "Any doubts?"
(c) The coach said to us, "Do you have any doubts?"
(d) The coach said, "Would you have doubts?"

Ans. (*c*)

6. He prayed that God might fulfill her wish.
(a) He said, "May God fulfill her wish."
(b) He said, "May God fulfill your wish."
(c) He said, "Might God fulfilled her wish."
(d) He said, "Might God fulfills her wish."

Ans. (*a*)

7. The reporter confirmed that that news was fake.
(a) The reporter said, "This news has been fake."
(b) The reporter said, "This news is fake."
(c) The reporter said, "The news was fake."
(d) The reporter said, "That news is fake."

Ans. (*b*)

8. Vikas ordered that I had to complete the presentation soon.
(a) Vikas said, "You must complete the presentation soon."
(b) Vikas said, "You shall complete the presentation soon."
(c) Vikas said, "You complete the presentation!"
(d) Vikas said, "Will you complete the presentation soon?"

Ans. (*a*)

9. He commanded me to guard the door.
(a) He said, "Guard the door."
(b) He requested, "Guard the door."

(c) He said, "Guarded the door."
(d) He told, "Guard the door."

Ans. (*a*)

10. Tina said that she might postpone the trip to the following year.
(a) Tina said, "I may postpone the trip to the following year."
(b) Tina said, "I might postpone the trip to the next year."
(c) Tina said, "I may postpone the trip to the next year."
(d) Tina said, "I may be postponing the trip to the next year."

Ans. (*c*)

11. Ms. Nita asked to reschedule the meeting to the following Monday.
(a) Ms. Nita asked, "Reschedule the meeting to next Monday."
(b) Ms. Nita said, "Reschedule the meeting to next Monday."
(c) Ms. Nita told, "The meeting to be rescheduled to next Monday."
(d) Ms. Nita said, "The meeting will take place on next Monday."

Ans. (*b*)

12. Julia said that she could not attend our wedding.
(a) Julia said, "I could not attend your wedding."
(b) Julia said, "I will not attend your wedding."
(c) Julia said, "I am not attending your wedding."
(d) Julia said, "I cannot attend your wedding."

Ans. (*d*)

13. Harish asked me if I would accompany him there.
(a) Harish said, "Will you accompany me there?"
(b) Harish said, "Would you accompany me there?"
(c) Harish said, "Would you like to accompany me there?"
(d) Harish said, "Won't you accompany me there?"

Ans. (*a*)

14. The suspect exclaimed that he was not guilty.
(a) The suspect said, "I wish I were not guilty!"
(b) The suspect said, "I was not guilty!"
(c) The suspect said, "I am not guilty!"
(d) The suspect said, "I am innocent!"

Ans. (*c*)

15. The teacher said that the wind is a renewable energy source.
(a) The teacher says, "The wind was a renewable energy source."
(b) The teacher said, "The wind is a renewable energy source."
(c) The teacher said, "The wind was a renewable energy source."
(d) The teacher says, "The wind is a renewable energy source."

Ans. (*b*)

PART 2
Subjective Questions

I. Change the following sentences into indirect speech.

Interrogative Sentences

1. The teacher said, "Good morning dear students! Have you done your homework?"

Ans. The teacher wished the students good morning and asked if they had done their homework.

2. Ahmad said to the magician, "What have I done to deserve so severe a blow?"

Ans. Ahmad asked the magician what he had done to deserve so severe a blow.

3. My friend said to me, "Will you take me to my office"?

Ans. My friend asked me if I would take him to his office.

4. She asked whether Jessica would arrive the following week.

Ans. She said, "Will Jessica arrive the next week?"

5. Farhan asked Geeta whether she could lend him a hundred rupees until the next day.

Ans. Farhan said to Geeta, "Could you lend me a hundred rupees until tomorrow?"

Statement Sentences

6. He said, "I have passed the examination."

Ans. He said that he had passed the examination.

7. The captain shouted, "Hurrah! We have won the match."

Ans. The captain exclaimed with joy that they had won the match.

8. Muneer said, "Let us play cricket".

Ans. Muneer proposed to play cricket.

9. Sadiq's uncle tried out, "Call the fire brigade: there's a fire next door".

Ans. Sadiq's uncle shouted for the fire brigade to be called as there was a fire next door.

10. The poet said, " What a bewitching sight !"

Ans. The poet exclaimed with wonder that it was a very bewitching sight.

11. He said, "By God, I am speaking the truth".

Ans. He swore by God and said that he was speaking the truth.

12. He said that he would not go with us.

Ans. He said, "I will not go with you."

13. The chairman said that it was his pleasure to be there that evening.

Ans. The chairman said, "It is my pleasure to be here this evening."

14. The teacher quoted that slow and steady wins the race.

Ans. The teacher said, "Slow and steady wins the race."

15. She said he had some work to complete.

Ans. She said, "He had some work to complete."

16. He prayed that his son might live long.

Ans. He said to his son, "May you live long"!

17. The teacher told the children to answer the question after closing their books.

Ans. The teacher said to the children, "Now close your books and answer my question".

18. Mr. Gupta said that he was busy that weekend.

Ans. Mr. Gupta said, "I am busy this weekend."

19. He told me that he might not be able to reach the court in time.

Ans. He said to me, "I may not be able to reach the court in time".

20. The audience exclaimed with wonder that she was singing very beautifully.

Ans. The audience said, How beautifully she is singing!"

Commands and Requests

21. He said to his servant, "Leave the room at once".

Ans. He ordered the servant to leave the room at once.

22. Zaira's mother said to her, "Cook the food properly".

Ans. Zaira's mother ordered her to cook the food properly.

23. The teacher said to a student, "Don't waste your time".

Ans. The teacher ordered a student not to waste the time.

24. The police man shouted to the man, "Stop or I will shoot you".

Ans. The police man ordered the man to stop and threatened that otherwise he would shoot him.

25. My elder brother said to me, "Please post this letter for me".

Ans. My elder brother requested me to post this letter for him.

26. I said to my brother, "Let us go to some hill station for a change".

Ans. I suggested to my brother that we should go to some hill station for a change.

27. The police officer ordered a culprit not to try to be clever.

Ans. The police officer said to a culprit, "Don't try to be clever".

28. The judge ordered the accused to hold his tongue.

Ans. The judge said to the accused, "Hold your toungue".

Integrated Grammar Exercises

Based on Whole Grammar Section

CATEGORY I Gap Filling

Directions (Q. Nos. 1-10) Fill in the blanks by with appropriate words.

A. 1. Mount Kailash—the Stairway to Heaven— (i) .... (is the most/ is the more) intriguing mountain range is the whole of Himalayas. As a matter of fact, Mount Kailash is 22,000 ft from the Tibetan Plateau, which (ii) .... (is largely/ is large) considered to be inaccessible. For Hindus and Buddhists, Mount Kailash is the physical embodiment of Mount Meru. It is one of the world's most sacred and mysterious mountain peak. Every year, thousands of pilgrims enter Tibet for pilgrimage to the holy Mount Kailash. A few (iii) .... (make/ makes) it to the region and a very few manage to finish circumambulating the hallowed peak.

2. We enjoy protection from Earth's magnetic field, (i) .... (generates/ generated) by our planet's rotation and its iron-nickel core. This teardrop-shaped field shields Earth from high-energy particles (ii) .... (launched at us/ launching at us) from the Sun and elsewhere in the cosmos. But due to the field's structure, some particles get funneled to Earth's Poles and (iii) .... (collide into the / collide with our) atmosphere, yielding Auroras, the natural fireworks show known by some as the Northern lights.

3. The Amazon rainforest is the world's largest tropical rainforest and does the critical task (i) .... (to providing/ of providing) Earth with 20% of its oxygen supply. Its dense vegetation acts like a giant air purifier, constantly (ii) .... (taking in/ taking inside) carbon dioxide and giving out oxygen. The rainforest is so big that it comprises more than half of the world's remaining rainforests even though it covers only 6% of the earth's surface. The Amazon rainforest (iii) .... (is located/ is locating) in South America and spreads over an astounding 5.5 million square kilometers.

4. Brahmins (i) .... (were the/ are the) highest ranking caste group and are the top of the varna system above Kshatriyas, Vaisyas and Sudras. Brahmins have traditionally been priests, either in temples or to particular families and (ii) .... (has/ have) traditionally been better educated, held high positions and had land and money. Many have worked as teachers, scribes, landowners and government clerks. Today they are employed in a number of professions. Many (iii) .... (fulfilling/ fulfil) their priestly duties only a part time basis.

5. A total of 152 million children – 64 million girls and 88 million boys – (i) are .... (estimated to be/ estimates to being) in child labour globally, accounting for almost one in ten of all children worldwide. Despite rates of child labour declining over the last few years, children (ii) .... (are still being/ were still been) used in some severe forms of child labour such as bonded labour, child soldiers, and trafficking. Across India child labourers (iii) .... (can be found/ could be finding) in a variety of industries: in brick kilns, carpet weaving, garment making, domestic service, food and refreshment services (such as tea stalls), agriculture, fisheries and mining.

6. (i) .... (An earlier/ The earliest) known dinosaurs appeared during the Triassic Period (approximately 250 to 200 million ago). Dinosaurs evolved into a very diverse group of animals with a vast array of physical features, including modern birds. Contrary to what many people think, not all dinosaurs (ii) .... (lived in/ lived during) the same geological period. Stegosaurus, for example, lived during the Late Jurassic Period, about 150 million years ago. Tyrannosaurus rex lived during the Late Cretaceous Period, about 72 million years ago. Stegosaurus (iii) .... (was extinct for/ was extinct from) 66 million years before Tyrannosaurus walked on Earth.

7. Earthquakes happen when two large pieces of the Earth's crust suddenly slip. This causes shock waves (i) .... (to shake/ to shook) the surface of the Earth in the form of an earthquake. Earthquakes usually occur (ii) .... (by the edges to/ on the edges of) large sections of the Earth's crust called tectonic plates. These plates slowly move over a long period of time. Sometimes the edges, which are called fault lines, can get stuck, but the plates keep moving. Pressure slowly starts to build up where the edges are stuck and, once the pressure gets strong enough, the plates will suddenly move (iii) .... (caused/ causing) an earthquake.

8. Global warming occurs when carbon dioxide and other air pollutants and greenhouse gases (i) ....(collect in/ collect into) the atmosphere and absorb sunlight and solar radiation that have (ii) .... (bouncing off/ bounced off) the earth's surface. Normally, this radiation would escape into space—but these pollutants, which can last for years to centuries in the atmosphere, trap the heat and cause the planet (iii) .... (to get hotter/ to get hot). That's what's known as the greenhouse effect.

9. Emperor Qin Shi Huang is often referred as the initiator of the Great Wall. Actually, it was (i) .... (him/ he) who first commanded the linking of the separate sections built by previous states. It (ii) .... (is surprising/ was surprised) to know that the decision for this huge project was made due to a rumor! After unifying central China and establishing the Qin Dynasty in 221BC, Emperor Qin Shi Huang (iii) wanted .... (to consolidating/ to consolidate) his power and rule the country forever.

10. Located 80 km North of Udaipur forest, Kumbhalgarh Fort (i) .... (was/ is) the second largest fort in Rajasthan after Chittorgarh Fort. The fort wall spans a length of 36 kilometers and is therefore known as "The Great Wall of India". Kumbhalgarh Fort (ii) .... (spread/ spreads) in the Aravalli range is the birthplace of Maharana Pratap, the famous king of Mewar. This is the reason that Rajputs (iii) .... (has/ have) a special place in the hearts of this fort. In 2013, the fort was declared a UNESCO World Heritage Site at the 37th session of the World Heritage Committee.

Directions (Q. Nos. 1-25) Fill in the blanks with the correct form of verbs given in the brackets.

B.1. The roadside from Agra to Firozabad .... (sprinkle) with crumbling Mughal era monuments juxtaposed with verdant fields.

2. I .... (book) a ticket online and left for Amritsar.

3. Meditation .... (mean) when the mind is without any agitation.

4. Remarkably, this is all that modern science .... (tell) about the horseshoe crab in Taunton Bay or anywhere else.

5. Tomorrow I .... (go) for an entrance test at B.B. Public School.

6. People from all over the world .... (come) to Kamakhya temple in Guwahati and pray.

7. There were .... (more) whales swimming in the ocean a long time ago.

8. Ali Baba reached the foot of the same mountain where the thieves .... (gather).

9. They .... (have) an excellent and qualified staff to look after their work.

10. This year Shimla Summer Camp .... (be) in the Pabber valley in the upper regions of Shimla.

11. The Army .... (attempt) unsuccessfully to throw up the Government.

12. Scientists .... (be) on the brink of a major breakthrough in career research.

13. The State Government .... (plan) to build a bypass for Bhubaneswar to speed up traffic on the main highway.

14. Gautam's outlook on life changed when he realised that the world .... (be) full of sorrows.

15. Rakesh .... (seem) unusually cast down after the game.

16. A large team of United Nations Inspectors .... (arrive) in India under the terms of the International Forestry Treaty.

17. The soldiers .... (receive) a military mandate to inspect all their vehicles before traveling.

18. Juan's friends found him in a jovial mood after he learnt he .... (be) the homecoming king.

19. With all of the recent negative events in her life, she .... (feel) malignant forces must be at work.

20. The fictitious rumors .... (do) a great deal of damage even though they turned out to be false.

21. When her schoolwork .... (get) to be too much, Pakhi had a tendency to delay, which always put her further behind.

22. If criminals .... (be) allowed to join electoral fray extortion is likely to increase.

23. While the demand is high for clay idols, people also prefer moulded idols .... (procure) in bulk from other cities.

24. Crocodile can .... (live) effortlessly both in water and on land.

25. Two of the accused were arrested against whom the police .... (have) registered a complaint.

CATEGORY II Editing

Directions (Q. Nos. 1-5) The following passages have not been edited. There is one error in each line. Identify the wrong word and write it with the correction in the space given. The first one has been done for you.

	Incorrect	Correct
1. A little political thinkers e.g.	A little	Some
(a) thinks that liberty	....	....
(b) and equality couldn't go together.	....	....
(c) They think that liberty implied the freedom	....	....
(d) to do what one may like to doing.	....	....

CBSE 2020

	Incorrect	Correct
2. Countries near on equator are e.g.	on	the
(a) much warmer then countries	....	....
(b) farthest to the North and South,	....	....
(c) as all know that Kerala is	....	....
(d) warm than Punjab	....	....
(e) on winter	....	....

CBSE 2019

	Incorrect	Correct
3. In the prisoner's room a candle is e.g.	is	was
(a) burning dimly. A prisoner himself	....	....
(b) sat by the table. Only him back,	....	....
(c) the hair by his head, and his	....	....
(d) hands are visible from outside	....	....
(e) through by window.	....	....

CBSE 2018

	Incorrect	Correct
4. One morning I finished one business at the bank e.g.		
(a) and was returning in pick up my motorbike which I had left	....	....
(b) in the parking lot outside. Suddenly he realised that I had	....	....
(c) lost the bike key. Upset, I searched about it in the bank. A bank	....	....
(d) employee tried to help me find it and in vain.	....	....

CBSE 2013

	Incorrect	Correct
5. Neil Armstrong was the commander for Apollo 11.		
(a) He was the first to walk over	....	....
(b) the moon. What many people do not knew	....	....
(c) is that, unlike most of their fellow	....	....
(d) astronauts, he was the civilian and not part of the military	....	....

CBSE 2017

CATEGORY III Dialogue Writing

Directions (Q. Nos. 1-5) Choose the correct options to fill in the blanks to complete the narrations.

A.1. Jane (i) .... how she was doing. Jane (ii) .... with all those classes she was becoming so boring. Jane agreed to this and went away. Anne asked Jane to wait and said that (iii) .... becoming so bored.

2. Kylie (i) .... she had outgrown those shoes. Her mom (ii) .... they were barely two weeks old. How it could be possible. She checked and said those fit fine. To this Kylie replied that (iii) .... outgrown them fashion-wise.

3. The grandson (i) .... how many times he could make a rock skip across the water. The grandpa thought and said that one time he got a rock to skip twenty three times. The grandson (ii) .... and asked if he could do it again right then. Grandpa (iii) .... he could only skip the rock that many times when the water was frozen over.

4. When Birbal arrived in the court, Akbar told him that he had lost his ring. It was very dear to him as his father had given it to him as a gift. He (i) .... find it. Birbal relaxed Akbar and (ii) .... find his ring right away. Birbal further said addressing His Majesty that (iii) .... It was with one of their courtiers. The courtier who had a straw in his beard had his ring.

Directions (Q. Nos. 1-5) Read the conversations and complete the passages that follow

B.1. Shylock : I am unwell

Duke : What can I do for you, sir?

Shylock : Will you take me to the doctor?

Duke : Yes, Sir.

Shylock told the Duke (a) .... The Duke asked (b) ....

Shylock asked the Duke (c) .... The Duke replied in affirmative.

2. Divya : I am planning to buy a car.

Arti : Which car do you intend to buy?

Divya : I intend to buy the latest model of any popular company.

Arti : It is a wise decision.

Divya told Arti that (a)............. Then Arti asked her (b) .... Divya said that (c)............. Arti said that (d) ....

3. Susan : Why have you not brought my party dress?

Jenny : I haven't brought it because I had gone to my uncle's house with my parents, so I forgot to keep it.

Susan : Don't give me silly excuses. I want to know the truth.

Jenny : I am sorry Susan. I was chatting with my friends till late. I forgot that you needed it urgently today.

Susan asked Jenny (a) .... Jenny said that she (b) .... Susan (c)............. Jenny said that (d)............. . She was chatting with her friends till late and (e)........... that Jenny needed it urgently that day.

4. Dilip : I have been watching the sea and there hasn't been any trace of a ship.

Rohan : I told you yesterday too that we'll be rescued, so have patience.

Dilip : Why do you ask me to keep quiet whenever I say something?

Rohan : Have you ever said anything sensible?

Dilip said that (a)........... the sea and that (b) .... any trace of a ship. Rohan replied that (c)........... that they (d)........... and asked him to have patience. Dilip angrily asked Rohan (e)........... to keep quiet whenever he said something to which Rohan wanted to know (f)............. .

5. Sanjay : I am surprised to see you here in Delhi. When did you come?

Madan : I came here yesterday. I have been offered a job here.

Sanjay told Madan (a) .... and asked (b) .... Madan replied that (c) .... and added that (d) ....

ANSWERS

Category I Gap Filling A.

1. (i) is the most · (ii) is largely · (iii) make
2. (i) generated · (ii) launched at us · (iii) collide with our
3. (i) of providing · (ii) taking in · (iii) is located
4. (i) are the · (ii) have · (iii) fulfil
5. (i) are estimated to be · (ii) are still being · (iii) can be found
6. (i) The earliest · (ii) lived during · (iii) was extinct for
7. (i) to shake · (ii) on the edges of · (iii) causing
8. (i) collect in · (ii) bounced off · (iii) to get hotter
9. (i) he · (ii) is surprising · (iii) to consolidate
10. (i) is · (ii) spread · (iii) have

B.1. is sprinkled · 2. booked · 3. means
4. tells · 5. will go · 6. come
7. many · 8. gathered · 9. have
10. is · 11. attempted · 12. are
13. plans · 14. is · 15. seems
16. will arrive · 17. received · 18. was
19. felt · 20. do · 21. got
22. are · 23. procured · 24. live
25. has

Category II Editing

	Incorrect	Correct	Incorrect	Correct
1.	(a) thinks	think	(b) couldn't	can't
	(c) implied	implies	(d) doing	do
2.	(a) then	than	(b) farthest	farther
	(c) all	we	(d) warm	warmer
	(e) an	in		
3.	(a) A	the	(b) him	his
	(c) by	on	(d) are	were
	(e) by	the		

	Incorrect	Correct	Incorrect	Correct
4.	(a) in	to	(b) he	I
	(c) about	for	(d) and	but
5.	(a) over	on	(b) knew	know
	(c) their	his	(d) the	a

Category III Dailogue Writing

A.1. (i) asked Anne · (ii) sighed and said that · (iii) she meant she was
2. (i) informed her mom that · (ii) got surprised and said that · (iii) she meant she had
3. (i) asked his grandpa · (ii) exclaimed with surprise · (iii) replied in negation that
4. (i) requested Birbal to help him · (ii) said that he would · (iii) the ring was there in that court itself
5. (i) informed the lady that · (ii) thought to herself · (iii) said that the detergent

B. 1. (a) that he was unwell   (b) what he could do for him

    (c) if he would take him to the doctor

2. (a) she was planning to buy a new car   (b) which car she intended to buy

    (c) she intended to buy the latest model of any popular company

    (d) it was a wise decision

3. (a) Why she had not brought her party dress

    (b) hadn't brought it as she had gone to her uncle's house with her parents so she had forgotten to keep it

    (c) told her not to give silly excuses and that she wanted to know the truth

    (d) she was sorry

    (e) had forgotten

4. (a) he had been watching   (b) there had not been

    (c) he had told him the day before   (d) would be rescued

    (e) why he asked him   (f) if he had ever said anything sensible

5. (a) that he was surprised to see him there in Delhi   (b) When he had come

    (c) he had come there the previous day   (d) he had been offered a job there

CHAPTER 01

Glimpses of India

In this Chapter...

- Chapter Summary
- Word Meaning
- Chapter Practice

I. A Baker from Goa

by Lucio Rodrigues

This part of the chapter is a pen-portrait of a traditional Goan village baker or 'Pader' who still has an important place in the Goan culture.

Chapter Summary

The Old Portuguese Days in Goa

In the old days of Goa, the Portuguese were famous for their loaves of bread. The Portuguese left Goa a long time ago but the traditional bakers and their furnaces (a machine for baking) still exist there.

The mixers, moulders and the people who bake the loaves still exist carrying on their business of baking. The sound of the baker's bamboo in the morning can still be heard in some places. These bakers are still known as pader in Goa.

The Traditional Baker during the Narrator's Childhood

The narrator recalls his childhood in Goa, when the baker used to be their friend, companion and guide. He came to their house twice a day. He came once in the morning while selling his bread and again in the evening after selling all his bread.

The baker used to arrive with a jingling sound of the bamboo stick that woke everyone up. As soon as the children heard the sound, they ran to meet the baker and get the bread bangles which was sometimes made of sweet bread.

The Baker's Arrival

The baker used to carry the bread basket on his head along with a bamboo stick. His one hand supported the basket and other hand banged the bamboo stick on the ground. As the baker came, he would great the lady of the house and put his basket on the stick.

The children would be pushed aside and the loaves would be delivered to the maid servant. Howerver, the children still found a way to peep into the basket. The author remembers the sweet fragrance of the bread and how they did not even brush their teeth before eating anything.

Importance of Bread in Traditional Ceremonies

The presence of a baker was essential during those times in Goa. Marriages or any festival were incomplete without the sweet bread known as bol. Sandwiches were prepared by the lady of the house for her daughter's engagement. Cakes and bolinhas were essential for Christmas and other festivals.

The Baker's Dress and Monthly Accounts

The baker in Goa wore a special dress known as Kabai. It was a single piece long frock that reached down to his knees. During the narrator's childhood, bakers wore shirts trousers which were shorter than full-length and longer than half pants. Even today in Goa, if anyone in the streets is seen wearing half pants, he is referred to as a pader.

The baker used to maintain his monthly accounts on a wall in pencil and collected his bills at the end of the month.

Baking : A Profitable Profession

In old days, baking was a profitable profession. A baker's family and servants were always happy and prosperous. Their plump body structure proved the fact that a baker and its family were never hungry.

Word Meanings

The given page nos. correspond to the pages in the prescribed textbook.

Word	Meaning
Page 85	
reminiscing nostalgically	thinking fondly of the past
vanished	to disappear
mixers	people who kneading the flour
moulders	people who give a particular shape to the bread
furnace	very hot enclosed chamber

Word	Meaning
extinguished	to end
thud	a dull and heavy sound
jingle	a light ringing sound
Page 86	
heralding	announcing
staff	stick
rebuke	disapproval or scolding
parapet	A low protective wall along the edge of a roof

Word	Meaning
fragrance	scent, smell
Page 87	
peculiar	particular, special
prosperous	marked success or economic well-being
plump physique	pleasantly fat body
open testimony	public statement about a character or quality

Chapter Practice

Objective Questions

• Multiple Choice Questions

1. The baker used to come ....
 (a) Once a day   (b) Twice a day
 (c) Once a week   (d) Twice a week

Ans. (*b*) The baker used to come twice a day - once in the morning with his basket full of breads and second in the evening with his empty basket.

2. From where did the 'jhang-jhang' sound come?
 (a) Basket of bread
 (b) Musical instrument used by baker
 (c) Noises of children
 (d) Specially made bamboo staff of baker

Ans. (*d*) The 'jhang-jhang' sound came from the specially made bamboo staff of baker.

3. What did the baker used to bring for children?
 (a) Loaves   (b) Bread Bangles
 (c) Sweet bread   (d) Sandwiches

Ans. (*b*) The baker used to bring bread bangles for children.

4. The author is .... when he says, "Loaves for the elders and the bangles for the children".
 (a) despairing   (b) proud
 (c) nostalgic   (d) regretful

Ans. (*b*) The author nostalgically remembers his childhood when the bakers in Goa used to come to their houses.

5. Match the following essentials required during various events as mentioned in 'A Baker from Goa'.

Events	Essentials
A. As marriage gifts	1. Sandwiches
B. For a party or feast	2. Cakes and bolinhas
C. For a daughter's engagement	3. Bol
D. For Christmas	4. Bread

Codes

	A	B	C	D			A	B	C	D
(a)	1	3	2	4		(b)	3	4	1	2
(c)	2	3	1	4		(d)	4	1	3	2

Ans. (*b*) 3412 is the correct matching sequence.

6. What do bakers used to wear during old Portuguese days?
 (a) Long shirt   (b) Long frock
 (c) Kabai   (d) Bol

Ans. (*c*) Bakers used to wear a very specific dress called kabai during old Portuguese days.

7. Who invites the comment – "he is dressed like a pader"?
 (a) Anyone who wears a half pant which reached just below the knees
 (b) Anyone who wears a long piece of frock till knees
 (c) Anyone who wears a shirt and trousers
 (d) Anyone who bakes bread

Ans. (*a*) Anyone who wears a half pant which reached just below the knees invites the comment – "he is dressed like a pader".

8. How is the traditional baker recognised?
 (a) With the thud and jingle of the bamboo
 (b) With his baking style
 (c) With his clothing style
 (d) None of the above

Ans. (*a*) The traditional baker is recognised with the thud and jingle of the bamboo.

9. Choose the option that lists the set of sentences that are not true according to the given extract.
 (i) The loaves of bread loved by the narrator are Portuguese.
 (ii) The loaves of bread are a special delicacy in Goa.
 (iii) The baker is a celebrated personality of Goa.
 (iv) Baking as a profession is dead in Goa.
 (v) The arrival of a baker is a special highlight of the day for the narrator.
 (vi) The narrator misses the loaves of Portuguese bread sellers.
 (a) 1 and 2
 (b) Only 4
 (c) Only 6
 (d) 3 and 5

Ans. (*b*) Only statement 4 – Baking as a profession is dead in Goa is false.

• Extract Based MCQs

1. Read the extract to attempt the questions that follow.

"Our elders are often heard reminiscing nostalgically about those good old Portuguese days, the Portuguese and their famous loaves of bread. Those eaters might have vanished but the makers are still there. We still have amongst us the mixers, the moulders and those who bake the loaves. Those age-old, time-tested furnaces still exist. The fire in these furnaces has not yet been extinguished. The thud and jingle of traditional baker's bamboo, heralding his arrival in the morning, can still be heard in some places."

CBSE Question Bank 2021

(i) The narrator says that the furnaces were 'time-tested' because
(a) they had been thoroughly tested each time, before being used
(b) they had proved the test of time and were working well
(c) they had been tested by modern day experts
(d) they had the power to withstand inexperienced usage

Ans. (*b*) The narrator says that the furnaces were time-tested because they had proved the test of time each time, before being used.

(ii) Those eaters might have vanished but the makers are still there.
Pick the option that expresses the tone of the narrator.

1. elated
2. morose
3. nostalgic
4. hopeful
5. sarcastic
6. critical
7. celebratory

(a) 1 and 7
(b) 2 and 6
(c) 3 and 4
(d) 4 and 5

Ans. (*c*) The author's tone is nostalgic for the Portuguese loaves of bread and at the same time is hopeful that these bread and the portuguese bakers exist in Goa.

(iii) Pick the idiom that brings out the same meaning of 'reminiscing' as used in the passage.
(a) Train of thought
(b) Commit something to memory
(c) A trip down memory lane
(d) Jog somebody's memory

Ans. (*c*) The idiom 'a trip down the memory lane' brings out the same meaning of 'reminiscing' as used in the passage.

(iv) Why do you think the baker came in with 'a thud and a jingle'?
(a) He wanted to make everyone alert and active with his presence
(b) He wanted to wake up everyone from their slumber and ask them to visit the bakery
(c) He was used to making a loud noise as most people responded to just that
(d) He wanted to make people aware that he had come around to sell his goods

Ans. (*d*) The baker came with a thud and jingle because he wanted to make people aware that he had come around to sell his breads.

(v) The 'fire in the furnaces has not yet been extinguished' implies that
(a) the furnaces are still being used to bake the loaves of bread
(b) the fire is in the process of being reviewed as a replaceable method for heating furnaces
(c) the furnaces are very strong and cannot be shifted for use in other areas
(d) the fire in the furnaces takes a long time to cease burning, once lighted

Ans. (*a*) The fire in the furnace has yet not been extinguished implies that the furnaces are still being used to bake the famous loaves of Portuguese bread.

2. Read the extract to attempt the questions that follow.

The baker made his musical entry on the scene with the 'jhang jhang' sound of his specially made bamboo staff. One hand supported the basket on his head and the other banged the bamboo on the ground. He would greet the lady of the house with 'Good Morning' and then place his basket on the vertical bamboo. We kids would be pushed aside with a mild rebuke and the loaves would be delivered to the servant. But we would not give up. We would climb a bench or the parapet and peep into the basket, somehow.

(i) How would the baker greet the lady of the house?
(a) With Good Evening
(b) With Good Morning
(c) With a Bow
(d) With a Smile

Ans. (*b*) The baker used to greet the lady of the house with Good Morning.

(ii) Choose the option that lists the set of statements that are not true according to the given extract.

1. The baker was a celebrated individual.
2. The children loved the loaves of bread.
3. The baker was very rude.
4. Only the servant would address the baker.
5. The baker entered with a musical sound.
6. The baker carried the loaves of bread in a box.

(a) 1, 2 and 4
(b) 2, 5 and 6
(c) 1, 3 and 5
(d) 3, 4 and 6

Ans. (*d*) Statements 3, 4 and 6 are not true.

(iii) What did the baker do first once he reached a house?
(a) Place the basket and deliver the loaves
(b) Place the basket on the vertical bamboo and deliver the loaves to the servant
(c) Deliver the loaves to the lady of the house
(d) None of the above

Ans. (*b*) Once the baker reached a house he put the basket on his vertical bamboo and deliver the loaves to the servant.

(iv) Why would the children not give up?

(a) Peeping into the basket

(b) Crying to peep into the basket

(c) To choose a bread bangle of their choice

(d) Pushing aside others to peep into the basket

Ans. (*c*) The children would not give up to choose the bread-bangle of their choice.

(v) Select the correct option for (1) and (2).

1. The baker used to push aside the children.

2. The bread loaves were delivered to the servant.

(a) (1) is the result of (2)

(b) (2) is the result of (1)

(c) (1) is independent of (2)

(d) (1) contradicts (2)

Ans. (*c*) Statement (1) is independent of (2).

PART 2
Subjective Questions

• Short Answer Type Questions

1. Is bread-making still popular in Goa? How do you know? **NCERT**

Ans. Yes, bread-making is still popular in Goa.

This is very clear from the narrator's statement that the Portuguese have gone away but the traditional bakers and their furnaces still exists. The mixers, moulders and the people who bake the loaves still exist in Goa.

2. What did the bakers wear **NCERT**

(i) in the Portuguese days?

(ii) when the author was young?

Ans. (i) The bakers usually wore a peculiar dress called Kabai. It was a single piece long frock reaching down to the knees.

(ii) When the author was young, he saw the bakers wearing a shirt and trousers. The trousers were shorter than full length and longer than half-pants.

3. When would the baker come everyday? Why did the children run to meet him? **NCERT**

Ans. The baker would come twice a day, once early in the morning and the second time when he returned after selling all his bread.

The children would run to meet him for those bread-bangles and sweet bread of special make, which they choose very carefully.

4. 'The tiger never brushed his teeth'. Why does the author say so?

Ans. The author said so because when the baker used to bring bangles for children, they did not even care to brush their teeth or wash their mouths properly. They did not like to take the trouble of pluching the mango leaf for the toothbrush. They did not feel it necessary to wash their mouths just take tigers who never brush their teeth before meals.

5. Why was the baker's furnace essential in a traditional Goan village? **CBSE 2010, 2020**

Ans. The baker's furnace was essential in a traditional Goan village because different kinds of breads were required for different occasions. Marriage gifts are meaningless without the sweet bread known as bol. The lady of the house must prepare sandwiches on the occasion of her daughter's engagement. Cakes and bolinhas are essential for Christmas as well as other festivals.

6. How do we know that Goa's bakers are very prosperous ? **CBSE 2019**

Ans. We know that Goa's bakers are very prosperous from their plump physique. Baking in Goa is an important profession as breads were an essential part of all festivities in Goa. As a result, the baker, his family and servants never starved. They were always happy and prosperous.

• Long Answer Type Questions

1. After reading the story 'A Baker from Goa', do you think our traditions, heritage, values and practices are the roots that nourish us? Why/why not? **CBSE 2015**

Ans. Yes, I think that our traditions, heritage, values and practices are the roots that nourish us. They shape our personality and provide us with emotional support. They make us mentally strong and enable us to face a difficult situation. They even impact our behavioural pattern towards the other people in the society. The story highlights the importance of the traditional practice of making breads at every occasion. In Goa, every occasion is incomplete without bread.

A marriage is incomplete if it does not include a sweet bread known as 'bol' All festival and feasts are incomplete without cakes and bolinhas. Even today, the elders remember those old famous breads baked by Portuguese bakers. From childhood till their old age, they remember the Portuguese bread. This shows that bread is an important part of the Goan life that continues even today. Thus, our traditional practices keep our past heritage alive and nourishes us.

2. 'During our childhood in Goa, the baker used to be our friend, companion and guide.' What does this statement tell us about the character of the baker?

Ans. The given statement tells us that the baker was a very respected person in Goan society. He would guide children about good behaviour. This happened when he mildly scolded them for peeping into his basket.

He taught children about giving respect to the elders. This was when he wished 'Good Morning' to the lady of the house. He was very informal with the children.

So the narrator considered him a friend and companion. He was not simply a vendor interested in selling what he made. Even though he scolded the children, he offered them bread bangles and sweet bread of their choice.

A party or feast lost its charm without bread. Cakes and bolinhas were a must for Christmas and other festivals. Presence of the baker's furnace in the village was absolutely essential. Thus, he was an important character in Goan society of those days.

3. Why were the children fascinated by the baker? How did they show their eagerness to see him?
CBSE 2020

Ans. The children according to the narrator, were eager to see him. They used to wake up whenever they heard the jingling sound of the bakers's bamboo stick. Whenever the baker greeted the lady of the house, children would surround the baker who would rebuke them and hand over the loaves to a servant.

Then, the children would climb over a chair to peep into the basket full of bread loaves. These children didn't even brush their teeth before taking the bread bangles that they could choose carefully. Their actions made it clear that the children were fascinated by the baker and were always eager to see him.

• Extract Based Questions

1. Read the extract to attempt the questions that follow.

We kids would be pushed aside with a mild rebuke and the loaves would be delivered to the servant. But we would not give up. We would climb a bench or the parapet and peep into the basket, somehow. I can still recall the typical fragrance of those loaves. Loaves for the elders and the bangles for the children.

(i) Who are 'we' in the extract?

(ii) Why were the children pushed aside?

(iii) Which word/phrase in the extract means the same as 'an expression of disapproval/a scolding'?

(iv) What was there in the basket?

(v) What did children do when they were pushed aside by the baker?

Ans. (i) 'We' in the extract refers to the narrator and his friends.

(ii) The children were pushed aside so that the bread can be delivered to the servant.

(iii) The word 'rebuke' from the extract means 'an expression of disapproval/a scolding'.

(iv) There were some loaves for the elders and some bangles for the children.

(v) When children were pushed aside by the baker then they climbed a bench or the parapet to peep into the baker's basket.

2. Read the extract to attempt the questions that follow.

The baker usually collected his bills at the end of the month. Monthly accounts used to be recorded on some wall in pencil. Baking was indeed a profitable profession in the old days. The baker and his family never starved. He, his family and his servants always looked happy and prosperous. Their plump physique was an open testimony to this. Even today any person with a jackfruit- like physical appearance is easily compared to a baker.
CBSE 2019

(i) Where did the baker record his accounts?

(ii) Why did the baker and his family never starve?

(iii) Which word in the extract is same in meaning of 'build'?

(iv) How can a baker be identified in Goa?

(v) "The monthly records were maintained an some walls in pencil". What does this show about the relationship between the baker and the Goan people.

Ans. (i) The baker recorded his accounts on some wall with pencil.

(ii) The baker and his family never starved because baking was a profitable profession.

(iii) 'Physique' from the extract is same in meaning of 'build'.

(iv) Any person with a jackfruit-like physical appearance or plump physique is easily identified to a baker.

(v) The baker and the Goan people shared a relationship based on trust and friendship as the baker did not require to remember the records of his sale.

II. Coorg

by Lokesh Abrol

This part of the chapter is a pen-portrait of Coorg. Coorg is a coffee growing area famous for its rain forests and spices.

Chapter Summary

A Heaven called Coorg

Coorg or Kodagu is the smallest district of Karnataka that lies between Mysore and the coastal town of Mangalore. It is a land of rolling stones that is inhabited by martial men, beautiful women and innumerable wild creatures.

Weather and Environment of Coorg

Coorg consists of evergreen forests which covers 30% of the district along with coffee and spice plantations.

The best time to visit Coorg starts in September and continues till March. During this time, the weather is pleasant with some amount of rainfall and the smell of coffee all around. With coffee estates and colonial bungalows hidden in corners the landscape seems like heaven on Earth.

The Origin of People of Coorg

The people of Coorg are possibly descendents of Greeks or Arabs. It is believed that Alexander's army moved South along the coast and settled there, when they were unable to return to their country. These people married among the locals and their culture can be seen in their martial traditions, marriages and religious rites.

The theory of the Arab descent can be proved by their traditional clothes. The Kodavus (residents of Coorg) wear a long black coat with an embroidered waist belt known as Kuppia. It resembles Kuffia worn by the Arabs and the Kurds.

Hospitality and Bravery Tales of Kodavus

Kodavus are known for their hospitality. Also, there are many tales of bravery related to the people of Coorg. The Coorg Regiment is one of the most decorated regiments of the Indian Army.

The first Chief of the Indian-Army, General Cariappa was a Coorgi. Even today Kodavus are the only people in India permitted to Carry Firearms without a licence.

River Kaveri and Wildlife in Coorg

The river Kaveri originates in the hills of Coorg. In the waters of the river, a large freshwater fish, Mahaseer can be found in abundance.

The land of Coorg is a home to a number of birds and animals including kingfishers, squirrels, langurs, elephants, slender loris, macaques, bees, butterflies, etc.

Tourism in Coorg

Coorg offers many adventurous activities such as river rafting, canoeing, rappelling, rock climbing, mountain biking and trekking. One can have a panoramic view of the entire Coorg by climbing the Brahmagiri hills. Other interesting places are the Nisargadhama and the largest Tibetan settlement of Buddhist monks at Bylakuppe.

Word Meanings

The given page nos. correspond to the pages in the prescribed textbook.

Word	Meaning
PAGE 90	
drifted	seperated
martial	having to do with war
commences	begins
invigorating	make one feel strong, healthy and full of energy
tucked	hidden
canopies	roof like coverings that form shelters
prime	the best
fiercely	powerfully
descent	origin
mainstream	a tradition which most people follow

Word	Meaning
PAGE 91	
hospitality	generous and friendly treatment of visitors and guests
tales of valour	stories of courage and bravery, usually in war
most decorated	having received maximum number of awards for bravery in war
permitted	allowed
abound	exist in large numbers
scrubbed	to rub for purpose of clean
mahouts	the keepers of elephants
laidback	relaxed

Word	Meaning
rafting	travelling in a river in a raft
canoeing	travelling in a river in a canoe
rappelling	going down a cliff by sliding down a rope
PAGE 92	
trails	paths created by walking
panoramic view	a view of a wide area of land
misty	filled with fog
ochre	a moderate yellow-orange to orange colour

PART 1
Objective Questions

• Multiple Choice Questions

1. According the lesson, Coorg is almost equidistant from ....
(a) Mangalore and Mysore   (b) Karnataka and Mangalore
(c) Bengaluru and Mysore   (d) Chennai and Karnataka

Ans. (*a*) According the lesson, Coorg is almost equidistant from Mangalore and Mysore.

2. The season of joy commences from September and continues till March. The given line suggests that
(a) September to March is the best time to visit Coorg
(b) September to March are the months of rainfall
(c) Coorg becomes even more beautiful between September and March
(d) Both (a) and (c)

Ans. (*d*) The given line suggests that September to March is the best time to visit Coorg and it becomes even more beautiful between September and March.

3. What was the embroidered waist-belt worn by Kodavus known as?
(a) Kuffia   (b) Kuppia
(c) Kurd   (d) Waist-belt

Ans. (*b*) Kuppia was the embroidered waist-belt worn by Kodavus.

4. The first chief of the Indian Army is from ....
(a) Coorg   (b) Goa   (c) Mysore   (d) Punjab

Ans. (*a*) The first chief of the Indian Army is from Coorg.

5. Who are the only people in India permitted to carry firearms without a license?
(a) Kodavus   (b) Kurds   (c) Arabs   (d) Greeks

Ans. (*a*) Kodavus are the only people in India permitted to carry firearms without a license.

6. The climb to the .... hills brings one into a panoramic view of the entire misty landscape of Coorg.
(a) Brahmagiri   (b) Himalayan
(c) Nilgiri   (d) Parvati

Ans. (*a*) The climb to the Brahmagiri hills brings one into a panoramic view of the entire misty landscape of Coorg.

7. Which of the following destinations are mentioned in the lesson 'Coorg'?
1. Mangalore   2. Mysore
3. Karnataka   4. Nisargadhama
5. Bylakuppe   6. Brahmagiri hills
(a) 1, 3, 4 and 6   (b) 2, 3, 4 and 5
(c) 1, 2 3 and 5   (d) All of these

Ans. (*d*) The following destinations are mentioned in the lesson 'Coorg'
• Mangalore   • Mysore
• Karnataka   • Nisargadhama
• Bylakuppe   • Brahmagiri hills

8. Which nationalities or ethnic groups have been mentioned in the chapter 'Coorg'?
1. Arabs   2. Kurds
3. Greeks   4. Coorgis
(a) Only 1   (b) 2 and 4
(c) 2 and 3   (d) All of these

Ans. (*d*) The nationalities or ethnic groups mentioned in the chapter 'Coorg' are: Arabs, Kurds, Greeks and Coorgis.

• Extract Based MCQs

1. Read the extract to attempt the questions that follow.
Midway between Mysore and the coastal town of Mangalore sites a piece of heaven that must have drifted from the Kingdom of God. This land of rolling hills is inhabited by a proud race of martial men, beautiful women and wild creatures. Coorg or Kodagu, the smallest district of Karnataka, is home to evergreen rain forests, spices and coffee plantations. Evergreen rain forests cover thirty per cent of this district. During the monsoons, it pours enough to keep many visitors away. The season of joy commences from September and continues till March. The weather is perfect, with some showers thrown in for good measure. The air breathes of invigorating coffee. Coffee estates and colonial bungalows stand tucked under tree canopies in prime corners.

(i) The weather is perfect, with some showers thrown in for good measure. The given line suggests that
(a) showers make the perfect weather more perfect
(b) showers are good for Coorg's weather
(c) showers help in making Coorg's weather pleasant
(d) None of the above

Ans. (*a*) The given line suggests that light showers make the perfect weather more perfect.

(ii) Select the suitable word from the extract to complete the following.
Pagaents : Beauty : Army : ....
(a) Martial   (b) Estates   (c) Colonial   (d) Prime

Ans. (*a*)

(iii) The author says that from September to March, some showers thrown in for a good measure.
This indicates that
1. The weather is pleasant
2. Rainfall adds to the beauty
3. Expect some rainfall during that time

4. Rainfall is scarce
5. One can visit during the time
(a) (1) and (5)　　　　　(b) (1), (2), 3 and (5)
(c) (2) and (3)　　　　　(d) (2), (4) and (5)

Ans. (*b*) The phrase as used by the author indicates that the rainfall is scarce from September to March which makes the weather pleasant and the scenes more beautiful. So, one should visit during this time.

(iv) Coorg or Kodagu, the smallest district of Karnataka, is home to ....
(a) evergreen rain forests and spices
(b) evergreen rain forests, spices and coffee plantations
(c) spices and coffee plantations
(d) evergreen rain forests and coffee plantations

Ans. (B) Coorg or Kodagu, the smallest district in Karnataka, is home to evergreen rainforests, spices and coffee plantations.

(v) The air breather of invigorating coffee means that
(a) there is coffee everywhere in Coorg
(b) there are many coffee plantations in Coorg
(c) the air smells of strong coffee
(d) All of the above

Ans. (*c*) The air in Coorg breathes of invigorating coffee means that the air smells of strong coffee.

2. Read the extract to attempt the questions that follow.

These people married amongst the locals and their culture is apparent in the martial traditions, marriage and religious rites, which are distinct from the Hindu mainstream. The theory of Arab Origin draws support from the long, black coat with an embroidered waist-belt worn by the Kodavus, known as Kuppia, it resembles the Kuffia worn by the Arabs and the Kurds.

(i) Which things show that Kodavus culture is distinct from Hindu mainstream in the above extract?
(a) Martial traditions　　　(b) Marriage
(c) Religious rites　　　　(d) All of these

Ans. (*d*) Martial tradition, marriage and religious rites show that Kodavus' culture is distinct from Hindu mainstream.

(ii) What is so similar between Kodavus and Arabs?
(a) A traditional dress with embroidery
(b) A modern dress with stonework
(c) A long black coat with an embroidered waist-belt resembling the Kuffia
(d) A short coat with a simple waist-belt resembling the Kuffia

Ans. (*c*) A long black coat with an embroidered waist-belt called Kuppia is the similarity between Kodavus and Arabs.

(iii) From the given options, identify the author's tone in the extract.
(a) Informative　　　　　(b) Nostalgic
(c) Reminiscent　　　　　(d) Joyful

Ans. (*a*) The author given us the information about Coorg in a matter of fact tone.

(iv) 'These people' in the above extract refers to
(a) Greeks　　　　　　　(b) Alexander's army men
(c) Arabs　　　　　　　(d) Kodavus

Ans. (*b*) 'These people' in the given extract refers to Alexander's army men.

(v) .... means 'related to war'.
(a) Mainstream　　　　　(b) Apparent
(c) Martial　　　　　　(d) Kurds

Ans. (*c*) Martial means related to war.

PART 2
Subjective Questions

• Short Answer Type Questions

1. Why is Coorg called the land of rolling hills?
CBSE 2020

Ans. Coorg is called the land of rolling hills because it is situated on the gentle sloping hills that are covered with lush green rainforests. The hills on which it is located seem to be rolling down to a beautiful panoramic view which make it look like a piece of heaven on Earth.

2. Describe Coorg's weather. When is it most pleasant for the tourists to visit Coorg?　　**CBSE 2012**

Ans. Coorg receives heavy rainfall during the monsoon which we can say extends from April and ends in August. The weather of Coorg is pleasant for the tourists during the months from September to March. At this time, the smell of coffee is spread all around.

3. Coorgis belong to a valorous and hospitable race. Comment on this statement with reference to the text.　　**CBSE Question Bank 2021**

Ans. Coorgis are said to belong to a valorous and hospitable race as their homes have tradition of hospitality. There are innumerable tales of courage related to the people belonging to Coorg. In fact, the Coorg Regiment is one of the most decorated in the Indian Army, and the first Chief of the Indian Army, General Cariappa, was a Coorgi. Even now, Kodavus are the only people in India permitted to carry firearms without a licence.

4. How is the Coorgi tradition of courage and bravery recognised in modern India?　　**CBSE 2019**

Ans. The Coorgi tradition of courage and bravery has been recognised in India by awarding the Coorg Regiment with the most number of gallantry awards. Besides, the Coorgis are the only Indians allowed to carry guns without a licence. The first Chief of the Indian Army, General Cariappa, was also a Coorgi.

5. Do adventure sports like river rafting and rock climbing require a person to possess just physical strength? Why/Why not? **CBSE Question Bank 2021**

Ans. No, adventure sports like river rafting and rock climbing does not require a person to possess just physical strength. It also requires alertness and mental toughness. As these sports are done in natural surroundings, one must be alert and cautious while performing them. A person needs to have excellent judgement and should have a quick response system to perform them effectively and safely.

6. Why does the author in 'Coorg' say that the visitors' search for the heart and soul of India would be found in Coorg? **CBSE Question Bank 2021**

Ans. The author in 'Coorg' says that the visitors' searching for the heart and soul of India would find it in Coorg because of its natural grandeur and different appearance of nature. Not only is the land of Coorg full of different species of flora and fauna but it also is a home to martial men and attractive women.

• Long Answer Type Questions

1. The Coorgis are the descendants of the Greeks or the Arabs and are still able to maintain their traditional practices. Do you agree that following these practices today is important? Why or why not?

Ans. After reading the text, I feel that it is important to follow the traditional practices. The reason is that it has kept the tradition of Coorgis known to the people even today. If the people of Coorg had not followed it, their tradition would have perished. Nobody, would have remembered them today without their culture and traditional practices.

According to the text, their traditions can be seen in the martial forms, religious rites and marriages. The Kodavus even wear the dress which resembles the dress of Arabs.

Traditional practices also play a very important role in maintaining values amongst people. They have an impact on shaping the behaviour of people. These practices bind us together in our social life. Just like the Kodavus who are bound to their ancestors even today, we are also bound to our ancestors because of the traditional values we have inherited from them.

2. How do Coorg's location, people and natural features add to the diversity of India? **CBSE 2016**

Ans. Coorg, the smallest district of Karnataka is among the most beautiful regions of India. It's location, people and natural features add to the diversity of India. Coorg is called a piece of heaven that must have drifted from the kingdom of God. It has beautiful rolling hillsides that is filled with evergreen rainforests, spice and coffee plantations. It also includes a river, Kaveri along with

many species of birds, insects, and animals. Nature here exists in its original glory.

Further, Coorg's culture is distinct from the Hindu traditions. Its martial traditions, rituals and rites show a mixture of Arabic and Greek culture owing to Greek and Arabic descendance. In addition, the land is a home to many courageous men as well as religious Buddhist monks. Also there are many other tourist destinations that add to its glory. All these features of Coorg together add to the diversity of the country.

• Extract Based Questions

1. Read the extract to attempt the questions that follow.

The river, Kaveri, obtains its water from the hills and forests of Coorg. Mahaseer — a large freshwater fish — abound in these waters. Kingfishers dive for their catch, while squirrels and langurs drop partially eaten fruit for the mischief of enjoying the splash and the ripple effect in the clear water. Elephants enjoy being bathed and scrubbed in the river by their mahouts.

(i) Which river flows from the hills of Coorg?

(ii) Why do the squirrels drop partially eaten fruit in the river?

(iii) Find the word in the extract which means same as 'wave'.

(iv) What do elephants enjoy by their mathouts?

(v) Which fish is found in abundance in Kaveri waters?

Ans. (i) The river Kaveri flows from the hills of Coorg.

(ii) The squirrels drop partially eaten fruit in the river because they enjoy the splash and ripple effect created by the fruit hitting the water.

(iii) Ripple from the extract means 'wave'.

(iv) Elephants enjoy being bathed and scrubbed by their mahouts.

(v) Mahaseer - a large freshwater fish is found in abundance in Kaveri waters.

2. Read the extract to attempt the questions that follow.

The most laidback individuals become converts to the life of high-energy adventure with river rafting, canoeing, rappelling, rock-climbing and mountain-biking. Numerous walking trails in this region are a favourite with trekkers. Birds, bees and butterflies are there to give you company. Macaques. Malabar squirrels, langurs and slender loris keep a watchful eye from the tree canopy. I do, however, prefer to step aside for wild elephants.

(i) How does Coorg change the most-laidback individuals?

(ii) Which high-energy adventure sports can be done in Coorg?

   (iii) Which animals can be found in Coorg?

   (iv) Which word in the extract is opposite to 'relaxed'?

   (v) What are favourites with trekkers?

Ans. (i) The most-laidback individuals get changed into high-energy adventurists when they visit Coorg.

   (ii) River rafting, canoeing, rappelling, rock-climbing and mountain-biking can be done in Coorg.

   (iii) Macaques, Malabar squirrels, langurs and slender laris can be found in Coorg.

   (iv) 'High-energy' is opposite to 'relaxed'.

   (v) Numerous walking trails in Coorg are a favourite with trekkers.

III. Tea from Assam

by Arup Kumar Datta

This part of the chapter is about tea plantations in Assam.

Chapter Summary

Pranjol and Rajvir Visit to Assam

Pranjol and Rajvir were classmates studying in the same school in Delhi. Pranjol belonged to Assam where his father was the Manager of a tea garden.

He had invited Rajvir to visit his home during the summer vacation. So, both of them were travelling to Assam by train. When the train had stopped on the way at a station, they bought tea from a vendor and started sipping it.

Popularity of Tea and Tea Gardens

While sipping tea, Rajvir told Pranjol that over 80 crore cups of tea drunk everyday around the world. It is, thus, a very popular drink.

As the train started moving, Rajvir looked out of the window. He was amazed to see the beautiful scenery of grenery outside. The soft rice fields gave way to tea bushes. Rajvir was fascinated by the vast stretch of the tea bushes.

On the other hand, Pranjol was reading his detective book. Pranjol was born and bought up in a tea plantation and thus was not as excited. However, he told Rajvir that Assam has the largest concentration of tea plantations in the world.

Rajvir's Knowledge of Tea

Rajvir told Pranjol that there are many legends or stories about the discovery of tea. According to a legend, a Chinese emperor discovered tea when he was boiling water for drinking.

When the water was put to boil, a few leaves of the twigs (stems) burning under the pot fell into the water. Thus, the boiled water got a delicious taste. It is believed that they were tea leaves.

Rajvir further told Pranjol that Tea was first drunk in China in 2700 BC and the words like 'tea', 'chai' and 'chini' are also Chinese. He also mentioned that tea first came to Europe in the sixteenth century and it was drunk more as medicine than as a beverage.

Rajvir also told Pranjol about another legend from India which said that Bodhidharma, an ancient Buddhist monk, cut off his eyelids because he felt sleepy during meditations. Ten tea plantations grew out of his eyelids. It is believed that the leaves of these plants, when put in hot water and drunk, banished sleep.

At the Dhekiabari Tea Plantation

Rajvir and Pranjol reached the Mariani Junction where Pranjol's parents received them. In car, they went to Dhekiabari, the tea estate managed by Pranjol's father.

On both the sides of the road, there were huge acres of tea bushes. Groups of tea-pluckers with bamboo baskets on their backs and wearing plastic aprons were plucking the newly sprouted leaves. Looking at the tea-pluckers, Rajvir told Pranjol's father that it was the second flush or sprouting season. He also told him that this season lasts from May to July and yields the best tea. Rajvir's knowledge surprises Pranjol's father to which Rajvir tells him that he expects to learn more there.

Word Meanings

The given page nos. correspond to the pages in the prescribed textbook.

Word	Meaning
PAGE 94	
steaming	very hot
buried his nose in	started reading
ardent	keen
backdrop	scenery at the back
densely	thickly

Word	Meaning
dwarfing	making something appear small
sturdy	strongly and solidly built
PAGE 95	
billowing	a moving cloud or mass of smoke

Word	Meaning
legends	a story from the past that is believed by many people but cannot be proved to be true
ascetic	a person with incredible self discipline
bamshed	get rid of

PART 1
Objective Questions

• Multiple Choice Questions

1. Who is the author of 'Tea from Assam'?
(a) Arup Kumar Datt   (b) Lokesh Abrol
(c) Lucio Rodrigues   (d) None of these

Ans. (*a*) Arup Kumar Datta is the author of 'Tea from Assam'.

2. Rajvir and Pranjol were going to Assam from ....
(a) Mumbai   (b) Delhi
(c) Pune   (d) Ahemadabad

Ans. (*b*) Rajvir and Pranjol were going to Assam from Delhi.

3. When Pranjol says, "You will see enough gardens to last you a lifetime!" he means that
(a) Rajvir would see many tea gardens in Assam that he would become bore at a point of time
(b) Assam has many tea gardens that Rajvir wouldn't be able to see all of them during his lifetime
(c) Rajvir would see enough tea gardens in Assam
(d) Rajvir would see many tea gardens in Assam that he could experience their essence throughout his life

Ans. (*d*) When Pranjol says, "You will see enough gardens to last you a lifetime!" He means that Rajvir would see many tea gardens in Assam that he could experience their essence throughout his life.

4. In Europe, tea was drunk as more of a .... than ....
(a) medicine, beverage   (b) beverage, medicine
(c) sleep waver, medicine   (d) sleep banisher, medicine

Ans. (*a*) In Europe, tea was drunk as more of a medicine than beverage.

5. The words like 'chai' and 'chini' are derived from ....
(a) Indi   (b) China
(c) France   (d) None of these

Ans. (*b*) The words like 'chai' and 'chini' are derived from China.

6. Pranjol's and Rajvir's train stooped at
(a) Dhekiabari Junction
(b) Dibrugarh Station
(c) Mariani Junction
(d) None of these

Ans. (*c*) Pranjol's and Rajvir's train stooped at Mariani Junction.

7. You seem to have done your homework before coming," Pranjol's father said in surprise. Which homework is he talking about?
(a) Holiday homework   (b) Tuition homework
(c) Knowledge about Assam   (d) All of the above

Ans. (*c*) Pranjol's father was talking about Rajvir's knowledge about Assam.

8. The second sprouting of tea lasts from
(a) May to July   (b) May to June
(c) June to July   (d) July to August

Ans. (*a*) The second sprouting of tea lasts from May to July.

• Extract Based MCQs

1. Read the extract to attempt the questions that follow.

"CHAI-GARAM... garam-chai," a vendor called out in a high-pitched voice.

He came up to their window and asked,"Chai, sa'ab?"

"Give us two cups," Pranjol said.

They sipped the steaming hot liquid. Almost everyone in their compartment was drinking tea too.

"Do you know that over eighty crore cups of tea are drunk every day throughout the world?" Rajvir said.

"Whew!" exclaimed Pranjol. "Tea really is very popular."

(i) Where were Rajvir and Pranjol going to?
(a) Meghalaya   (b) Assam
(c) Sikkim   (d) Manipur

Ans. (*b*) Rajvir and Pranjol were going to Assam.

(ii) How many cups of tea are drunk everyday throughout the world?
(a) Over eighty crore   (b) Over eighty
(c) Over seventy crore   (d) About eighty crore

Ans. (*a*) Over eighty crore cups of tea are drunk everyday throughout the world.

(iii) Choose from the following options, how did Pranjol feel when he said, "Whew! Tea really is very popular."
(a) Relived   (b) Shocked
(c) Surprised   (d) Angry

Ans. (*c*) Pranjol felt surprised when he said, "Whew! Tea really is very popular."

(iv) Which word in the passage means the same as 'chinked'?
(a) Steaming   (b) Sipped   (c) Liquid   (d) Drink

Ans. (*b*) Sipped means the same as 'chinked'.

(v) Pick out the option that classifies the statements as Facts (F) and Opinions (O) as said by students.
1. I think tea is very popular all over the world.
2. I feel that everyone should drink tea.
3. I think Rajvir was very excited for seeing tea gardens.
4. I think Rajvir and Pranjol were classmates.
(a) F-2, 3 and O-1, 4   (b) F-1, 2, 4 and O-3
(c) F-3, 4 and O-1, 2   (d) All are facts

Ans. (*c*) F-3, 4 and O-1, 2

2. Read the extracts and answer the questions that follow.

"Tell me another!" scoffed Pranjol.

"We have an Indian legend too. Bodhidharma, an ancient Buddhist ascetic, cut off his eyelids because he felt sleepy during meditations. Ten tea plants grew out of the eyelids. The leaves of these plants when put in hot water and drunk, banished sleep."

"Tea was first drunk in China," Rajvir added, "as far back as 2700 B.C.! In fact, words such as tea, chai and chini are from the Chinese. Tea came to Europe only in the sixteenth century and was drunk more as medicine than as beverage."

CBSE Question Bank 2021

(i) What is the main idea of this extract?
   (a) Tea as a popular beverage in Europe and how it spread
   (b) Origin of tea in India and why it became popular in Europe
   (c) Importance of India in popularising tea and influencing Europe
   (d) Indian legend on tea and how it travelled from China to Europe

Ans. (*d*) The main idea of the extract is Indian legend on tea and how it travelled from China to Europe.

(ii) Why do you think Pranjol 'scoffed'?
   (a) He was upset with the legend Rajvir shared
   (b) He was mocking Rajvir for his lack of knowledge
   (c) He was mocking and tickled at what Rajvir shared
   (d) He was impressed with what Rajvir had shared

Ans. (*c*) Pranjol scoffed because he was amused and tickled at what Rajvir shared about tea.

(iii) Pick the option that includes the tea label information that corresponds to the given sentence.

"The leaves of these plants when put in hot water and drunk, banished sleep."

(1) Its calming effects may be attributed to an antioxidant called apigenin, which is found in abundance in chamomile tea. Apigenin binds to specific receptors in your brain that may decrease anxiety and initiate sleep.	(2) It increases levels of a neurotransmitter called Gamma-Aminobutyric Acid (GABA) and improves overall sleep quality by shortening the time it takes to fall asleep and decreasing night-time awakenings.
(3) It interferes with REM sleep, has some unwanted side effects, keeps sleep away and allows the possibility of inducing hours of sleeplessness and increased night-time awakenings.	(4) It alleviates anxious thoughts and soothes the spirit before bedtime. It improves energy levels and helps banish stress and results in a better nights sleep, naturally.

   (a) Option (1)   (b) Option (2)
   (c) Option (3)   (d) Option (4)

Ans. (*c*) The given lines focus on how tea banished sleep which is also the central concern of options (3).

(iv) Based on the inference from the extract, which of these is not true about tea drinking in the sixteenth century Europe? Dr. Smith is a doctor of sixteenth century Europe.
   (a) Dr. Smith encouraged drinking of green tea whenever available, to reduce chances of tooth loss.
   (b) Dr. Smith prescribed regular tea drinking to all his patients with a weak heart.
   (c) Dr. Smith always served tea as refreshment when he has guests, as they all enjoyed this beverage.
   (d) Dr. Smith usually recommended black tea to reduce inflammation in the body.

Ans. (*c*) It is stated in the passage that tea was drunk as a medicine in Europe and not as a beverage. Hence, option (c) is correct.

(v) Based on this extract, how do you think Rajvir felt while narrating?
   (a) (i) excited (ii) agitated
   (b) (i) hysterical (ii) nervous
   (c) (i) nervous (ii) agitated
   (d) (i) enthusiastic (ii) passionate

Ans. (*d*) Rajvir was feeling enthusiastic and passionate while narrating legends about tea to Pranjol.

PART 2
Subjective Questions

• Short Answer Type Questions

1. Where were Rajvir and Pranjol going and why?

Ans. Rajvir and Pranjol were going to Assam. Pranjol had invited Rajvir to spend the summer vacation there. Pranjol's father was the manager of a tea garden in Assam. So, he wanted Rajvir to visit the tea gardens and know about how tea is grown.

2. Rajvir was very fond of reading detetive stories. Why did he not like read then during his journey?

CBSE 2020

Ans. Rajvir did not like to read detective stories during his journey because at that moments he was keep on looking at the beautiful scenery. It was green everywhere-soft paddy fields and then come tea bushes. It was a magnificent view for Rajvir to see greenery as far as his eyes could see.

3. Pranjol buried his head in his detective book while Rajvir was eager to look at the beautiful scenery during the train journey. Why was there a difference in their attitude?

CBSE Question Bank 2021

Ans. Pranjol buried his head in his detective book because he belonged to Assam and had travelled on the route and seen the green tea plantations many times. So he was not eager to see the scene outside. Whereas Rajvir was travelling to Assam for the first time. So, rather than reading a book, he was interested in looking at the beautiful scenery during the train journey.

4. What did Rajvir see while looking outside from the train?

Ans. While looking outside from the window of the train, Rajvir saw greenary all around. First he saw the green paddy (rice) fields which gave way to the tea bushes. Against the backdrop of densely wooded hills, he saw a sea of tea gardens that were pruned to the same height. The beautiful view amazed and fascinated him.

5. Why did Pranjol not share Rajvir's excitement on seeing the tree plantation?   **CBSE 2013, 2019**

Ans. Pranjol did not share Rajvir's excitement on seeing the tree plantation because Pranjol had been born and brought up on a tea plantation. He was familiar with the tea gardens. On the other hand, Rajvir had never visited any tea plantation ever before. So, the vast expanse of green tea bushes fascinated him.

The magnificent view, orderly rows of tea bushes amazed Rajvir while Pranjol was used to such sights.

6. 'This is a tea country now'. Explain this with reference to Assam.   **CBSE 2013**

Ans. Assam is known as 'tea country'. It has the world's largest concentration of tea plantations in the world. A large number of tea gardens can be found there. Everywhere in Assam, a sea of tea bushes can be seen as far as the eye could see. Most of the tea grown in Assam is supplied all over the world.

7. In what ways is China related to tea?

Ans. China is related to tea in many ways. According to a legend, tea was first discovered in China by a Chinese Emperor who always boiled water before drinking .

One day, a few leaves of the tea twigs fell into the water and gave it a delicious flavour. It is believed that they were tea leaves. Further, the words 'tea', 'chai' and 'chini' are from China.

8. Why did Pranjol's father say that Rajvir had done his homework before visiting Assam?

Ans. Pranjol's father said the Rajvir had done his homework before visiting Assam because he told Pranjol's father many facts about the growing of tea and its popularity.

9. Rajvir did his study before his visit to the tea plantation. Is it good to do one's research before the start of a new venture or does it take away from the thrill of discovery? Elucidate your stance.
    CBSE Question Bank 2021

Ans. The fact that Rajvir did his study before his visit to the tea plantation and his knowledge about the land he was visiting shows that it is good to do research before starting a new venture.

By doing so, not only does one gets an idea about the destination but one can also plan the journey accordingly. One can also identify places or activities of ones interest. It does not take one away from the thrill of discovery, instead it helps in planning a better holiday.

• Long Answer Type Questions

1. According to the text, Assam is said to be 'tea country'. Do you believe that Assam has some of the best tea plantations in the world that makes it a unique place?

Ans. Yes, I believe that Assam has some of the best tea plantations in the world that makes it a unique place. In India, some crops such as tea and coffee are grown in huge quantities. India is also home to many spices like haldi. While Assam is home to tea, Coorg is home to coffee.

One can see enough tea gardens in Assam. Between May and July, it is the best time to yield the best tea. On both sides of the roads of Assam, there are acre of tea-bushes, all neatly trimmed to the same height.

These plantations further use the traditional agriculture practices of India. Thus, these plantations make India a unique country which has traditional spices and beverage plants growing within it.

2. Inspired by the diversity in the chapter, 'Glimpses of India', you wrote an article for your school magazine on the topic, 'Diversity-the Uniqueness of India'. Write a paragraph, sharing two key opinions from the article.

Ans.   'Diversity-the Uniqueness of India'
                            XYZ

India is a land of different cultures and traditions. No doubt, it's called the land of Unity in Diversity. Each and every culture in this land has its own uniqueness. The geographical and cultural dissimilarities of each region makes every place distinct from the other. While on one hand, we have the beauty and bravery of Coorg which exemplifies martial bravery, beautiful women and magnificent landscapes full of flora and fauna.

On the other, Assam's geographical features make it appropriate for tea production. In the similar way stands the cultural heritage of Portuguese in Goa. Every region is identified by its own lifestyle which makes its diversity full of unique combinations.

3. The culture, lifestyle and traditions of a place are influenced by the people who lived or settled there at some point of time. Cultural assimilation adds flavour to the existing structure of a society. Summarise your opinion on the given idea.

Ans. The culture, lifestyle and traditions of a place are influenced by the people who lived or settled there at some point of time. Cultural assimilation or the amalgamation of another culture adds flavour to the existing structure of a society. This is especially true for the land of India. Starting from Goa to Coorg or Assam, this cultural assimilation is visible everywhere. The Portuguese culture and its Baker has become an essential part of the Goan landscape.

The people of Coorg are of Greek or Arabic descent which brings its mark in the martial traditions, clothing, marriage and religious rites, which are distinct from the Hindu mainstream. Even the Assam Tea landscape derive its bounty due to the development of Tea in China.

• Extract Based Questions

1. Read the extract to attempt the questions that follow.

We have an Indian legend too. Bodhidharma, an ancient Buddhist ascetic, cut off his eyelids because he felt sleepy during meditations. Ten tea plants grew out of the eyelids. The leaves of these plants when put in hot water and drunk banished sleep. "Tea was first drunk in China," Rajvir added, "as far back as 2700 BC! In fact words such as tea, 'chai' and 'chini' are from Chinese. Tea came to Europe only in the 16th century and was drunk more as medicine than as beverage.

  (i) Why is the story called a legend?

  (ii) What does the given lines show is about Rajvir?

  (iii) Find the word in the extract which means the' get rid of'.

  (iv) When and where was tea first drunk?

  (v) Why did Bodhidharma cut off his eyelids?

Ans. (i) The story of discovery of tea by Bodhidharma is called a legend because there is no way through which the authenticity of the story could be proved.

  (ii) The given lines show in that Rajvir was deeply interested in tea. He had read a lot about it and wanted to explore more about it.

  (iii) 'Banish' from the extract means 'get rid of'.

  (iv) Tea was first drunk in China as far back as 2700 BC.

  (v) Bodhidharma cut off his eyelids because he felt sleepy during meditations.

2. Read the extract to attempt the questions that follow.

Pranjol's father slowed down to allow a tractor, pulling a trailer-load of tea leaves, to pass. This is the second-flush or sprouting period, isn't it, Mr. Barua? Rajvir asked, "It lasts from May to July and yields the best tea." "You seem to have done your homework before coming", Pranjols father said in surprise, "Yes, Mr. Barua", Rajvir admitted. "But I hope to learn much more while I'm here."

  (i) Why did Mr. Barua feel surprised?

  (ii) How did Rajvir want to spend his stay there?

  (iii) Which word in the extract means agreed?

  (iv) What is the sprouting period of tea?

  (v) Who was Mr. Barua?

Ans. (i) Mr. Barua was surprised to know that Rajvir already knew a lot about the tea gardens of Assam.

  (ii) Rajvir wanted to spend his time discovering the beauty of Assam. He wanted to learn more about the tea plantations of Assam.

  (iii) 'Admitted' from the extract means 'agreed'.

  (iv) The sprouting period or the second-flush of tea lasts from May to July.

  (v) Mr. Barua was Pranjol's father and the manager of a tea-garden in Uper Assam.

Madam Rides the Bus

by Vallikkannan

In this Chapter...

- Chapter Summary
- Word Meaning
- Chapter Practice

Chapter Summary

Valli and Her Desire to Ride the Bus

Valliammai was an eight year old girl who was fondly called Valli. She was a curious girl and her time pass involved standing at the front door of her house, watching the happenings on the street. She had no playmates of her own age so, she just enjoyed looking out. For her, it was just as fun and enjoyable as the games that children played.

Valli was most fascinated by the bus that travelled from her village to the nearest town. The sight of the bus with new passengers every hour filled Valli with joy and soon she started to desire a bus ride. The desire to ride the bus turned into a longing as Valli saw the bus passing through her street everyday.

Valli's Planning to Ride the Bus

For many days and months, Valli used to listen carefully the conversations between her neighbours and the regular travelers of bus. Some times she would ask them questions to collect information about the bus and its journey.

In this manner she gathered various small details about the bus journey such as distance between her village and town, fare of the bus, i.e. thirty paise for one side. She got to know that the bus took 45 minutes to reach the town. She calculated the timings of her journey, planned and replanned her trip. She carefully saved her coins for months resisting her temptations to buy toys, toffees and riding merry-go round in the village fair. At last, she collected sixty paise for the bus. Then she planned to go for the ride after lunch time when her mother took a nap for about three to four hours.

Valli's First Bus Journey

One day, as the bus was about to leave the village stop Valli stopped the bus and got on it.

Valli acted like an adult lady while boarding the bus. The conductor, who was jolly natured man was amused by Valli's behaviour and started referring to her as 'Madam'. He showed her, seat and as soon as Valli sat down the bus started moving.

There were only six or seven passengers in the bus. It was a new bus with soft and luxurious seats and nice paint. Valli stood up on her seat to enjoy the views outside the window.

Views Outside the Bus

The bus passed along the banks of a canal. On one side of the narrow road there were palm trees, grasslands, distant mountains and blue sky. On the other side of the bus, there was a deep ditch and beyond it were acres of green fields. While she was enjoying the greenery, she heard an old man asking her to sit down on her seat.

Valli felt annoyed at the old man for thinking of her to be child. She told him that she had paid full fare like others and then asked the conductor to give her the ticket. The conductor and the passengers were amused at an 8 year old child acting like an adult. They laughed at her actions while the conductor handed her the ticket. He also explained her that she needed to sit down or she would get hurt.

The Journey Continues

Soon the bus stopped at a bus stop and some new passengers got inside. Valli took her seat in fear of losing it. An elderly woman sat beside her and asked Valli about her travelling alone in the bus. Valli found that lady ugly and unpleasant. Valli got irritated with her questions and started to look out of the window.

The bus was moving smoothly, leaving all the obstacles behind. Suddenly, Valli saw a young cow running in the middle of the road, in front of the bus. The driver slowed down the bus and blew horn but the cow got scared and ran even faster. Valli found it very amusing and laughed heartily. Finally, the cow moved off the road.

The Halt at The Town

The bus then passed through the railway crossing and the train station. Then, it reached the nearest town to Valli's village. All the passengers got off the bus except Valli. The conductor asked her to got down and explore the street and nearby sights, but Valli refused and informed him that she would be going back to the village in the same bus. The conductor also offered her cold drink but she refused it.

Valli's Return Journey

The bus started going towards the village and Valli saw the same beautiful sights again with same excitement. Then her sight fell upon the dead cow which had been struck by some speeding vehicle.

The scene dejected her and she no longer wanted to look out of the window. The bus reached her village at three forty. She bid a good bye to conductor and conductor warmly did the same. She got down the bus and ran towards her home.

As she entered her house, she saw her mother talking to one of her aunt. They were conversing about the everyday things and those that were beyond their knowledge and understanding. Valli affirmed with them, smiled and went inside the house.

Word Meaning

The given page nos. correspond to the pages in the prescribed textbook.

Word	Meaning
PAGE 118	
crept	make way
overwhelming	(here) strong
wistfully	longingly
kindle	set alight (a fire) here, feelings
slang	a type of language consisting of words and phrases that are regarded as very informal
discreet	not likely to be seen or noticed by many people
PAGE 119	
crawl	to move slowly
jolly	happy and cheerful
slack	a time when there is not much work
PAGE 120	
roar	to move at high speed making a loud prolonged sound
gleaming	shining brightly
overhead	above someone's head
devoured	absorbed fully
canvas blind	curtain of thick cloth
peered	looked carefully
ditch	a pothole

Word	Meaning
startle	surprise
PAGE 121	
haughtily	proudly
chimed in	to break into a conversation or discussion
mimicking	copying the speech of someone
repulsive	causing strong dislike or disgust
PAGE 122	
curtly	sharply
drivel	talk in a very foolish or silly way
bother	worry
painstaking	diligent care and effort
thriftily	to spend money carefully
temptation	a strong urge or desire to have or do something
resolutely stifled	controlled with determination
excursion	a short trip, especially for pleasure
PAGE 123	
ventured out	went cautiously, courageously
hamlet	small village
gobbling up	hitting

Word	Meaning
pedestrian	a person travelling on foot
glee	joy
honked	sounded the horn
galloped	(of an animal) to run very fast
PAGE 124	
speck	a very small size
rattle	to make a rapid succession of short, sharp noises
traversed	travelled across or through
thoroughfare	a main road in a town
glittering	shining
gape	to look in surprise or wonder
merchandise	things for sale
PAGE 125	
shrugged	expressed indifference
spreadeagled	lying with arms and legs stretched out
haunted	returned repeatedly to the mind
dampening	reducing
PAGE 126	
chatterbox	talkative persson
chit of a girl	immature girl
pokes her nose	take an interest in something that does not concern her

Chapter Practice

Objective Questions

• Multiple Choice Questions

1. "Valli would stare wistfully at the people who got on or off the bus." What is the meaning of wistfully?
(a) Longingly
(b) Fearfully
(c) Carefully
(d) Willingly

Ans. (*a*) "Valli would stare wistfully at the people who got on or off the bus." The word 'wistfully' means longingly, a strong desire.

2. Which word was used by Valli and her friends as a slang expression for disapproval?
(a) Okay! Okay!
(b) Yeah! Yeah!
(c) Proud! Proud!
(d) Oh okay!

Ans. (*c*) 'Proud! Proud!' was used as a slang expression for disapproval by Valli and her friends.

3. The conductor called Valli as ....
(a) Baby
(b) Madam
(c) Child
(d) Daughter

Ans. (*b*) The conductor called Valli as madam.

4. From the following options, identify the conductors intention behind calling Valli 'Madam'.
(a) Hatred
(b) Envy
(c) Joke
(d) Sarcasm

Ans. (*a*) By calling Valli as 'Madam', the conductor wants to make a joke and amuse everyone.

5. Select the correct option for (i) and (ii).
(i) Valli found the elderly woman repulsive.
(ii) The woman had large piercings in her ears, wore ugly earrings and chewing betel nut.
(a) (ii) is true (i) is false
(b) (i) is true (ii) is false
(c) Both (i) and (ii) are false
(d) (ii) is the cause for (i)

Ans. (*d*) (ii) is the cause for (i), i.e. Valli found the old woman repulsive because the old woman had large piercings in her ears, wearing ugly earrings and chewing betel nut.

6. What was the timing of the afternoon nap taken by Valli's mother?
(a) 1 to 3
(b) 1 to 4
(c) 2 to 4
(d) 2 to 3

Ans. (*b*) 1 to 4 after lunch was the timing of the afternoon nap taken by Valli's mother.

7. What was the next challenge once she'd saved enough money?
(i) Know about the timings of the bus
(ii) Buy a ticket
(iii) To sneak out of the house
Codes
(a) Only (i)
(b) Only (iii)
(c) Only (ii)
(d) All of these

Ans. (*c*) The next challenge for Valli once she'd saved enough money was to sneak out of the house.

8. What does the phrase 'a fixed stare from its lifeless eyes' from 'Madam Rides the Bus' mean?
(a) The animal was asleep
(b) The animal was dead
(c) The animal was watching sky
(d) The animal was staring at Valli

Ans. (*b*) The phrase 'a fixed stare from its lifeless eyes' means that the animal was dead.

9. What does it tell you about Valli when she refused to accept the conductor's treat?
(a) Responsible
(b) Stubborn
(c) Rude
(d) Disrespectful

Ans. (*a*) Valli was responsible and mature enough to take care of herself in the outside world.

10. What thoughts do generally come in mind of an eight-year old child before travelling alone?
(i) I should go for an adventure alone.
(ii) What if I get lost and will never be able to come back to my parents and family!
(iii) I should not go without my parents' permission.
(iv) I am grown up enough to take care of things myself.
Codes
(a) (i) and (iv)
(b) (ii) and (iii)
(c) (i), (ii) and (iii)
(d) (ii), (iii) and (iv)

Ans. (*b*) Statements (ii) and (iii) are the general thoughts that come to the mind of an eight-year old child before travelling alone.

11. Given below is the list of some adjectives. Choose the ones which can be associated with Valli based on the chapter 'Madam Rides the Bus'.

1. Intelligent	2. Cunning
3. Mature	4. Responsible
5. Cranky	6. Mannerless
7. Curious	8. Active listener

(a) 1, 3, 4, 7, 8   (b) 2, 3, 5, 6, 7
(c) 1, 2, 3, 4, 5, 6   (d) 2, 3, 4, 7, 8

Ans. (*a*) Valli was intelligent, mature, responsible, curious, active listener.

12. Rearrange Valli's bus journey in order as given in the story.
 (i) The bus passed the train station.
 (ii) The bus started from village.
 (iii) The bus moved along the canal.
 (iv) The bus moved through a busy and crowded street.
 (v) The bus reached the town.

Codes
(a) (i), (ii), (iii), (iv) and (v)
(b) (v), (iii), (ii), (iv) and (i)
(c) (ii), (iii), (i), (iv) and (v)
(d) (iii), (iv) (i), (ii) and (v)

Ans. (*c*) (ii), (iii), (i), (iv) and (v) is the correct sequence of Valli's bus journey.

• Extract Based MCQs

1. Read the extract to atempt the questions that follow.

"Day after day she watched the bus and gradually a tiny wish crept into her head and grew there: she wanted to ride on that bus, even if it was just once. This wish became stronger, until it was an overwhelming desire. Valli would stare wistfully at the people who got on and off the bus when it stood at the street corner. Their faces would kindle in her longings, dreams and hopes. If one of her friends happened to ride the bus and tried to describe the sights of the town to her. Valli would be jealous to listen and would shout, in English: "Proud! Proud!"

CBSE Question Bank 2021

 (i) Valli would stare wistfully at the people as she
 (a) had been watching the bus for a long time
 (b) was inspired by the people travelling on the bus
 (c) had a strong desire to take a ride on the bus
 (d) envied the people who could travel on the bus

Ans. (*c*) Valli would stare at the people wistfully as she had a strong desire to take a ride on the bus.

 (ii) Pick the option that shows the list of words that collocate with 'overwhelming' (e.g. overwhelming desire)

1. response	2. lies
3. support	4. majority
5. pets	6. places

(a) 1, 5 and 6   (b) 1, 3 and 4
(c) 2 and 5   (d) 3, 5 and 6

Ans. (*b*) Response, support and majority collocates with the word 'overwhelming'.

 (iii) 'Valli would be jealous to listen...' This indicates Valli's
 (a) longing to ride the bus
 (b) nature as an envious person
 (c) denial to accept her situation
 (d) inclination to trouble travellers

Ans. (*a*) 'Valli would be jealous to listen…' This indicates that Valli had a longing to ride the bus.

 (iv) A part of the extract has been paraphrased. Choose the option that includes the most appropriate solution to the blanks.

The desire became so (i) .... that it transformed into an (ii) .... one. Valli would look (iii) .... at people who boarded the bus and got off.

 (a) (i) active ii) overt iii) longingly
 (b) (i) vigorous (ii) overpowering (iii) cheerfully
 (c) (i) staunch (ii) overt (iii) joyfully
 (d) (i) vigorous (ii) overpowering (iii) longingly

Ans. (*d*) (i) vigorous (ii) overpowering (iii) longingly

 (v) What does the line "gradually a tiny wish crept into her head and grew there", mean?
 (a) The wish developed in her head over a period of time
 (b) The wish was a feeling of wanting to prove her strength
 (c) The wish was planted in her head by someone's suggestion
 (d) The wish was small and was overpowered by a sense of doubt

Ans. (*a*) The line "gradually a tiny wish crept into her head and grew there" means that the wish developed in her head over a period of time.

2. Read the extract to attempt the questions that follow.

Over many days and months, Valli listened carefully to conversations between her neighbours and people who regularly used the bus and she also asked a few discreet questions here and there. This way she picked up various small details about the bus journey. The town was six miles from her village.

 (i) How did Valli picked up small details about the bus journey?
 (a) Listening to convcrsations of neighbours.
 (b) Asking a few discreet questions.
 (c) Both (a) and (b)
 (d) None of the above

Ans. (*c*) Valli picked up the small details about the bus journey by listening to the conversations of neighbours and asking a few careful questions about the bus and journey.

(ii) What was Valli's overwhelming desire?
   (a) To have friends
   (b) To travel by bus
   (c) To top the class
   (d) None of these

Ans. (*b*) Valli's overwhelming desire was to travel by bus.

(iii) Choose the option that can describe Valli with reference to above extract.
   (i) Curious
   (ii) Intelligent
   (iii) Active listener
   (iv) Irritating
   (v) Cautious
   (vi) Interrupting
   Codes
   (a) (ii), (iii) and (vi)
   (b) (i), (ii), (iii) and (v)
   (c) (iii), (iv), (v) and (vi)
   (d) (i), (ii) and (iv)

Ans. (*b*) Valli was curious, intelligent, active listener and cautious.

(iv) Select the correct option for (i) and (ii).
   1. Valli listened to the conversations between her neighbours and the regular passengers of the bus.
   2. Valli wanted to travel in the bus.
   (a) Both 1 and 2 cannot be inferred from the extract
   (b) 2 is true 1 is false.
   (c) 1 contradicts 2.
   (d) 2 is the cause for 1.

Ans. (*d*) (2) is the cause for (1), i.e., Valli wanted to travel in the bus, so she used to listen the conversations between her neighbours and the regular passengers of that bus.(d) 2 is the cause for 1.

(v) The synonym of 'discreet' is
   (a) Carefully
   (b) Details
   (c) Cautious
   (d) Regularly

Ans. (*c*) The synonyms of discreet is 'cautious'.

PART 2
Subjective Questions

• Short Answer Type Questions

1. Who was Valli? Why did she keep standing in front of the door?

Ans. Valli was an eight year old girl who was very curious. Valli kept standing in front of the door as there were no playmates of her age. So, she used to keep on watching the street outside her house.

2. What was the most fascinating thing that Valli saw on the street? **CBSE 2019**

Ans. The most fascinating thing that Valli saw on the street was the bus that travelled between her village and the nearest town. It passed through her street each hour, once going to the town and once coming back.

3. What did Valli find out about the bus journey? How did she find out these details? **NCERT**

Ans. Valli found out that the town was six miles away from her village. The trip to town would take forty five minutes and the fare of one way was thirty paise.

Valli found out these details by listening carefully to the conversations between her neighbours and people who regularly ride the bus. She also asked a few questions from them.

4. How did Valli save money to travel by bus? **CBSE 2013**

Ans. Valli saved the money to travel by bus by controlling every temptation to buy peppermints, toys, balloons and even a ride on the merry-go round at the village fair to save money for her bus journey.

5. Why does the conductor call Valli 'madam'? **NCERT**

Ans. The conductor calls Valli 'madam' because she behaved like a mature woman. She declined his help and was very quick in her answers to the conductor's questions. The conductor was amused at her behaviour and to tease her calls her 'madam'.

6. Describe the bus in which Valli sat.

Ans. The bus in which Valli sat was new. Its outside was painted a gleaming white with some green stripes along the sides. Inside, the overhead bars shone like silver.

There was a beautiful clock above the windshield and its seats were soft and luxurious.

7. Why does Valli stand up on the seat? What does she see now?

Ans. Valli stands up on the seat because she found her view blocked by the canvas that covered the lower part of the window. In order to have a better view, she stood up on the seat and looked over the canvas.

Valli can now see that the road was narrow. On one side of the road was a canal beyond which there were palm trees, grasslands, distant mountains and the blue sky. On the another side, she sees that there was a deep ditch and many acres of green fields.

8. During her journey, Valli absorbed the natural beauty and clapped her hands in happiness on seeing a young cow running very fast. What does this reveal about Valli? **CBSE Question Bank 2021**

Ans. During her journey, Valli absorbed the natural beauty and clapped her hands in happiness on seeing a young cow running very fast. This shows that although Valli was a mature and a responsible girl, she was still a child at heart.

Valli may have behaved like adults while boarding the bus but her childish nature and joy gets revealed when she reacts by clapping her hands on seeing a cow running in front of the bus.

9. Why didn't Valli want to make friends with the elderly woman? **NCERT**

Ans. Valli did not want to make friends with the elderly woman because she looked quite repulsive. She had big earholes and was wearing ugly earrings. Apart from this, she was chewing betel and it seemed that the juice of the betel would spill out of her mouth.

10. Valli didn't like the way adults treated her during her bus journey. Describe how you would feel and react if you were to find yourself in a similar situation.

CBSE Question Bank 2021

Ans. In a situation wherein adults are constantly ordering me during a journey, I would also react like Valli did because I would consider myself to be responsible enough to take the journey by myself. Just like Valli thought that she could take care of herself, I would also think the same and so, would dislike being interrupted by elders.

11. What did Valli see on her way that made her laugh? **NCERT**

Ans. Valli saw a young cow, running very fast in the middle of the road in front of the bus. The horn of the bus frightened the animal. The more the driver horned, the more faster the cow ran in front of the car. This all seemed very funny to Valli and she laughed heartily.

12. Why didn't Valli get off the bus when the bus stopped at the town?

Ans. When the nearest town had reached, everyone got off the bus except Valli because she wanted to return home in the same bus. She only wanted to take a ride on a bus. So, she gave the conductor the fare to return home in the same bus.

13. Why didn't Valli want to go to the stall and have a drink? What does this tell you about her?

Ans. Valli didn't want to go to the stall and have a drink because she did not have the money to pay for it.

This tells us about her that she was a well-mannered and self-respecting girl.

14. How did Valli feel on seeing the dead cow on the road? **CBSE 2014**

Ans. On seeing the dead cow on the road, Valli felt sad. She thought that a lovable, beautiful creature just a little while ago had now suddenly lost its charm and its life. It looked so horrible and frightening. After that, she did not even look outside the bus.

• Long Answer Type Questions

1. Age is not a barrier when it comes to doing something different and great. Which characteristics of Valli help her achieve the wonder of visiting the town at such a tender age? **CBSE 2014**

Ans. In today's era, age is no more a barrier. Children are doing wonders at a very young age. Same goes with Valli. At an age of 8 years, Valli was able to pursue her dream all alone by travelling in the bus to town. She was no different from others, except that she had certain characteristics that made her fulfil her dreams.

Valli was a very confident and a bold girl. She had a knowledge of proper planning and execution. She controlled her wishes to save money for the bus ride. Also, she was a very good observer and learner. All these qualities made her realise the dream of visiting the town. Hence, one should always remember that there is no age to learn and experience new things.

2. Once we decide to achieve something, so many difficulties come in our way. With focused attention we can make that achievement. How did Valli succeed in fulfilling her desire of riding a bus? **CBSE 2017**

or How did Valli fulfill her desire to ride a bus to the town and back? **CBSE 2020**

Ans. It is true once we decide to achieve something, many difficulties came in our way to stop us from doing our best to achieve our goals. However, with focused attention we can make our achievement. The story 'Madam Rides the Bus' proves this fact to be true.

In the story, Valliammai or Valli, an eight year old girl develops a strong desire to take a ride on the bus that travelled from her street everyday. As a confident and bold girl Valli not only gathered all knowledge about the journey but also meticulously planned her trip.

With extreme self-control, Valli saved the money she would require for a round trip in the bus. She controlled her desire to buy peppermints, toys, balloons and even did not take a ride on the merry-go-round in the village fair. Then she properly plans to take the journey quietly when her mother is taking her afternoon nap. Finally, she was able to fulfill her dream.

Her passion, self-dependence and self-respecting nature helped her to take the journey safely. Thus, it is true that with focussed attention, determination and planning one can achieve everything in life.

3. What kind of person is Valli? Illustrate your answer from the text that you have read. **CBSE 2012**

or "Valli was a mature girl ahead of her age." Justify the statement with instances from the text. **CBSE 2020**

Ans. Valliammai or Valli was an eight year old curious girl who developed a strong desire to take a bus ride. In the story, Valli emerged as a clever, sensitive, self-respecting and fun loving girl. With determination and passion she worked towards fulfilling her desire.

Not only did she just gather all the information she would require for the bus journey but also sacrificed many things to achieve it. She controlled her simple desires of buying toys, balloons, etc to take a ride on the bus. During the bus journey, Valli proved to be mature, confident, bold and practical girl beyond her age. She was full of excitement and enthusiasm with which she enjoyed the scenes outside the bus.

Even the cow filled her with extreme joy. Valli was also a keen observant intelligent and sensitive girl, she was friendly, polite as well as careful. She not only refuses to take a cold drink from a strange man but also shows her good manners while talking to the conductor.

Her nature is evident when she is saddened by the dead cow lying by the roadside. All these characteristics shows that Valli is different from other children of her age.

4. Valli's dream was to enjoy a ride on the bus to the nearest town. What preparations did she make to realise her dream? **CBSE 2019**

Ans. Valli planned her bus ride by listening carefully to conversations between her neighbours and people who regularly used the bus. She also asked a few questions from them.

She found out that the town was six miles from her village, the bus fare was thirty paise for one way and the bus trip took forty-five minutes. She also thought that if she stayed in the bus and came back by the same bus, it would cost her sixty paise.

She saved up the fare by controlling herself from buying toys, peppermints etc. She did not even take a ride on the merry-go round at the village annual fare to save money. Finally, she was able to save sixty paise for her journey.

● Extract Based Questions

1. Read the extract to attempt the questions that follow.

But for Valli, standing at the front door was every bit as enjoyable as any of the elaborate games other children played. Watching the street gave her many new unusual experiences.

(i) Why did Valli kept on standing at the doorway?

(ii) How did Valli feel while standing at the doorway?

(iii) Find a word from the extract which means 'not very common'.

(iv) How was Valli different from children of her age?

(v) What did other children do on street?

Ans. (i) Valli kept on standing at the doorway to watch the happenings of the street outside.

(ii) Watching the street gave Valli many new experiences. She felt joyous standing at the doorway.

(iii) 'Unusual' from the extract means 'not very common'.

(iv) Valli was different from children of her age as she was not interested in playing any elaborate games.

(v) Other children used to play elaborated games on the street.

2. Read the extract to attempt the questions that follow.

The most fascinating thing of all was the bus that travelled between her village and the nearest town. It passed through her street each hour, once going to the town and once coming back. The sight of the bus, filled each time with a new set of passengers, was a source of unending joy for Valli.

(i) How many times did the bus pass?

(ii) What was the source of unending joy for Valli?

(iii) Find a word from the extract which means 'ever casting'.

(iv) What was the most fascinating thing for Valli?

(v) What happened when Valli see the bus everyday?

Ans. (i) The bus passed through Valli's street once in an hour.

(ii) The sight of the bus, filled each time with a new set of passengers, was a source of joy for Valli.

(iii) 'Unending' from the extract means 'ever lasting'.

(iv) The most fascinating thing for Valli was watching the bus that travelled between her village and the nearest town.

(v) Valli slowly developed a desire to ride the bus on seeing the bus passing through her village everyday.

The Sermon at Benares

—by Betty Renshaw

In this Chapter...

- Chapter Summary
- Word Meaning
- Chapter Practice

Chapter Summary

Gautama's Early life

Gautama Buddha was born as a prince named Siddhartha Gautama in Northern India. When he was twelve years old, he was sent for schooling in the Hindu sacred scriptures. Four years later, he returned home and got married to a princess with whom he had a son. He lived a royal life for ten years protected from all the sufferings of the world.

Gautama Feels Sufferings of the World

Gautama was 25 years old when he saw the sight of sufferings present in the world. One day, on his way to hunt, he saw a sick man, an aged man, a funeral procession and then a monk begging for alms. The sights had a deep impact on Gautama and he gave upon his royal life and went out to seek enlightenment.

Gautama Seeks Enlightenments

Gautama travelled aimlessly for seven years and then he sat under a *peepal* tree until he attained enlightenment. He got enlightened after seven days and renamed the tree as 'Bodhi Tree' (Tree of wisdom). He began to teach his new understandings and came to be known as Buddha.

As Buddha, Gautama gave his first Sermon in Benares, the holiest of the dipping places on the river Ganges. The Sermon reflects Buddha's wisdom about a kind of suffering.

Story of Kisa Gotami

Kisa Gotami's only son had died. She was so grieved that she carried her dead son and went door to door asking for medicines for her dead child. Eventually she met a man who directed her towards lord Buddha who could possibly have a solution for her problem. She went to Buddha and asked him to cure his son. Buddha asked her to bring a handful of mustard seeds from a house where no one had lost a family member.

Kisa Gotami went from house to house in search of mustard seeds but she could not find any house where no one had ever died. Tired and hopeless she sat down at the wayside. As she saw the city lights flickering in darkness, she realised that human life has the same fate. She realised that death is everywhere and nobody can escape from it.

Certainty of Death

Buddha held that our life is full of pain and sufferings. Everyone who is born has to die. It is not possible to avoid death. Everyone irrespective of the difference has to die as death is inevitable for all mortals. He further adds that wise men understand the unavoidability of death. They do not lament, grieve or complaint and are thus peaceful and away from sorrow. If one keeps on grieving, one will suffer both physically and mentally, only those who move on are blessed.

World Meaning

The given page numbers correspond to the pages in the prescribed textbook.

Word	Meaning
PAGE 133	
sacred	holy
scriptures	the holy writings of a religion
befitted	appropriate
heretofore	before now
alms	money or food given to poor people
enlightenment	a state of high spiritual knowledge
chanced upon	came across by chance
wandered	moved in a leisurely or aimless way

Word	Meaning
vowed	a serious promise to do something
PAGE 134	
awakened	enlightened
sermon	a talk on a religious or moral subject
inscrutable	impossible to understand or interpret
repaired	went
procure	obtain
beloved	dearly loved
weary	feeling or showing extreme tiredness
flickered	shone unsteadily

Word	Meaning
extinguished	put out
valley of desolation	place filled with deep sorrow
mortals	those bound to die
PAGE 135	
earthen	made of baked or fired clay
kinsmen	near relatives
lamenting	expressing sorrow, regret or unhappiness about something
slaughter	the killing of animals for their meat
afflicted	affected

Chapter Practice

Objective Questions

• Multiple Choice Questions

1. The lesson talks of Buddha's life as prince to show that ....
(a) he lived a happy and fulfilling life
(b) he was a prosperous man
(c) he was a pampered and a wealthy man
(d) he was ignorant to the sufferings of the world

Ans. (*b*) The lesson talks of Buddha's life as a prince to show that he lived a happy and fulfilling life with his parents, wife and son.

2. Prince Siddhartha lived for ten years as <u>befitted royalty</u>. What does the underlined phrase mean?
(a) Royal person
(b) Someone who lives by royal treasures
(c) Someone who lives as a king or a queen should
(d) None of the above

Ans. (*c*) 'Befitted royalty' means someone who lives as a king of a queen should.

3. What could be the reason that Prince Siddhartha was shielded from the sufferings of the world?
(a) To prevent him from becoming a great spiritual leader as foretold on his birth.
(b) He was unable to accept the truth about the sufferings of the world.
(c) He did not want to see the sufferings of the world.
(d) None of the above

Ans. (*a*) Prince Siddhartha was shielded from the sufferings of the world to prevent him from becoming a great spiritual leader as foretold on his birth.

4. For how much time did Gautama sit under the peepal tree?
(a) Seven years
(b) Six years
(c) Seven days
(d) Four days

Ans. (*c*) Gautama sat for seven days under the peepal tree and got enlightened.

5. What does the word 'enlightenment' mean in the context of the chapter 'The Sermon at Benares'?
(a) A state of being innocent
(b) A state of high spiritual knowledge
(c) A state of deserted brain
(d) A state of begging alms

Ans. (*b*) Enlightenment means a state of high spiritual knowledge.

6. What does the sermon in the chapter 'The Sermon at Benares' reflect?
(a) Buddha's wisdom
(b) Buddha's enlightenment
(c) Story of Kisa Gotami
(d) Death is common to all

Ans. (*a*) The sermon in the chapter 'The Sermon at Benares' reflects the Buddha's wisdom about one inscrutable kind of suffering.

7. Why did Kisa Gotami want to bring her dead child back to life? Choose the least possible reason.
(a) She could not accept the truth that her only son was dead.
(b) She believed in rebirths.
(c) She believed that medicine could cure her son.
(d) None of the above

Ans. (*b*) The least possible reason for Kisa Gotami to bring her dead child back to life is she believed in rebirths.

8. "She has lost her senses. The boy is dead." – Who is 'she' and 'the boy' in the given sentence?
(a) Kisa Gotami and her dead husband
(b) Kisa Gotami and Gautam Buddha
(c) Kisa Gotami and her dead son
(d) Kisa Gotami and a man from neighbourhood

Ans. (*c*) In the given line 'she' is Kisa Gotami and the 'boy' is her dead son.

9. Why do you think Gautam Buddha ask Kisa Gotami to bring mustard seeds from the house where no one had ever died?
(a) To put her down.
(b) To make her realise that death is common to all.
(c) To keep her busy till he was cured her son.
(d) All of the above

Ans. (*b*) Gautam Buddha asked Kisa Gotami to bring mustard seeds from the house where no one had ever died to make her realise that death is common to all.

10. Those who do not grieve are ……… …
(a) arrogant   (b) proud   (c) happy   (d) wise

Ans. (*d*) Those who do not grieve are wise.

11. Which of the following statement is not true in accordance with the chapter 'The Sermon at Benares'?
(i) The real name of Gautam Budhha was Prince Devdatt.
(ii) The sight of a monk begging alms moved the prince towards the path of enlightenment.
(iii) Kisa Gotami was grieving for her dead husband.
(iv) It took Gautam Buddha ten years to gain enlightenment.
(v) Prince Siddhartha was married at the age of sixteen.
(vi) Prince Siddhartha was shielded from the sufferings of the world till twenty five years of his life.
(a) (i), (iv) and (v)   (b) (i), (iii) and (iv)
(c) (ii), (v) and (vi)   (d) (i), (ii) and (iii)

Ans. (*b*) Statements (i), (iii) and (iv) are not true. The real name of Gautam Buddha was Prince Siddhartha. Kisa Gotami was grieving for her dead son. It took Gautam Buddha seven days to gain enlightenment.

12. Which of the following are the teachings of Buddha as mentioned in the chapter 'The Sermon at Benares'?
(i) The life of mortals in this world is troubled and brief and combined with pain.
(ii) There is no means by which those that have been born can avoid dying.
(iii) The fate of men is like city lights which flicker up and then extinguish again in darkness.
(iv) Not from weeping nor from grieving will anyone obtain peace of mind.
(a) Option (i)
(b) Option (ii) and (iii)
(c) Options (i), (ii) and (iv)
(d) None of these

Ans. (*c*) Options (i), (ii) and (iv)

• Extract Based MCQs

1. Read the extract to attempt the questions that follow.

At twelve, he was sent away for schooling in the Hindu sacred scriptures and years later he returned home to marry a princess. They had a son and lived for ten years as befitted royalty.

At about the age of twenty-five, the prince here to fore shielded from the sufferings of the world, while going out on hunting, chanced upon a sick man, then an aged man, then a funeral procession, and finally a monk begging for alms. These sights so moved him that he at once became a beggar and went out into the world to seek enlightenment concerning the sorrows he had witnessed.

(i) What was the unintended effect of the sights Buddha see?
(a) He felt dejected and sorrowful
(b) He renounced royalty
(c) He decided to become an ascetic
(d) He decided to consult a pandit

Ans. (*a*) The sight of sufferings had a deep impact on Gautama. He wanted to see answer and so renounced or left his royal life to become a wanderer.

(ii) What did the prince see while he was out on hunting?
(a) He saw a sick and aged man.
(b) He saw a funeral procession.
(c) He saw a monk begging for alms.
(d) All of the above

Ans. (*d*) While the prince was out on hunting, he saw a sick man, an aged man, a funeral procession and a monk begging for alms.

(iii) Choose the option that lists the set of statements that are NOT TRUE according to the given extract.
(i) He was Lord Buddha.
(ii) He was kept away from sorrows of life.
(iii) He was just ten years old when he left the kingdom.
(iv) He became a beggar because he was dethroned.
(v) He gained enlightenment.
(vi) His son was ten years old when he left the kingdom.
(a) (iii) and (iv)   (b) (i) and (iv)
(c) (ii) and (v)   (d) (ii) and (vi)

Ans. (*a*) Statements 3 and 4 are not true. He was 25 years old when he left the kingdom. He became a beggar in search of enlightenment.

(iv) Pick the option that correctly classifies Fact/s(F) and Opinion/s (O) given below.
1. He was born a prince and was kept away from sorrows.
2. He should not have taken such a rash decision.
3. His wife and son must have hated him.
4. He was the enlightened one.
(a) F- 1, 3 and O-2, 4   (b) F-2, 3 and O-1, 4
(c) F-1, 4 and O-2, 3   (d) F-1 and O-2, 3, 4

Ans. (*c*) Statements 1 and 4 are facts because they are directly mentioned in the text. Statements 2 and 3 are opinions because they are not mentioned in the text.

(v) He decided to seek
(a) self-consciousness   (b) enlightenment
(c) cure for people from pain   (d) helpless people from sorrow

Ans. (*b*) He decided to seek enlightenment.

2. Read the extract to attempt the questions that follow.

Poor Kisa Gotami now went from house to house, and the people pitied her and said, "Here is mustard-seed; take it!" But when she asked, "Did a son or daughter, a father or mother, die in your family?" they answered her, "Alas! the living are few, but the dead are many. Do not remind us of our deepest grief." And there was no house but some beloved one had died in it.

CBSE Question Bank 2021

(i) The community's response to Kisa in the above extract was somewhat different from before. Why do you think that was the case?

   (a) They had learnt from Buddha's sermons.
   (b) They were able to help Kisa in some way this time.
   (c) They understood parental grief.
   (d) They liked Kisa and enjoyed talking to her.

Ans. (*b*) The community's was different from before because this time they were able to help Kisa in some way; they could give her handful of mustard seeds. However, due to Buddha's condition, she could not take them.

(ii) Which of the following options represent the correct understanding of the word 'poor' in the phrase "Poor Kisa Gotami"?

   (a) In need of money   (b) Weak
   (c) Unfortunate   (d) Inferior

Ans. (*c*) 'Unfortunate' represents the correct understanding of word 'poor' in the phrase 'Poor Kisa Gotami'.

(iii) "Do not remind us of our deepest grief." The tone of the speaker(s) is

   (a) disillusioned   (b) sceptical
   (c) ironic   (d) solemn

Ans. (*d*) The tone of the speaker in given line is solemn, i.e., serious.

(iv) Pick the option that explains — '…the living are few, but the dead are many.'

   (a) It shows the high death rate and low birth rate in the city of Benares.
   (b) It highlights the holy status of Benares where many Hindus go to die.
   (c) It throws light on the numerous loved ones the villagers had lost over time.
   (d) It reflects that many children who had died in the village for various reasons.

Ans. (*c*) "The living are few, but the dead are many" throws light on the fact the villagers had lost numerous loved ones over time.

(v) Imagine you are a photo journalist visiting the city at the time Kisa Gotami went from house to house. You documented her experience given in the above extract in a photo series.

Your publisher wants to publish the photo series in three parts wherein Part 1 shows Kisa's visits to the houses; Part 2 depicts her conversations with people, and Part 3 captures Kisa's reflections at the end of the day sitting by the wayside.

The publisher would also like you to choose titles for the series and its three parts.

Look at the titles given below, and choose the options that provide the most appropriate set of titles.

(1) Series Title – From Darkness to Light.
    Part I – Living in Loss; Part II – A Mother's Journey; Part III – Mustard Seed

(2) Series Title – Mustard Seed.
    Part I – A Mother's Journey; Part II – From Darkness to Light; Part III – Living in Loss

(3) Series Title – A Mother's Journey.
    Part I – Mustard Seed; Part II – Living in Loss; Part III – From Darkness to Light

(4) Series Title – Living in Loss.
    Part I – From Darkness to Light; Part II – Mustard Seed; Part III – A Mother's Journey

   (a) 1 and 2   (b) 2 and 3
   (c) 3 and 4   (d) 1 and 4

Ans. (*b*) 2 and 3

PART 2
Subjective Questions

• Short Answer Type Questions

1. What do you know about the early life of Buddha?

Ans. The early life of Buddha was filled with royal pleasure and happiness. Lord Buddha was born in a royal family as Siddhartha Gautama. At the age of twelve, he was sent away for schooling in Hindu sacred scriptures. Four years later, he got married to a princess and had a son.

2. What was the effect of observing the sufferings of the world on Buddha?

Ans. The sights of suffering sick man, old man, funeral process and a beggar had a deep impact on Buddha. He was so affected by the sufferings that he at once left his royal life in search of enlightenment and an understanding of the world around him.

3. What did the Buddha do after he had attained enlightenment?

Ans. After the Buddha had attained enlightenment, he started teaching and sharing his new understandings. He spread his preachings far and wide so that people could come to know the truth. He wanted people to understand the world so that they could live peacefully.

4. When her son dies, Kisa Gotami goes from house to house. What does she ask for? Does she get it? Why not? **NCERT**

Ans. When Kisa Gotami's son died, she went from house to house, and asked for some medicine that would cure her child.

No, she did not get it because her child was dead and no medicine could have brought him back to life.

5. Kisa Gotami again goes from house to house after she speaks with the Buddha. What does she ask for, the second time around? Does she get it? Why not? **NCERT**

Ans. After talking to Lord Buddha, Kisa Gotami again went house to house to get mustard seed from a family wherein no one has died.

No, Kisa Gotami could not get anything because there is no person or family in the world wherein there has been no death. Everyone has faced the loss of a beloved member.

6. What does Kisa Gotami understand the second time that she failed to understand the first time? Was this what the Buddha wanted her to understand? **NCERT**

Ans. Kisa Gotami understood the second time that death is common to all. She understood that she was being selfish in her grief. There was no house where some beloved had not died.

Yes, this was what the Buddha wanted her to understand.

7 According to Kisa Gotami, what is the greatest grief of life? **CBSE 2014**

Ans. According to Kisa Gotami, the greatest grief in life is the death of one's loved ones. Therefore, instead of lamenting on it, the wise should accept the truth of death. Weeping will only increase the pain and disturb the peace of mind of a person.

8. How did Kisa Gotami realise that life and death is a process? **CBSE 2016,2019**

Ans. Kisa Gotami realised that life and death is a normal process when she went from house to house but was unable to find one house where nobody had died. It was when she sat down that she realised that death is common to everyone. Those who are born will die one day.

9. According to Buddha, who are wise men?

Ans. According to Buddha, wise men are those people who never complain or lament over their loss. They accept the truth and move on such people are calm and composed. They lead a blessed and peaceful life.

10. How do you usually understand the idea of 'selfishness'? Do you agree with Kisa Gotami that she was being 'selfish in her grief'? **NCERT**

Ans. I usually understand the idea of selfishness as being concerned only about one's own interests. I also understand it to mean showing complete disregard for others' interests.

Yes, I agree with Kisa Gotami that she was being 'selfish in her grief'. In her son's death, she was unable to see that death is something that strikes all living beings.

11. Elucidate any one quality that Siddhartha demonstrated when he gave up his status and family. Explain your choice. **CBSE Question Bank 2021**

Ans. Siddhartha demonstrated compassion, kindness and his determination in his decision to leave behind his family and prince hood. He felt sympathetic towards others. He was disturbed to see people's sufferings and wanted to find out a solution to eradicate their sufferings and diseases.

12. Do you think being enlightened placed a far greater responsibility on the Buddha than being king would have? Justify your stance. **CBSE Question Bank 2021**

Ans. Yes, enlightenment placed far greater responsibilities than being a king would have on Buddha. As a king, he was more concerned with the physical well-being of only his countrymen but now he had an obligation to take care of the whole of humanity.

As Buddha, he owed the responsibility of preaching and educating the people about the truth that he had realised.

● Long Answer Type Questions

1. Describe the journey of Siddhartha Gautama becoming the Buddha. **CBSE 2020**

Ans. Gautama Buddha was born in 563 BC in a royal family. His name was Siddhartha Gautama. At the age of twelve, he was sent away for schooling. He studied all the sacred Hindu scriptures. At the age of sixteen, he married a princess and later they had a son. He lived a royal life for ten years and was shielded from the sufferings of the world.

However, when he was twenty five, he saw a sick man, then an aged man and a funeral procession. Finally, he came across a monk begging for alms. This was his first encounter with the harsh realities of life. These sights made him so sad that he decided to renounce the worldly pleasures. He left his family and became a monk. He went out into the world to seek spiritual knowledge.

Siddhartha Gautama wandered for seven years in search of wisdom and truth. Finally, he sat down under a big peepal tree to mediate. He vowed to stay there until he got enlightenment. After seven days, Gautama got enlightenment. He became known as 'The Buddha' which means 'enlightened' or 'the awakened'. He began to teach and spread his message of wisdom and truth.

2. Life is full of trials and tribulations. Kisa Gotami also passes through a period of grief in her life. How does she behave in those circumstances?

or Why did Gotami go to the Buddha? What lesson did he teach her? **CBSE 2019**

or How did the Buddha make Kisa Gotami realise the reality of death? **CBSE 2020**

Ans. After the death of Kisa Gotami's only child, she became very sad. She carried her dead child to her neighbours in order to get medicine to bring him to life. Her neighbours thought that she had gone insane as she was unable to accept the fact that her child is dead. It was then that someone suggested her to meet Gautama Buddha.

When she met Gautama Buddha, he gave her an exercise to do. She was asked to collect mustard seeds from a house where no one had ever died. She went from one house to another but was unable to find a single house in the town where no one had died. This way she realised that death is a part of life and anyone who is born is bound to die one day.

Thus, Buddha changed her understanding of death by this exercise. Buddha told her that only the wise do not grieve and they accept the reality. Mourning brings only pain and sufferings to the body. One, who is composed, obtains peace of mind and will be free from sorrow and be blessed. This gave her strength to overcome grief.

3. Through the story of Kisa Gotami what did the Buddha try to preach to the common man?

CBSE 2020

Ans. The lesson on death and suffering that Buddha taught Gotami was that, these are part and parcel of life. No one can avoid this truth. One has to meet one's destined end one day. Whoever has come into this world will die one day. Thus, in the hour of grief for a loved one who has died, one must remain calm and composed. Then one doesn't occupy himself with grief. Otherwise, they will feel the pain more.

However, those persons who are wise never complain or lament over their loss. They never try to bring back to life their loved ones who are dead, as Gotami wanted to do. They accept the truth and overcome their sorrow. Persons who overcome their sorrow will be blessed. So, wisdom is in the fact that people should not get distressed with pain, suffering or death.

4. What lesson did Kisa Gotami learn the second time that she had failed to learn the first time?

CBSE 2020

Ans. Kisa Gotami had lost her only son and in grief, she carried her dead son to all her neighbours to get him cured and restored back to life. Finally, she went to the Buddha asking him for medicine to cure her boy. The Buddha felt that she needed to be enlightened about the truth of life that death and sorrow are inseperable.

He could see that grief had blinded her, and it would be difficult for her to accept the truth. So, the Buddha told her to procure mustard seeds from a house where none had died. Kisa Gotami went door to door. Then, she realised that there was no house where no one had died and that death is common to all.

She came back to the Buddha where he told her that life in this world is troubled and filled with sorrows. He gave her examples of ripe fruits and earthen vessels whose

'lives' are short. This way he made her realise the second time that death is unavoidable and none even the near and dear ones can save anyone from death.

● Extract Based Questions

1. Read the extract to attempt the questions that follow.

He wandered for seven years and finally sat down under a peepal tree, where he vowed to stay until enlightenment came. Enlightened after seven days, he renamed the tree the Bodhi Tree and began to teach and to share his new understandings. At that point he became known as the Buddha.

(i) What was the name of the peepal tree under which Buddha sat?

(ii) What did Siddhartha do while sitting under the tree?

(iii) Find the exact word from the extract which means 'solemnly promise to do a specified thing'.

(iv) After how many days Siddhartha got enlightenment?

(v) Siddhartha come to known as .... after enlightenment.

Ans. (i) The name of the peepal tree under which Buddha sat was Bodhi Tree.

(ii) Siddhartha began to teach and share his new understandings while sitting under the tree.

(iii) 'Vowed' from the extract means 'solemnly promise to do a specific thing'.

(iv) Siddhartha got enlightenment after seven days of his vow that he would sit until enlightenment came.

(v) Siddhartha came to know as Gautama Buddha after enlightenment.

2. Read the extract to attempt the questions that follow.

The Buddha preached his first sermon at the city of Benares, most holy of the dipping places on the River Ganges; that sermon has been preserved and is given here. It reflects the Buddha's wisdom about one inscrutable kind of suffering.

(i) Where did Buddha preach his first sermon?

(ii) What does the sermon preached by Buddha reflect?

(iii) Find the exact word from the extract which means 'impossible to understand'.

(iv) How Benares is described in the lesson?

(v) What do you understand by the term Buddha?

Ans. (i) Buddha preached his first sermon at Benares.

(ii) It reflects Buddha's wisdom about one inscrutable kind of suffering.

(iii) 'Inscrutable' from the extract means 'impossible to understand'.

(iv) Benares is described in the lesson as the holiest of the dipping places on the river Ganges.

(v) Buddha means the awakened or the enlightened.

The Proposal (Play)

—by Anton Chekov

In this Chapter...

- Chapter Summary
- Word Meaning
- Chapter Practice

Chapter Summary

Lomov at Chubukov's House

The play begins in a drawing room of Chubukov's house. Ivan Lomov comes to meet Chubukov. Chubukov is extremely happy to meet him. He is surprised to see Lomov wearing a formal dress and asks him if he is going somewhere. Lomov informs him that he has come to meet him because he needs his help. Chubukov thinks that Lomov must have come to borrow money from him and states that he wouldn't give him any money. Finally, Lomov tells that he has come to ask for Natalya's (Chubukov's daughter) hand for marriage.

Chubukov's Reaction to the Proposal

Chubukov gets very excited after hearing about the proposal. He hugs and kisses Lomov. He informs Lomov that he has been waiting for this proposal since a long time. He even guarantees that Natalya would also agree to the proposal and goes to call her.

Lomov Thinks about Natalya and His Life

As chubukov leaves, Lomor is left alone in the drawing room. He starts talking to himself. He finds Natalya to be a good housekeeper. She is well educated and not bad looking. He thinks that he needs to get married now because he is thirty-five years old and needs to live a quiet and peaceful life. He also thinks that he is always restless and cannot sleep properly. Infact, we (as readers) find Lomov getting over excited and getting nervous while stating the proposal.

Natalya Meets Lomov

Natalya enters the drawing room and is surprised to see Lomov. She welcomes Lomov and starts talking about the work in the fields. Suddenly, she notices Lomov's dress and enquires if he is going to a ball (party).

Lomov tells her the purpose of his visit. But instead of talking about the proposal, Lomov tells her about the good relations between Lomovs and Chubukovs. He also mentions about Oxen Meadows that he has inherited from his aunt.

Argument over Oxen Meadows

After hearing Lomov calling Oxen Meadows as his own, Natalya tells Lomov that the Oxen Meadows do not belong to him. They actually belong to Chubukov. An argument begins over the Oxen Meadows. Both of them constantly state that the Meadows are owned by them.

Lomov offers to show documents to prove his claims. He clarifies that the Oxen Meadows were once a subject of dispute between their families. His aunt's grandmother gave its free use to the peasants of Natalya's father's grandfather. The peasants used to make bricks for the grandmother. Since peasants used the meadows for forty years, Chubukovs started considering the land to be their own. But now they belong to Lomov.

Argument Continues between Natalya and Lomov

Natalya does not agree and sticks to her point that those meadows belong to them. She insists that the land has been owned by them for nearly 300 years.

Both Lomov and Natalya insist that the land is not worth a lot of money but they want the land as a matter of principle. Lomov offers to make meadows as a present to Natalya. Natalya also says that she can make meadows a present to Lomov.

Chubukov Joins the Argument

Chubukov enters the room and gets to know the reason for the argument. He supports Natalya and tells Lomov that Oxen Meadows are owned by them. The quarrel increases to such an extent that Lomov and Chubukov start abusing each other and their families.

Chubukov asks Lomov not to talk to him so disrespectfully as he is twice of his age. Lomov calls Chubukov a land grabber and threatens to take Chubukov to the court.

This angers Chubukov who sates that Lomov's grandfather was a drunkard and his younger aunt Nastasya ran away with an architect. He also calls Lomov a villain, a scarecrow and a monster who has the courage to propose. All this excites Lomov and his health deteriorates. Finally, Chubukov asks Lomov to leave his house and never come back again.

Natalya Gets to Know about the Proposal

As soon as Lomov leaves, Chubukov tells Natalya that Lomov had come to propose her for marriage. When Natalya hears this, she almost faints and starts crying. She blames Chubukov for irritating Lomov and asks him to bring Lomov back. Chubukov goes to get Lomov back.

Another Argument over Dogs

Lomov enters the house again. Natalya tells him that the Oxen Meadows belongs to Lomov and shifts the conversation. Then, they start talking about dogs. Lomov tells Natalya that his dog 'Guess' is the best dog. Natalya again objects to Lomov's claims and calls her dog 'Squeezer' to be better than Guess. Again, an argument begins. Both of them list the qualities of their dogs and claim their dog to be better than the other. Chubukov also joins the argument and again it grows to such an extent that they start abusing each other.

Chubukov Asks Lomov to Marry Natalya

While they are arguing, Lomov's condition worsens and he falls onto an arm chair. Both Natalya and Chubukov think that he has died and start crying. They think that Natalya's chance of getting married has gone. After sometime, Lomov comes to his senses. Chubukov tells Lomov that Natalya is ready for marriage and that they should get married soon.

He does not want to lose even a single moment and joins their hand. He asks them to kiss each other and blesses them. But again, they start arguing about their dogs while Chubukov calls everyone for Champagne to try to quiet her daughter.

Word Meaning

The given page nos. correspond to the pages in the prescribed textbook.

Word	Meaning
PAGE 144	
get up	dress
pardon	to excuse
to count on	to depend on
PAGE 145	
by jove	used to express surprise or emphasis
off my balance	excited
consent	to give permission for something
trembling	to shake slightly as you are afraid, nervous, excited etc
egad	expressing surprise, anger or affirmation
PAGE 146	
palpitation (of the heart)	to beat quickly and strongly and often in a way that is not regular because of excitement, nervousness etc
twitch	to make a slight, sudden movement that is not controlled or deliberate

Word	Meaning
lunatic	a crazy person
neglige	gown
shelling	removing shells
stacked	stored
PAGE 147	
regard	a feeling of respect and admiration for someone
meadow	a place for grazing cattle
marsh	a place with loose earth and water
wedged	to force into a narrow space, squeeze
perpetuity	the state of continuing for a long time
reckon	believed
PAGE 148	
dessiatins	a currency
implore	to make a very serious or emotional request to someone
make head or tail	understand

Word	Meaning
threshing	process of separating the grains from the plant
gypsie	a homeless person
impudent	failing to show proper respect and courtesy
carafe	a water container
PAGE 149	
mower	a person who cuts grass
clutch	to hold with the hand
hoarse	loud
restrain	to stop somebody from doing something
excruciating	very painful; causing great mental or physical pain
PAGE 150	
accustomed	habitual
agitating	disturbing, exciting or angering someone
PAGE 151	
pettifogger	one who argues about small issues

Word	Meaning
embezzlement	to steal the money of your employer
drunkard	a person who is drunk or who often gets drunk
hump-backed	having a hump at the back
guzzle	fat or drink (something) greedily
gambler	one who gambles
intriguer	cheater
malicious	having or showing a desire to cause harm
stagger	to move unsteadily from side to side
rascal	a cruel or dishonest man
scarecrow	a person who is very badly dressed, odd-looking or thin
impudence	quality of not showing respect for others
confounded	used for emphasis, especially to express anger or annoyance
wizen-faced	wrinkle-faced

Word	Meaning
frump	a colourless person
PAGE 152	
wail	to cry
hysterics	a wildey emotional and exaggerated reaction
fetch	to go after and bring back someone
heated	angry
PAGE 153	
lame	having an injured leg or foot that makes walking difficult or painful
twisted	forced out of its natural or proper shape
pedigree	the history of the family members in an animal's past especially when it is good or impressive
thoroughbred	of pure and unmixed breed
overshot	having the upper jaw extending the lower
worn-out	tired
pretend	assume

Word	Meaning
PAGE 154	
bursting	to break open or into pieces
rot	(here) rubbish
well-sprung	rounded
purebred (of an animal)	having parents that are of the same breed
muzzle	the usually long nose and mouth of an animal
neck and neck	very close (as in a race)
verst	a Russian unit of distance equal to 1.067 kilometres
PAGE 155	
worrying	(here) following
liable to	likely to
tracking	(here) hunting
partridge	a bird
milksop	a man who lacks courage
jesuit	one who cheats
PAGE 156	
damned	used to say that something is not important
bliss	complete happiness

Chapter Practice

Objective Questions

• Multiple Choice Questions

1. What is the play about?
   (a) Tendency of wealthy families to seek ties with other wealthy families
   (b) Tendency of wealthy families to increase their estates
   (c) Encouragement of marriages that make good economic sense
   (d) All of the above

Ans. (*d*) The play is about tendency of wealthy families to seek ties with other wealthy families to increase their estates and encouragement of marriages that make good economic sense.

2. The word 'proposal' has several meanings can you guess what sort of proposal the play is about?
   (a) A suggestion, plan or scheme for doing something
   (b) An offer for a possible plan or action
   (c) The act of asking someone's hand in marriage
   (d) None of the above

Ans. (*c*) The play is about, the act of asking someone's hand in marriage.

3. Chubukov (aside) He's come to borrow money. Shan't give him any.

   The given line reflects that Chubukov is ....
   (a) selfish   (b) pretentious
   (c) greedy   (d) hypocrite

Ans. (*c*) The given lines show that even though Chubukov meets Lomov very pleasantly, he in reality dislikes him and only pretends to like him.

4. What was Lomov wearing when he entered the scene?
   (a) Dress-jacket and white gloves
   (b) Evening coat with hat
   (c) Waistcoat and trousers
   (d) Shirt and trousers

Ans. (*a*) Lomov was wearing dress-jacket and white gloves when he entered the scene.

5. Chubukov was blessing Lomov because he ....
   (a) gave Oxen Meadows to Chubukov
   (b) gave his pet dog guess to Natalya
   (c) asked Chubukov's daughter's hand in marriage
   (d) None of the above

Ans. (*c*) Chubukov was blessing Lomov because he asked Chubukov's daughter's hand in marriage.

6. Identify the setting of the scene.
   (a) Chubukov's drawing room (b) Lomov's bedroom
   (c) Natalya's bedroom   (d) Oxen Meadows

Ans. (*a*) The entire scene of the play is set in Chubukov's drawing room.

7. What was the first point of disagreement between Natalya and Lomov?
   (a) Pet dog   (b) Oxen Meadows
   (c) House   (d) None of these

Ans. (*b*) Oxen Meadows was the first point of disagreement between Natalya and Lomov.

8. When does Natalya falls into the chair and demands to call Lomov back?
   (a) When she gets to know that Lomov had come to propose her
   (b) When she gets to know that Lomov suffers from excitement attacks
   (c) When Natalya get to know that he has actually left the place
   (d) None of the above

Ans. (*a*) When Natalya gets to know that Lomov had come to propose her, she falls into the chair and demands to call Lomov back.

9. "Dear one, why yell like that? You won't prove anything just by yelling." Who said this to whom in the play?
   (a) Chubukov to Natalya   (b) Chubukov to Lomov
   (c) Lomov to Natalya   (d) Natalya to Lomov

Ans. (*b*) The given line is said by Chubukov to Lomov.

10. Natalya's pet dog Squuezer was a thoroughbred animal, the son of ....
   (a) Harness and Chisles   (b) Harness and Volchantesky
   (c) Chisles and Volchantesky (d) Chisles and cab-horse

Ans. (*a*) Natalya's pet dog Squuezer was a thoroughbred animal, the son of Harness and Chisles.

11. What is the theme of the play?

   (i) Human nature
   (ii) Rich people
   (iii) Physical weakness
   (iv) Arguments and disputes
   (v) Double faced people
   (vi) Feelings for dogs

(a) (i), (iv), (v) and (vi)   (b) (ii), (iii) and (iv)
(c) (i), (ii), (iii) and (v)   (d) All of these

Ans. (*d*) All of these

12. Select the most appropriate option for (1) and (2).

   1. Natalya and Lomov would not be a happily married couple.
   2. Lomov does not Love Natalya.

(a) Both (1) and (2) are true
(b) (2) is the opposite of (1)
(c) (1) furthers the premise of (2)
(d) Both (1) and (2) are false

Ans. (*a*) Both (1) and (2) are true

• Extract Based MCQs

1. Read the extract to attempt the questions that follow.

"Natalya Stephenova is an excellent housekeeper, not bad looking, well-educated. What more do I want? But I'm getting noise in my ears from excitement. (Drinks) And it's impossible for me not to marry. In the first place, I'm already 35–a critical age so to speak. In the second place, I ought to lead a quiet and regular life."

(i) Who is the speaker of the given lines?
   (a) Chubukov
   (b) Ivan
   (c) Ivan's brother
   (d) Chubukov's friend

Ans. (*b*) Ivan is the speaker of the given lines.

(ii) When the speaker says, 'What more do I want?', he means that
   (a) he wants to get married soon.
   (b) Natalya is a good match for him.
   (c) he and Natalya are both quarrelsome.
   (d) Natalya would add to his glory.

Ans. (*b*) When the speaker says, 'What more do I want?' he means that Natalya is a good match for him.

(iii) What does the given lines tell us about the speaker?
   (a) He suffered from many illnesses.
   (b) He lived a very social life.
   (c) He wanted a beautiful wife.
   (d) He wanted to lived a very quiet and regular life.

Ans. (*d*) The given lines tell us that the speaker wanted to live a regular life.

(iv) The statement that is true about the speaker, according to the passage is
   (a) he is an old man.
   (b) he suffers from attacks of excitements.
   (c) he wants to make Natalya his business partner.
   (d) he wants to travel to the world.

Ans. (*b*) "The speaker suffers from attacks of excitement" is true.

(v) Choose a word from the extract to complete the following.
Critical : Safe : : ……… : Indifference
   (a) Excellent   (b) Educated
   (c) Excitement   (d) Quiet

Ans. (*c*) Critical : Safe : : Excitement : Indifference. This is because critical and safe are antonyms and so do excitement and indifference.

2. Read the extract to attempt the questions that follow.

LOMOV Never mind about my people! The Lomovs have all been honourable people, and not one has ever been tried for embezzlement, like your grandfather!

CHUBUKOV You Lomovs have had lunacy in your family, all of you!

NATALYA All, all, all!

CHUBUKOV Your grandfather was a drunkard, and your younger aunt, Nastasya Mihailovna, ran away with an architect, and so on...

LOMOV And your mother was hump-backed. [Clutches at his heart] Something pulling in my side... My head.... Help! Water!

CHUBUKOV Your father was a guzzling gambler!

           CBSE Question Bank 2021

(i) Choose the option that correctly identifies the tone of the characters in the given extract.
   (1) antagonism   (2) humour
   (3) contempt   (4) irony
   (a) (1) and (2)   (b) (2) and (4)
   (c) (1) and (3)   (d) (3) and (4)

Ans. (*c*) The tones of the characters can be described as antagonism and contempt.

(ii) The playwright's intention in the given extract is to
   (a) throw light upon the weaknesses of the rich in any society.
   (b) emphasise that family history is important in a marriage proposal.
   (c) satirise the superficiality of the upper class in Russian society.
   (d) send a message that ego is not healthy in any relationship.

Ans. (*c*) The playwright's intention in the given extract is to satirise the superficiality of the upper class in Russian society.

(iii) If according to Chubukov and Natalya, Lomovs are not 'honourable people', why do they still consider Lomov's proposal?

   (a) Natalya can take care of her father if she marries close by.

   (b) They were exaggerating in the argument and didn't mean it.

   (c) They understand that honour is superficial and overrated.

   (d) Lomov's status in society supersedes everything.

Ans. (*d*) Chubukov and Natalya still consider Lomov's proposal because of his status in society superseded everything.

(iv) Imagine you found the playwright's notes for each scene in the play and noticed that some of the words were missing. Choose the option that fills the missing words most appropriately.

A conversation that starts pleasantly quickly turns into a (i) .... argument. With (ii) .... of Oxen Meadows at the heart of the matter, Lomov and Natalya quarrel and are later joined by Chubukov. Thus, begins a (iii) .... of insults, accusations and name-calling. All (iv) .... disappears. Eventually, Lomov leaves clutching at his heart, his foot numb.

   (a) (i) petty ; (ii) history ; (iii) series; (iv) politeness

   (b) (i) vicious ; (ii) ownership ; (iii) circus ; (iv) civility

   (c) (i) curious ; (ii) land ; (iii) outpouring ; (iv) laughter

   (d) (i) ugly ; (ii) neighbourhood ; (iii) barrage; (iv) goodness

Ans. (*b*) (i) vicious ; (ii) ownership ; (iii) circus ; (iv) civility

(v) Which of the following options comes closest to the meaning of 'tried' as used in the extract?

   (a) She mastered the game through a process of trial and error.

   (b) He followed the trial closely and was seen in court every day.

   (c) This had been a tried and tested formula for the organisation.

   (d) They tried with all their might to repeat their earlier successes.

Ans. (*b*) Sentence (b) is closes to the word 'tried' used in the above extract.

PART 2
Subjective Questions

• Short Answer Type Questions

1. What does Chubukov at first suspect that Lomov has come for? Is he sincere when he later says "And I've always loved you, my angel, as if you were my own son"? Find reasons for your answer from the play. **NCERT**

Ans. At first, Chubukov suspected that Lomov had come to borrow money.

Chubukov was not sincere when he told Lomov that he had always loved him and that he was like his own son, because he had decided to not give any money to Lomov.

If he truly meant what he said he would not have thought of not giving him money. He said so only because Lomov had asked for his daughter's hand in marriage.

2. How does Lomov come to Chubukov's house? For what does he come? How is he received? **CBSE 2012**

Ans. Lomov came to Chubukov's house in the evening dress with gloves on.

Lomov came to propose Chubukov's daughter Natalya for marriage.

Lomov is treated with respect by Chubukov, who also felt happy.

3. How does Chubukov react when Lomov to asked for the hand of his daughter in marriage? **CBSE 2019**

Ans. When Lomov says that he has come to ask for the hand of his daughter in marriage, Chubukov gets excited with joy.

He hugs and kisses Lomov, sheds a tear of joy and calls for God's blessing for Lomov and Natalya.

4. Why did Natalya feel surprised when Lomov paid her a visit to her house? **CBSE 2019**

Ans. Natalya felt surprised when Lomov paid a visit to her house because Lomov was wearing an evening dress-a-dress, jacket and white gloves. Usually one does not visit ones' neighbours in a formal dress.

5. Why did Lomov want to get married?

Ans. Lomov wanted to get married as he was already 35 years old. He felt that now he should lead quiet and peaceful life with a well educated, beautiful Natalya. Moreover, he was suffering from a weak heart and sleep-sickness and wanted company of someone to look after him.

6. When Natalya comes to meet Lomov, she quotes her father's words – "and papa said", "Go; there's a merchant come for his goods." What do you think Chubukov meant? **CBSE Question Bank 2021**

Ans. When Natalya comes to meet Lomov, she quotes her father's words – 'and papa said', "Go; there's a merchant come for his goods." These words of Chubukov represents that Lomov had come to propose marriage with Natalya.

7. What happens to Lomov when he is in an excited state?

Ans. When Lomov is in an excited state, his heartbeat increases, his lips tremble and there is a twitch in his right eyebrow. When he goes to sleep in such a state, something pulls him from his left side and he jumps like a lunatic.

8. "The Lomovs and the Chubukovs have always had the most friendly, and I might almost say the most affectionate, regard for each other." How would you evaluate Lomov and Chubukov's relationship as neighbours?   **CBSE Question Bank 2021**

Ans. The statement that "The Lomovs and the Chubukovs have always had the most friendly, and I might almost say the most affectionate, regard for each other" may seem true at first. Both Lomov and Chubukov have been neighbours for years and for this very reason, Lomov comes to Chubukov's house with a proposal of marrying Natalya.

However, as one moves ahead, the relationship may not be as affectionate as it seems. They constantly quarrel with each other over trivial issues and do not trust each other even a bit. They insult each other, call each other names but still maintain a façade of happy relationship.

9. Describe Oxen Meadows. How were they a source of quarrel between Lomov's and Natalya's family?

Ans. Oxen Meadows is a land wedged between Birchwoods and the Burnt Marsh.
It becomes the source of quarrel between Lomov's and Natalya's family as both of them lay claim over it.

Lomov tries to prove that the Oxen Meadows were given to Natalya's great grandfather's peasants for free use. Because of using it for 40 years, they had started thinking that the Meadows belonged to them while Chubukov's contest (contradict) Lomov's claims.

10. How does Natalya react when she comes to know that Lomov had come to propose her?   **CBSE 2014**

Ans. When Natalya comes to know that Lomov had come there to propose her, she was shocked. She cries, changes her stance and asks her father to bring Lomov back. When he proposed her, she became very happy as she also wanted to marry him.

11. Why do you think Natalya Stepanova asked her father to call Lomov back when she heard that he had come with a proposal?   **CBSE Question Bank 2021**

Ans. Natalya Stepanova asked her father to call Lomov back when she heard that he had come with a proposal because she had secretly loved Lomov. She may have always hoped that Lomov would love her and propose her.

12. To what end does the playwright employ Lomov's palpitations in the play?   **CBSE Question Bank 2021**

Ans. The play 'The proposal' as the name suggests is about Lomov proposing to Natalya for marriage. However, all the characters in the play engage in trivial arguments which delays the purpose of Lomov. Lomov's palpitations, then has been employed by the playwright to meet the purpose of proposal. It is only after Lomov gets unconscious due to his palpitations, that the proposal is made and accepted.

● Long Answer Type Questions

1. Among neighbours we should have cordial relations and not lose our temper. How do Natalya and Lomov lose their temper on trivial issues ?   **CBSE 2018**

Ans. Neighbours must have a cordial relationship which Lomov and Natalya lacked. When Lomov came to Chubukov's house to ask for Natalya's hand in marriage, Chubukov became extremely happy.

When Natalya entered the house, she also talked politely with Lomov. At the moment, when they started talking about a stretch of land called 'Oxen Meadows', they started arguing over its ownership claiming the land to be theirs. Chubukov also started arguing in favour of Natalya and cursed Lomov.

As soon as this argument got over, Lomov and Natalya again started arguing over whose dog was better. These arguments show that they both lost their tempers on trivial issues and forgot about the marriage proposal.

They should have followed the principle of forgive and forget. They should have been courteous to each other. They should not complaint and blame each other for trivial things. They should develop mutual understanding and help each other.

2. The proposal of the marriage was forgotten amidst the arguments over petty things. Which right approach should have been followed by Lomov and Natalya ?   **CBSE 2020**

Ans. Lomov came to Chubukovs to ask Natalya's (his daughter's) hand for marriage. They were neighbours since long and at the right age to marry. When Lomov was about to propose Natalya; they started arguing over a piece of land called Oxen Meadows claiming it to be theirs. Her father also got into the argument and cursed Lomov.

All this while they forgot about the proposal. But when Lomov left, Chubukovs remembered about the proposal and told Natalya about it.

She immediately called Lomov back and then they again started to argue over their dogs. All three of them claimed their dog to be better than others. Again they forgot about the proposal amidst fighting over trivial things.

This would not have happened if they had followed a right approach to talk calmly to each other. Natalya and Lomov should have understood that Oxen Meadows would have belonged to both if they got married to each other.

They should have been polite and patient to each other instead of being rude and stubborn. Oxen Meadows and dogs are pity things to argue over in front of a marriage proposal.

3. Neighbours must have a cordial relationship which Lomov and Natalya do not have. Describe the first fight between them.   **CBSE 2015**

Ans. Neighbours must have a cordial relationship which Lomov and Natalya lack. Lomov comes to his neighbour Chubukov house to ask for his daughter, Natalya's hand in marriage.

When he meets Natalya, it seems that they do share a cordial relationship as both of them talk about Natalya's fields. However, they both soon start quarrelling over the ownership of a piece of land called Oxen Meadows.

The quarrel starts when Lomov calls the Oxen Meadows his own. On hearing this, Natalya objected and claimed that the Oxen Meadows belongs to her family. Lomov even claimed to have the documents that proved that the land was his property.

He also tells Natalya that his aunt's grandmother gave those meadows to her father's grandfather for free use. Now, because the peasants had used the land for forty years, they started thinking it and their own. But Natalya refuses to believe it and insists that they belonged to her family.

This quarrel is even joined by Chubukov, Natalya's father. However, instead of resolving the issue he gets into an argument with Lomov. They even started abusing each other and after some time, Lomov leaves their house. All of these show that they do not share a cordial relations with each other and fight over small issues.

• Extract Based Questions

1. Read the extract to attempt questions that follow.

LOMOV Hear me out, I implore you! The peasants of your father's grandfather, as I have already had the honour of explaining to you, used to bake bricks for my aunt's grandmother. Now my aunt's grandmother, wishing to make them a present.

NATALYA I can't make head or tail of all this about aunts and grandfathers and grandmothers. The Meadows are ours, that's all.

LOMOV Mine.

NATALYA Ours! You can go on proving it for two days on end, you can go and put on fifteen dress jackets, but I tell you they're ours, ours, ours! I don't want anything of yours and I don't want to give anything of mine. So there!

(i) Why were Natalya and Lomov arguing?

(ii) Find the exact word from the extract which means 'to beg someone desperately to do something'.

(iii) What did the peasants of Natalya's father's grandfather do?

(iv) Find out the idiom given in the extract and write its meaning also.

(v) What did Lomov forget in the midst of the argument?

Ans. (i) Natalya and Lomov were arguing over the ownership of Oxen Meadows.

(ii) 'Implore' from the extract means 'to beg someone desperately to do something'.

(iii) The peasants of Natalya's father's grandfather used to bake bricks for Lomov's aunt's grandmother.

(iv) The given idiom is 'can't make head or tails' which means unable to understand anything.

(v) Lomov forgot about marriage proposal for Natalya in the midst of the argument.

2. Read the extract to attempt questions that follow.

"But, please, Stephen Stepanovitch, how can they be yours ? Do be a reasonable man ! My aunt's grandmother gave the Meadows for the temporary and free use of your grandfather's peasants. The peasants used the land for forty years and got accustomed to it as if it was their own, when it happened that ...."

(i) Who is the speaker of the above lines ?

(ii) Why did his aunt's grandmother give the meadows ?

(iii) Why did the peasants treat the land as their own ?

(iv) What light do these lines throw on the speaker's character ?

(v) How does the listener react to the speaker?

Ans. (i) Lomov is the speaker of these lines.

(ii) His aunt's grandmother gave the meadows for the temporary and free use of the peasants employed by Stephan Chubukov's grandfather in return for which they were to make bricks for her.

(iii) The peasants treated the land as their own because they used the land for forty years and got accustomed to using it as their own land.

(iv) These lines tell that speaker is logical, rational and polite.

(v) The listener, Chubukov politely refutes the speakers assertion.

CHAPTER 01

Amanda

—by Robin Klein

In this Chapter...

- Stanzawise Explanation
- Word Meaning
- Chapter Practice

Stanzawise Explanation

Stanza 1

> Don't bite your nails, Amanda!
> Don't hunch your shoulders, Amanda!
> Stop that slouching and sit up straight,
> Amanda!

Word Meanings

Hunch : raise shoulders and bend the upper portion of body in forward position; **Slouching :** sitting in a lazy, drooping way

Explanation In these lines, Amanda, a little girl is being scolded and instructed by her mother for her actions.

Amanda is asked to stop biting her nails. She is also instructed to sit straight without bending her shoulders because her mother wants her to sit in the right posture.

The last word 'Amanda!' is used with an exclamation mark, to shows the irritation and frustration of Amanda's mother.

Stanza 2

> (There is a languid, emerald sea,
> where the sole inhabitant is me—
> a mermaid, drifting blissfully.)

Word Meanings

Languid : reluctant to exert itself; **Mermaid :** an imaginary sea creature having a woman's head and body with a fish's tail instead of legs; **Drifting :** a slow and steady movement

Explanation Amanda is lost in her world of imagination while her mother is instructing her. In her world, she imagines that she is a mermaid who lives alone in the beautiful green sea.

She imagines that as a mermaid she would move in the soft waves of the sea. She believes that as a mermaid, her life would be peaceful and relaxing.

Stanza 3

> Did you finish your homework, Amanda?
> Did you tidy your room, Amanda?
> I thought I told you to clean your shoes,
> Amanda!

Word Meanings

Tidy : arrange neatly and in order

Explanation In these lines, Amanda is being inquired about her work.

Amanda's mother is asking if she has finished her homework and whether she has cleaned her room or not. Amanda is also reminded that she was told to clean her shoes.

Stanza 4

> (I am an orphan, roaming the street.
> I pattern soft dust with my hushed, bare feet.
> The silence is golden, the freedom is sweet.)

Word Meanings

Orphan : a child whose parents are dead; **Roaming :** to move about aimlessly, **Hushed :** very quiet and still

Explanation Again, Amanda is not paying any attention to her mother. Amanda is in her world of imagination. She imagines that she is an orphan child who is freely roaming around on the street.

She has no shoes on her feet and is making patterns on the soft dust with her quiet and bare feet. She is loving the silence and freedom to do anything in her world of imagination.

Stanza 5

Don't eat that chocolate, Amanda!

Remember your acne, Amanda!

Will you please look at me when I'm speaking to you, Amanda!

Word Meanings

Acne : common skin disease characterised by pimples, especially on face

Explanation In these lines, Amanda is instructed by her mother to not eat chocolates. She is reminded that eating chocolates had previously caused her acne. However, as Amanda is lost in her own thoughts, she is not paying attention to her mother. So, her mother strictly asks her to look at her when she is talking to her.

Stanza 6

(I am Rapunzel, I have not a care;

life in a tower is tranquil and rare;

I'll certainly never let down my bright hair!)

Word Meanings

Rapunzel : Rapunzel is the name of a girl in a German fairy tale who was made to live alone in a high tower and had very long, beautiful golden hair. She was held captive by a witch who used to come up to the tower by climbing her long hair; **Tranquil :**free from any trouble or anxiety, to be in a peaceful state of mind.

Explanation Amanda is still in her world of imagination. Now, she dreams of herself as Rapunzel who lived alone in a tower. As Rapunzel, she would not have to worry about anything and her life would be calm and peaceful in the tower. She emphasises that unlike Rapunzel, she would never let her hair down and permit anyone to come to her.

Stanza 7

Stop that sulking at once, Amanda!
You're always so moody, Amanda!
Anyone would think that I nagged at
you, Amanda!

Word Meanings

Sulking : to be upset about something; **Nagged :** to irritate someone by complaining about his or her habits again and again

Explanation In these lines, Amanda is not reacting on her mother's instructions. It seems that she is annoyed due to constant instructions.

Amanda's mother is asking her to stop being upset and moody. Her mother says that her upset behaviour will show everyone that she is disturbed due to her mother's constant instructions.

Chapter Practice

Objective Questions

• Multiple Choice Questions

1. What does the poem 'Amanda' inform us about the speaker?
   (a) Loves giving instructions
   (b) Physical beauty is important
   (c) Wants to control Amanda
   (d) All of the above

Ans. (*d*) The poem informs us that the speaker loves giving instructions, physical beauty is important for her and she tries to control Amanda.

2. Emerald sea means ....
   (a) clear sea
   (b) green sea
   (c) sea filled with emeralds
   (d) None of the above

Ans. (*b*) Emerald sea means green sea.

3. A transferred epithet is a literary device where the modifier or epithet is transferred from the noun it is meant to describe to another noun in the sentence. Based on the given definition of 'transferred epithet', choose the option that lists an example of transferred epithet.
CBSE Question Bank 2021

   (a) soft dust
   (b) hushed (bare) feet
   (c) freedom (is) sweet
   (d) silence (is) golden

Ans. (*b*) Hushed (bare) feet is an example of transfer epithet.

4. Which option completes the popular adage given below? .... silence is gold.
CBSE Question Bank 2021

   (a) Precious are words for
   (b) Speech is silver
   (c) Silver is the tongue
   (d) Ideas may be precious but

Ans. (*b*) Speech is silver silence is gold.

5. Will you please look at me when I'm speaking to you, Amanda!
Read the given lines and tell why is Amanda not looking at the speaker?
   (a) Amanda listening to music
   (b) Amanda is playing
   (c) Amanda is sleeping
   (d) Amanda is lost in her own thoughts

Ans. (*d*) Amanda is not looking at the speaker because she is lost in her own thoughts.

6. What causes acne to Amanda according to the speaker?
   (a) Biting nails   (b) Cleaning the room
   (c) Eating chocolates   (d) Eating pizzas

Ans. (*c*) Eating chocolates cause acne to Amanda.

7. In the poem 'Amanda!', the speaker is so worried about acne. What does it show?
   (a) This shows importance is given to physical beauty.
   (b) This shows her concern towards Amanda.
   (c) This shows Amanda's carelessness.
   (d) Both (a) and (b)

Ans. (*a*) The speaker is worried about the acne. This shows that the speaker gives importance to physical beauty.

8. What do the words tranquil and rare signify?
   (a) Pleasant surrounding   (b) Freedom and peace
   (c) Music and excitement   (d) Peace and no nagging

Ans. (*d*) Tranquil and rare signify peace and nagging.

9. Why has the poet used bracketed lines in the poem 'Amanda'.
   (a) To show they are important.
   (b) To show mother's words
   (c) To show Amanda's imagination.
   (d) To show poet's words.

Ans. (*c*) The poet has used bracketed lines in the poem to show Amanda's imagination.

10. Amanda wants to be Rapunzel because ....
   (a) She wants to have long hair.
   (b) She wants a prince to save her.
   (c) She wants to lead a care free life.
   (d) She wants to be a princes.

Ans. (*c*) Amanda wants to be Rapunzel because she wants to lead a carefree life.

11. What all things did Amanda imagine while her mother was giving her instructions?

1. To be a mermaid
2. To be an orphan
3. to be Rapunzel

(a) Only 1   (b) 1 and 2
(c) 2 and 3   (d) All of these

Ans. (*d*) Amanda imagined being a mermaid, an orphan, Rapunzel while her mother was giving her instructions.

12. When Amanda's mother says, "stop that sulking at once, Amanda!" She means that

(i) Amanda is annoyed by her mother's constant nagging.
(ii) Amanda is ignoring the instructions given by her mother.

(a) (i) is correct (ii) is incorrect
(b) (i) is incorrect (ii) is correct
(c) Both (i) and (ii) are correct
(d) Neither (i) nor (ii is correct

Ans. (*c*) When Amanda's mother says, "Stop that sulking at once, Amanda!" she means that Amanda is annoyed by her mother's constant nagging. She is ignoring the instructions given by her mother.

• Extract Based MCQs

1. Read the extract to attempt the questions that follow.

(I am an orphan, roaming the street.
I pattern soft dust with my hushed, bare feet.
The silence is golden, the freedom is sweet.)

CBSE Question Bank 2021

(i) The tone of the given lines is
(a) analytical   (b) despairing
(c) peaceful   (d) nervous

Ans. (*c*) The tone of the given lines is peaceful.

(ii) Read the statements A and B given below, and choose the option that correctly evaluates these statements.

Statement A The figure 'I' imagines a less than realistic view of being an orphan.

Statement B The figure 'I' does not like the speaker.

(a) A is true, B is false, according to the extract
(b) A is true, B cannot be clearly inferred from the extract.
(c) A cannot be clearly inferred from the extract, B is false.
(d) A is true and can be inferred from the poem, B is true too.

Ans. (*b*) A is true, B cannot be clearly inferred from the extract.

(iii) The golden silence is contrasted with the ....
(a) chaos of the street
(b) constant instructions received
(c) sweetness of freedom
(d) hushed, bare feet

Ans. (*b*) The golden silence is contrasted with the constant instructions received from the smother.

(iv) The rhyme scheme 'aaa' in the above extract is followed in all other stanzas of the poem that are written in parenthesis, i.e. (). Why?

Read the reasons given below, and choose the option that lists the most accurate reasoning.

(1) It shows the simplicity of the child's thoughts.
(2) It reflects the harmony and rhythm of the child's inner world.
(3) It mirrors a child's expression.
(4) It highlights the poet's aesthetic sensibility.

(a) (1) and (4)   (b) (1) and (2)
(c) (2) and (3)   (d) (3) and (4)

Ans. (*c*) Statements (2) and (3) are the possible reasons.

(v) Pick the option that lists the usage of the word 'pattern', as in the extract above.
(a) That is a lovely pattern for a wallpaper.
(b) He decided to wear a patterned shirt to the party.
(c) Poetry is a form of pattern making.
(d) She patterned her hair after her favourite celebrity.

Ans. (*d*) Option (d) is the correct answer.

2. Read the extract to attempt the questions that follow.

Don't bite your nails, Amanda!
Don't hunch your shoulders, Amanda!
Stop that slouching and sit up straight, Amanda!   **CBSE Question Bank 2021**

(i) The purpose of the speaker's words in the given extract is to
(a) show the speaker's power over the listener.
(b) make the listener a better human being.
(c) advise the listener as an elder.
(d) improve the listener's posture and habits.

Ans. (*d*) The purpose of the speaker's words in the given extract is to improve the listener's posture and habits.

(ii) Pick the option that lists the image which correctly corresponds to the speaker's mood in the extract.

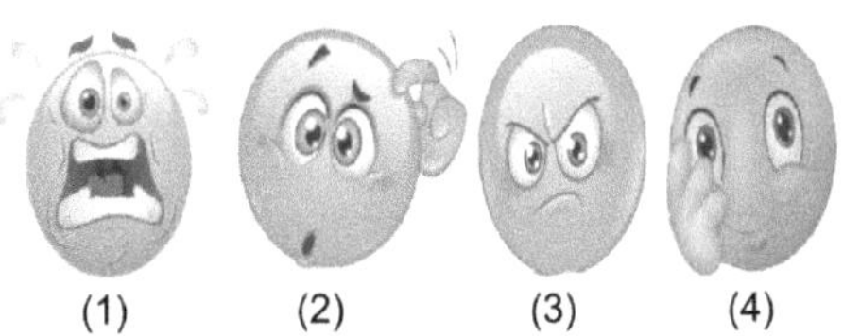

(1)   (2)   (3)   (4)

(a) Image (1)
(b) Image (2)
(c) Image (3)
(d) Image (4)

Ans. (*c*) Image (3)

(iii) Alliteration is a literary device used in the extract. Which of the following options DOES NOT include examples of this literary device?

    (a) The moon and the shimmering stars watched over us

    (b) With that charming chat, Catherine chose comfort

    (c) Away ran the pathetic pooch pouting like a princess

    (d) Dee dee was driving down day after day

Ans. (*a*) Option (a) does not use alliteration.

(iv) What does the repetition of 'Amanda!' at the end of each line reflect?

    (a) It describes who the speaker is talking to.

    (b) It represents the absent-mindedness of the listener.

    (c) It shows the frustration of the speaker.

    (d) It helps create a rhyme scheme.

Ans. (*c*) The repetition of 'Amanda!' at the end of each line reflects the frustration of the speaker.

(v) Select the option that fits with the following:

Slouching : Straight:: .... : ....

    (a) Transparent: Translucent

    (b) Lazy: Agile

    (c) Forgetful: Lively

    (d) Generous: Liberal

Ans. (*b*) Lazy: Agile is the correct answer.

PART 2
Subjective Questions

• Short Answer Type Questions

1. How old do you think Amanda is? How do you know this?   **NCERT**

Ans. Amanda is a little, middle aged (8-12 years) school going girl. We know this because of the reference of a mermaid and Rapunzel. Also, the instructions given to her, for doing homework, nail biting, correcting posture, etc are generally given to children of such an age group.

2. Who do you think is speaking to her?   **NCERT**

Ans. Any one of Amanda's elder's or parents is speaking to her. From the instructions given to Amanda, one can say that it is most probably Amanda's mother or governess.

3. Why are stanzas 2, 4 and 6 given in parenthesis? **NCERT**

Ans. Stanza 2, 4 and 6 are given in parenthesis because they reflect the inner thoughts of Amanda. Amanda is lost in her dream world and is not listening to what her mother is asking/telling her.

4. Who is the speaker in stanzas 2, 4 and 6? Do you think this speaker is listening to the speaker in stanzas 1, 3, 5 and 7?   **NCERT**

Ans. The speaker in stanza 2, 4 and 6 is the child, Amanda.

No, Amanda is not listening to the speaker of stanza 1, 3, 5 and 7, as she is lost in the world of her imagination.

5. What kind of an image does "languid, emerald sea" evoke?   **CBSE Question Bank 2021**

Ans. "Languid, emerald sea" evokes an image of a calm and green sea. 'Languid means moving slowly with little energy, often in an attractive way. 'Emerald' is a green coloured gemstone that refers to the green colour of sea water.

6. What does the girl yearn for? What does this poem tell you about Amanda?   **NCERT**

Ans. The girl Amanda yearns or desires for freedom and peace in life.

According to the poem, Amanda feels that her freedom has been limited by her mother. She is fed up of the constant scolding and instructions by her mother. She wants to go away and live a peaceful life.

7. Why does Amanda wish to be a mermaid, an orphan, or Rapunzel?

Ans. Amanda wishes to be a mermaid, an orphan and Rapunzel to live a life of freedom. She is constantly scolded by her mother. So, she escapes into her own world of imagination wherein she lives a peaceful life, all alone. As a mermaid she would be the sole resident of a beautiful sea and as an orphan, she would enjoy freedom. Finally, as Rapunzel she would live a carefree life.

8. Why does Amanda seem moody most of the time?   **CBSE 2016**

Ans. Amanda seems moody most of the time because she is so involved in her world of imagination that she does not pay attention to her mother. Amanda often escapes from reality into her world of fantasy to get away from the continuous scoldings. Her day dreaming makes her look moody and uninterested.

9. List the things about which Amanda's mother nag her.

Ans. *Amanda's mother nag or scold her about the following things*

• She continuously ask her to sit properly and to not bite her nails.

• Amanda is instructed to not eat chocolates and to clean her room as well as shoes.

• Amanda is also asked to finish her homework.

• Amanda is also pointed out for not paying attention to her mother and for her sulking and moody behaviour.

10. Justify the title of the poem 'Amanda'.

Ans. The title of the poem 'Amanda' is very appropriate. The poem is about a little girl, Amanda who is constantly scolded by her mother. Throughout the poem, the focus is on Amanda and her world of imagination. In this world, she lives a free and peaceful life without any interruptions.

11. Do you think it is Amanda's fault in the poem? Justify your answer.

Ans. No, Amanda is not at fault. In the poem, Amanda is constantly instructed and scolded by her mother. Her mother restricts her freedom. Amanda desires the peace and freedom which is not granted to her. So, she escapes into her own world where she enjoys the calmness.

12. What is the central theme of the poem?

Ans. The central theme of the poem Amanda by Robin Klein is that children love freedom. They do not want any restrictions on their activities. The poem points out that in the endeavour to make their children well-behaved, parents often give too many instructions. Such a scolding behaviour is resented by children and adversely affects their development.

13. Does Amanda's mother have a nagging behaviour. Justify your answer.

Ans. Amanda's mother really have a nagging behaviour. She is always instructing Amanda and finding faults within her. Her mother constantly tell her the do's and don'ts.

Such a nagging behaviour affects Amanda who feels that her freedom is restricted. Amanda's mothers responsibility to instill (develop) good manners in the child makes Amanda retreat (escape) into her imagination where she seeks peace and freedom.

14. Would you call Amanda a disrespectful child? Provide one reason to justify your opinion.
CBSE Question Bank 2021

Ans. Yes, we can call Amanda a disrespectful child because she does not respond to her parent's repeated instructions. She is lost in her imagination and does not even look towards her mother when she is yelling at her.

15. What does the line "never let down my bright hair" tell us about Amanda?

Ans. The line "never let down my bright hair." tell that Amanda does not want anyone to come and disturb her. She wants to live alone in the silence and hates chaos.

16. The reader sympathises with the speaker in the poem. Support this opinion with a reason.
CBSE Question Bank 2021

Ans. The speaker (probably Amanda's mother) is worried about Amanda as she is lost in her thoughts. Amanda does not pay attention to what her mother says and this makes the reader sympathise with her mother.

● Long Answer Type Questions

1. Discuss the importance of proper upbringing with reference to the poem 'Amanda' by Robin Klein.

Ans. Upbringing plays an essential role in personality development of a child. Whenever we wish to admire or criticise someone, we talk about the upbringing of that person. Robin Klein's poem 'Amanda' highlights the problems of 'proper' upbringing of a child. To instil good values and moral principles in a growing child is the foremost duty of the parents. However, the poem shows how a child feels upset because of constant instructions.

Amanda, the little girl in the poem goes through such a situation. She is instructed and scolded for her habits. She gets no freedom and space for herself. As a result, she enters her world of imagination. This world proves to be her defence against her scolding mother. In her world, she seeks freedom and peace. She imagines herself as a mermaid who is the sole resident of a beautiful sea.

Then, she imagines herself as an orphan who is free to do anything. Finally, she wants to be Rapunzel and live a peaceful life in a tower. Therefore, elders/parents must maintain a balance. While instilling good manners, they should also give some freedom to their children.

2. How does Amanda tackle the nagging nature of her mother? Explain with examples from the poem.

Ans. In the poem, 'Amanda', the little girl named Amanda often escapes into her own world. Her world of dreams give her the freedom and peace that she seeks in reality where she is constantly nagged by her elders. Her mother continuously instruct and scold her for her ill-manners and laziness.

She is asked not to bite her nails, not to eat chocolates, to clean her room and so on. As Amanda's mother is giving her instructions, she is lost in her daydreams.

The persistance of Amanda's mother leave a harmful impression in her mind. Her retreat, then, is her way of tackling her mother.

It is her shield and defence against the harsh realities that she goes through. In her reality, her freedom is restricted. Her need for freedom and peace, finds expression in her dreams where she imagines a carefree and happy life as an orphan, mermaid and Rapunzel, without her mother. Amanda may seem moody and upset, to her mother, but is not really so. The nagging nature of her mother makes her escape into a world away from the realities of her life.

3. State the key points in the poem 'Amanda'. What do you learn from it?
CBSE 2016

Ans. The key point highlighted in the poem 'Amanda' is that every child is special in itself and it requires a great amount of patience and love to make them understand this.

To create such an understanding, parents must give freedom to their children as they learn the best from their own experiences. In this process, children may learn some bad habits which needs to be removed. This undoing also requires a great level of understanding and the right approach. Parents judging each action of a child does more harm.

In the poem, the little girl Amanda goes through constant scoldings for her habits. Everything she does is corrected by her mother and she can't do anything at her will. Consequently, the girl seeks/desires freedom and a choice. The lack of freedom makes Amanda upset and moody as she escapes her world of imagination. She enjoys the things in her imagination, which she is deprived of in reality.

Therefore, in Amanda, we witness a failed approach of her parents and get a lesson that the parents need to take a more gentle/kind approach to teach their child.

4. Amanda wants to be a Rapunzel, a beautiful princess living in a tranquil tower. Whrite a character sketch of Amanda in the light of this remark? **CBSE 2020**

Ans. The given statement shows that Amanda yearns for freedom. She was frustrated and irritated by contant nagging of her mother. She always imagined situations and places in which she wished to remain alone.

In one such imagination, she thought of Rapunzel and felt that she must have had a happy life alone in that tower.

She wants to be Rapunzel to live a peaceful life in tower. Her world of dreams give her the freedom and peace that she seeks in reality where she is constantly nagged by her elders.

Amanda did not want to follow the instructions given by her mother and want to live her life on her own terms. This behaviour shows that teenagers do not like to be instructed all the time. They want to take their own decisions and explore the world themselves.

• Extract Based Questions

1. Read the extract to attempt the questions that follow.

(There is a languid, emerald sea,
where the sole inhabitant is me—
a mermaid, drifting blissfully.) **CBSE 2019**

(i) Who does 'me' stand for?
(ii) How does 'me' feel?
(iii) Who is 'me' compared to?
(iv) Which word in the extract means opposite of 'sorrowfully'?
(v) Why does Amanda want to be a mermaid?

Ans. (i) Here, 'me' stands for Amanda.

(ii) 'Me' feels lonely and imagines to bea mermaid who lives alone in a beautiful green sea. She would move in the soft waves of the sea.

(iii) Here, 'me' is compared to a 'mermaid'.

(iv) 'Blissfully' is opposite of sorrowful.

(v) As mermaid sails in a sea carelessly and effortlessly, similarly Amanda longs to do so in a place where she is all by herself.

2. Read the extract to attempt the questions that follow.

Don't eat that chocolate, Amanda!
Remember your acne, Amanda!
Will you please look at me when I'm speaking to you, Amanda! **CBSE 2016**

(i) Why is Amanda not looking at the speaker?
(ii) The speaker is so worried about acne. What does it show?
(iii) Which word in the extract means the same as 'to gaze'?
(iv) Why does the speaker want Amanda to look at her?
(v) Why is Amanda being reminded about her acne?

Ans. (i) Amanda is lost in her own thoughts and is paying no attention to instructions being given to her. That is why she is not looking at the speaker.

(ii) The speaker being worried about acne shows how much importance is given to physical beauty in a household.

(iii) To look continuously means the same as 'to gaze'.

(iv) The speaker wants Amanda to look at her to make sure that Amanda is listening to her and following her instructions.

(v) Eating chocolates causes acne to Amanda, thus, she is being reminded about the same.

3. Read the extract to attempt the questions that follow.

(I am Rapunzel, I have not a care;
life in a tower is tranquil and rare;
I'll certainly never let down my bright hair!)

(i) Does Amanda live on a tower?
(ii) Why will Amanda not let down her bright hair?
(iii) Which poetic device is used in this stanza?
(iv) Find from the stanza a word which means the same as 'serene'.
(v) Why does Amanda want to live like Rapunzel?

Ans. (i) No, Amanda stays at her place. Here, she is imagining herself to be Rapunzel who lived in a tower.

(ii) Amanda is aware about the story of Rapunzel. In the story of Rapunzel, all the mishappening and misfortunes are brought to her by letting down the hair. Amanda also wishes to live alone and carefree, without any disturbance.

(iii) The poet has used allusion here as the underlying poetic device.

(iv) The word 'tranquil' means the same as serene.

(v) Amanda wants to live like Rapunzel because she had a carefree life in the tower, all alone by herself.

CHAPTER 02

Animals

—by Walt Whitman

In this Chapter...

- Stanzawise Explanations
- Word Meaning
- Chapter Practice

Stanzawise Explanations

Stanza 1

I think I could turn and live with animals, they are
so placid and self-contain'd,
I stand and look at them long and long.

Word Meanings

Placid : quiet, calm; **Self-contain'd :** – in full control of self

Explanation In these lines, the poet says that he wants to turn into an animal and live with them. According to the poet the animals are calm, peaceful and self contended. They never complain about any problem. Due to these qualities of animals, the poet stands and looks at them for a very long time.

Stanza 2

They do not sweat and whine about their condition,
They do not lie awake in the dark and weep for their
sins,
They do not make me sick discussing their duty to
God.

Word Meanings

Sweat and whine – to complain/cry; **Sins** – misdeeds

Explanation In these lines, the poet says that animals do not complain and cry about their condition like humans do. Unlike humans, animals do not stay awake in the night and weep for their sins. Further, he says that animals do not make him feel sick by discussing their duties to God.

Stanza 3

Not one is dissatisfied, not one is demented with
the mania of owning things,
Not one kneels to another, nor to his kind that lived
thousands of years ago,
Not one is respectable or unhappy over the whole
earth.

Word Meanings

Demented – affected with madness; **Mania** – obsession;
Owning –possessing; **Kneels** – bends (as a sign of respect)

Explanation In these lines, the poet says that he does not find any animal that may appear to be dissatisfied. There is not single animal who suffers from the obsession of possessing more and more things.

Animals do not show respect or bow their heads to other animals or to their ancestors like humans do. According to the poet, all animals are equal. So for the animals no one is more respectable or unhappy on the earth.

Stanza 4

So they show their relations to me and
I accept them,
They bring me tokens of myself, they evince
them plainly in their possession
I wonder where they get those tokens,
Did I pass that way huge times ago and negligently
drop them?

Word Meanings

Tokens – innate qualities; **Evince** – to show a particular feeling,
quality or attitude; **Possession** – ownership

Explanation In these lines, the poet says that the animals show
their similarities to him which he accepts happily. He feels that
animals represent human beings in some way.

They seem to have innate qualities, that humans once had, i.e.
virtues like kindness, self-containment and innocence. Animals
remind the poet of these qualities that symbolise the lost values of
the humans.

The poet wonders about how animals had got these qualities. The
poet believes that the humans carelessly dropped these virtues a
long time ago and have forgotten all about them in their madness
to possess more things.

Chapter Practice

PART 1

Objective Questions

• Multiple Choice Questions

1. Which of the following options shows the poet's
love towards animals?
(a) He stands and looks at the animals for a very long time.
(b) He admires the animals
(c) He praises their inner qualities
(d) His desire to turn into one of them and live with them

Ans. (*d*) All the given statements show the poet's love towards
animals.

2. The line "They do not sweat and whine about their
condition" means
(a) Animals do not cry for their conditions
(b) They do not blame others for their conditions
(c) They remain happy and accept whatever comes in their
lives
(d) All of the above

Ans. (*d*) The line "They do not sweat and whine about their
condition" means that animals do not cry for their
conditions, they do not blame others for their conditions,
remain happy and accept whatever comes in their lives.

3. The literary device used in the line "I think I could
turn and live with animals" is ....
(a) Simile
(b) Assonance
(c) Metaphor
(d) Alliteration

Ans. (*b*) The literary device used in the line "I think I could
turn and live with animals" is assonance.

4. Name the poetic device used in the following lines:
"They do not sweat and whine about their
condition,
They do not lie awake in the dark and weep for
their sins,
They do not make me sick discussing their duty to
God,"
(a) Anaphora
(b) Assonance
(c) Metaphor
(d) Alliteration

Ans. (*a*) Anaphora is a literary device in which a word or
phrase repeats in the beginning of sentence. Herein,
'They' is repeated.

5. How do human beings make the poet feel sick?
(a) By boasting their welfare works
(b) By discussing their duties
(c) By boasting and discussing their good deed in the
name of God and religion
(d) By discussing their personal lives with him

Ans. (*c*) Human beings make the poet feel sick by boasting and
discussing their good deed in the name of God and
religion.

6. The poet says animals are not dissatisfied.
This means that animals are
(a) unconcerned
(b) satisfied
(c) instinctive
(d) content

Ans. (*d*) The poet believes that animals are content in their
lives with what they have and thus are not concerned
with satisfaction or dissatisfaction.

7. What craze do animals never display?
   (a) Craze of owning things
   (b) Craze of crying over sin in the dark
   (c) Craze of complaining about their situation
   (d) None of the above

Ans. (*a*) Animals never display craze of owning things.

8. "Not one is <u>demented</u> with the mania of owning things" – the underlined word means
   (a) Suffering from dementia   (b) Irrational behaviour
   (c) Suffering from obsessions (d) Both (b) and (c)

Ans. (*b*) The underlined word 'demented' means irrational behaviour.

9. 'Ancestors of human beings shared token of love and understanding in the remote past making them divine and worshipped' – the given line is paraphrase of which line? Choose the correct option.
   (a) They do not sweat and whine about their condition
   (b) Did I pass that way huge times ago and negligently drop them?
   (c) Not one is respectable or unhappy over the whole earth.
   (d) Not one kneels to another, nor to his kind that lived thousands of years ago

Ans. (*d*) The given line is paraphrase of not one kneels to another, nor to his kind that lived thousands of years ago.

10. Choose the option which tells the qualities of animals that humans should adopt from them.
   (a) Animals spend most of their time in sleeping and eating, they show rudeness and ignorance towards each other.
   (b) Animals learn to stand immediately after birth, fighting for one's territory.
   (c) Animals do not idle away their time discussing their duties to God, they show qualities of innocence and simplicity.
   (d) None of the above

Ans. (*c*) The qualities of animals that humans should adopt from them are
   • Animals do not idle away their time discussing their duties to God
   • They show qualities of innocence and simplicity

11. Which qualities have the man taken over 'the token' refered in the poem?
   (a) Materialism   (b) Immorality
   (c) Selfishness   (d) All of these

Ans. (*d*) All of these

12. The last line of the poem is a question. What do you think is its purpose?
   (a) To allow readers to think about it
   (b) To ask listeners about when
   (c) For poetic diction
   (d) To show his thinking nature

Ans. (*a*) To allow readers to think about it

• Extract Based MCQs

1. Read the extract to attempt the questions that follow.

They do not sweat and whine about their condition,
They do not make me sick discussing their duty to God,   **CBSE 2015**

   (i) Why do humans lie awake in the dark?
   (a) Donot feel sleepy   (b) Feel guilty
   (c) Worried   (d) Cry for their sins

Ans. (*d*) Human beings lie awake in the dark to cry for their sins.

   (ii) What does the word 'whine' mean here?
   (a) Pleased   (b) Angry
   (c) High complaining cry   (d) Utter softly

Ans. (*c*) The word 'whine' means high complaining cry.

   (iii) They are referred to ………… here.
   (a) Animals   (b) Human beings
   (c) Small children   (d) Birds

Ans. (*a*) 'They' are referred to animals here.

   (iv) Why does the poet feel sick?
   (a) Human's running after money
   (b) Always complaining
   (c) Always criticising others
   (d) Sermonising themselves

Ans. (*d*) On seeing the people sermonizing themselves, the poet feels sick.

   (v) What is the purpose of the given lines?
   (a) To highlight the importance of moral virtues.
   (b) To compare humans and animals.
   (c) To highlight the virtures possessed by animals.
   (d) To represent nostalgia regarding the good old days.

Ans. (*b*) The purpose of the given lines is to compare humans and animals.

2. Read the extract to attempt the questions that follow.

Not one is dissatisfied,
not one is demented with
the mania of owning things,
Not one kneels to another, nor to his kind thatlived thousands of years ago,
Not one is respectable or unhappy over the whole earth.   **CBSE Question Bank 2021**

   (i) The repetition of 'not one' in the given extract signifies the poet's
   (a) effort to create a sense of continuity.
   (b) attempt at musicality and rhythm.
   (c) sense of disappointment and frustration.
   (d) feelings of anger and vengeance.

Ans. (*c*) The repetition of 'not one' in the given extract signifies the poet's sense of disappointment and frustration.

(ii) Which of the following set of qualities does the poet attribute to animals in the given extract?

   1. Discontented, furious, respectful
   2. Fearless, materialistic, reputable
   3. Contented, equal, non-acquisitive
   4. Happy, self-serving, intelligent

  (a) Option (1)　　　　(b) Option (2)
  (c) Option (3)　　　　(d) Option (4)

Ans. (*c*) The animals are contended, equal and non-acquisitive as per the poet.

(iii) Pick the option that completes the following
Dementia : Demented :: Mania: ....

  (a) Maniac　　　　(b) Manically
  (c) Manical　　　　(d) Maniacal

Ans. (*d*) Dementia: Demented : : Mania : Maniacal.

(iv) Choose the option that contains a statement which CANNOT be conclusively inferred from the extract.

  (a) Man is miserable
  (b) Man is materialistic.
  (c) Man is power-hungry.
  (d) Man is curious.

Ans. (*d*) 'Man is curious' cannot be conclusively inferred from the extract.

(v) Which of the following characterises the poet's attitude towards animals in the given extract?

  (a) Admiration　　　　(b) Nostalgia
  (c) Jealousy　　　　(d) Enthusiasm

Ans. (*a*) The poet admires the animals in the given extract.

PART 2
Subjective Questions

• Short Answer Type Questions

1. Notice the use of the word 'turn' in the first line, "I think I could turn and live with animals...". What is the poet turning from?

Ans. In this line, the poet wants to turn from a human into an animal. This turning represents the poet's desire to get away from the depressing, selfish and false world of humans and stay with animals.

2. Why does the poet wants to turn and live with animals? **CBSE 2018, 2020**

Ans. The poet likes/prefers animals for their calm and self-controlled nature.

He is impressed with animals because unlike human beings, they don't desire to own things and are satisfied with their lives.

The poet wants himself to turn into an animal and live with animals as they have retained the basic good values lost by humans.

3. What is the difference between animals and humans regarding their attitude towards sin and God?

or Why do humans keep awake in the dark and weep for their sins while animals never do such things?

Ans. In the poem, the poet states that animals are simple and innocent creatures who commit no sins. Therefore, they do not have to worry about forgiveness from God. However, humans commit sins of greed, possession etc. As a result, they can't sleep peacefully all night and pray to God for forgiveness.

4. Explain the satisfaction that animals have and humans don't. **CBSE 2014**

Ans. Animals do not have the desire to possess worldly things and thus, are satisfied with what they have. They live happily in their natural surroundings. However, humans desire to own as many things as possible and thus, are dissatisfied forever.

5. Explain "No One kneels to another… Not one is respectable …"

Ans. In the poem 'Animals', "No one kneels to another… Not one is respectable…" refers to the good values possessed by animals.

It states that there is no concept of respect or insult among animals. They are all equal and don't get involved in unnecessary activities and formalities.

6. What is the relevance of 'tokens' in the poem 'Animals'? Who brings them to the poet?

Or Why does the poet say "They bring me tokens of myself"? Who owns those tokens?

Ans. In the poem 'Animals', the poet states the animals bring him/show him 'tokens' of himself. Tokens here refers to the good virtues which includes satisfaction, self-containment, innocence, etc. The poet believes that these virtues were present in both humans and animals but humans have forgotten them. Animals still retain these tokens or virtues and remind the poet about them.

7. What message does the poet Walt Whitman want to give through this poem?

Ans. Through the poem, 'Animals', the poet Walt Whitman wants to convey the message of superiority of animals over humans. In the poem, the poet states that with advancement, humans have forgotten all the nobel virtues. They have degraded themselves while animals still retain those noble virtues. So, they appear to be noble as compared to humans.

8. What is the central idea of the poem, 'Animals' ?
CBSE 2020

Ans. In the poem animals, Walt Whitman frankly tells that he feels more comfortable with animals rather than humans. According to him, humans have become corrupted and had lost all the good values of kindness, equality and peace. Animals have yet retained all the positive values and thus are superior to humans.

9. What vices in human being does Whitman notice?
CBSE 2020

Ans. Whitman notices that human beings have been self-centred and do not respect other beings. They weep for their sins and pray to God to ask for forgiveness. Human beings are dissatisfied with their lives. They suffer from the obsession of possession and want to rule the world.

10. Does Whitman believe that animals and humans are essentially similar? Provide one reason to support your opinion. **CBSE Question Bank 2021**

Ans. Yes, Whitman believes that animals and humans are essentially similar. According to him, humans too possessed the same qualities like calmness, self, restraint etc. Initially that are possessed by animals. However, with the passage of time they have lost them.

11. Calling someone 'an animal' usually has a negative connotation. How does the poet invert it?
CBSE Question Bank 2021

Ans. Calling someone an animal means he/she is uncivilised. The poet inverts this by high lighting the qualities of calmness and self-restraint possessed by animals. By this he brings about the fact that animals are far more civilised than human who are greedy and sinful.

12. Whitman's ode to animals is merely a yearning for a simpler life. Do you agree? Justify your answer.
CBSE Question Bank 2021

Ans. Yes, I agree that to animals is merely a yearning for a simpler life. In the poem 'Animals, Whitman urges man to slowdown and lead a peaceful life. He believes that man's lust for greed is taking a toll on his quality of life.

• Long Answer Type Questions

1. Why do you think the poet has called the desire to own things, as a mania? Is the poet right in doing so? Write your own views.

Ans. In the poem 'Animals', the poet uses the word 'mania' to refer to the never-ending desire of human beings to possess things.

According to the poet, humans desire to possess as many things as possible and thus, never get satisfied. The acquisition of material things is a rat race in which all human beings participate forever.

The more a human gets, the more he/she desires. There is no end to their greed.

Yes, the poet is right in doing so. The greed or desire to possess things drives all humans mad. They madly try to acquire more and more but are never satisfied. So the poet states, animals are better than humans.

They do not have any desire to possess physical things and are happy with what they have. Unlike animals, humans always worry and complain. Thus, the poet is right in calling the desire to own things as a mania.

2. "Human beings are called the most civilised species in the entire world. But sometimes they lack the virtues which are better exhibited by the animals." Elucidate with reference to the poem 'Animals'.

Ans. Human beings are called the most civilised species in the entire world, yet they lack good virtues. Human beings are devoid of virtues of being respectable, happy, self contained and calm. In the poem 'Animals', the poet believes that it is with civilisation that humans have lost their true nature.

They have become selfish, jealous, restless, unhappy and greedy creatures. They always complain about their lives, cry over their sins and discuss their duty to God. They have become false to their true identity.
Unlike humans, animals are peaceful, self-contained, and happy.

They are satisfied with their lives. They do not have the mania of owning things nor do they have the concept of respect or insult. Animals, thus retain all those good virtues that were present even in humans, very long time ago.

3. The key to happiness is 'Do not complain but accept the situation'. Elaborate it in the context of the poem 'Animals'. **CBSE 2015**

Ans. It is true that the key to happiness is 'Do not complain but accept the situation. 'The poet, Walt Whitman in the poem 'Animals' justifies the given statement.

In the poem, animals are compared to human beings to highlight the differences between them. On the basis of their characteristics of happiness, equality, simplicity and many more 'tokens', animals have been ranked much superior and nobler to humans.

The poet explains his belief by stating that animals are simple creatures who never complain about their situations. They have accepted their natural surroundings and thus, are happy and satisfied with their lives.

Humans, on the other hand, have never accepted nature. They are always complaining about it and so, try to change it. Thus, they lead an unhappy life. The ever increasing expectations of human beings and their demanding, greedy and selfish nature leads to their unhappiness.

4. Imagine that Walt Whitman and Nelson Mandela are invited to engage in a discussion on the topic - 'Man's Journey – Vices, Virtues and Vision'.

Based on your reading of 'Animals' and 'Nelson Mandela: Long Walk to Freedom', present the similarities and differences in their viewpoints and vision of human beings in the form of a conversation.

Or Nelson Mandela is more hopeful about human kind than Walt Whitman. Do you agree? Support your opinion based on your reading of 'Animals' and 'Nelson Mandela: Long Walk to Freedom'.

CBSE Question Bank 2021

Ans. Nelson Mandela's 'Long Walk to Freedom' talks about the value of freedom. He states that a human being who has not enjoyed freedom know its value better than one who is free. He believed that the oppressed and the oppressor both were equally to be blamed. Nelson Mandela believed in the power of humans to unite and fight against evils like social and racial discrimination.

Walt Whitman in the poem 'Animals' says that human beings are inferior to animals as they no longer possess the qualities of contentment, kindness etc. that they possessed once. he states that they are not free creatures as they are bound by greed, over-ambition, arrogance, etc.

He wants to leave the human world and take refuge in the animal kingdom as animals still possess the noble qualities. So, we can say that Walt Whitman is less hopeful about human kind than Nelson Mandela.

• Extract Based Questions

1. Read the extract to attempt the questions that follow.

I. I think I could turn and live with animals, they are so placid and self-contain'd,

I stand and look at them long and long.

(i) What does the poet want to turn into?

(ii) Which qualities of animals attract the poet?

(iii) Which word is similar to the word 'calm'?

(iv) Explain the successive use of the word 'long' twice and bring out its significance.

(v) Why does the poet want to live with animals?

Ans. (i) The poet wants to turn into an animal.

(ii) The poet is attracted to the calmness and poise of the animals.

(iii) The word 'placid' is similar to the word 'calm'.

(iv) The successive use of the word 'long' makes the line significant; the first 'long' denotes 'time' whereas the other, 'a desire'.

(v) The poet wants to live with animals because they are calm and self-contained.

2. Read the extract to attempt the questions that follow.

They do not sweat and whine about their condition,

They do not lie awake in the dark and weep for their sins,

They do not make me sick discussing their duty to God,

(i) Why do humans lie awake in the dark?

(ii) What do humans do about their condition?

(iii) What does the phrase 'make me sick' mean?

(iv) Find a word from the stanza that is an antonym of 'Thanking'.

(v) How do human beings make the poet feel sick?

Ans. (i) Humans lie awake in the dark weeping for their sins.

(ii) They regret and cry about their condition.

(iii) The phrase means to make someone feel angry or upset.

(iv) The word 'whine' is an antonym of 'Thanking'.

(v) Human beings make the poet feel sick by discussing their good deeds done I the name of God.

3. Read the extract to attempt questions that follow.

So they show their relations to me and I accept them,

They bring me tokens of myself, they evince them plainly in their possession

I wonder where they get those tokens,

Did I pass that way huge times ago and negligently drop them? **CBSE 2019**

(i) Explain the line: "They bring me tokens of myself".

(ii) What does the poet accept?

(iii) What similarities does the poet find between the human beings and the animals?

(iv) What does the poet wonder about?

(v) Which poetic device is used in the line – "I wonder where they get those tokens"?

Ans. (i) The poet here means that the animals remind him of true values of the human nature such as love and understanding.

(ii) The poet accepts the bonding with animals and their love.

(iii) The poet finds that animals have virtues of truthfulness, kindness, and innocence just like human beings. However, human beings have long lost these virtues.

(iv) The poet wonders if the animals got their virtues from humans when they dropped them for their greed and selfishness.

(v) Alliteration is used in the given line.

CHAPTER 03

The Tale of Custard the Dragon

—by Ogden Nash

In this Chapter...

- Stanzawise Explanations
- Word Meaning
- Chapter Practice

Stanzawise Explanations

Stanza 1

Belinda lived in a little white house,
With a little black kitten and a little grey mouse,
And a little yellow dog and a little red wagon,
And a realio, trulio, little pet dragon.

Word Meaning

Wagon : a carriage, a cart; **Realio :** really; **Trulio** – truly.

Explanation Belinda lived in a little white house with her four pets – a little black kitten, a little grey mouse, a little yellow dog, and a little dragon. She also had a little red wagon. In the last line of the stanza, 'realio' and 'trulio' are used by the poet as an expression for the little dragon meaning 'really' and 'truly respectively.

Stanza 2

Now the name of the little black kitten was Ink,
And the little grey mouse, she called him Blink,
And the little yellow dog was sharp as Mustard,
But the dragon was a coward, and she called him Custard.

Explanation The name of the little black kitten was Ink and the name of the little grey mouse was Blink. The name of the little dog was Mustard because its colour was sharp yellow just like that of mustard. The dragon was a coward whom Belinda called Custard.

Stanza 3

Custard the dragon had big sharp teeth,
And spikes on top of him and scales underneath,
Mouth like a fireplace, chimney for a nose,
And realio, trulio, daggers on his toes.

Word Meaning

Spikes : a thin pointed structures on the body; **Scales :** small hard flat pieces of skin on the bodies of animals; **Fireplace :** the place where fire is burnt to keep the house warm; **Chimney :** a long pipe that opens on the roof to let out the smoke released from the fireplace; **Dagger :** small sword

Explanation Custard, the dragon has big sharp teeth, spikes on his top and scales on his stomach. His mouth has been compared to a fireplace because dragons can release fire from their mouth. His nose is compared to a chimney from which smoke comes out. His toes are so pointed and sharp that they could cut anything like a dagger.

Stanza 4

Belinda was as brave as a barrel full of bears,
And Ink and Blink chased lions down the stairs,
Mustard was as brave as a tiger in a rage,
But Custard cried for a nice safe cage.

Word Meaning

barrel : drum (usually used for keeping liquids); **rage :** anger

Explanation In these lines, the poet compares the bravery of all the characters of the poem.

Belinda's bravery has been compared to the bravery of a group of bears. Ink and Blink, despite being so small in size, have the power to chase away lions down the stairs. Mustard's bravery has been compared with that of an angry tiger. But, Custard is completely opposite to all of them. He was a coward who always demanded a safe cage.

Stanza 5

Belinda tickled him, she tickled him unmerciful,
Ink, Blink and Mustard, they rudely called him Percival,
They all sat laughing in the little red wagon
At the realio, trulio, cowardly dragon.

Word Meaning

Tickle : to touch (a body part) lightly to cause laughter;
Percival : a warrior in king Arthur's court;

Explanation Belinda used to tickle Custard cruelly. Ink, Blink and Mustard made fun of Custard by comparing him to Percival. Percival was one of the best knights of King Arthur's court who was known for his courage and bravery. All of them sat together in the little red wagon and made fun of Custard. They used to laugh at his cowardice.

Stanza 6

Belinda giggled till she shook the house,
And Blink said Weeck!, which is giggling for a mouse,
Ink and Mustard rudely asked his age,
When Custard cried for a nice safe cage.

Word Meaning

Giggling : laughing

Explanation Belinda laughed a lot at the dragon. She laughed so hard that it seemed that the house was shaking due to her laughter. Blink, the mouse used to laugh and make a sound of 'Weeck'. Ink and Mustard rudely asked the dragon's age to make fun of him, while the dragon cried for a nice safe cage for himself.

Stanza 7

Suddenly, suddenly they heard a nasty sound,
And Mustard growled, and they all looked around.
Meowch! cried Ink, and Ooh! cried Belinda,
For there was a pirate, climbing in the winda.

Word Meaning

Nasty : unpleasant; **Growled :** the sound by animals; **Pirate :** dacoit, robber; **Winda :** window

Explanation While all of them were busy making fun of the dragon, they heard an unpleasant sound in the house. Mustard, the dog started growling and they all looked around. Ink cried 'Meowch' and Belinda cried 'Ooh' as they saw a pirate climbing the window of the house.

Stanza 8

Pistol in his left hand, pistol in his right,
And he held in his teeth a cutlass bright,
His beard was black, one leg was wood;
It was clear that the pirate meant no good.

Word Meaning

Cutlass : a small sword with a slightly curved blade

Explanation The appearance of the pirate seemed very dangerous. He was carrying pistols in both hands and he was carrying a small sword between his teeth. He had black beard and

his one leg was of wood. His looks made it very clear to the housemates that the pirate meant to harm the people and pets living there.

Stanza 9

Belinda paled, and she cried, Help! Help!
But Mustard fled with a terrified yelp,
Ink trickled down to the bottom of the household,
And little mouse Blink strategically mouseholed.

Word Meaning

Paled : became pale yellow due to fear; **Yelp :** cry; **Trickled :** stepped down; **Mouseholed :** holes made by a mouse (it is not a word but has been made into a word to fit the rhyming scheme)

Explanation Belinda became pale with fear after seeing the pirate and cried for help. All her brave pets could not help her and everyone ran away from there. Mustard made a huge cry and ran away. Ink ran down towards the bottom of the house and Blink very smartly ran into his hole.

Stanza 10

But up jumped Custard, snorting like an engine,
Clashed his tail like irons in a dungeon,
With a clatter and a clank and a jangling squirm
He went at the pirate like a robin at a worm.

Word Meaning

Snorting : huge sound made through nose; **Clashed :** striked; **Dungeon :** an underground prison; **Clatter and a clank and a jangling :** sounds of two metals striking; **Squirm :** to move in a twisted manner; **Robin :** a bird.

Explanation When everyone ran away on seeing the pirate, it was the coward dragon, Custard, who came to rescue Belinda and fought the pirate bravely.

He jumped in front of the pirate and made a loud snorting sound through his nose like an engine. He started to move his tail powerfully producing a sound like iron or metals striking in a dungeon (prison). With all these dangerous sounds, he followed the pirate like a bird follows a worm.

Stanza 11

The pirate gaped at Belinda's dragon,
And gulped some grog from his pocket flagon,
He fired two bullets but they didn't hit,
And Custard gobbled him, every bit.

Word Meaning

Gaped : stared with mouth wide open;
Gulped : swallowed; **Grog :** wine;
Flagon : a container made of silver in which drink is stored;
Gobbled : swallowed

Explanation The pirate was shocked by the dragon's reaction. He stared at Belinda's dragon with his mouth open.

He drank some wine from a container that he carried in his pocket. The pirate then took out his pistol and fired two bullets at Custard. But, he failed to hit him. Finally, Custard ate the pirate.

Stanza 12

Belinda embraced him, Mustard licked him,
No one mourned for his pirate victim
Ink and Blink in glee did gyrate
Around the dragon that ate the pirate.

Word Meaning

Embrace : to hug; **Licked :** to touch with tongue;
Mourned – to grieve; **Glee :** happiness;
Gyrate : make circular movements.

Explanation Everyone celebrated the death of the pirate. Belinda hugged Custard and Mustard licked him affectionally.
No one felt sorrow for the pirate's death. Ink and Blink started dancing in joy around the dragon who had eaten the pirate.

Stanza 13

But presently up spoke little dog Mustard,
I'd have been twice as brave if I hadn't been flustered.
And up spoke Ink and up spoke Blink,
We'd have been three times as brave, we think,
And Custard said, I quite agree
That everybody is braver than me

Word Meaning

Flustered : got nervous

Explanation The incident clarifies who is coward and who is brave. Mustard said that he would have been twice as brave as Custard if he had not been panicked. After this, Ink and Blink said that they would have been thrice as brave as Custard. Custard agreed and said that everybody was braver than him.

Stanza 14-15

Belinda still lives in her little white house, with her
little black kitten and her little grey mouse,
And her little yellow dog and her little red wagon,
And her realio, trulio little pet dragon.
Belinda is as brave as a barrel full of bears,
And Ink and Blink chase lions down the stairs,
Mustard is as brave as a tiger in a rage,
But Custard keeps crying for a nice safe cage.

Explanation Stanza 14 and 15 are an almost repetition of Stanza 1 and 4. There is only one difference that stanza 1 and 4 present the condition of the housemates in the past and stanza 14 and 15 present their condition after the pirate incident. The situation has not changed at all. Everything has gone back to normal with Belinda and her three 'brave' pets making fun of the "coward", pet dragon.

Chapter Practice

Objective Questions

• Multiple Choice Questions

1. The Tale of Custard the Dragon poem narrating a story in short stanzas is called a/ an ....
(a) free verse
(b) ballad
(c) lyric
(d) epic

Ans. (*b*) A poem or song narrating a story in short stanzas is called a ballad.

2. Name the poetic device used in the line "And the little yellow dog was sharp as mustard."
(a) Oxymoron
(b) Metaphor
(c) Assonance
(d) Simile

Ans. (*d*) The poetic device used is simile.

3. .... was sarcastically compared to the brave knight Percival.
(a) Ink
(b) Blink
(c) Belinda
(d) Custard

Ans. (*d*) Custard was sarcastically compared to the brave knight Percival.

4. A cage means captivity. Why is Custard inclined to remain in a cage despite what it symbolises?

This is so because he viewed it as a

CBSE Question Bank 2021

  (i) sanctuary
  (ii) guardhouse
(iii) cubicle
(iv) refuge
 (v) booth
(a) (i), (ii) and (v)
(b) (i) and (iv)
(c) (iii), (iv) and (v)
(d) (iii) and (v)

Ans. (*b*) Custard viewed cage as a sanctuary and refuge.

5. What is the theme of the poem "The Tale of Custard the Dragon"?
 1. Appearance vs reality
 2. Hypocrisy
 3. Courage
 4. Jealousy
(a) Only 4
(b) 2 and 3
(c) 1, 2 and 4
(d) All of these

Ans. (*d*) Appearance vs reality, hypocrisy, courage and jealousy are the themes of the poem.

6. Pick an option that best fits the usage of the word' trickled' as used in the line. Ink trickled down to the bottom of the household. **CBSE Question Bank 2021**
(a) The water trickled down the tap and filled the trough.
(b) Students trickled into the classroom as the teacher entered.
(c) Tears trickled down her cheeks as she heard the sad news.
(d) His enthusiasm for the task slowly trickled away.

Ans. (*b*) Option (b) is the correct answer.

7. "And he held in his teeth a cutlass bright" what is a cutlass?
(a) A short sword with a curved blade
(b) A big hammer
(c) A short axe
(d) A very sharp bladed saw

Ans. (*a*) A cutlass is a short sword with a curved blade.

8. 'He went at the pirate like a robin at a worm. Why has this comparison been used here? Just like the robin catches the worm, **CBSE Question Bank 2021**
(a) Custard attacked the pirate after careful observation.
(b) Custard attacked the pirate without delay.
(c) Custard attacked the pirate valourously.
(d) Custard attacked the pirate stealthily.

Ans. (*b*) Just like the Robin catches the worm, Custard attacked the pirate without delay.

9. "The pirate gaped at Belinda's dragon" means that
(a) the pirate was looking at the dragon
(b) the pirate was shocked to see such a big dragon
(c) the pirate got scared on seeing the dragon
(d) None of the above

Ans. (*b*) "The pirate gaped at Belinda's dragon" means that the pirate was shocked to see such a big dragon.

10. What did the pirate do to prepare himself for the fight?
(a) Gulped some liquor
(b) Had some breath
(c) Shouted a war cry
(d) Made up his mind

Ans. (*a*) The pirate gulped some liquor to prepare himself for the fight.

11. "Belinda is as brave as <u>a barrel full of bears</u>" what does the underlined phrase mean?
(a) A person without fear of what may happen
(b) A barrel which contains bears inside
(c) A group of bears
(d) None of the above

Ans. (*a*) A barrel full of bears means a person without fear of what may happen.

12. Pick the option with the correct matches for columns A and B.　　　**CBSE Question Bank 2021**

	Column A		Column B
A.	Chuckle	1.	To smile in a half- suppressed mocking way
B.	Snigger	2.	To smile in an irritating, conceited manner.
C.	Smirk	3.	To let out a quiet and suppressed laugh.
D.		4.	To let out a laugh heartily and loudly

(a) A-4, B-1, C-3
(b) A-3, B-1, C-2
(c) A-2, B-4, C-3
(d) A-1, B-3, D-4

Ans. (*b*) 3 1 2 is the correct matching sequence.

• Extract Based MCQs

1. Read the extract to attempt the questions that follow.

Belinda giggled till she shook the house,

And Blink said Weeck! which is giggling for a mouse,

Ink and Mustard rudely asked his age,

When Custard cried for a nice safe cage.

Suddenly, suddenly they heard a nasty sound,

And Mustard growled, and they all looked around.
　　　　　　　CBSE Question Bank 2021

(i) What can you infer from the repetition 'suddenly, suddenly' in the above extract?
(a) There was an immediate change in the scene.
(b) It focuses on the hasty attack and the loud noise.
(c) It emphasises that an unexpected noise was heard.
(d) It draws our attention to the loud cry that occurred.

Ans. (*c*) The repetition of the word 'suddenly' emphasises that an unexpected noise was heard.

(ii) Why has the poet used the word 'weeck' to signify the giggling of the mouse? The poet
(a) uses it to add suspense in the poem.
(b) has imagined how the mouse would sound in this mood.
(c) has mocked at the mouse for giggling at Custard.
(d) uses it to create a scary effect for readers.

Ans. (*b*) The poet has imagined how the mouse would sound in the mood described in the given extract.

(iii) Select a word from the extract to complete the following.

Whimper : Giggle : : Purr : ………
(a) Weeck　　　　　　　(b) Heard
(c) Shook　　　　　　　(d) Growl

Ans. (*d*) Whimper : Giggle : : Purr : Growl. This is because whimper is the antonym of giggle and so do purr and growl.

(iv) Which belief about dragons is in contrast to Custard's behaviour in the extract?
(a) Dragons are brave and feared.
(b) Dragons can grant wishes.
(c) Dragons can become invisible at will.
(d) Dragons are soft-hearted and kind.

Ans. (*a*) Dragons are brave and feared, but, in the poem, Custard, the dragon is described as a coward.

(v) A hyperbole is a literary device where the poet/writer/speaker purposely and obviously exaggerates to an extreme.

Choose the option that includes an example of hyperbole, from the extract.
(a) And Mustard growled, and they all looked around
(b) Ink and Mustard rudely asked his age,
(c) Belinda giggled till she shook the house,
(d) When Custard cried for a nice safe cage.

Ans. (*c*) Belinda giggled till she shook the house is an example of hyperbole.

2. Read the extract to attempt the questions that follow.

"Ink trickled down to the bottom of the household,

And little mouse Blink strategically mouseholed.

But up jumped Custard, snorting like an engine,

Clashed his tail like irons in a dungeon,

With a clatter and a clank and a jangling squirm,

He went at the pirate like a robin at a worm"
　　　　　　　CBSE Question Bank 2021

(i) Which option lists the quotes that support the ideas in the extract?
　1. Fear makes strangers of people who would be friends.
　2. If you're brave enough to start, you're strong enough to finish.
　3. Courage doesn't mean you don't get afraid. Courage means you don't let fear stop you.
　4. You get in life what you have the courage to ask for.
　5. Fear has a large shadow, but he himself is small.
(a) 1 and 5
(b) 2, 3 and 4
(c) 2 and 3
(d) 1, 3 and 5

Ans. (*d*) Quotes 1, 3 and 5 support the ideas in the extract.

(ii) What is the poet's purpose of using the onomatopoeia words given in the extract?

    (a) It is to emphasise on the might and boldness of Custard.

    (b) It is to introduce the character Custard to the readers.

    (c) It is to impress upon the readers that Custard was ready.

    (d) It is to make Custard bold enough to face the situation.

Ans. (*a*) The poet used onomatopoeia words to emphasise on the might and boldness of Custard.

(iii) Select the option that fits with the reaction of the characters in the context of the extract.

    Ink: terrified : : Blink : i) .... Pirate: ii) ....:: Custard: undaunted

    (a) (i) shocked (ii) displeased   (b) (i) petrified (ii) wondered

    (c) (i) upset (ii) dazed   (d) (i) petrified (ii) shocked

Ans. (*d*) Blink was terrified, Pirate was shocked and Custard was undaunted.

(iv) Pick the option that does not display a simile from the extract.

    (a) Clashed his tail like irons…

    (b) …at the pirate like a robin at a worm.

    (c) …custard, snorting like an engine…

    (d) …trickled down to the bottom…

Ans. (*d*) "Trickled down to the bottom" does not have simile.

(v) The extract mentions 'irons' in dungeons. According to this extract, 'irons' is a reference to

    (a) iron racks for scared books.

    (b) iron cases housing treasures.

    (c) iron chains holding the prisoners captive.

    (d) iron coffins for burying the royal dead.

Ans. (*c*) The 'irons' in the extracts refer to iron chains holding the prisoners captive.

PART 2

Subjective Questions

• Short Answer Type Questions

1. Where did Belinda live and with whom?

Ans. Belinda lived in a little white house with her four pets and a red wagon. She had a black kitten named Ink, a grey mouse named Blink, a yellow dog named Mustard and a coward dragon named Custard.

2. What did Custard look like?   **CBSE 2016**

Ans. Stanza three of the poem 'The Tale of Custard the Dragon' describes the physical appearance of the dragon. Custard, the dragon has big sharp teeth. He has spikes on top and scales underneath him. His mouth is like a fireplace and his nose is like a chimney. He has daggers on his toes.

3. Did Custard match his physical appearance?

Ans. No, Custard did not match his appearance, as he looked dangerous but actually he was a coward. He always cried for a nice and safe cage, while everyone laughed at him for his cowardice.

4. Why did Custard cry for a nice safe cage? Why is the dragon called 'cowardly dragon'?

Ans. Custard cried for an nice safe cage because he was a 'coward' who wanted peace and safety.

He is called a 'cowardly dragon' because apart from him, all other pets are described as very brave. Belinda is as brave as a big group of bears, Ink and Blink can chase lions and Mustard is like an angry tiger.

Compared to all of them, the dragon demanded nice safe cage so it is called 'Cowardly dragon'.

5. Why was Custard, the dragon teased as Percival?

Ans. Custard, the dragon is teased as Percival by Ink, Blink and Mustard for his timidity.

They teased him as Percival because unlike Custard, he was a courageous and brave knight of King Arthur. Custard on the other hand, was meek (submissive) and always cried for a nice safe cage.

6. What did everyone do when the pirate came?

Ans. When the pirate came, Belinda cried for help and became pale with fear.

Mustard ran away with a terrified cry and Ink hid himself in the bottom of the house, while Blink disappeared in his hole. It was only Custard who jumped in front of the pirate to fight him and showed the courage to face the pirate.

7. How did Custard face the pirate?

Ans. When the pirate came in Belinda's house, all of her pets except Custard hid themselves. Custard jumped infront of the pirate to fight him. He even clashed his tail. During this fight, the pirate shot two bullets at him which missed its aim. Finally, Custard ate him and left no trace of him.

8. Were Belinda and her pets grateful to Custard for killing the pirate? How did Custard react to their reactions?

Ans. Yes, Belinda and her pets were grateful to Custard for killing the pirate, but it was only temporary. Soon after expressing gratitude, Mustard, Ink and Blink started giving excuses for their cowardice and things went back to normal, as it was before the pirate incident. Custard, the dragon reacted in a humble manner and accepted that all other pets are braver than him.

9. Was everyone really as brave as they claimed?

Ans. Belinda and her three pets, excluding Custard, were very proud of their bravery but, they were not really brave. It was only Custard, who had the courage to face the pirate and fight him. So, among all, only Custard was brave.

10. The poet has employed many poetic devices in the poem. For example "Clashed his tail like iron in a dungeon" — the poetic device here is a simile. Can you, with your partner, list some more such poetic devices used in the poem? **NCERT**

Ans. In the poem, 'The Tale of Custard, the Dragon', the poet has used a lot of poetic devices. Following are some of the devices used

(i) **Simile** Mouth like a fireplace.

(ii) **Repetition** The repetitive use of the word 'little' in stanza 1.

(iii) **Onomatopoeia** Use of sound words such as 'weeck' and 'meowch'.

(iv) **Metaphor** Use of comparison such as 'Nose for a Chimney'.

11. How did Custard accept his cowardice and others bravery? **CBSE 2020**

Ans. Custard accepted his cowardice by asking for safe cage and accepted other's bravery when they boasted of how brave they could be infront of the pirate.

But, in real, Custard was the bravest of all because he was the one who killed the pirate and saved everyone in the house. However, he chose to be humble and modest instead of boasting about himself.

12. Custard humbly accepts that other animals are braver than him. Give a reason to support your stance that humility is a virtue worth possessing. **CBSE Question Bank 2021**

Ans. Custard humbly accepts that other animals are braver than him because humility is a virtue worth possessing because it helps us in not placing too much importance to our achievements. It also allows us to accept our vulnerabilities.

13. The usage of words like 'realio trulio' creates a wonderful poetic effect. How?

Ans. The words 'realio trulio' create a wonderful poetic effect by making the poem interesting to read. In actual there are no such words as 'realio' and 'trulio'. They actually mean 'really' and 'truly', respectively.

14. Why is it fair to say that Custard could be the 'poster-boy' for the belief that the real nature of a person is revealed at times of the greatest difficulty? **CBSE Question Bank 2021**

Ans. Custard could be the perfect poster-boy for the belief that the real nature of a person is revealed at times of the greatest difficulty. This is because Custard showed his true courageous nature when he fought fiercely with the pirate. He was considered as cowardly by his house mates before this incident.

15. State the reason you think the poet named the animals Ink, Blink, Mustard and Custard?

Ans. The poet named the animals Ink, Blink, Mustard and Custard to make the poem interesting to read and to maintain the rhyming scheme of the poem. Mustard was named so because he was yellow in colour.

• Long Answer Type Questions

1. The dragon, Custard was considered a coward. The humble dragon proved his bravery in adversity. Analyse that certain qualities like bravery and courage are situational and spontaneous. Express your views with reference to the poem, "The Tale of Custard, the dragon".

Ans. It is true that bravery and courage are situational and spontaneous. This fact has been aptly conveyed in the poem "The Tale of Custard the Dragon". wherein the dragon was considered a coward. He was laughed at for crying for a nice safe cage. He never boasted of his bravery and courage, unlike Belinda and her other pets do.

Everyone else, including Belinda, Ink, Blink and Mustard claim to be brave. They even made fun of Custard's cowardice.However, when the time to show their courage came, none of them could face the danger.

They hid themselves in some corner of the house. It was only Custard who dared to face the frightening pirate. He not only fought the pirate but also ate him up. It was a dangerous situation to which Custard spontaneously responded. His courage and bravery came out in a threatening situation. Hence, it is true that qualities like courage and bravery are situational and spontaneous.

2. Do you think that one should be made fun of because of their preferences and choices in life? Explain in the context of Custard, the dragon.

Ans. According to me, one should never make fun of anyone on the basis of their lifestyle and their choices.

One must always remember that choices and preference can depend on unexplanable factors.

In the poem 'The Tale of Custard the Dragon', Custard makes one such choice of wishing for a 'nice safe cage'. He prefers comfort and safety. However, Belinda and her other pets always laugh at him.

They think of him as a coward for choosing to stay in cage and make fun of him. Custard, the dragon soon proved that his choice of comfort doesn't make him a coward. Infact, instead of all the 'brave' pets of Belinda, it was Custard who fought the pirate. It was Custard who showed courage to face the pirate and kill him.

Therefore, one must never judge anyone for choice. Appearance may be deceptive. Just like the dragon who appeared to be a coward but was actually courageous, another person might also be different from what show him/her to be his/her preferences.

3. Do you find 'The Tale of Custard the Dragon' to be a serious or a light-hearted poem? Give reasons to support your answer. **NCERT**

Ans. 'The Tale of Custard the dragon' is a very light hearted funny poem that is meant to be enjoyed by everyone. The fixed rhyme scheme and the use of wrong spelling to maintains and it, makes it easy and enjoyable to read. Even the names of the pets are rhyming and evokes laughter.

The description of Belinda and her pets makes the poem entertaining. Belinda's bravery is described as equal to a group of bears. The smallest of her pets, her kitten Ink and mouse Blink have been shown so brave that they can scare a lion.

The dog Mustard is like an angry tiger. But the biggest of them all, the dragon is nice and cowardly. He is always crying for a safe cage. In addition, the reactions of these characters to the dangerous pirate, also makes it funny.

• Extract Based Questions

1. Read the extract to attempt the questions that follow.

Now the name of the little black kitten was Ink,

And the little gray mouse, she called her Blink,

And the little yellow dog was sharp as Mustard,

But the dragon was a coward, and she called him Custard. **CBSE 2019**

(i) Name the poem and the poet.

(ii) What is the colour of Belinda's dog?

(iii) What were the kitten and the mouse called?

(iv) Which word in the stanza is an antonym of 'dull'.

(v) Name the poetic device used in the line – "And the little yellow dog was sharp as Mustard".

Ans. (i) The name of the poem is 'The Tale of Custard the Dragon' and the name of the poet is Ogden Nash.

(ii) Belinda's dog is yellow as mustard.

(iii) The kitten is called Ink and the mouse is called Blink by Belinda.

(iv) The word sharp is the correct antonym of dull.

(v) Simile is used in the line – "And the little yellow dog was sharp as Mustard".

2. Read the extract to attempt the questions that follow.

Belinda was as brave as a barrel full of bears,

And Ink and Blink chased lions down the stairs,

Mustard was as brave as a tiger in a rage,

But Custard cried for a nice safe cage.

(i) How brave were the kitten and the mouse?

(ii) Why did Custard cry for a nice safe cage?

(iii) Which word is similar to 'anger'?

(iv) Which figure of speech has been used in the first and the third line of the stanza.

(v) Why was the dragon called the cowardly dragon?

Ans. (i) The kitten and the mouse were so brave that they could scare away lions.

(ii) Custard cried for a nice safe cage because he was a coward.

(iii) The word is 'rage'.

(iv) Figure of speech used in first and third line is 'Simile'.

(v) The dragon was called cowardly dragon because in spite of having immense strengths and potential , he always cried for a nice safe cage.

3. Read the extract to attempt the questions that follow.

Belinda tickled him, she tickled him unmerciful,

Ink, Blink and Mustard, they rudely called him Percival,

They all sat laughing in the little red wagon

At the realio, trulio, cowardly dragon. **CBSE 2018**

(i) Who was tickled by Belinda?

(ii) Why did she tickle 'him'?

(iii) Who are Ink, Blink and Mustard?

(iv) Why did they all laugh at 'him'?

(v) What does realio, trulio mean?

Ans. (i) Custard, the dragon, was tickled by Belinda.

(ii) She tickled him to tease and make fun of him.

(iii) Ink is a little black kitten, Blink is a grey mouse and Mustard is a little yellow dog. They all are Belinda's pets.

(iv) They are laughed at him because they all thought him to be a coward.

(v) Realio, trulio actually means really and truly. The words have been changed by the poet so as to give rhythm to the poem.

CHAPTER 01

The Making of a Scientist

—by Robert W Peterson

In this Chapter...

- Chapter Summary
- Word Meaning
- Chapter Practice

Chapter Summary

Richard's Success at Young Age

Richard HEbright and his college roommate were the first college students to get their article published in the 'Proceedings of the National Academy of Science'.

Richard was only 22 when he and his roommate explained the theory of how cells work. This achievement is one of the many that Richard got in the field of science.

Richard's Childhood

Richard lived in Pennsylvania, USA and was the only child of his parents. As there was no one to play football or baseball with him, he developed a habit of collecting things such as rocks, fossils and coins. He also took interest in astronomy and loved to gaze the stars all night.

Richard's Mother : His True Companion

Richard lost his father when he was in third grade so his mother was his only companion. His mother encouraged his interest in learning.

She took him on trips and bought him telescopes, microscopes, cameras, mounting materials and many other equipments. She also supported him in his hobbies and invited his friends to play with him.

Even when Richard didn't have things to do, she found work for him. She supported his driving curiosity, bright mind and his desire to learn. As result, Richard earned top grades in school.

Richard Reads 'The Travels of Monarch X' Book

Richard was deeply interested in butterflies since his early childhood. When he was in second grade, he had collected all 25 species of butterflies found around his hometown. He had gotten bored of collecting butterflies. But his mother gifted him the book 'The Travels of Monarch X.' The book opened up a new world of science for Richard.

Tagging Butterflies for Research

At the end of the book, Richard found an invitation for studying the migration of butterflies. Readers were told to tag butterflies for research by Dr. Frederick A Urquhart of University of Toronto, Canada.

After his mother wrote to Dr. Urquhart, Richard started tagging butterflies. However, soon he started raising them. He caught a female monarch and took her eggs. As the butterflies grew, he tagged their wings and freed them. For many years, this process was continued and his basement was a home to butterflies. Soon, his interest was lost because he did not receive much feedback.

Richard's Entry in the County Science Fair

Richard was in seventh grade when he got to know, what true science is. At the county science fair, everyone else won awards except him. It was then that he realised that all other had done real experiment while he had just show a neat slide of frog tissues. The failure filled Ebright with competitive spirit.

Richard's Eighth Grade Project

For his next project, he wrote to Dr. Urquhart for ideas and recieved many suggestions. Soon, Richard achieved his first success.

In Richard's eighth grade project, he had tried to find the cause of a viral disease that kills monarch caterpillars. Richard thought that the disease might be carried by a beetle. He tried raising caterpillars in presence of beetles but he failed. However, he won a prize in the county fair.

Richard's Next Project on Viceroy Butterflies

Richard's next project was testing the theory that viceroy butterflies copy monarch butterflies. Viceroys butterflies do so to protect themselves from birds as birds don't like to eat monarchs while they like to eat Viceroys.

He found that a bird Starling would only eat monarch butterflies and not ordinary bird food. That project was placed first in the zoology division and third in overall county science fair.

Richard's Discovery of a Hormone

In his second year of high school, Richard discovered an unknown insect hormone which also led to his new theory on the cell life. The purpose of the original project was to know the reason behind the twelve tiny gold spots on monarch's pupa.

Richard along with another science student built a device which showed that the spots were producing a hormone necessary for the butterfly's full development. That project won Richard first place in county science fair and entry into the International Science and Engineering Fair. There he won third place for zoology and also got a chance to work at the entomology laboratory of the Walter Reed Army Institute of Research.

Richard Continues his Research on Monarch Pupa

As a high school junior, Richard continued his advanced research on the monarch's pupa. He won first prize at International Science Fair that year. In his senior year, he grew cells from monarch's wing in a culture.

He showed that the cells would develop into normal butterfly wings scales only when they were fed the hormones produced by the gold spots. This experiment got him first prize in zoology at the international fair. Throughout, he continued working in the army laboratory and he also got a chance to work at the laboratory of US department of agriculture.

Richard's Study of Cell and DNA

Richard joined Harvard University where he continued his research on the gold sports. There using the advanced technology at department of Agriculture, he could identify the hormone's chemical structure.

In his junior years he got the idea of his new theory about cell life while looking at the X-ray photos of chemical structure of a hormone. He believed that his study could tell how the cell can read the blueprint of its DNA.

Richard and his college room-mate James R. Wong worked all night constructing the plastic models of molecules showing how it could happen. Later, they together wrote a paper explaining their theory.

Highest Honours in Harvard

Richard graduated with second position in a class of 1510 students. He became a graduate student researcher at Harvard Medical School where he started experimenting to prove his new theory. If his theory is correct it can lead to new ways of preventing some types of cancer and other diseases.

Richard: An all Rounder

Richard was not just a scientist. He was an all rounder. He was a champion debator and a public speaker. He was also a good canoeist and an outdoor person. He was also a great photographer.

In his high school, he was a part of the Debating and the Model United Nations Clubs. There, he found Richard A Weiherer, his social studies professor and advisor to both clubs, whom he admired a lot.

Richard : A True Scientist

Mr. Weiherer praised Richard for his hard work. He also praised Richard's healthy competitiveness which was just for the sake of doing his best. Richard had all the qualities that made him a true scientist. He had a first rate mind, curiosity and a will to win for all the right reasons.

Word Meaning

The given page nos. correspond to the pages in the prescribed textbook.

Word	Meaning
Page 32	
scout	a member of the scout association
journal	a newspaper or magazine that deals with a particular subject
making the big leagues	becoming part of a successful or important group
Page 33	
variegated	having patches, stripes or marks of different colours
crescent	a shape that is curved, wide at its center and pointed at its two ends like a crescent moon
species	a group of animals or plants that are similar and can produce young animals or plants

Word	Meaning
fritillary	a butterfly with orange-brown wings that are chequered with black
Page 34	
adhesive	able to stick fast to a surface or object; sticky
monarch and viceroy	types of butterflies found in North America
tedious	boring and too slow or long
Page 35	
stack	large number
starling	a dark brown or black bird that is common in Europe and the US
zoology	the branch of science that involves the study of animals and animal behaviour

Word	Meaning
Page 36	
hormone	a natural substance that is produced in the body and that influences the way in which body grows or develops
pupa	an insect that is in the stage of development between larva and adult
entomology	a branch of science that deals with the study of insects
culture	the growing of cells in a specially prepared nutrient medium
eureka	a cry of joy when one discovers something
blueprint	a design plan
Page 37	
canoeist	person paddling a canoe
sake	for the purpose of

Chapter Practice

Objective Questions

• Multiple Chocie Questions

1. Richard Ebright published his cell theory in ....
(a) Proceedings of the National Academy of Science
(b) Proceedings of the National Academe Sciences
(c) Minutes of the National Academy of Science
(d) Minutes of the International Journal of Science

Ans. (*a*) Richard Ebright published his cell theory in the Proceedings of the National Academy of Science.

2. Why could Richard not play football or baseball?
(a) Because he didn't know how to play.
(b) Because he didn't want to play.
(c) Because his mother didn't allow him to play.
(d) Because he had nobody to team up with.

Ans. (*d*) Richard could not play football or baseball because he had nobody to team up with.

3. "I was his only companion until he started school." Who said this in the context of 'The Making of a Scientist'?
(a) Richard E. Bright   (b) Richard's mother
(c) Dr. Urquhart   (d) James R. Wong

Ans. (*b*) The given dialogue was said by Richard's mother.

4. Among the butterflies that Ebright captured in his hometown, which were not a part of the list?
(a) Bog Copper   (b) Red Admiral
(c) Pearl Crescent   (d) Olympia

Ans. (*b*) Among the butterflies that Ebright captured in his hometown, 'Red Admiral' were not a part of the list.

5. The book 'The Travels of Monarch X' told how monarch butterflies migrate to ....
(a) Northern America
(b) Canada
(c) Central America
(d) Pennsylvania

Ans. (*c*) The book 'The Travels of Monarch X' told how monarch butterflies migrate to Central America.

6. Which project won Ebright first prize in the county fair?
(a) Device that showed the golden spots on monarch were producing a hormone necessary for the butterfly's full development.
(b) How the cell can read the blueprint of its DNA.
(c) Discovery of unknown insect hormone.
(d) All of the above

Ans. (*a*) Device that showed the golden spots on monarch were producing a hormone necessary for the butterfly's full development, won Ebright first prize in the county fair.

7. Which entomology lab did Richard get the opportunity to work at?
(a) Walter Reed Army Institute of Research
(b) Model United Nations Club
(c) Army Laboratory
(d) U.S. Department of Agriculture

Ans. (*a*) Richard got the opportunity to work at Walter Reed Army Institute of Research.

8. Which experiments did Richard continue as a high school junior?
(a) Experiments on Cells
(b) Experiments on DNA
(c) Experiments on Monarch pupa
(d) Experiments on Viceroy butterflies

Ans. (*c*) Experiments on Monarch pupa were continued by Richard as a high school junior.

9. DNA is the substance in the nucleus of a cell that controls ....
(a) Blueprint   (b) Information
(c) Heredity   (d) Identity

Ans. (*c*) DNA is the substance in the nucleus of a cell that controls heredity.

10. Mr. Weiherer said, "For the right reasons he wants to be the best." What did he mean by the given statement?
A. Richard was not interested in winning prizes.
B. Richard did not want to win the first prize for the sake of winning.
C. Richard wanted to do his best job for the welfare of people.
(a) Only A   (b) A and B
(c) B and C   (d) None of these

Ans. (*c*) Mr. Weiherer meant by the given statement that Richard did not want to win the first prize for the sake of winning but he wanted to do his best job for the welfare of people.

11. Who was Richard's Social Studies teacher?

(a) Mr. Weiherer   (b) Dr. Urquhart
(c) James R. Wong   (d) None of these

Ans. (*a*) Mr. Weiherer was Richard's Social Studies teacher.

12. Arrange the achievements of Richard Ebright from 'The Making of a Scientist'.

(i) Tried to discover the disease caused by a virus that nearly killed most of the monarch caterpillars every year.
(ii) Started his scientific research about the discovery of a mysterious insect hormone.
(iii) His brand-new theory on the life of cells took place.
(iv) Tried to find the main purpose of the twelve tiny golden spots on a monarch pupa.
(v) Got an opportunity to work at the entomology lab in Walter Reed Army Institute of Research.

(a) (i), (ii), (iii), (iv) and (v)   (b) (iv), (iii), (v), (ii) and (i)
(b) (v), (ii), (iii), (i) and (iv)   (d) (iv), (v), (ii), (iii) and (i)

Ans. (*a*) (i), (ii), (iii), (iv) and (v) is the correct matching sequence.

13. Which other qualities than being a scientist did Richard possessed?

(i) Debater   (ii) Photographer
(iii) Public Speaker   (iv) Cannoeist

(a) (i), (ii) and (iii)
(b) (ii), (iii) and (iv)
(c) (i), (iii) and (iv)
(d) (i), (ii), (iii) and (iv)

Ans. (*d*) Richard was all rounder. Other than being a scientist, he was a photographer, debater, canoeist and a public speaker.

14. What is the conclusion of the story 'The Making of a Scientist'?

(a) We should be perseverant
(b) We should be dedicated towards our work
(c) Anyone can become a scientist
(d) Both (a) and (b)

Ans. (*d*) The conclusion of the story is that we should be perseverant and dedicated towards our work.

15. Select the correct option for (i) and (ii).

(i) Richard's mother motivated him and his scientific curiosity.
(ii) Richard was a graduate from Harvard Medical School.

(a) (i) is the result of (ii)
(b) (i) and (ii) are independent of each other
(c) (ii) is the result of (i)
(d) (i) is true (ii) is false

Ans. (*b*) Statements (i) and (ii) are independent of each other.

● **Extract Based MCQs**

1. Read the extract to attempt the questions that follow.

"I didn't get any real results," he said. "But I went ahead and showed that I had tried the experiment. This time I won." The next year his science fair project was testing the theory that viceroy butterflies copy monarchs. The theory was that viceroys look like monarchs because monarchs don't taste good to birds.

Viceroys, on the other hand, do taste good to birds. So, the more they look like monarchs, the less likely they are to become a bird's dinner. Ebright's project was to see whether, in fact, birds would eat monarchs. He found that a starling would not eat ordinary bird food. It would eat all the monarchs it could get.   **CBSE Question Bank 2021**

(i) Choose the option listing Ebright's qualities as depicted by the above extract.

1. Persevering   2. Visionary
3. Determined   4. Liberal
5. Conceited

(a) 1, 2   (b) 3, 5
(c) 1, 3   (d) 4, 5

Ans. (*c*) As per the given extract, Ebright was preserving and determined.

(ii) According to the dictionary, 'fair' as a noun, shows the following meanings. Choose the option that lists the meaning similar to the usage to that in the extract.

(a) A gathering of stalls and amusements for public entertainment.
(b) A competitive exhibition showcasing products or ideas.
(c) A periodic gathering for the sale of goods.
(d) An annual exhibition of livestock, agricultural products, etc., held by a town, county, or state.

Ans. (*b*) Option (b) lists the similar meaning to fair as it is used in the extract.

(iii) Choose the option that is true for the two statements given about the information in the extract.

Statement 1 Starling feeds on viceroys.

Statement 2 Starling does not eat seeds and insects.

Codes
(a) Both statements are clearly mentioned in the extract.
(b) Statement 1 cannot be clearly inferred from the text and statement 2 is true.
(c) Statement 1 is false and statement 2 cannot be clearly inferred from the extract.
(d) Both the statements need to be inferred from the given extract.

Ans. (*c*) Statement 1 is false and statement 2 cannot be clearly inferred from the extract.

(iv) Choose the statements that are TRUE for the given extract contextually.
1. Ebright didn't get any results for the experiment he conducted on butterflies.
2. Monarchs tasted awfully to the birds.
3. Ebright wanted to explore the possibility of monarchs getting eaten by birds.
4. He wanted to prove that viceroys are look alikes of monarchs.

(a) 1, 2   (b) 2,
(c) 1, 3   (d) 2, 4

Ans. (*b*) Statements 2 and 3 are true.

(v) Four friends bring their pets to a pet show. Choose the option that mentions the friend with a starling as a pet.

Friend 1 has a turtle named Missy.
Friend 2 has a dragonfly named Majesty.
Friend 3 has a rabbit named Molly.
Friend 4 has a bird named Mitch.

(a) Friend 1   (b) Friend 2
(c) Friend 3   (d) Friend 4

Ans. (*d*) Friend 4

2. Read the extract to attempt the questions that follow.

Surprising no one who knew him, Richard Ebright graduated from Harvard with highest honours, second in his class of 1510. Ebright went on to become a graduate student researcher at Harvard Medical School. There he began doing experiments to test his theory. If the theory proves correct, it will be a big step towards understanding the processes of life. It might also lead to new ideas for preventing some types of cancer and other diseases. All of this is possible because of Ebright's scientific curiosity. His high school research into the purpose of the spots on a monarch pupa eventually led him to his theory about cell life.

(i) Which theory is being talked about in the above extract?
(a) Ebright's theory of gold spots on monarch's pupa
(b) Ebright's theory of cell life
(c) Ebright's theory about insect hormone
(d) Ebright's theory about viceroys and monarchs

Ans. (*b*) Ebright's theory of cell life is being talked about in the given extract.

(ii) "All this is possible because of Ebright's scientific curiosity" suggests that
(a) One can discover many things in life.
(b) Ebright was an intelligent man.
(c) Curiosity to know more leads to important discoveries.
(d) Scientific curiosity was required to make Ebright world famous.

Ans. (*c*) "All this is possible because of Ebright's scientific curiosity" suggests that curiosity to know more leads to important discoveries.

(iii) How might his theory benefit the world?
(a) By providing new ideas for preventing some types of cancer and other diseases.
(b) By providing information about DNA.
(c) By providing information about monarch butterflies.
(d) By providing information about viceroy butterflies.

Ans. (*a*) His theory might benefit the world by providing new ideas for preventing some types of cancer and other diseases.

(iv) How did Rechard Ebright graduate?
(a) With highest honours   (b) As second in a class of 1510
(c) From Harvard University   (d) All of the above

Ans. (*d*) Richard Ebright graduated from Harvard University with highest honours, second in his class of 1510.

(v) Why was no one surprised at Ebrights graduation?
(a) Because everyone knew Ebright would do so.
(b) Because Ebright had already acheved fame.
(c) Because every believed in Ebright.
(d) Because Ebright was intelligent.

Ans. (*a*) No one was surprised at Ebright's graduation because everyone knew Ebright would do so.

PART 2
Subjective Questions

• Short Answer Type Questions

1. What rare achievement did Richard manage at the age of twenty-two?

Ans. Richard had a rare achievement at the age of twenty-two. He wrote an article with his friend about a theory of how cells work. The article was published in the scientific journal 'Proceedings of the National Academy of Science.' It was the first time that this journal had ever published the work of college students.

2. Richard became a collector at an early age. How?

Ans. Richard was the only child of his parents. He had no company at home to play with. So, he started collecting things in his spare time. He would collect coins, fossils, rocks and butterflies as a hobby. In this way, Richard became a collector at an early age.

3. Why did Ebright lose interest in tagging bufferflies?
CBSE 2020

Ans. Richard raised thousands of butterflies, tagged them and released them to study their migration. But soon, he lost interest because only two of his tagged butterflies were recaptured and they had travelled only seventy-five miles.

4. How dsid Ebright's mother help him in becoming a scientist? **CBSE 2019, 2020**

Ans. Richard Ebright's mother helped him in becoming a scientist by encouraging his interest in learning.

She took him on trips and bought scientific equipment for him. She spent all her time in setting up challenges for him. This helped Richard to learn a lot. She presented him the book 'The Travels of Monarch X'. The book changed Richard's life forever.

5. How did the book become a turning point in Richard Ebright's life?

Ans. The book 'The Travels of Monarch X' became a turning point in Richard Ebright's life as after reading it, he became interested in studying the migration of butterflies. It opened the world of science for Richard.

6. What lesson did Ebright learn when he entered the county science fair in the seventh garde? **CBSE 2020**

Ans. When Ebright entered the county science fair he learnt what science was all about. He learnt that science was not a neat and tidy display of tissues on a slide. It was about the real experiments that were performed to get some real results.

7. What experiments and projects does Richard undertake? **NCERT**

Ans. Richard Ebright undertook many projects and experiments. His first project was to prove that a beetle carries a viral disease that kills monarch caterpillars.

Then, he tried to prove that viceroy butterflies copy monarchs. Later, he studied the twelve golden spots on monarch pupa and discovered a new hormone. Also, he found out how cells read their DNA.

8. Who was Dr. Frederick A Urquhart? Why did Richard Ebright look to him for fresh ideas?

Ans. Dr. Frederick A Urquhart was a scientist and teacher at the University of Toronto, Canada. He was doing research on butterfly migrations. Ebright sent him many tagged butterflies for his research work.

Richard looked to him for fresh ideas and suggestions because the suggestions sent by Dr. Urquhart helped in shaping Ebright's career as a scientist.

9. Why do viceroy butterflies copy the monarch butterflies?

Ans. Birds eat viceroy butterflies because they taste good to them, whereas monarch butterflies do not. So, the viceroys try to copy the monarchs to protect themselves from the birds.

10. Mention any two of Ebright's contributions to the world of science. **CBSE 2011**

Ans. The two contributions of Ebright to the world of science were

- Ebright built a device that showed that the spots on monarch butterflies wings produce a hormone that is necessary for the growth of the butterfly.
- His other important contribution was his study of how cells read their DNA.

11. In addition to science, what were the other interests of Richard?

Ans. Apart from science, Richard was a good debater and a public speaker as well as a canoeist and an outdoor person. He also loved photography and likes to collect different kinds of things and butterflies.

12. Mr Weiherer pays a glowing tribute to Richard. What did he say?

Ans. Mr Weiherer was Ebright's social studies teacher and the advisor to the clubs that Richard Ebright had joined. He praised him for his brilliant mind, his curiosity and a will to win for the right reason. He also admired Richard for his spirit to do his best all the time.

13. Hobbies play a very important role in one's life. Elaborate this with reference to 'The Making of a Scientist'. **CBSE 2016**

Ans. It is true that hobbies play a very important role in one's life. It was Richard Ebright's hobbies that led him into the field of science.

His hobbies were encouraged by his mother who always motivated him to learn new things.

Further, it is because of his hobbies that he became a curious all rounder, always ready to participate in things that he loved to do.

14. How can one become a scientist, an economist, a historian …? Does it simply involve reading many books on the subject? Does it involve observing, thinking and doing experiments? **NCERT**

Ans. Reading of books is important for becoming a scientist, an economist and a historian.

However, it is not enough. Apart from the knowledge gained from books, one must be able to think independently.

Yes, one also requires a keen interest in observing, thinking and doing experiments and gain as much practical knowledge as possible to be successful in their fields.

15. Do you think Richard's mother was too indulgent when she bought him things like cameras, telescopes, microscopes? Give two reasons to support your answer. **CBSE Question Bank 2021**

Ans. I don't think that Richard's mother was too indulgent when she bought him things like cameras, telescopes, etc. due to the following reasons

(a) She knew that Richard was highly curious and had a bright mind.

(b) He wanted to learn things. Thus, Richard's mother was justified in providing him the appropriate equipment to help him in the process.

16. Suggest two ways by which you feel scientific temperament can be developed in a child.
CBSE Question Bank 2021

Ans. Scientific temperament is all about questioning. It can be developed in a child in the following ways

(a) By encouraging him/her to ask questions rather than making him/her accept somethingblindly.

(b) Logical thinking is another way to develop scientific temperament in children.

● Long Answer Type Questions

1. Richard's mother had a great influence on him. Discuss.

or Discuss the role of Ebright's mother in making him a scientist.
CBSE 2011, 2019

Ans. Richard's mother played a huge role in making him a great scientist. She would take him on trips to encourage learning. He was a single child. After his father died, his mother made him the focus of her life.

She would buy him all kinds of microscopes, telescopes and other equipments. After dinner, she gave him problems to solve. This helped Richard to learn a lot.

She was his only companion for a long time. She always tried to give him work that required no physical labour but those which enhanced his learning skill.

It was his mother who got him the book 'The Travels of Monarch X'. This book opened the world of science for Richard. She also wrote to Dr Urquhart to guide her son. The scientist helped Richard and guided him. Thus, his mother shaped him into an extraordinary scientist.

2. Richard Ebright displayed a well-rounded personality. Do you agree? Elucidate in the context of the given text.
CBSE 2016

Ans. Richard Ebright displayed a well-rounded personality from his childhood. His genius was obvious by the time he was in second grade. He not only collected butterflies but also collected rocks, fossils and coins. He had managed to collect all the twenty-five species of butterflies that were found in his hometown and had classified them. Science was not his only passion. He was an active member of his school's debating club and Model United Nations Clubs and was also an effective debator and public speaker.

He was an enthusiastic canoeist and an all-round outdoor person with a keen interest in photography. Because of his interest and hobbies, it was simple for him to devote time and energy to many other interests.

He was a champion, not because of his desire to win for the sake of winnings but for attempting to do his best. All of these qualities make him a well-rounded personality.

3. How did Ebright use determination and perseverance to achieve him aim of becoming a scientist?
CBSE 2019

Ans. Richard Ebright had been a curious child since he was in kindergarten. His curiosity prompted him to collect rocks, fossils, coins and butterflies. His mother's encouragement and his bright mind also contributed to making him a successful scientist.

His mother got him all that he needed to develop his scientific bent of mind. His response to Dr Fredrick A. Urquhart to collect butterflies for his research gave him an opportunity in his endeavours.

Then in the seventh grade, he got a hint of what real science is when he entered a country science fair and lost. He realised that winners had tried to do real experiments, not simply made a neat display.

Thereafter, Ebright worked sincerely on every science project he got every year in school. Then he stood first in a county fair that gave him entry into international science and engineering fair where he won third place. He then went on to win the highest honours and graduated from Harvard.

His High School research into the purpose of the spots on a monarch pupa eventually led him to his theory about cell life and DNA. He never lost his perseverance and determination and thus always kept on moving in life keeping all his failures aside and thus, he became a renowned scientist.

4. 'Richard Ebright had all the ingredients required for the making of a scientist." Elaborate
CBSE 2019

Ans. Ebright was a keen observer and a hardworking child. He was sharp-minded and had great curiosity. He started working when he was very young, i.e. in kindergarten. He collected all 25 species of butterflies found around his hometown by the time he was in second grade. He raised a flock of butterflies and tagged them to help Dr. Fredrick to study their migration.

In the seventh grade, when he lost in county science fair he learnt that actual science was about real experiments which give results. His competitive spirit derived him to perform real experiments. In his high school, he led to the discovery of new theory on the life of cells.

With his perseverance, dedication and continuous hard work to achieve his aim, he could determine that DNA is the blueprint for life. This discovery helped him to become a renowned scientist all over the world.

Thus, Richard Ebright had all the ingredients required for the making of a scientist-analytical mind, providing ideas through experiment, a strong will to win and work for the benefits of others.

5. Give a brief character sketch of Ebrights mother.

CBSE 2020

Ans. Richard H Ebright's mother was a gentle and kind lady who encouraged and inspired Ebright's interest in learning. It was she who laid the foundation of his success as a scientist. After her husband's death, her son, who was studying in the third grade, became her life. She encouraged her son's keen interest in learning. She understood that her son had a curious and a bright mind.

She recognised his son's scientific temper, so she made sure that her son had everything that he needed. She took him on trips and bought him telescopes, microscopes, cameras, mounting material and all other equipments.

She was his only companion before Richard started going to school. When Richard's school started it was she who encouraged him to make friends. She would invite his friends to their house. She would sit with him at night.

Even when Richard did not have any work to do, his mother made sure that she finds something to engage her son. It was she who got him the book "The Travels of Monarch X" and opened the world of science for him.

She knew that her son had a passion and did all things possible to fulfill them. This support, guidance, care and concern of Ebright's mother made him into the prodigal and successful scientist.

• Extract Based Questions

1. Read the extract to attempt the questions that follow.

So he did, and did he ever! Beginning in kindergarten, Ebright collected butterflies with same determination that has marked all his activities. He also collected rocks, fossils and coins. He became an eager astronomer, too, sometimes star-gazing all night. From the first he had a driving curiosity along with a bright mind. He also had a mother who encouraged his interest in learning. She took him on trips, bought him telescopes, microscopes, cameras, mounting materials and other equipment and helped him in many other ways.

(i) What does 'he did' in the extract refer to?

(ii) What else did he collect other than butterflies?

(iii) Find a word from the extract which means 'resoluteness'.

(iv) How did Richard's mother encourage his interest in learning?

(v) How did Richard develop an interest in collecting things?

Ans. (i) 'He did' refers to Richard's habit of collecting various things.

(ii) He collected fossils, coins and rocks other than butterflies.

(iii) 'Determination' is a word from the extract which means 'resoluteness'.

(iv) Richard's mother encouraged his interest in learning. She took him on trips, bought him telescopes, microscopes, cameras, mounting materials and other equipment.

(v) Since, Richard had no one to play with, he developed a habit of collecting things.

2. Read the extract to attempt the questions that follow.

So the next step for Ebright was to raise a flock of butterflies. He would catch a female monarch, take her eggs and raise them in his basement through their life cycle, from egg to caterpillar to pupa to adult butterfly. Then he would tag the butterflies' wings and let them go. For several years his basement was home to thousands of monarchs in different stages of development.

(i) Why did Ebright raise butterflies?

(ii) Find the word which has the same meaning as the word 'rear' from the extract given above.

(iii) Why did Ebright lose interest in tagging butterflies?

(iv) Why was he tagging butterflies?

(v) Whom did he have to send the tagged butterflies to?

Ans. (i) Ebright raised butterflies as it was difficult to catch many butterflies one by one.

(ii) 'Raise' is the similar meaning word as 'rear' from the extract.

(iii) Ebright lost interest in tagging butterflies because he didn't get much feedback and it was a tedious work.

(iv) He was tagging butterflies to study their migration pattern.

(v) He had to send the tagged butterflies to Dr. Urquhart.

CHAPTER 02

The Necklace

—by Guy De Maupassant

In this Chapter...

- Chapter Summary
- Word Meaning
- Chapter Practice

Chapter Summary

Matilda Loisel and her Unhappiness

Matilda Liosel was a pretty married lady who had high ambitions. She wished to be wealthy and dreamt of a marvellous life. However, she was born into a family of clerks. She was also married to a clerk, M Liosel who worked in the office of Board of Education.

Matilda believed that she was born for a life of luxury. She always used to dream of elegant dinners, fine crockery, beautiful frocks and delicious dishes.

However, her reality was poverty and this made her miserable. She was always dissatisfied with her life and envied her rich friend.

M Loisel brings an Invitation

One evening Matilda's husband, M Loisel returned from his office with a large envelope. The envelope consisted of an invitation to a ball (party) at the Minister's residence. M Loisel thought that his wife would be happy to read the invitation but Matilda threw the invite away in anger.

When her husband informed Matilda of his intention, she spitefully told him that she does not have a fancy dress to wear to the ball. She even refuses her husband's idea of a dress she has and asks him to give the invite to a colleague.

New Dress was Bought

After realising Matilda's distress, her husband M. Loisel told her that she could buy a new dress. He gave 400 francs that he had saved to buy a gun, to Matilda so that she could buy a new dress.

Matilda was still Unhappy

Matilda bought a new dress but she was still unhappy. When her husband asked about the reason of her unhappiness, Matilda told him that she did not have any jewellery to wear with her dress. Her husband suggested natural flowers.

But Matilda was not convinced and replied that she would look shabby among the rich women. Finally, her husband advised her that she should go to Mme Forestier, her rich friend to borrow her jewellery.

Matilda Gets Necklace from Mme Forestier

Next day, Matilda went to her friend's house. She told Mme Forestier her problem. So, Mme Forestier brought her jewel case and asked Matilda to make her choice. Matilda tried various pieces of jewellery but ultimately decided to borrow a diamond necklace.

Matilda at the Night of Ball

The night of the ball arrived and Matilda looked very beautiful. Everyone liked her and she was the centre of attraction. She danced with great enthusiasm and happiness. At 4 am, they hired an old carriage and returned home.

The Necklace was Lost

When Matilda returned home and was changing her dress, she wanted to have a final view of herself before the mirror. Suddenly, she noticed that the necklace was not around her neck. She cried out and informed her husband about the same.

Her husband searched for the necklace everywhere they went last night. He went to the police and the cab offices. He also put an advertisement in the newspapers offering reward, but the necklace was not found. So he advised his wife to write a letter to her friend telling her that the clasp of the necklace was broken and she needed some time to get the necklace repaired.

Matilda Replaces the Necklace

At last, Matilda and her husband decided to replace the necklace. They searched for a similar necklace everywhere and found it in a shop at Palais Royal.

The necklace cost them 36000 Francs. Her husband gave his 18000 francs which his father had left for him. He also took loans of the remaining amount and purchased a diamond necklace. Finally, Matilda returned the necklace to her friend.

Life of Poverty

After replacing the necklace, Matilda and her husband lived in poverty. They sent away the maid, changed their lodgings and rented some rooms in an attic. Matilda had to do all the household work. She started dressing simply and even went to get her grocery.

Her husband worked day and night. He spent his evening putting the books of some merchants and did some copying at night. Finally, they were able to pay off their debt after ten years.

Matilda had Changed

After ten years, Matilda had changed. She had became an old, strong and hard woman. Her hair was nessy, her skirts were uneven, her hands were red and she used to speak in a loud tone. She also often wondered of the life she would have lived is she had not lost the necklace.

The Truth of Necklace Revealed

One Sunday while Matilda was walking in the Champs-Elysees, she saw Mme Forestier. She was looking charming and beautiful as she had looked ten years before.

Matilda was hesitant but decided to tell Mme Forestier about her necklace. Initially, Mme Forestier did not recognise her, upon introduction, she was shocked.

When she got to know about Matilda's misery and her necklace, she was even more surprised. She told Matilda, that the necklace she had replaced was fake and cost around only 500 francs.

Word Meaning

The given page nos. correspond to the pages in the prescribed textbook.

Word	Meaning
Page 39	
petty	of lesser rank or importance
incessantly	continuously
tureen	a deep bowl with a cover used for serving soup
exquisite	finely made
despair	a complete loss of hope
elated	to be extremely joyful
Page 40	
spitefully	hurtfully

Word	Meaning
dismay	a feeling of unhappiness and disappointment
Page 41	
vexed	annoyed, frustrated or worried
ecstatic	very happy and excited
Page 42	
salon	a room used for entertaining guests
modest	not expensive
cloak	a sleeveless garment that hangs loosely from shoulders

Word	Meaning
Page 43	
bewilderment	confusion
chaplet	a string of (diamonds)
usurer	money lender
Page 44	
attic	a space or room inside the roof a building
crude	very simple
sou	a French coin of low value
perceived	noticed, spotted
personage	name

Chapter Practice

Objective Questions

• Multiple Choice Questions

1. Where did Loisel used to work?
(a) Board of Education
(b) Board of Public Instruction
(c) Ministry of Public Instruction
(d) Ministry of Education

Ans. (*a*) Loisel used to work Board of Education.

2. Matilda was .... regarding the invite.
(a) doubtful   (b) stressed   (c) confused   (d) dejected

Ans. (*b*) The poverty of her life and the invite to a rich and lavish bass dejected Matilda.

3. Identify the option that aptly describes M Loisel.
(a) Greedy yet kind   (b) Considerate and selfless
(c) Proud and honourable   (d) Brilliant but lawless

Ans. (*b*) Considerate and selfless

4. Why did Matilda need the jewels?
(a) To go to a party of rich people
(b) For a photoshoot
(b) To get a replica made
(d) for wearing them at home

Ans. (*a*) Matilda needed the jewels to go to a party of rich people at Minister's residence.

5. What made Mme Liosel cry out in joy?
(a) Her husband's suggestion.
(b) Her husband's permission.
(c) The thought of looking good.
(d) Her husband's promotion.

Ans. (*a*) Mme Loisel cried out in joy on her husband's suggestion.

6. What does Matilda's husband suggest her?
(a) That she does not wear any jewellery.
(b) That she should go out and buy a piece of beautiful jewellery.
(c) That she should wear what she has.
(d) That she sould borrow jewels from her rich friend.

Ans. (*d*) Matilda's husband suggested her that she should borrow jewels from her rich friend Mme Forestier.

7. Which of the following sentences tell us that Matilda greatly desired the necklace?
1. Her heart began to beat with uncontrolled desire.
2. Her hands trembled as she took it. She fastened it around her neck and stood lost in ecstasy.
3. Then she asked anxiously, hesitating, "Would you lend me this, just this?"
4. She threw her arms around her friend's neck embraced her with passion, then went away with her treasure.
(a) Only 1   (b) 2 and 4
(c) 3 and 4   (d) All of these

Ans. (*d*) All the given sentences tell us that Matilda greatly desired the necklace.

8. Where did Loisel sleep when his wife was enjoying the party?
(a) At his own house   (b) At the venue of the party
(c) In a little salon   (d) Outside in a carriage

Ans. (*c*) Loisel slept in a little salon when his wife was enjoying the party.

9. Loisel had to reach office after the party at ....
(a) Seven o'clock   (b) Ten o'clock
(c) Eight o'clock   (d) Nine o'clock

Ans. (*b*) Loisel had to reach office after the party at ten o'clock.

10. Select the correct option for (i) and (ii).
(i) Loisels suffered for ten long years to repay the rent.
(ii) Mme Loisel was regretting her decision of borrowing the necklace.
(a) (i) is true (ii) is false
(b) (ii) is true (i) is false
(c) Both (i) and (ii) are false
(d) (ii) furthers the meaning of (i)

Ans. (*d*) (ii) furthers the meaning of (i), i.e., Mme Loisel regretted her decision of borrowing a necklace from Mme Forestier as its replacement led to Loisels suffering for ten years.

11. Where did Matilda find her friend Mme Forestier after ten years of sufferings?
(a) Drury Lane   (b) On the street
(c) At minister's ball   (d) Champs-Elysees

Ans. (*d*) Matilda found her friend Mme Forestier after ten years of sufferings at Champ-Elysees.

12. How do you think Mme Loisel feel when she got to that the necklace she borrowed was fake? Choose the correct option.

(i) Mme Forestier cheated with me!

(ii) I should have told the truth to Mme Forestier.

(iii) She should have told me that the necklace was fake.

(iv) How stupid I am! I wasted ten years of my life because of that fake necklace!

(a) (i) and (ii) (b) (i), (ii) and (iv)

(c) (ii), (iii) and (iv) (d) All of these

Ans. (*c*) Statements 2, 3 and 4 depict the feelings of Mme Loisel.

• Extract Based MCQs

1. Read the extract to attempt the questions that follow.

"She suffered incessantly, feeling herself born for all delicacies and luxuries.

She suffered from the poverty of her apartment, the shabby walls and the worn chairs. All these things tortured and angered her.

When she seated herself for dinner opposite her husband who uncovered the tureen with a delighted air, saying, "Oh! the good potpie! I know nothing better than that...," she would think of elegant dinners of shining silver; she thought of the exquisite food served in marvellous dishes. She had neither frocks nor jewels, nothing. And she loved only those things. She had a rich friend, a schoolmate at the convent, who she did not like to visit- she suffered so much when she returned. She wept for whole days from despair and disappointment." **CBSE Question Bank 2021**

(i) Choose the option that list the set of statements that are NOT TRUE according to the given extract.

1. Matilda was very pleased with her life.

2. Matilda envied her friend for being well-off.

3. M Loisel didn't appreciate what Matilda cooked.

4. Matilda despised the fact that she lived a life of poverty.

5. Matilda never felt troubled, though she desired a luxurious life.

6. Matilda thought of grand dinners and silverware sitting at the dinner table.

7. Matilda felt depressed after visiting her friend.

(a) 1, 3, 6 (b) 3, 5, 7

(c) 1, 3, 5 (d) 2, 4, 7

Ans. (*c*) Statements 1,3 and 5 are not true.

(ii) Which word does 'delicacies' NOT correspond to?

(a) Etherealness (b) Elegance

(c) Exquisiteness (d) Robustness

Ans. (*d*) Delicacies mean fineness or intricacy of texture or structure. Robustness means the quality or condition of being strong and in good condition. Thus, it does not correspond to delicacies.

(iii) Choose the characteristic displayed by M Loisel in the extract.

(a) Conceited (b) Contended

(c) Appeased (d) Subdued

Ans. (*b*) M. Loisel, Matilda's husband was contended with what he had.

(iv) Choose the answer that lists the correct option of what a 'tureen' is?

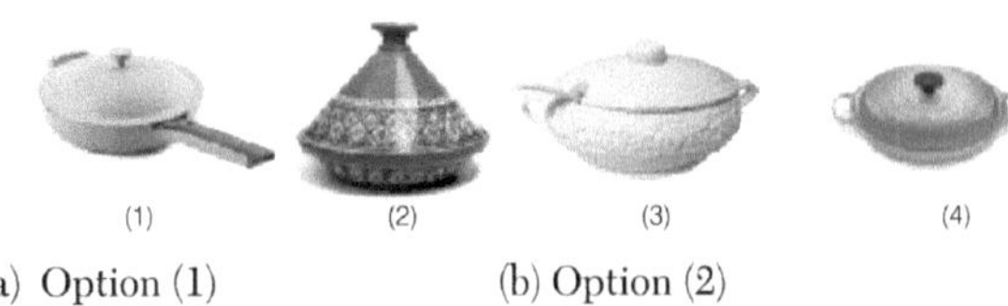

(a) Option (1) (b) Option (2)

(c) Option (3) (d) Option (4)

Ans. (*c*) Option (3)

(v) The extract uses the phrase 'elegant dinners'. Which of the following expressions is incorrect with respect to the word 'elegant'?

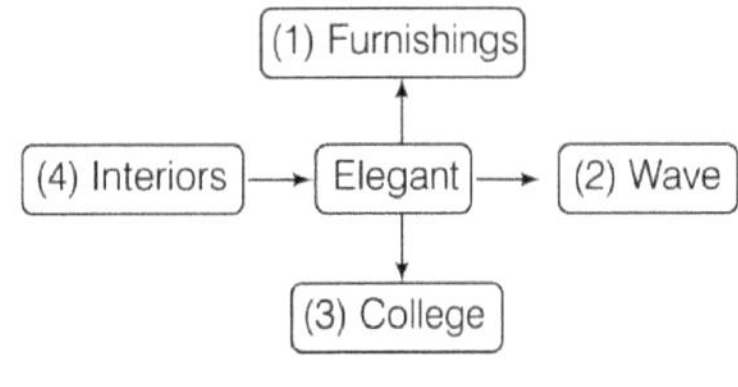

(a) Option (1) (b) Option (2)

(c) Option (3) (d) Option (4)

Ans. (*c*) Option (3)

2. Read the extract to attempt the questions that follow.

"He was silent, stupefied, in dismay, at the sight of his wife weeping. He stammered, "What is the matter? What is the matter?" By a violent effort, she had controlled her vexation and responded in a calm voice, wiping her moist cheeks, "Nothing. Only I have no dress and consequently I cannot go to this affair. Give your card to some colleague whose wife is better fitted out than I." He was grieved, but answered, "Let us see, Matilda. How much would a suitable costume cost, something that would serve for other occasions, something very simple?" She reflected for some seconds thinking of a sum that she could ask for without bringing with it an immediate refusal and a frightened exclamation from the economical clerk." **CBSE Question Bank 2021**

(i) What does 'economical clerk' indicate?

(a) M Loisel was a spend thrift even though he earned a lot.

(b) M Loisel was thrifty as he had a meagre income.

(c) M Loisel calculated money all the time as he was a clerk.

(d) M Loisel was stingy about money and didn't spend it.

Ans. (*b*) The phrase 'economical clerk' indicates that M Loisel was thrifty as he had a meager income.

(ii) Pick the correct set that matches with the feelings of the highlighted words related to the characters:

Matilda By : a **violent effort**, she had controlled...

M Loisel : He was **grieved**....

(1) Matilda felt aggressive; M Loisel was troubled

(2) Matilda was irritated; M Loisel was upset and cried

(3) Matilda tried extremely hard; M Loisel felt intense sorrow

(4) Matilda was quite calm; M Loisel's heart ached for love

(a) Option (1)   (b) Option (2)

(c) Option (3)   (d) Option (4)

Ans. (*c*) Option (3) that Matilda tried extremely hard to control her irritation and M Loisel felt intense sorrow – matches with the feelings of the highlighted words related to the characters.

(iii) Choose the option that gives the most appropriate response to the statement made by the speaker.

M Loisel over-pampered his wife and readily accepted her demands.

(a) I think Matilda was being unreasonable and unrealistic.

(b) I feel that M Loisel loved Matilda and wanted her to be happy.

(c) In my opinion M Loisel was being too harsh with Matilda.

(d) I feel that M Loisel should not have brought the invite home.

Ans. (*b*) Option (b) gives the most appropriate response to the statement made by the speaker.

(iv) Pick the option that correctly classifies Fact's (F) and Opinion's (O) of the people below:

(a) F-1, 2 and O-3, 4

(b) F-3, O-1,2, 4

(c) F-2, 4, O-1,3

(d) F-2, 3, 4, O-1

Ans. (*b*) F-3, O-1,2, 4

(v) M Loisel was astonished seeing his wife's reaction. He writes a diary entry that night. Complete the entry by choosing the correct option.

> 11th January, Monday 9:00 pm
>
> I thought Matilda would be _____(i)_____ seeing the invitation in my hand. However, her reaction has left me _____(ii)_____. I don't know how I would be able to _____(iii)_____ a new dress for her.

(a) (i) vexed (ii) disturbed (iii) bring

(b) (i) elated (ii) disturbed (iii) afford

(c) (i) keen (ii) depressed (iii) bring

(d) (i) elated (ii) distressed (iii) afford

Ans. (*d*) (i) elated (ii) distressed (iii) afford

PART 2
Subjective Questions

• Short Answer Type Questions

1. Why was Mme Loisel always unhappy?

CBSE 2020, 2019

Ans. Mme Loisel was always unhappy because she felt that she was, by mistake, born in the family of clerks. She felt that she was born for all the delicacies and luxuries in life. She remain disappointed as she was married to a clerk.

She always dreamt of a luxurious life filled with elegant dresses, jewellery, exquisite foods served in silver dining. She felt tortured and angered with her present living conditions and suffered incessantly.

2. Why do you think M. Loisel was a loving husband?

CBSE 2019

Ans. M. Loisel was a loving husband as he cared about his wife's emotions. He looked after all needs and desires of his wife. He made her buy a new dress for the party.

When his wife lost her diamond necklace, he did not lose his cool and helped her in returning the necklace by replacing it with a diamond necklace. He helped in repaying the debt by working in the evenings and night to earn extra money.

3. Why did Matilda throw the invitation spitefully?

Ans. Matilda was simply displeased when her husband showed her the invitation. She felt humiliated and threw the invitation spitefully, as she had nothing beautiful enough to wear at the ball.

4. How is the problem of jewel solved?   **NCERT**

Ans. Matilda Loisel's husband, M Loisel came to solve Matilda's problem. First, he suggests her to wear fresh flowers. Then, he advises her to borrow jewels from her rich friend, Mme Forestier. Thus, the problem is solved as Mme Forestier lends her a beautiful diamond necklace.

5. Do you think Mme Loisel had an enjoyable evening at the ball? Give reasons for your answer. **CBSE 2014**

Ans. Mme Loisel was the centre of attention at the ball. Her beauty, her grace, her joy and the gorgeous smile attracted all. She danced happily. Hence, she had a successful enjoyable evening at the ball.

6. Why did Matilda leave the ball in a hurry ? What does it show about her character? **CBSE 2018**

Ans. Matilda left the ball in a hurry because she did not want to be seen with the ordinary wrap that she carried. She believed that the poor looks of her wrap contrasted with the elegance of the other ladies, who were wrapping themselves in rich furs.

This shows that she only wanted to keep up the appearance just to flatter her pride without being in touch with the real truth of her life.

7. What do M. and Mme Loisel do when Matilda lost the necklace?

Ans. Loisel did everything to find the necklace. M. Loisel went back and searched for the lost necklace. Then, he went to the police and to the cab offices. Also, they put out an advertisement in the newspapers and offered a reward to anyone who finds the necklace. But, all their efforts went in vain.

8. What excuse did Loisels put up to explain the delay in returning the necklace?

Ans. Loisels had lost the necklace and needed time to find an identical one. Thus, Mme Loisel wrote a letter to Mme Forestier with an excuse that the clasp of the necklace had got broken and she needed time to get it repaired.

9. How do they replace the necklace? **NCERT**

Ans. After all other efforts fail, Loisel decided to buy a new identical necklace to replace the lost one. M Loisel gave eighteen thousand Francs that his father had left for him and took a loan for the rest.

Then the couple managed to buy the new necklace for thirty six thousand francs and returned it to Mme Forestier.

10. The course of the Loisel's life changed due to the necklace. Comment.

Ans. It is true that the necklace changed the course of the Loisel's life. It took the Loisels ten years to pay back the money they had borrowed to buy the necklace. It changed everything for them.

They had to move to the poorest quarters of the city. With no maids or assistance, Matilda had to cook, clean, mend, sew and bargain with the grocer and butcher to save every sou (a french coin of low value) just for their mere survival.

The husband had to work in the evening and night to pay their debt.

11. Describe Mme Loisel after ten years.

Ans. Ten years of poverty and hardship stole away Matilda's youth and beauty. She became a strong and hard woman, who was poorly dressed with untidy hair and red ragged hands. Her skirts were awry (uneven) and she spoke in a loud voice. She had become a commoner who had to do all things by herself.

12. Why was Matilda's friend astonished to see her at the end of the story? **CBSE 2012**

or Why did Jeanne not recognise her friend, Matilda?

Ans. Jeanne Forestier, Matilda's friend, could not recognise her at the end of the story as she seemed an old and worn out poor woman. Matilda was no longer her former beautiful and joyous self. She had lost her charm and was living an unfortunate life.

13. What was the cause of Matilda's ruin? How could she have avoided it? **NCERT**

Ans. The cause of Matilda's ruin was her over ambitiousness and dissatisfaction from life. She expected too much from life. But unfortunately, she was married to an ordinary man who could not provide her with all the materialistic luxuries.

She could have avoided it if she had told the fact to her friend that she had lost the necklace. Moreover, she should have been satisfied with what she had instead of imitating rich people.

14. What would have happened to Matilda if she had confessed to her friend that she had lost her necklace? **NCERT**

Ans. If Matilda had confessed to her friend that she had lost her necklace, she might have been in lesser trouble than what she faced after having replaced the necklace. Her friend would have been angry with her and most probably would have asked Matilda to replace it.

She would have given her the details from where she bought the necklace and how much it had cost her. Matilda would thus have known that the jewels in the necklace were not real diamonds. Matilda would thus have saved herself and her husband from all the trouble they went through.

15. Mme Loisel now knew the horrible life of necessity. Do you think Mme Loisel accepted this change willingly? Give two reasons in support of your answer. **CBSE Question Bank 2021**

Ans. Yes, I think Mme Loisel accepted this change willingly due to the following reasons

  (i) She understood that in order to pay the debt, she would have to cut down on her luxuries.

  (ii) She learned the work of kitchen, washed the clothes, brought up the water from the street and sent away the maid to help save money to pay off the debt.

16. Mention two things you would have done, other than what M Loisel did, to help resolve the problem of the lost necklace. **CBSE Question Bank 2021**

Ans. The two things I would done, other than M Loisel did, to help resolve the problem of the lost necklace are

(i) I would have told Mme Forestier the truth about what happened and asked for her forgiveness.

(ii) I would also have promised her to replace the necklace as soon as possible.

• Long Answer Type Questions

1. Mme Loisel's disposition invites her doom. Comment in the context of the text you've read.

or Matilda wanted to live a life above her status. How did this desire of her's led to her sufferings?

CBSE 2019

Ans. Mme Loisel belonged to a family of clerks but wanted to live a life above her status. They lived on small income, enough for meeting the basic needs but not to fulfil aspirations. She got married to a clerk and was so caught up with her dreams of wealth and pleasure that she was out of touch with the truths of her real life.

In order to keep up appearances and just to flatter her pride, she blowed up four hundred francs on a gorgeous dress. She also went on borrowing a necklace from her friend. All of this was just to impress the wealthy and the rich with her beauty and glamour (even if on loan). No doubt, her pride was flattered and her wish of fine dining and wearing expensive dresses and jewels was satisfied. But it came at a great price.

Unfortunately, the necklace was lost and the couple had to cough up their entire inheritance and borrow as well to replace it. Repayment of the debt ate away the next ten years of their youth. They lived in utter poverty and had to work very hard to repay the loan.

If she had accepted her reality and remained happy with what she had, she would not have suffered so badly. Therefore, one can say that it was her disposition that led her to doom.

2. Mme Forestier proved to be a true friend. Elucidate. **CBSE 2015, 2020**

Ans. Mme Forestier is a true friend of Mme Loisel. She plays a very vital role in the story. As a friend to Matilda, we find her to be really genuine.

She helps Matilda in the hour of her need. When Mme Loisel needed to borrow jewels, she turned to Mme Forestier. Mme Forestier does not refuse. Displaying her generosity, she opens up the entire case of her jewels for Matilda to choose from. Also, she was considerate when the Loisels delayed the return of the necklace. At the end of the story, she concludes the entire narrative.

Mme Forestier reveals to Matilda that her necklace was just a fake. She is not at all worried in the light of the fact that she may have to return the necklace. It shows her honesty. She was a true friend who, feels bad for Matilda at her unnecessary suffering.

3. Was Matilda's dream fulfilled at the ball? Why did all men notice and wanted them to be presented to her?

Ans. Yes, Matilda's dream was fulfilled at the ball. Matilda always dreamt of grandeur, luxuries and delicacies in her life. She had prepared for the ball so thoroughly as **befitted a grand occasion**. She didn't want to present a poverty-stricken image of her, amidst rich ladies and gentlemen.

She made her husband buy a new dress for the party. She borrowed a necklace from Madame Forestier to adorn herself like a graceful and distinguished lady. She proved to be a grand success at the ball and her dream was fulfilled. She was the centre of attraction for all ladies as well as men who were present there.

Matilda danced with enthusiasm. She was intoxicated with pleasure as she loved to be admired and appreciated. At the party, Matilda was the prettiest of all and that is why all the men noticed her. They couldn't avoid the temptation of noticing her and wanted to be presented to her.

4. Do you think the story is aptly titled? Justify your answer.

Ans. The whole narrative of the story 'The Necklace' revolves around a young woman Matilda, who in her foolish pride borrows a necklace inviting misery and sorrow for herself as well as for her husband. The 'necklace' has lost and the Loisels fall into a tremendous debt. They spend the next ten years of their life in paying debt for the replacement of the lost necklace. Their entire life moves around impoverished everyday saga of misery and hunger and the necklace, in fact, changes the very course of their life.

Also, it is against the back drop of the necklace that Matilda's pride and dishonesty are highlighted. At the same time, the necklace serves a twist at the end as it turns out to be a fake one. The story is, hence, most aptly titled as the necklace is, in fact, the leading character of this ironic tale of desire, the doom and the tragedy.

5. What changes occurred in Matilda's lifestyle after she had lost the necklace? **CBSE 2020**

Ans. When Matilda lost the necklace she borrowed from Mme Forestier, she bought a new diamond necklace on loan. The repayment of debt changed Matilda's life drastically. The Loisels became poor, they had to send away their maid and changed their lodgings to room in an attic. Matilda learnt the household chores. She learned to do the dishes, wash the soiled linens, clothes and dishcloths.

She had to walk to the street to bring up the water. She had to dress like an ordinary woman and had to go to grocerer, butcher and fruit seller all by herself keeping in mind to save each and every penny she could. Her husband also worked in the evenings. He used to put the books of some merchants in order and at night, he did copying at five sous a page. This miserable life lasted for ten years to repay the debt.

6. Read the following quote.

"We are too involved in materialistic things, and they don't satisfy us. The loving relationships we have, the universe around us, we take these things for granted."
- Mitch Albom

Matilda was never satisfied with her life and desired more. The given quote reflects her character. Justify.

CBSE Question Bank 2021

Ans. Matilda always wished for more than what she had She wanted exquisite food, shining silver, frocks and jewels. She only loved and longed for these rich things. She cared much less for her husband's happiness.

He got an invitation from the minister hoping it would make her happy. Instead, she only cared about lack of clothes and jewels.

Her husband gave her the money he had saved just to make her happy but even after spending it in buying a dress, she yearned for jewels. This yearning led to troubles in her and husband's life and they spent 10 years in poverty. While she did all her household tasks. M. Loisel worked day and night.

In the end, she looked old and troubled, and discovered that the necklace didn't even cost so much and that all their troubles and debt was for nothing.

If she had accepted and been happy with what they have, none of her troubles would have occured. She could have chosen to see her husband's love and care for her instead of what they didn't have and been truly happy.

● Extract Based Questions

1. Read the extract to attempt the questions that follow.

He threw around her shoulders the modest wraps they had carried whose poverty clashed with the elegance of the ball costume. She wished to hurry away in order not to be noticed by the other women who were wrapping themselves in rich furs. Loisel detained her, "Wait," said he. "I am going to call a cab." But she would not listen and descended the steps rapidly. When they were in the street, they found no carriage; and they began to seek for one, hailing the coachmen whom they saw at a distance.

(i) 'She' wished to hurry away. Why?
(ii) Why did Loisel detain Matilda?
(iii) Why did Matilda did not stop?
(iv) Which figure of speech is used in 'rich furs'?
(v) Find the word in the extract which is opposite in meaning to the word 'grandiose'?

Ans. (i) 'Matilda' did not wish to shatter the illusion of her grandeur that she had so successfully managed to convey others by putting on such a shabby wrap. So, she wished to hurry away to escape the notice of the rich women.

(ii) Loisel asked Matilda to wait so that he could call a cab as it was four o'clock in the morning.

(iii) Matilda did not stop in order to avoid getting noticed by the rich ladies.

(iv) Synecdoche is used in 'rich furs'. They mean expensive coats or cloak worn by British women.

(v) Modest is opposite in meaning to grandiose.

2. Read the extract to attempt the questions that follow.

She learned the odious work of a kitchen. She washed the dishes. She washed the soiled linen, their clothes and dishcloths, which she hung on the line to dry; she took down the refuse to the street each morning and brought up the water, stopping at each landing to catch her breath.

And, clothed like a woman of the people, she went to the grocer's, the butcher's and the fruiterer's, with her basket on her arm, shopping, haggling to the last sou of her miserable money. The husband worked evenings, putting the books of some merchants in order, and nights he often did copying at five sous a page. And this life lasted for ten years. At the end of ten years, they had restored all.

(i) How does she live?
(ii) Why did she have to learn the household work?
(iii) What changes took place in 'she'?
(iv) What is the meaning of the word 'haggling'?
(v) How did the husband manage to work?

Ans. (i) 'She' lives in extreme poverty and misery.

(ii) She had to learn the household chores because she and her husband had to repay the loan borrowed to replace Mme Foretsier's diamond necklace.

(iii) She, Matilda, became a crude owman, she used to dress simply and do all the work herself. She started looking old.

(iv) Haggling means bargaining persistently over the cost of something.

(v) The husband, M Loisel worked day and night to repay the loan, after office he used to manage the books of a merchant and then he used to copying work during nights.

CHAPTER 03

The Hack Driver

—by Sinclair Lewis

In this Chapter...

- Chapter Summary
- Word Meaning
- Chapter Practice

Chapter Summary

The Narrator's Job

The Narrator was a young lawyer who became a Junior Assistant Clerk in a magnificent law firm. He had been assigned the duty to serve summons on witnesses. But he hated his job because he had to go to dirty and shadowy places to serve summons. Also, sometimes he was beaten. Consequently, he thought of going back to his home town where he could have been a real lawyer.

The Narrator went to New Mullion

One day, the narrator was sent to a town named New Mullion to serve summons on Oliver Lutkins who was a witness in a law case. The narrator was very excited to visit a small and beautiful town but his excitement ended by the dull appearance of the town. The streets were full of mud and there were shabby wooden shops all around.

The only cheerful thing that the narrator found was a delivery man (hack driver) at the station. He was about forty years old, had a fat body and a red face. His clothes were dirty but he seemed friendly. So, the narrator went to him.

The Narrator Met the Hack Driver

The narrator told the hack driver that he wanted to find Oliver Lutkins. The hack driver told him that he had seen Lutkins about an hour ago and that he was hard to catch. In his opinion, Lutkins was always busy doing one thing or another.

The hack driver told the narrator that Lutkins must be playing poker game in the back of Fritz's shop. The driver also told the narrator that he drives a carraige and would help him find Lutkins.

The Hack Driver Tells about Oliver Lutkins

The narrator bargained the fare money to two dollars per hour and the search for Lutkins began.

As they left to search for Lutkins, the hack driver told the narrator that Lutkins owed money to a lot of people but he never paid them off. He also told that Lutkins owe him fifty cents on a poker game. The narrator was impressed with hack driver's friendly nature. He also got confident of finding Lutkins with the help of the hack driver.

Looking for Lutkins

The hack driver introduced himself to the narrator as Bill. At Fritz's shop, the hack driver asked the lawyer to follow him. He inquired about Oliver Lutkins and got to know that Lutkins had gone to Gustaff's for a shave.

At Gustaff's, they got to know that Lutkins had spend all his credit and had left the place without getting his shave. So, they went to Gray's where they got to know that Lutkins had gone to the poolroom.

However, by the time both the hack driver and the lawyer reached the poolroom, Lutkins had already left.

The Narrator Enjoys the Driver's Company

It was lunch time, so the narrator offered to take Bill to a restaurant. But Bill wanted to go home to his wife for lunch. Bill told the narrator that his wife would pack a lunch for the narrator for half a dollar. So, they had lunch at the Wade's Hills. The narrator was enjoying the company of the hack driver who was telling him about people of New Mullion.

The simplicity and humour of the driver influenced the narrator so much that he planned to settle down in the town.

The Driver and the Narrator Visit Oliver's Mother

Both the hack driver and the lawyer looked for Lutkins for a long time. Then one of Lutkin's friends suggested that they should look for Oliver at his mother's place. So, they both went to Lutkins' mother's place. One the journey, the hack driver described Lutkins' mother as a nine feet tall and four feet thick quick lady.

When they reached Lutkin's mother's house and enquired there for Luktins, the mother took a hot iron rod and threatened to burn them. The two escaped to save themselves. However, they searched the house, the stable, the barn, but failed to find Lutkins anywhere.

The Narrator Returns to Town

When the narrator returned to town without serving the summons, his chief got very angry with him. They needed Lutkins as an important witness in their case. He decided to send another man who knew Lutkins with the narrator to the town to bring him.

The Narrator Serves Summons on Lutkins

The narrator and his companion went to the village the next day. They found the hack driver at the station laughing and joking with Lutkin's mother. The narrator pointed out the driver to his companion and explained how the driver helped him in trying to find Lutkins.

His companion then told the narrotor that the driver was Lutkins himself. The narrator served summons on Lutkins who along with his mother was making fun of the narrator.

Word Meaning

The given page nos. correspond to the pages in the prescribed textbook.

Word	Meaning
Page 47	
summons	an order to appear before a judge
agreeable sight	pleasant sight
PAGE 48	
cent	a monetary unit in various countries, equal to one-hundredth of a dollar.
PAGE 49	
part with	to give to some one (money, property, control etc.).

Word	Meaning
lingered	to stay somewhere longer than is necessary
swede	a native of Sweden
PAGE 50	
creek	a narrow area of water that flows into the land from the sea
meadow	a piece of grassland
PAGE 51	
seized	got hold of
retreat	an act of moving back or withdrawing

Word	Meaning
barn	a large farm building used for storing hay/grain etc
swearing	rude or offensive language that someone uses, especially when they are angry
peering	to look carefully or with difficulty
PAGE 52	
loafing	to spend one's time in an aimless, idle way

Chapter Practice

Objective Questions

• Multiple Choice Questions

1. Why was the lawyer sent to serve summon to Oliver Lutkins?
 (a) He was needed as a witness in a law case.
 (b) He was a criminal and had to be arrested.
 (c) He was summoned to clear the legal matters against him.
 (d) None of the above

Ans. (a) The lawyer was sent to serve summon to Oliver Lutkins because he was needed as a witness in a law case.

2. The village folks used to call the hack driver ....

 (a) Fraudster   (b) Magnuson
 (c) Oliver   (d) Lutkins

Ans. (b) The village folks used to call the hack driver Magnuson.

3. Bill initially thought that the narrator had come in search of Lutkins because
 (a) He owed fifty cents to Lutkins.
 (b) He wanted to serve summons on Lutkins.
 (c) He had to collect money from Lutkins.
 (d) None of the above

Ans. (c) Bill initially thought that the narrator had come in search of Lutkins because he had to collect money from Lutkins.

4. Which of the following people were described by Bill while roaming the city with the lawyer?
 (a) Minister's wife who sang the loudest in church.
 (b) Boys who came back from college in fancy clothes.
 (c) Lawyer whose wife could never succeed in getting him to put on both a collar and a tie on the same day.
 (d) All of the above

Ans. (d) Following people were described by Bill while roaming the city with the lawyer:
 • Minister's wife who sang the loudest in church.
 • Boys who came back from college in fancy clothes.
 • Lawyer whose wife could never succeed in getting him to put on both a collar and a tie on the same day.

5. Where did Lutkins' friend directed the hack driver and the narrator for Lutkins' mother' farm?
 (a) Three miles South   (b) Six miles North
 (c) Three miles North   (d) Seven miles East

Ans. (c) Lutkins' friend directed the hack driver and the narrator to go three miles North for Lutkins' mother' farm.

6. How did Lutkin's mother react when Bill and the narrator enquired about Lutkins?
 (a) She threatened to burn them
 (b) She threatened to kill them
 (c) She abused them
 (d) She chased them away

Ans. (a) Lutkin's mother threatened them to burn Bill and the narrator when they enquired about Lutkins.

7. The Chief hinted that the narrator might do well at ....
 (a) Serving summons
 (b) Digging ditches
 (c) Beating up criminals
 (d) Getting beaten up by criminals

Ans. (b) The Chief hinted that the narrator might do well at digging ditches.

8. Why were Lutkins and his mother laughing at the narrator in the end?
 (a) Because the narrator was befooled by Lutkins.
 (b) Because they were of jovial nature.
 (c) Because they were sharing jokes with each other.
 (d) None of the above

Ans. (a) Lutkins and his mother were laughing at the narrator in the end because the narrator was befooled by Lutkins.

9. Why did Lutkins beg the narrator to go with them to a neighbour's house for a cup of coffee?
 (a) They wanted to host an evening snack for the narrator.
 (b) They were the only folks in the town that missed seeing the narrator the previous day.
 (c) The hack driver wanted to eat at the neighbour's place.
 (d) All of the above

Ans. (b) Lutkins begged the narrator to go with them to a neighbour's house for a cup of coffee because they were the only folks in the town that missed seeing the narrator the previous day.

10. What can you infer about the lawyer after reading 'The Hack Driver'?

  (i) Innocent
  (ii) Befooled by the hack driver
  (iii) Trusts people blindly
  (a) Only (i)　　　　　　(b) (i) and (ii)
  (c) (ii) and (iii)　　　　(d) All of these

Ans. (*d*) The lawyer was an innocent man who trusted people blindly which let him getting befooled by the hack driver.

11. Given below are some adjectives. Choose the ones which can be associated with Oliver Lutkins from 'The Hack Driver'.

  1. Deceptive　　　　　2. Clever
  3. Cunning　　　　　　4. Short-tempered
  5. Friendly　　　　　　6. Jolly
  7. Quick-witted　　　　8. Hack driver
  (a) 3, 4, 7 and 8　　　　(b) 1, 2, 5, 6, 7 and 8
  (c) 2, 3, 4 and 5　　　　(d) 1, 3, 4, 6 and 7

Ans. (*b*) Oliver Lutkins was deceptive, clever, friendly, jolly, quick-witted, hack driver.

12. Pick the option that correctly classifies Facts (F) and Opinions (O) of the students given below.

  1. I feel everyone in the village was making a fool of the narrator.
  2. I think the narrator was not happy with his work and city life.
  3. I think the narrator should not have trusted anyone blindly.
  4. I think Oliver Lutkins took advantage of the narrator's innocence.
  (a) F-1 and O-2, 3 and 4　　(b) F-1, 2 and O-3, 4
  (c) F-1, 2, 4 and O-3　　　(d) F-3, 4 and O-1, 2

Ans. (*c*) Statements 1, 2 and 4 are facts as they are directly mentioned in the text and statement 3 is opinion.

• Extract Based MCQs

1. Read the extract to attempt the questions that follow.

After graduating with honours, I became a junior assistant clerk in a magnificent law firm. I was sent, not to prepare legal briefs, but to serve summons, like a cheap private detective. I had to go to dirty and shadowy corners of the city to seek out my victims. Some of the larger and more self confident ones even beat me up. I hated this unpleasant work, and the side of city life it revealed to me.

CBSE Question Bank 2021

  (i) The law firm that the narrator joined was
  (a) splendid　　　　　(b) philanthropic
  (c) reputable　　　　　(d) contemporary

Ans. (*a*) The law firm that the narrator joined was splendid.

  (ii) 'Like a cheap private detective' is a reference to the fact that the speaker
  (a) wasn't drawing as good a salary as a detective.
  (b) was upset about working in the private sector.
  (c) wasn't trying to be an established detective.
  (d) was disappointed with his allotted work.

Ans. (*d*) The speaker was disappointed with his work.

  (iii) Which of the following options was NOT a part of this unpleasant work?
  (a) Searching for law-breakers
  (b) Serving summons
  (c) Getting beaten up
  (d) Preparing legal documents

Ans. (*d*) Preparing legal documents was not a part of his unpleasant work.

  (iv) The shadowy corners of the city conjure up images of places?
  (a) With many trees to provide shade.
  (b) Where crime is not uncommon.
  (c) Which receive absolutely no sunlight.
  (d) With tall buildings and their shadows.

Ans. (*b*) The shadowy corners of the city conjure up images of places where crime is not uncommon.

  (v) Choose the option that is NOT TRUE.
  The speaker found this side of the city life unpleasant because it revealed people who had
  (a) robbed others of their belongings.
  (b) threatened others.
  (c) swindled the innocent.
  (d) served summons for a case.

Ans. (*a*) robbed others of their belongings.

2. Read the extract to attempt the questions that follow.

Fritz looked at me, hiding behind Bill. He hesitated, and then admitted, "Yes, he was in here a little while ago. Guess he's gone over to Gustaff's to get a shave." "Well, if he comes in, tell him I'm looking for him."

We drove to Gustaff's barber shop. Again, Bill went in first, and I lingered at the door. He asked not only the Swede but two customers if they had seen. Lutkins. The Swede had not. He said angrily, "I haven't seen him, and don't care to. But if you find him you can just collect that dollar thirty-five, he owes me." One of the customers thought he had seen Lutkins walking down Main Street, this side of the hotel.　　**CBSE Question Bank 2021**

  (i) Fritz's hesitation was on account of wanting to
  (a) take a moment to comprehend and fall in with the prank.
  (b) understand what was being asked and answer accordingly.
  (c) pretend ignorance at the question asked to waste time.
  (d) confirm that it was him being addressed, before replying.

Ans. (*a*) Fritz's hesitation was on account of wanting to take a moment to comprehend and fall in with the prank.

(ii) The narrator hovered near the door because he
  (a) wanted to eavesdrop on the conversation.
  (b) didn't trust Bill to enquire sternly.
  (c) had been asked to remain there by Bill.
  (d) found the interior too stuffy.

Ans. (*c*) The narrator hovered near the door because he had been asked to remain there by Bill.

(iii) One person mentioned that he had seen Lutkins walking down Main Street. This was an example of
  (a) being taken to the cleaners.
  (b) sending someone on a wild goose chase.
  (c) stretching the truth.
  (d) making scales fall off someone's eyes.

Ans. (*b*) The given sentence is an example of sending someone on a wild goose chase which means to direct one to go on a prolonged or chaotic search for something that is difficult or impossible to find, often because it does not exist.

(iv) The extract is an example of writing in the style of a
  (a) personal narrative (b) biography
  (c) historical fiction (d) research article

Ans. (*a*) The extract is an example of writing in the style of a personal narrative.

(v) The extract is an example of writing in the style of a
  (a) personal narrative
  (b) biography
  (c) historical fiction
  (d) research article

Ans. (*a*) personal narrative

PART 2
Subjective Questions

• Short Answer Type Questions

1. Why did the lawyer hate his work?
                          CBSE Question Bank 2021

or Why did the lawyer call his work 'unpleasant'
                          CBSE 2019

Ans. The narrator called his work unpleasant and hated his work because unlike expectation of practicing law, he was sent to serve summons. He had to go to all sorts of dirty and dangerous places to meet criminals. At times, he was also beaten by those people to whom he had to serve summons.

2. Why is the lawyer sent to New Mullion? What does he first think about the place?   **NCERT**

Ans. The lawyer was sent to New Mullion to serve summons on Oliver Lutkins, who was needed as a witness in a law case.

The lawyer thought that the place must be a beautiful and peaceful country village.

3. Explain how the narrator's expectations fell short of what he'd expected when he was sent to New Mullion?   **CBSE Question Bank 2020**

Ans. The narrator wished to see a sweet and simple country village but when he reached New Mullion, he was disappointed. He saw streets that looked like rivers of mud, with wooden shops, on the side, that were either painted brown or not painted at all.

4. What does Bill say about Lutkins?

Ans. Bill told the lawyer that Lutkins was a hard person to find as he was always busy in some activity or the other. He owed money to many people, including Bill himself but he had never paid back anybody. He also tells the lawyer that Lutkins played a lot of poker and was good at deceiving people.

5. 'But he was no more dishonest than I'. Explain.

Ans. The lawyer says the following words because the hack driver was charging him a large amount to search for Lutkins.

However, just like the hack driver, he was also going to charge the firm for the expenses of visiting New Mullion. Therefore, both of them were equally dishonest.

6. What does the hack driver do to help the lawyer to look for Oliver Lutkins?   **CBSE 2019**

Ans. A hack driver at the station, who called himself Bill Magnuson, befriends the lawyer. Bill told the lawyer that he knew Lutkins and would help in finding him.

Bill took him to all the places where Lutkins was known to be present. He took the lawyer to Fritz's shop, where Lutkins played a lot of poker; to Gustaff's barber shop and then to Gray's barber shop; to the poolroom and several other places before finally taking him to Lutkins' mother's farm. However, Oliver Lutkins was not found any where.

7. What about the delivery man appealed to the young junior assistant clerk from the city?   **CBSE Question Bank 2021**

Ans. When the narrator reach New Mullion, the delivery man was the only agreeable sight to the narrator. His presence appealed the narrator for he had a friendly and open manner. It filled the young junior assistant clerk with warmth. This kindness and his smile made the clerk feel like he was an old friend.

8. Why did Lutkins pretend to be Bill Magnuson?

CBSE 2015

Ans. Lutkins pretended to be Bill Magnuson as he did not want to accept the summons and be a witness in the case. So, he pretended to help the lawyer in finding Lutkins and wandered everywhere.

9. Explain why Bill's offer wasn't 'entirely a matter of brotherly love'. **CBSE Question Bank 2021**

Ans. When the narrator became hungry, Bill offered to bring lunch that his wife would make. It was not entirely a matter of brotherly love because he was charging money from the narrator. The narrator was paying Bill for his time and also for the lunch.

10. Why do you think Lutkins' neighbours were anxious to meet the lawyer? **NCERT**

Ans. Lutkins' neighbours were anxious to meet the lawyer because almost the entire village had enjoyed Lutkins making a fool of the lawyer. Only they (Lutkins' neighbours) had not seen the lawyer but had come to know what had happened. They wanted to see the gullible man whom Lutkins had taken for a ride.

11. Why did the young lawyer wish to return to New Mullion? **CBSE Question Bank 2021**

Ans. The young lawyer wished to return to New Mullion to practice law. He was overjoyed by the ride given by hack driver. He was happy with Bill's wisdom and quick wittedness. He thought of living with wise neighbours in New Mullion. He pictured an honest and happy life beyond the strict limits of universities and law firms.

12. What do you think inspired the minister's wife to sing the loudest in church when she was most in debt? **CBSE Question Bank 2021**

Ans. Bill told the narrator that the minister's wife sang the loudest when she was most in debt. It was probably so that God would hear her first and help her settle the debt as soon as possible.

13. The young man earned for himself the ire of his office people on his return from New Mullion. Explain why. **CBSE Question Bank 2021**

Ans. The young man earned for himself the ire of his office people on his return from New Mullion because his task remained incomplete. He went to New Mullion to serve summons on Oliver Lutkins, who was needed as a witness. When he failed to find him, everybody in the office got upset with him.

14. When the lawyer reached New Mullion, did 'Bill' know that he was looking for Lutkins? When do you think 'Bill' came up with his plan for fooling the lawyer?

Ans. When the lawyer reached the station, 'Bill' at once got to know that the lawyer was looking for him. When the lawyer told and confirmed Bill's opinion that he was looking for Oliver Lutkins, he made a plan to fool the lawyer.

15. Do you think the lawyer was gullible? How could he have avoided being taken for a ride? **NCERT**

Ans. Yes, the lawyer was gullible (innocent). He believed every word of what Oliver Lutkins said. He should have asked about Lutkins from other villagers also, instead of depending completely on the hack driver.

• Long Answer Type Questions

1. In life, people who easily trust others are sometimes made to look foolish. One should not be too trusting. Describe how Oliver Lutkins made a fool of the young lawyer. **CBSE 2018**

Ans. It is true that in life people who easily trust others are easily made to look foolish. One must remember that not everyone is honest and thus one should not trust everyone blindly.

In the story, 'the Hack Driver', Oliver Lutkins using this characteristic of the lawyer makes him a fool, throughout his first visit to the village.

First, he introduced himself as Bill at the railway station and assured the lawyer that they would together search for Lutkins. He told the lawyer that he knew most of the places where Lutkins used to hang out.

In succession, he took the narrator to Fritz, then to the barber's shop, then to Gray's shop and finally to Lutkins' mother, whom he called a 'terror'. He deceived the lawyer throughout and also made money by taking the lawyer around. Thus, because of Lutkins' desire to not be a witness to a case, he made a plan to fool the gullible lawyer and broke his trust.

2. Lutkins openly takes the lawyer all over the village. How is that no one lets out the secret? (*Hint :* Notice that the hack driver asks the lawyer to keep out of sight behind him when they go into Fritz's). Can you find other such subtle ways in which Lutkins manipulates the tour? **NCERT**

Ans. Lutkins never allows the lawyer to reach the place where the imaginary Lutkins is supposed to be present at a given time. The way he weaves stories about Lutkins' vagabond nature and the way he scares the lawyer about Lutkins' mother are ways of fooling the lawyer devised by the hack driver. Everywhere he does not allow the lawyer to ask about Lutkins but he himself pretends to ask about him, which the villagers are knowing is a pretence. So, the villagers also join in the whole drama. Lutkins it can be said manipulates the tour cleverly. At every place he takes the lawyer, he asks him to either stay outside or stay behind him. With his effective place he is able to prove his honesty and Lutkins dishonesty.

3. Write a character sketch of the hack driver.

CBSE 2020

Ans. **Cheerful and Friendly** The hack driver, named Bill was a red-faced, fourty years old man with a cheerful and a pleasant personality. The narrator met the hack driver when he had come to New Mullion to serve summons on Oliver Lutkins. Initially, the narrator found Bill to be a friendly, wise and an agreeable fellow.]

Helful A great schemer When the narrator informed Bill about his visit, Bill readily accepted to help him and took him to all the places where Lutkins could be found.

However, later the narrator get to know that Bill was a clever fellow. Bill had all the arts with him to win the confidence of gullible (innocent) people like the lawyers and fool them.

A Great Schemer Bill himself was Oliver Lutkins and as soon as he got to know about the lawyer's visit, he devised a plan. He pretended to help the lawyers.

All of this show that Bill was a great schemer. He cleverly fooled the lawyer into believing that he was trying to help. But in reality, he never allowed the lawyer to come directly in touch with the people. Therefore, Bill perfectly played a double role and outwitted the narrator.

4. What did the hack driver tell the narrator about Lutkins' mother? How did she treat the narrator?

CBSE 2020

Ans. While going to Lutkins' mothers house, the hack driver informed the narrator that Lutkins' mother was a terror. He told him that she was about nine feet tall and four feet thick lady who was as quick as a cat.

He also told him that once he had taken a trunk for her at her farmhouse and she had almost taken his skin off. All this information frightened the narrator but he still went to look for Lutkins at his mother's place.

When they reached Lutkins mother's house, they were faced with an enormous and cheerful old woman. Bill went to her and informed her about their visit. Lutkins' mother bluntly told them that shee did not know anything about Lutkins. When Bill pressed for searching the house as it was their legal right, she went inside and came out with a hot iron rod to attack them. Consequently, both of them ran away from the location.

• Extract Based Questions

1. Read the extract to attempt the questions that follow.

He was so open and friendly that I glowed with the warmth of his affection. I knew, of course, that he wanted the business, but his kindness was real. I was glad the fare money would go to this good fellow. I managed to bargain down to two dollars an hour and then he brought from his house nearby a sort of large black box on wheels. He remarked,

"Well, young man, here's the carriage" and his widesmile made me into an old friend. These villagers are so ready to help a stranger. He had already made it his own task to find Oliver Lutkins for me.

(i) Who is 'he' in these lines?

(ii) Give an instance of his kindness.

(iii) Find a word from the extract which means 'a gentle feeling of fondness'.

(iv) Pick out the qualities of the hack driver with context to the above extract.

(v) What did the narrator mean by saying "these villagers are so ready to help a stranger"?

Ans. (i) 'He' in these lines is Bill Magnuson, the hack driver.

(ii) He offered to take the narrator through the village and find Lutkins.

(iii) 'Affection' from the extract means 'a gentle feeling of fondness'.

(iv) The hack driver was open, friendly, affectionate, kind and ready to help the narrator.

(v) The narrator means that the village people are friendly and they made strange people's task as their own in order to help them heartily.

2. Read the extract to attempt the questions that follow.

So we pursued him, just behind him, but never catching him, for an hour till it was past one o' clock. I was hungry. But I had so enjoyed Bill's rough country opinions about his neighbours that I scarcely cared whether I found Lutkins or not. "How about something to eat?" I suggested. "Let's go to a restaurant and I'll buy you lunch." "Well, I ought to go home to the wife. I don't care much for these restaurants — only four of them and they're all bad. Tell you what we'll do. We'll get the wife to pack up a lunch for us.

(i) Who was pursuing whom?

(ii) Why were they pursuing him?

(iii) What do you understand by Bill's rough country opinions?

(iv) Why do you think Bill suggested the narrator to get their lunch packed by Bill's wife?

(v) How much charge did Bill tell for getting the lunch packed by his wife?

Ans. (i) The narrator and Bill were pursuing Lutkins.

(ii) They were pursuing him because the lawyer had to serve him summons.

(iii) Bill's rough country opinions means the opinions he had for the people of his town and the way he pictured the image of everyone in the town.

(iv) Bill suggested so in order to earn more money from the narrator.

(v) Bill told that his wife would not charge more than a dollar.

CHAPTER 04

Bholi

—by KA Abbas

In this Chapter...

- Chapter Summary
- Word Meaning
- Chapter Practice

Chapter Summary

Bholi as a Child

Bholi's real name was Sulekha but from her childhood everyone called her Bholi. She was the fourth daughter out of the seven children of Ramlal, Numberdar of the village. When Bholi was 10 months old she had fallen off the cot which had damaged some part of her brain. Since then she remained a backward child.

Further, when she was two years old, she suffered from an attack of small pox and her entire body was disfigured by deep black pock-marks. She learned to speak at the age of five and stammered while speaking. So, children used to make fun of her.

Bholi's Family

Bholi's father was a rich farmer who sent his sons to the city for studies. The eldest daughter, Radha was already married whereas Mangla and Champa were good looking and healthy girls. Ramlal was worried only about Bholi as she was neither beautiful nor intelligent.

Bholi Goes to School

Bholi was seven years old when a primary school opened in their village. The Tehsildar who had come to inaugurate the school advised Ramlal to send his daughter to school to set an example for others. Ramlal could not say no to him. His wife objected that no one would marry the girls if they would go to school. But then she felt that Bholi was ugly and nobody would marry her. So, they decided to send Bholi to school.

Bholi Prepares for School

Next day, Bholi was dressed to go to school. Bholi was given new clothes for the school. Earlier she used to wear old clothes of her sisters. She was given a bath and oil was rubbed into her dry hair. Bholi didn't know where she was being taken but was happy that her mother got her ready.

Bholi was filled with fear when her father went back to village after handling her to the headmistress. Her headmistress asked her to sit in a corner in one of the classrooms. She was glad to see girls of her own age at school.

Bholi's First Day at School

Bholi was attracted to the colourful pictures on the wall. She was much impressed by the realistic pictures of birds and animals. The teacher asked her name. Bholi stammered and then started crying.

After the class was over, the teacher went back to Bholi. She called her lovingly and encouraged her to tell her name. This time Bholi tried to speak her name and was successful. The teacher told Bholi to come to school everyday.

The Teacher Gives her a Book

The teacher gave a book to Bholi which had pictures of dog, cat, goat, etc. The teacher told her that she would be able to read like everyone else and then no one would laugh at her. Bholi way happy as the teacher encouraged Bholi and gave her a hope of a new life.

Progress of Village

Many years passed, the village progressed and converted into a small town. The primary school became a high school. There were now a cinema under a tin shed and a cotton ginning mill. The mail train began to stop at their railway station.

Bholi's Marriage Proposal

One night after dinner Ramlal and his wife were talking about a marriage proposal for Bholi. Bishamber was forty five or fifty years old and lame widower. He had grown up children from his first wife. Bishamber was rich and had not demanded any dowry. Ramlal was not very happy from this proposal but his wife believed that it was the best marriage proposal for Bholi.

She told Ramlal that since Bishamber was from another village, he didn't know about Bholi's pockmarks and lack of sense. So, they fixed her marriage with Bishamber.

Wedding Procession

On the day of the wedding, Bishamber came as a bridegroom with his friends and family with a lot. When he was about to put garland around Bholi's neck he saw her face. On seeing her pock marks. Bishamber asked for a dowry of five thousand rupees and threatened to leave without marrying Bholi, if not given.

Ramlal pleaded to him but at last he brought the amount of Rs 5,000. Seeing this, Bholi put away her veil and threw the garland in the fire. She refused to marry Bishamber and asked her father to take the money back. The guests started murmuring and shaming Bholi, but she took a firm stand.

The Courageous Bholi

When Bisamber and everyone went away, Ramlal asked Bholi what she would do with her future. Bholi told him that she would not marry and take care of her parents in their old age. She also told them that she would teach at the school just like her teacher.

Sulekha's teacher who was watching all this drama approved Bholi's decision. She smiled at her with satisfaction just like an artist who is satisfied after completing her masterpiece.

Word Meaning

The given page nos. correspond to the pages in the prescribed textbook.

Word	Meaning
PAGE 54	
pock-marks	marks on the skin left by the small-pox disease
mimicked	copy the behaviour or speech of other people in order to make fun of them
stammered	to speak with many pauses or repetitions because of having a speech problem
disfigured	spoiled or damaged
PAGE 55	
revenue	the income that a government receives regularly, or an amount representing such income
PAGE 56	
matted (of hair)	tangled into a thick mass

Word	Meaning
squatted	sat on their heeds
PAGE 57	
scurried	to move quickly with short steps
soothing	having a gently calming effect
PAGE 58	
blossomed a tree or plant	to produce flowers
heart was throbbing	heart was beating much harder and faster than usual due to excitement
PAGE 59	
witless	very foolish or stupid
grocer	one who sells food and household goods
prompted	to cause (someone) to do something
poised	not moving but ready to move

Word	Meaning
humiliate	to make someone feel very ashamed or foolish
muttered	to speak quietly so that it is difficult for other people to hear what you say.
PAGE 60	
triumphant	victorious
prospective	likely to be or become something specified in the future
like a streak of lightening	very quickly
contempt	a strong feeling of disregard for someone
PAGE 61	
thunderstruck	extremely surprised or shocked
contemplating	thinking deeply or carefully about something

Chapter Practice

Objective Questions

• Multiple Choice Questions

1. What do you mean by the word 'simpleton' as used in the chapter to describe Bholi?
(a) Simple
(b) Foolish
(c) Basic
(d) None of these

Ans. (b) The word 'simpleton' as used in the chapter to describe Bholi means foolish.

2. Why did Bholi talk very little?
(a) She stammered
(b) Other kids mimicked her and made fun of her
(c) She was an introvert
(d) None of the above

Ans. (b) Bholi talked very little because other kids used to mimic her and make fun of her.

3. How was Bholi treated in the family?
(a) She was not given new clothes
(b) None cared to wash her clothes
(c) None cared to comb her hair
(d) All of the above

Ans. (d) Bholi was not treated well in her family. She was not given new clothes, no one cared to wash her clothes or comb her hair.

4. What was the name of the cow that Bholi had?
(a) Lakshmi   (b) Gayatri   (c) Ganga   (d) Gayya

Ans. (a) Bholi had a cow named Lakshmi.

5. "What's the matter with you, you fool? I am only taking you to school." Who said this to whom?
(a) Tehsildar to Ramlal
(b) Teacher to Bholi
(c) Ramlal to Bholi
(d) Head-mistress to Bholi

Ans. (c) Ramlal said the given line to Bholi.

6. Whose paintings did she see on the classroom wall?
(a) Cow
(b) Goat
(c) Parrot
(d) All of these

Ans. (d) Bholi saw the paintings of cow, goat and parrot on the classroom wall.

7. What do you think how Bholi used to feel about herself before she started to going to school?
(i) Nobody loves me.
(ii) I'm a burden on my family.
(iii) I am of no good to anyone.
(iv) I wish I could speak and look like other children of my age.
(a) (i) and (ii)
(b) (ii) and (iv)
(c) (iii) and (iv)
(d) All of the above

Ans. (d) Before going to school, Bholi was under-confident and felt low about herself. She must have felt that nobody loves her, she's a burden on her family, no good to anyone and wished that she could speak and look like other children of her age.

8. Why did the garland remain poised in Bishamber's hands?
(a) On seeing pock-marks on Bholi's face
(b) He was shocked to see Bholi
(c) On hearing Bholi's stammering
(d) On seeing veil over bride's face

Ans. (a) On seeing pock-marks on Bholi's face, the garland remain poised in Bishamber's hands.

9. Ramlal went and placed his turban at Bishamber's feet. Here 'his turban' means ....
(a) a piece of cloth
(b) his honour
(c) his money
(d) None of the above

Ans. (b) Ramlal went and placed his turban at Bishamber's feet. Here 'his turban' means 'his honour'.

10. How did Bholi react when Bishamber was about to place garland round her neck?
(a) She happily accepted the garland.
(b) She flung the garland into sacred fire.
(c) She stood up and threw away her veil.
(d) Both (b) and (c)

Ans. (d) Bholi flung the garland into sacred fire, stood up and threw away her veil when Bishamber was about to place garland round her neck.

11. Choose the option that gives the most appropriate response to the statement made by the speaker.

Ramlal was more concerned about his izzat than Bholi's life.

(a) I think Ramlal and his wife were right at their point.
(b) I think Bholi took the right decision by calling off the marriage.
(c) I think Bholi should not have called off the wedding.
(d) I think Bholi should not have said a word.

Ans. (b) Option (b) is the most appropriate response to the statement made by the speaker.

12. Choose the correct option for (i) and (ii).
   (i) Everyone was shocked on hearing Bholi at the time of her wedding.
   (ii) Bholi spoke without any stammering.
   (a) (i) is true (ii) is false   (b) (ii) is true (i) is false
   (c) (i) is the result of (ii)   (d) Both (i) and (ii) are false

Ans. (c) (i) is the result of (ii), i.e., everyone was shocked on hearing Bholi at the time of her wedding because she spoke without any stammering.

• Extract Based MCQs

1. Read the extract to attempt the questions that follow.

"What's the matter with you, you fool? Shouted Ramlal. "I am only taking you to school." Then he told his wife, "Let her wear some decent clothes today or else what will the teachers and the other school girls think of us when they see her?

New clothes had never been made for Bholi. The old dresses of her sisters were passed on to her. No one cared to mend or wash her clothes. But today she was lucky to receive a clean dress which had shrunk after many washings and no longer fitted Champa. She was even bathed and oil was rubbed into her dry and matted hair. Only then did she believe that she was being taken to a place better than her home! When they reached the school, the children were already in their classrooms." **CBSE Question Bank 2021**

(i) Why did Ramlal call Bholi a fool? This was because
   (a) Bholi had become hysterical and was screaming.
   (b) Bholi shouted in fear and pulled her hand away.
   (c) Bholi was behaving foolishly and was running away.
   (d) Bholi had been behaving very strangely with her father.

Ans. (b) Ramlal called Bholi a fool because Bholi shouted in fear and pulled her hand away.

(ii) Pick the option that best describes how Bholi felt at the end of her first day in school.
   (a) lost and scared   (b) calm and peaceful
   (c) elated and peaceful   (d) hopeful and elated

Ans. (d) At the end of her first day at school, Bholi felt hopeful and elated.

(iii) Why was Bholi's hair matted?
   (a) It was entangled and oiled.
   (b) It was never oiled or combed.
   (c) It was not combed regularly.
   (d) It was unkempt and oiled.

Ans. (b) Bholi's hair was matted because it was never oiled or combed.

(iv) The phrase 'passed on' is similar to ....
   (a) hand-me-down   (b) nearly new
   (c) rubbish   (d) scrap

Ans. (a) The phrase passed on is similar to hand-me down which means wearing someone's old clothes.

(v) Pick the sentence that brings out the meaning of 'decent' as used in the extract.
   (a) He gets a decent amount of salary.
   (b) One must be decent when having a conversation with strangers.
   (c) She was dressed in a decent manner for the interview.
   (d) It was very decent of him to lend me some money.

Ans. (c) She was dressed in a decent manner for the interview.

2. Read the extract to attempt the questions that follow.

"Ramlal stood rooted to the ground, his head bowed low with the weight of grief and shame. The flames of the sacred fire slowly died down. Everyone was gone. Ramlal turned to Bholi and said, "But what about you, no one will ever marry you now. What shall we do with you?"

And Sulekha said in a voice that was calm and steady. "Don't you worry, Pitaji! In your old age I will serve you and Mother and I will teach in the same school where I learnt so much. Isn't that right, Ma'am?" The teacher had all along stood in a corner, watching the drama. "Yes, Bholi, of course," she replied. And in her smiling eyes was the light of a deep satisfaction that an artist feels when contemplating the completion of her masterpiece."

CBSE Question Bank 2021

(i) Ramlal stood rooted to the ground because he
   (a) was moved by what he heard.
   (b) was influenced by Bholi's words.
   (c) was in a state of shock.
   (d) was in an immovable position.

Ans. (c) Ramlal stood rooted to the ground because he was in a state of shock.

(ii) Bholi had refused to get married as
   (a) her father couldn't afford the dowry that was demanded.
   (b) the bridegroom had been greedy and was disrespectful.
   (c) the bridegroom had insulted her father.
   (d) her father was getting her married to a man older to her.

Ans. (b) Bholi refused to get married as the bridegroom had been greedy and was disrespectful.

(iii) Pick the sentence that brings out the meaning of 'contemplating' as used in the extract.
   (a) Contemplating sharing my belongings with someone is definitely tough.
   (b) She took some time to respond as she was contemplating what to say.

(c) I was contemplating my reflection in the mirror and was speechless.

(d) She was contemplating though the pages of the document that was with her.

Ans. (b) Option (b) picks out the meaning of contemplating as used in the extract.

(iv) Why did the teacher stand in one corner watching the drama?

(a) She was elated to see what was happening.

(b) She wanted to see what Bholi would be doing.

(c) She didn't want to interfere in a family matter.

(d) She had faith in Bholi standing up for herself.

Ans. (d) The teacher was standing in one corner watching the drama because she had faith in Bholi standing up for herself.

(v) Pick the option that includes the correct matches of Column A with Column B.

Column A	Column B
A. Bholi	1. independent and confident
B. Ramlal	2. burden less and free
C. Teacher	3. sense of contentment and accomplishment
	4. embarrassed and anxious

(a) A-2; B-4; C-3   (b) A-1; B-4; C-3

(c) A-3; B-2; C-1   (d) A-3; B-2; C-4

Ans. (b) 1 4 3 is the correct matching sequence.

PART 2
Subjective Questions

• Short Answer Type Questions

1. Why is Sulekha called 'Bholi'?

Ans. Sulekha is called 'Bholi' because she is a simpleton who had suffered some brain damage after falling off a cot when she was ten months old. As a result, she is slow in learning things and also stammered while speaking.

2. Ramlal was worried about Bholi as she didn't have good looks. Counter the belief that it's important for a girl to be good looking and give a reason for the same. **CBSE Question Bank 2021**

Ans. The belief that it's important for girl to be good looking, is wrong. It is not good looks that bring a person comfortable and prosperous life. It is a person's good behaviour, intelligence, pure heart and courage that ensures that he/she lives a happy life. Good looks doesn't stay forever, whether in a boy or a girl, it's a persons virtues that stay forever and thus, are more important.

3. How did you feel when you read about Bholi being ignored and ill-treated by her parents as a child? **CBSE Question Bank 2021**

Ans. I fell terribly sorrowful when I read about Bholi being ignored and ill-treated by her parents for no fault of her. All the problems faced by Bholi were not caused by her, they were accidents and mishaps. In this case, her parents behaviour was not justified.

4. For what unusual reason is Bholi sent to school? **CBSE 2018**

Ans. Bholi was sent to school because when the primary school opened in their village the Tehsildar advised her father to send his daughter to the school as an example for the villagers. After talking with his wife, it was decided that if the ugly Bholi went to school, it would not harm their other daughter's marriage prospects.

5. Does Bholi enjoy her first day at school? **NCERT**

Ans. Initially, Bholi was scared to go to school. She cried and sat in the corner of her classroom. However, she was fascinated by the colourful pictures on the walls which were very realistic.

Therefore, Bholi was not completely afraid in the school but did enjoy some part of it because of the kind teacher and the new life that it would bring.

6. Does she find her teacher to be different from the people at home? **NCERT**

Ans. Yes, Bholi found her teacher to be different from the people at home. At home, she was neglected and no one paid attention to her. She never bathed nor were her clothes washed. She was criticised and everyone made fun of her. Her teacher was entirely different. She was kind, soft and affectionate. She encouraged her and filled her with a hope of new life.

7. What filled Bholi', a dump cow, with a new hope in her? **CBSE 2015**

or Bholi's heart was overflowing with a 'new hope and a new life'. What does the phrase 'a new hope and a new life' mean to Bholi ? **CBSE 2020**

Ans. Bholi's heart was overflowing with 'a new hope and a new life'. This means that the new hope which came into Bholi's life was the hope of education when Bholi went to school, her teacher showed her the path of a new life through education. She assured Bholi that she would be able to speak without stammer, and that she would be the most learned person in the village and no one would laugh at her instead they would respect her.

8. What objections does Ramlal have to Bishamber's proposal?

Ans. Ramlal was not very happy with Bishamber's proposal. He did not like the fact that Bishamber was of his age.

He had a limp (lameness, difficulty in walking) and his children from his first wife were quite grown up.

It was not a very satisfactory proposition. But he could not do anything for her as Bholi was not beautiful like his other daughters.

9. Why do Bholi's parents accept Bishamber's marriage proposal? **CBSE 2015/2019**

Ans. Bholi's parents accepted Bishamber's marriage proposal Bishamber was a well-to-do person. He had a big shop, owned a house and he was not asking for dowry as well. He did not know about Bholi's pock marks also. Moreover, Bholi was considered to lack sense and she used to stammer also.

10. Why did Bholi dislike Bishamber? **CBSE 2020**

or Why did Bholi not marry Bishamber? **CBSE 2020**

Ans. Bholi did not marry Bishamber because, on seeing her pock-marked face, he asked for a dowry of five thousand rupees in order to marry her and insulted her father. This made Bholi refuse to marry him.

11. What kind of mother was Ramlal's wife? **CBSE 2014**

Ans. Ramlal's wife (Bholi's mother) was a traditional housewife who believed that daughters should not be educated as it would be difficult to find grooms for them. She neglected Bholi as she was ugly and dumb and wanted to get rid of her by marrying her off to anyone.

12. How did Bholi's teacher play an important role in changing the course of her life? **NCERT**

Ans. Bholi used to stammer and was afraid to speak when she attended school in the beginning. Her teacher treated her kindly and encouraged her to have confidence.

She taught Bholi to read and write and made her an independent girl who was aware of her rights. It was because of her teacher's guidance that Bholi developed her personality. Thus, with her kindness, love and affection she changed Bholi's life.

13. Bholi's real name is Sulekha. We are told this right at the beginning. But only in the last but one paragraph of the story is Bholi called Sulekha again. Why do you think she is called Sulekha at that point in the story? **NCERT**

Ans. The word 'Bholi' means a simpleton. Throughout the story she had been a simpleton who hardly expressed her opinion on any matter. The word Sulekha means 'a person with a beautiful sense of letters'. In this story, this word has a larger meaning of being a literate, intelligent and mature individual. After her education, Bholi has really changed to Sulekha and her assertion at the time of her marriage is her announcement to the world that she is no more a Bholi, but is a Sulekha.

14. How would you have reacted if you were one of the guests witnessing Bholi's wedding when she refused to marry Bishamber Nath? **CBSE Question Bank 2021**

Ans. I would have been very proud that she took a stand for herself. It is important for us to understand that no one can humiliate a person like this just because they are not good looking. I would definitely praise Bholi for being so brave.

15. Do you think Bholi's father would have agreed to the match if her mother hadn't insisted upon it? Why/why not? **CBSE Question Bank 2021**

Ans. I think Bholi's father would have agreed to the match even if her mother didn't insist upon it. It is clear that he was thinking about it as he had been worried about her looks when her sister was getting married. He had already thought that because of her looks and less intelligence the chances of Bholi's marriage will be very less.

• Long Answer Type Questions

1. Bholi chose a dignified life of service rather than surrendering herself to a greedy old man for the rest of her life. Education provides the required stimulus to overcome one's personal barriers.

Explain the role of education in shaping the life of a child with respect to the lesson 'Bholi'. **CBSE 2012**

or How did education change Bholi's personality? **CBSE 2020**

Ans. Education brought about a huge change in Bholi's personality. Bholi was a backward child. As a kid, she was a meek girl who had pockmarks all over her body and used to stammer. She could not speak until she was 5 years old. Because of these reasons, she was a neglected child of her family. No one cared for her and she lost all the confidence in herself. When her father was forced to send one of his daughters to school for education, Bholi was the first option. In the school, Bholi bloomed. The teacher treated her with love and care which she had never seen before.

She encouraged the little girl and guided her into becoming a strong-minded girl. Bholi learned to read and write and speak without stammering. As a result, she became confident and independent while being aware of her rights.

She learnt to fight against what she thought was wrong. It was because of her education that she could speak up against the groom and refused to marry a greedy man.

The now independent Bholi told her parents that she would teach at the school and take care of her parents in their old age. This Bholi stands in sharp contrast to the old weak Bholi, all because of her education.

2. Bholi is a child different from others. This difference makes her an object of neglect and laughter. Elaborate.   **CBSE 2019**

Ans. Bholi was a child different from others. She suffered from a weak mind due to her accident (falling from the cot) when she was ten months old. She also started to a stammer while speaking.

Then, she became ugly due to the pock-marks on her face and body on contracting the smallpox disease. All these made her family and other children treat her badly, resulting in her becoming an introvert.

To help such children face the world bravely, we must treat them with love and affection and encourage them to join the mainstream society. We must not mock their disabilities, instead we should give them hope that they can be as good as the other children by motivating and uplifting them.

As we know that every child is special, proper guidance and support should be given to boost up their morals and encourge them to do good in their lives. There are a lot of children like Bholi in our society who need utmost care and affection. We must help them to improve their lives to excel in their future.

3. What do you know about Bishamber Nath? Why did Bholi refuse to marry him?   **CBSE 2020**

Ans. Bishamber Nath was a well-to-do prosperous grocer who was of the same age as Bholi's father. He was a widower who had a shop and a house of his own along with a big bank balance. With grown up children from his first wife, Bishamber decided to get married again and agreed to the proposal of marrying Bholi.

On the day of the marriage, Bishamber came to the venue with his friends and family. He entered the venue with much pomp and show.

At the time of the ceremony, Bholi entered the venue and her veil was slipped. Initially, Bishamber had not asked for any dowry but after looking at Bholi's pock-marked face, he asked Bholi's father to give ₹ 5000 as dowry. Ramlal, Bholi's father started crying and bought out ₹ 5000. Satisfied with the dowry, Bishamber proceeded with the ceremony, but Bholi refused to marry him. She told her father that she would not marry a greedy man such as Bishamber. She would rather take care of her parents in their old age.

4. How did Bholi's teacher help her to overcome her fear of school and become a confident girl?

                                    CBSE 2020

Ans. Bholi was a meek girl. She had pockmarks all her body. She was a slow learner and used to stammer while speaking. When Bholi was sent to school for the first time, she did not know anything about the school. On reaching school she sat down in the corner of her class. When teacher asked her name, she stammered and could not tell her name.

All the girls laughed at her and Bholi felt hesitant and ashamed. After school got over, the teacher came to Bholi and again asked her name. Bholi, with so much stammering, finally spoke and told her name to the teacher. The teacher boosted her confidence by appreciating her effort. She assured Bholi that with time, she would be able to speak confidently. The teacher started by giving her a picture book and then help her reading and writing and learning other big books.

Her kind attitude towards Bholi, her affection and encouragement motivated Bholi to overcome the fear of school and become a confident girl.

5. After reading Bholi's story you decide to write a blog on the importance of educating the girl child and how it empowers her. Write that blog expressing your views.   **CBSE Question Bank 2020**

Ans. **Importance of Educating the Girl Child**

Right to Education is one of the Fundamental Rights as recognised by our Constitution. And yet, in many parts of our country girls are not send to school by their parents.

For the longest time, education has been treated as 'privilege' which only the boy child deserved because people thought girls should only focus on household chores and taking care of their family. And, because of this lack of education, they have been ill-treated even more, for they never learnt what is right and what is wrong.

This understanding comes from education and thus, it's imperative that we educate the girls. It will help them understand what is good for them and will also empower them to stand and fight for their rights. It will stop the mistreatment as it has done for many.

Only then can they be truly safe and happy. Education can also help them become independent, thus, helping them become more confident and self-dependent rather than depending on their family which only leads to more ill treatment and resentment.

● Extract Based Questions

1. Read the extract to attempt the questions that follow.

When she was two years old, she had an attack of small-pox. Only the eyes were saved, but the entire body was permanently disfigured by deep black pockmarks. Little Sulekha could not speak till she was five, and when at last she learnt to speak, she stammered. The other children often made fun of her and mimicked her. As a result, she talked very little.

   (i) What did Sulekha later on come to be known as?

   (ii) Why did children make fun of her?

   (iii) What does the word 'mimicked' mean?

   (iv) Why was Bholi a backward child?

   (v) How was Bholi at the time of birth?

Ans. (i) Sulekha later on came to be known as Bholi.

(ii) Children made fun of her because she stammered while speaking.

(iii) The word 'mimicked' means to copy the speech of others.

(iv) Bholi was a backward child because when she was ten months old, she fell of a cot on her head which damaged some part of her brain.

(v) Bholi was a fair and pretty looking child at the time of birth.

2. Read the extract to attempt the questions that follow.

The next day Ramlal caught Bholi by the hand and said, "Come with me. I will take you to school." Bholi was frightened. She did not know what a school was like. She remembered how a few days ago their old cow, Lakshmi, had been turned out of the house and sold. "N-n-n-n No, no-no-no," she shouted in terror and pulled her hand away from her father's grip. "What's the matter with you, you fool?" shouted Ramlal. "I am only taking you to school."

(i) Why was Bholi being taken to school?

(ii) Why did Bholi shout in terror?

(iii) How was Bholi treated by her family on the first day of her school?

(iv) What did Bholi know about school?

(v) Find the word in the extract which means scared.

Ans. (i) Tehsildar had asked Ramlal to send his daughters to school to set an example in front of the village as Ramlal was the numberdar of the village. So, Bholi was sent to school.

(ii) Bholi shouted in terror as she thought that her father would throw her out of the house and sell her.

(iii) Bholi was given new clothes, her hair were washed and oil was rubbed in her dry and matted hair.

(iv) Bholi did not know anything about school, how it looked and what is being done there.

(v) Frightened is the word which means scared.

3. Read the extract to attempt the questions that follow.

The lady teacher who was in class was saying something to the girls but Bholi could understand nothing. She looked at the pictures on the wall. The colours fascinated her — the horse was brown just like the horse on which the Tehsildar had come to visit their village; the goat was black like the goat of their neighbour; the parrot was green like the parrots she had seen in the mango orchard; and the cow was just like their Lakshmi. And suddenly Bholi noticed that the teacher was standing by her side, smiling at her.

(i) Where was Bholi?

(ii) Why could Bholi not understand anything?

(iii) Why was Bholi sent to school?

(iv) How did Bholi feel when she reached the school?

(v) Whom did Ramlal hand Bholi over to?

Ans. (i) Bholi was in the classroom in the primary school of her village.

(ii) She could not understand anything as it was her first day at school.

(iii) Bholi's parents thought that since she was not good looking and lacked intelligence, no one would marry her and hence, sending her to school was the best option.

(iv) Bholi was scared as she did not know what happened at the school.

(v) Ramlal handed Bholi over to the headmistress of the school, who then took her to her classroom.

4. Read the extract to attempt the questions that follow.

In the other corner of the courtyard, Bholi lay awake on her cot, listening to her parents' whispered conversation. Bishamber Nath was a well-to-do grocer. He came with a big party of friends and relations with him for the wedding. A brass-band playing a popular tune from an Indian film headed the procession, with the bridegroom riding a decorated horse. Ramlal was overjoyed to see such pomp and splendour. He had never dreamt that his fourth daughter would have such a grand wedding. Bholi's elder sisters who had come for the occasion were envious of her luck.

(i) Which conversation was Bholi listening to?

(ii) Who was Bishamber Nath?

(iii) How did Bishmaber come to the wedding procession?

(iv) Why were Bholi's sisters envious of her luck?

(v) Find the word from the extract which is opposite in meaning to modesty?

Ans. (i) Bholi was listening to her parents' conversations about her marriage with Bishamber Nath.

(ii) Bishamber Nath was a well-to-do grocer, a 45-50 years old lame widower from another village.

(iii) Bishamber came to the wedding procession with a big party and a great pomp and show.

(iv) Bholi's sisters were envious of her luck because her bridegroom came with lot of splendor and was riding a decorated horse and he was a well-to-do grocer.

(v) Splendour is the word opposite in meaning to modesty.

Prose

• Objective Questions

Answer the following questions by choosing the correct option.

1. "Our elders are often heard <u>reminiscing nostalgically</u> about those good old Portuguese days" what do you understand by the underlined phrase?
(a) Thinking about future days
(b) Remembering childhood
(c) Thinking fondly of the past
(d) All of the above

2. Where do Coorg's nearest railheads meet?
(a) At Mysore, Mangalore and Hassan
(b) At Mysore and Hassan
(c) At Mangalore and Hassan
(d) At Mysore and Mangalore

3. "The train <u>pulled out</u> of the station" what does the underlined phrase mean?
(a) To enter
(b) To leave
(c) To take a halt
(d) None of these

• Subjective Questions
Extract Based Questions

Directions Read the passage given below and answer the questions that follow.

Oh, please don't be angry with me, my fine madam," he said. "Here, have a seat right up there in front. Everybody move aside please — make way for madam." It was the slack time of day, and there were only six or seven passengers on the bus. They were all looking at Valli and laughing with the conductor. Valli was overcome with shyness. Avoiding everyone's eyes, she walked quickly to an empty seat and sat down. "May we start now, madam?" the conductor asked, smiling. Then he blew his whistle twice, and the bus moved forward with a roar.

1. What do you understand by the 'slack time of the day'?

2. Why did Valli avoid everyone's eyes when she got on the bus?

3. The line "Oh, please don't be angry with me, my fine madam," suggests about the conductor?

4. Why did the conductor blow his whistle?

5. Choose a word from the extract to complete the following.
Overwhelm : Overcome : : Hesitation : ....

Short Answer Type Questions

1. How did the baker ensure that he got his money for the bread supplied?

2. Coorg is the soul of India. Comment.

3. Why India called a country of tea?

4. What did Valli do when the conductor asked her to get down the bus on reaching the town?

Long Answer Type Questions

1. The traditional practices in Goa show us how important they are in maintaining our roots. Do you think children should be taught these practices starting from their childhood? Why?

2. On seeing the dead cow Valli felt very bad. Do you think there are people even today who feel bad for the animals? Why do you think such accidents happen?

3. "The way Chubulov, Natalya and Lomov fought over petty issues is against the behavior and mannerisms of neighbours." Comment. What would you have done to resolve the issue if you were in place of Chubukov?

4. Do you think that forgiveness is better than arguing? Give reasons supporting your answer.

Answers

Objective Questions

1. (c)   2. (a)   3. (b)

Poetry

• Objective Questions

1. The constant nagging by elders can make children ....
(a) annoyed   (b) irritated
(c) argumentative   (d) All of these

2. The poem suggests that
(a) Children should be allowed to make their own decision with the guidance of elders.
(b) Parents should impose discipline over children.
(c) Parents should constantly instruct their children to do one thing or another.
(d) Children should become revel and argument at each and every trivial matter.

3. How are human beings described in the poem?
(a) True and simple
(b) Loving and understanding
(c) Complicated and false
(d) Violent

4. The pirate .... at Custard.
(a) threw his cutlass
(b) threw his liquor
(c) threw his pistols
(d) fired two bullets

5. Why couldn't Mustard fight the pirate?
(a) He did not about the pirate
(b) He felt panicked
(c) He did not see the pirate
(d) The pirate had three weapons

• Subjective Questions
Extract Based Questions

Not one kneels to another, nor to his kind that lived thousands of years ago,
Not one is respectable or unhappy over the whole earth.
So they show their relations to me and I accept them,

1. Who does not kneel to another?

2. How do 'they' show their relations to the poet?

3. Why does the poet happily accept 'them'?

4. Find the word in the extract to complete the following.
Reputable : Respectable : : Bow : ....

5. What does the line 'Not one kneels to another' suggests?

Short Answer Type Questions

1. What do you think about the speaker after reading the poem?

2. Why does the poet become sick when one discusses one's duty to God?

3. Why do human beings so dissatisfied in this world?

4. Why is the poem 'The Tale of Custard the Dragon' called a ballad?

5. What is the true nature of Custard the dragon?

Long answer Type Questions

1. Amanda loves to live in a dream world and does not appreciate any interference. A parent tries to bring her back to the real world. Therefore, there is always a conflict going on. Elaborate.

2. Is the poet right in picturing humans in so many negative colours? Do you think humans are like that or are they better?

3. What does bravery mean to you? Who is a real brave heart?

4. Justify the aptness of the title of the poem.

Answers

Objective Questions

1. (d)   2. (a)   3. (c)   4. (d)   5. (b)

Supplementary

• Objective Questions

1. Which ingredients are required in the making of a scientist?
(a) A first-rate mind
(b) Curiosity
(c) Will to win for the right reasons
(d) All of the above

2. Why did Loisel think that Matilda would be happy on seeing the invitation?
(a) Matilda did not use to go out
(b) Matilda could attend a fine party as she used to dream of
(c) Matilda would have a chance to buy a new dress
(d) Matilda could have a chance to buy a new jewel

3. When did Matilda find that she had lost the necklace?
(a) When she wanted to have a final look before returning it to her friend
(b) When she was coming back form the party
(c) When she sat in the carriage
(d) When she was dancing enthusiastically at the ball

• Extract Based Questions

The book was full of nice pictures and the pictures were in colour — dog, cat, goat, horse, parrot, tiger and a cow just like Lakshmi. And with every picture was a word in big black letters.

"In one month you will be able to read this book. Then I will give you a bigger book, then a still bigger one. In time you will be more learned than anyone else in the village. Then no one will ever be able to laugh at you. People will listen to you with respect and you will be able to speak without the slightest stammer. Understand? Now go home, and come back early tomorrow morning."

Bholi felt as if suddenly all the bells in the village temple were ringing and the trees in front of the school-house had blossomed into big red flowers. Her heart was throbbing with a new hope and a new life.

1. How did Bholi find the teacher at school different from people at her home?

2. What does the line 'Her heart was throbbing with a new hope and a new life' means?

• Answers

Objective Questions

1. (d)   2. (b)   3. (a)

3. How could Bholi become more learned than anyone else in the village?

4. Who is the speaker in the above lines?

5. Choose a word from the extract to complete the following.

.... : Pulsate : : Stammer : Stutter.

Short Answer Type Questions

1. Richard showed that he was not an average boy in second grade. How?

2. What was heart-warming about the competitive spirit in Richard?

3. Describe Matilda's feelings and thoughts as she returned the box of the necklace to her friend.

4. Why did Ramlal not send all his daughters to school?

5. What did Bholi decide to do in her future?

Long Answer Type Questions

1. Although Richard does not win anything at the science fair, it was a stepping stone for his success. In the light of the above statement, give your comments whether competitions are for the sake of winning or to give your best at work.

2. Imagine yourself to be a newspaper reporter. You came to know of Matilda's sorry tale from Mme Forestier and decided to write an article on the ills of vanity and virtues of leading a life of simplicity, truth and honesty for your readers.

3. Sending Bholi to school was a 'blessing in disguise'. Do you agree? Support your answer on the basis of the text.

4. The story, 'Bholi', throws light on some social evils being practiced in our society. Bholi took a stand and succeeded in overcoming the social barriers. What can you contribute to change the social attitudes illustrated in the story?

Practice Paper 1*
(Unsolved)

General Instructions

■ Time : 2 Hours
■ Max. Marks : 40

1. The question paper contains three sections A, B and C.
2. **Section A** Reading section has 14 questions. Attempt a total of 10 questions as per specific instructions for each passage.
3. **Section B** Grammar section has 7 questions. Attempt a total of 5 questions and writing section has 2 questions. Attempt questions as per specific instructions for each.
4. **Section C** Literature section has extract based questions, short answer type questions and long answer type questions. Internal choice is given for individual questions.
5. Marks are mentioned against each question.

** As exact Blue-print and Pattern for CBSE Term II exams is not released yet. So the pattern of this paper is designed by the author on the basis of trend of past CBSE Papers. Students are advised not to consider the pattern of this paper as official. It is just for practice purpose.*

Section A   Reading

I Read the passage given below.

1. Time management is the act of planning and managing time that is spent on various activities. It helps to increase the effectiveness and efficiency of the time utilised. It helps us to work smarter instead of harder and also enables us to get more work done in less amount of time. Planning the time may seem as a wastage of time in itself; however, the benefits of time management are enormous. It results in less stress, increased productivity, efficiency, professional and personal growth, etc.

2. Time is limited and hence, it is important that we plan our time wisely and make the best use of the limited hours in a day. Time is something that we cannot store or save for later use. We cannot retrieve the time that has been wasted; hence, we need to learn to use it effectively. If we have to manage time effectively, we need to be organised and focused.

3. With the help of time management techniques, we can accomplish more with lesser efforts. Time management includes effective planning of activities, setting of goals, setting deadlines, delegating work, prioritising our activities, etc.

4. Most people feel that they always have too much to do and within too little time. Managing time wisely will help to find the right balance between time and work. A few people resort to multi-tasking in order to get the work done within the specified time limit.

5. At times, this may result in poor performance in the various tasks assigned. The major mistake committed while working is when one is in a rush to meet the deadline without taking proper breaks for rest or relaxation. It is impossible for anyone to focus on work and to produce good results without considering any break in between. It helps to perform better if one takes five minutes of break every two hours of work. One can either take a walk, enjoy a cup of coffee or simply meditate.

Proper time management is the cornerstone of a successful life and ensures achievement of one's goals in a healthy manner.

6. When it comes to harnessing your time, time management books are a must. They are a great way to learn from an expert and understand your time better than ever before. Many of the best lessons can be picked from these books. And it just so happens that many of those life-changing books are listed on the internet.

7. So, whether you are looking for time management for school/college students, stay-at-home parents, business executives, or anyone else looking to better utilise their time, reading these books is a wise way to learn the skill of managing your time.

Based on your understanding of the passage, answer **any five** out of the seven questions by choosing the correct option. **5 × 1 = 5**

1. According to the author, what, from the following are the consequences of time management?
(a) It diminishes stress
(b) It increases productivity and efficiency
(c) It contributes in overall growth of a person
(d) All of the above

2. Select the option that suitably completes the dialogue with reference to the above passage.

Dia: I have so much work to do this weekend. There are not enough hours in a Day ! I don't think it's possible.

Sona : Of course, it is. All you have to do is ....
(a) learn how to manage your time according to your work
(b) let go of all the tension and start from scratch every time you feel troubled
(c) learn to let go of all stress
(d) divide your work with your family. That way you will have lessen your burden.

3. Choose the option that best conveys the meaning of 'Time is limited'.
(a) Time is a renewable resource
(b) Since the end of the world is near, we don't have much time
(c) There are only 24 hours in a day and we must make the most of them
(d) There is enough time for everyone in the world

4. What is /are the problem(s) that may be the result of multi-tasking ? Choose one option from the following.
(a) Failure to focus in one's work
(b) Poor performance in time management
(c) Poor performance in the tasks
(d) Both (a) and (c)

5. Select the option with the underlined words that can suitably replace 'cornerstone' (Paragraph 5).
(a) Trust is the <u>fundamental element</u> of a healthy friendship.
(b) Officials held a ceremony to lay the <u>foundation stone</u> for a new library.
(c) Let's hide this game at our secret place in the <u>hidden bedrock</u> in the school playground.
(d) It's finally complete. They are just putting in the <u>final piece</u> in place.

6. Alliteration refers to the occurrence of the same letter or sound at the beginning of adjacent or closely connected words.

From the options given below, select a phrase from the above passage that can be an example of alliteration.
(a) 'Effective planning of activities'
(b) 'Store or save for later use'
(c) 'Prioritising our activities'
(d) 'Find the right balance'

7. Select the option that lists the activities included in time management.
1. Crashing deadlines 2. Abortive planning
3. Setting of goals 4. Proper planning
5. Assigning of work
(a) 2, 4 and 5 (b) 2, 3 and 4
(c) 1, 3 and 5 (d) 3, 4 and 5

II. Read the passage given below.

1. "Teenagers? Stress? You must be joking." This is probably the reaction when asked whether teenagers get fretful and apprehensive. For, it is generally believed that they have "no responsibilities, no worries and no duties." But that is not true.

2. In today's competitive world, one needs to struggle and fight to make it in this dynamic, yet uncertain environment that is both stressful and anxiety inducing. Teenagers face a myriad of pressures, three of which are briefly discussed here. The pressure to perform i.e. to do well academically comes principally from parents, teachers and peers.

3. The lack of aptitude tests or respecting the students' preferences push them into fields which may not interest them or for which they are not equipped. Apart from the pressure to perform well, they are often burdened with the pressure to conform to the norms laid down by society. Next, teenagers are pressurised to reform themselves. This is commonly experienced especially by students in the age group of 13 to 17 years.

Everybody is telling them when to wake up and what to do. As a result of pressure, teenagers are often found to be very anxious. Here's what you can do to deal with these pressures. A sign of anxiety is holding one's breath. The easy way out is to take deep breaths at regular intervals, trying to calm your mind.

4. Modern life's competitiveness and challenges put a tremendous load of work on teenagers. They need to understand that they are strong enough to handle the tough challenges in life, studying and assignments being two of them. Procrastinators i.e. people who habitually delay and postpone doing their work, need to cultivate 'the art of starting' and this involves dealing with the minor discomfort experienced while beginning a task. Once a job has started, it is much easier to continue.

5. Some students worry about factors like social and financial status, intelligence and habits that might make them different from their peers. Effective stress management lies in having a healthy attitude towards competition, work, friends and acquaintances. It lies in taking life as it comes, doing your best and being prepared for the worst.

Based on your understanding of the passage, answer **any five** out of the seven questions by choosing the correct option.   **5 × 1 = 5**

8. The purpose of the passage is to ......

Choose the correct option.
(a) Understand the problems that teenagers deal with
(b) Criticise everyone for the problems that the teenagers face
(c) Suggest few solutions to the teenagers' problems
(d) Both (a) and (c)

9. Select the option that gives the correct meaning of the following statement.

"Once a job has started, it is much easier to continue."
(a) No matter the difficulty of a job, it is easy to do.
(b) Continuation of an activity is much easier that attempting it.

(c) All things, in life, are easy to do.
(d) Both (a) and (b)

10. According to the passage, the way to deal with anxiety is to ....
(a) try to calm one's mind
(b) take deeps breaths all the time
(c) take deep breaths at regular interval
(d) try to develop a strong aptitude

11. Choose the option that lists the correct answer for the following.

1. Ajay is a 13 year old boy who is taking up small cooking courses as he wants to pursure a cooking career.

2. Rajan is a 15 year old boy who is into books and has frequent breakdowns.
(a) Both are under the stress of competition
(b) Both Ajay and Rajan are devoid of stress
(c) Rajan is stressed while Ajay is enjoying life
(d) Ajay is stressed while Rajan is enjoying his life

12. Which of the following factors become a source of worry for many students?
1. Social status   2. Financial status
3. Intelligence   4. Habits
5. Career   6. Relationships
(a) 1 and 5   (b) 2 and 4
(c) 3 and 5   (d) All of these

13. In what, from the following, way can one deal with procastination?
(a) By beginning the task
(b) By postponing the work
(c) By facing challenges in life
(d) By habitually delaying attempting their work

14. The passage suggests that ...... obstructs and stresses the teenagers in life. Select the correct options
(a) anxiety and its discomfort
(b) peer pressure from their classmates
(c) pressure from their parents and teachers
(d) Both (a) and (c)

Section B
Grammar

III. Attempt **any five** questions out of the following seven questions.

(i) He said that he ...... get up early in the morning.

(ii) The rag-pickers of India ...... (present) a pitiable sight.

(iii) He applied for and was ...... (grant) legal aid by the Labour Ministry.

(iv) I need ...... space for any luggage.

(v) You are such ...... good dancer.

(vi) Change the given sentence into Indirect speech.

The Principal said, 'well done ! My boys'.

(vii) Change the given sentences into Direct speech.

He asked her if she could lend him her umbrella.

Writing

IV. Write a letter to the Manager, ABC Company, cancelling your order of office stationery since it is not delivered in stipulated time. You are XYZ, Purchasing Officer of A–Z. Company.   **2**

Or

Write a letter to the Manager, Jeevan Industries, Ltd., Delhi enquiring about the car exchange scheme offered by their company. You are Ravi Verma, a resident of B -46, Rohini, Delhi. .

V. A survey was conducted to find out how the teenagers spend free time. Using the data given in the pie chart, write an analytical paragraph.

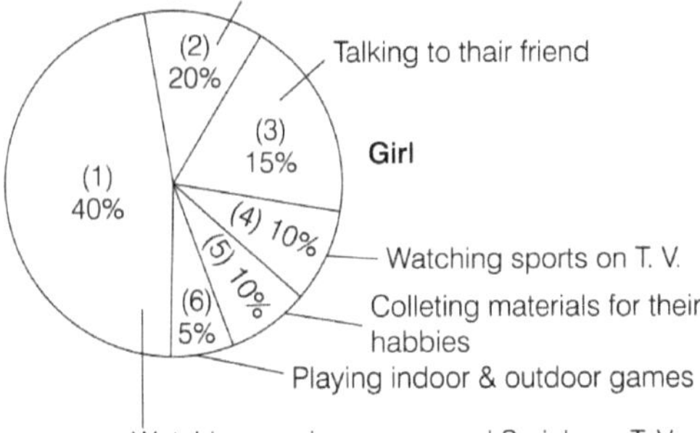

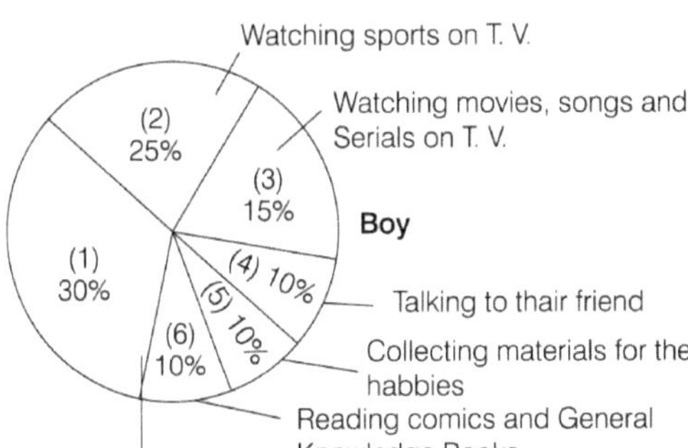

Or

A bar graph is given which shows the calorie source for UK males at different life periods. Using the data given, write an analytical paragraph .

Calorie Source for UK males at different life periods.

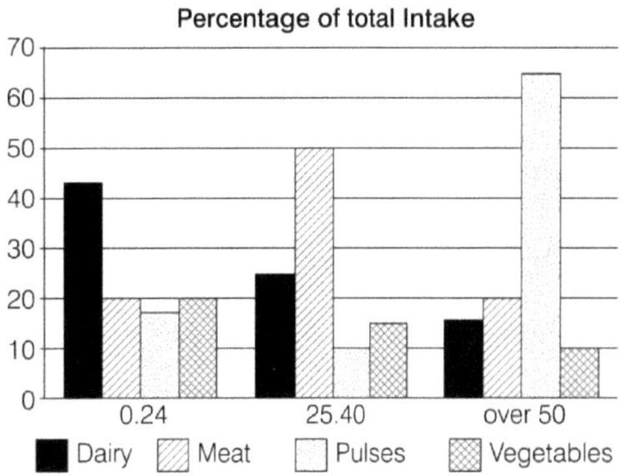

Section C   Literature

VI. Read the following extract and answer the questions that follow.

I can still recall the typical fragrance of those loaves. Loaves for the elders and the bangles for the children. Then we did not even care to brush our teeth or wash our mouths properly.

And why should we? Who would take the trouble of plucking the mango leaf for the teeth brush? And why was it necessary at all? The tiger never brushed his teeth. Hot tea could wash and clean up everything so nicely, after all!   **3 × 1 = 3**

(i) Who brought the loaves and bangles for the elders and the children respectively?

(ii) Why, according to the author, he did not need to brush his teeth?

(iii) Are those loaves of bread still available?

Or

Don't bite your nails, Amanda!

Don't lunch your shoulders, Amanda!

Stop that slouching and set-up straight, Amanda!

(i) Why is Amanda receiving the instructions?

(ii) How is Amanda's posture?

(iii) Which literary device is used in the given lines?

VII. Read the following extract and answer the questions that follow.

Ebright and his college roommate, James R wong, worked all that night drawing pictures and constructing plastic models of molecules to show how it could happen. Together they later wrote the paper that explained the theory.

Surprising no one who knew him, Richard Ebright graduated from Harvard with the highest honours, second in his class of 1510. $3 \times 1 = 3$

(i) Who was Wong?

(ii) Why was no one surprised at Ebright's graduation?

(iii) …… is a synonym of rank.

Or

She was not convinced. 'No', she replied, "there is nothing more humiliating than to have a shabby air in the midst of rich women."

Then her husband cried out, "How stupid we are! Go and find your friend Madame Forestier and ask her to lend you her jewels."

She uttered a cry of job. 'Its true!' She said! "I had not thought of that."

(i) Why did she need jewels?

(ii) What did her husband suggest her?

(iii) Shabby air means ……… .

VIII Answer the following questions. (Attempt any 2)

(i) Why did the conductor call Valli 'madam'?   3

(ii) How are animals different from humans?   3

(iii) What information about Lutkins did the hack driver give to the narrator?   3

IX. Answer the following questions.

(i) What do you learn about bravery after reading the poem 'The Tale of Custard the Dragon'?   4

Or

A little help and guidance to those who are experiencing grief may help them understand and overcome it. It is a big relief for the grieving person if support and care are extended to them. Explain citing examples from the lesson 'The Sermon at Benares.'

(ii) What characteristics does one need to become a scientist, an economist, a historian. …… ? Does it simply involve reading many books ? Justify   4

Or

The story teaches us that education plays an important role in making us aware of our rights and duties. Should people be aware of their rights and duties? What are some of the ways in which society treats girls differently ?

ANSWERS

I. 1. (d)   2. (a)   3. (c)   4. (c)   5. (a)   6. (b)   7. (b)

II. 8. (d)   9. (b)   10. (c)   11. (c)   12. (d)   13. (a)   14. (c)

Practice Paper 2*
(Unsolved)

General Instructions

■ Time : 2 Hours
■ Max. Marks : 40

1. The question paper contains three sections A, B and C.
2. **Section A** Reading section has 14 questions. Attempt a total of 10 questions as per specific instructions for each passage.
3. **Section B** Grammar section has 7 questions. Attempt a total of 5 questions and writing section has 2 questions. Attempt questions as per specific instructions for each.
4. **Section C** Literature section has extract based questions, short answer type questions and long answer type questions. Internal choice is given for individual questions.
5. Marks are mentioned against each question.

** As exact Blue-print and Pattern for CBSE Term II exams is not released yet. So the pattern of this paper is designed by the author on the basis of trend of past CBSE Papers. Students are advised not to consider the pattern of this paper as official. It is just for practice purpose.*

Section A   Reading

I. Read the passage given below.

1. The Walt Disney Company became the first major media company to ban advertisements for candy bars and junk food on its television channels, radio stations and websites, to stop food manufacturers from peddling nutritionally challenged fattening junk for kids. The ban covers food with too much sugar, too much salt or a full meal more than 600 calories. Predictably, the outraged public said that banning smoking in public places and artery-blocking transfats in food was bad enough, but stopping them from guzzling comfort drinks by the litres was almost a human rights violation.

2. It seems most people are not just happy choosing their own poison. They also want it in super sized doses, guaranteed to kill sooner than later. After tobacco use, obesity is the biggest public health bugbear that triggers more avoidable diseases and deaths than malnutrition. Overweight and obesity are the leading causes of global deaths, killing 2.8 million adults each year. Worldwide, obesity has more than doubled since 1980. The reasons for poor lifestyle choices are many, with almost all driven by socio-economic causes such as low education and limited income. Like killer infections, obesity and the resultant type-2 diabetes affect the poor more than the affluent, largely because processed and fast food are cheaper and take less or no time to prepare than healthy home-cooked meals.

3. Limiting food choices, however, is not enough. The need is to get children off their chairs and into the playgrounds. Too much screen time, social - networking, followed by online and video gaming and television, are making healthy children fat and putting them at risk of type-2 diabetes in the second decade of their lives. The lifestyle disease that interferes with the way the body metabolises glucose typically affects people in their fifties and sixties and is linked with a host of complications.

4. The official measure of obesity in adults is Body Mass Index (BMI), which is calculated by dividing a person's weight in kilograms by the square of his height in metres (kg/m^2). The WHO definition is: a BMI greater than or equal to 25 is overweight, 30 is obese, but the cut-offs for South Asians are 23 for overweight and 25 for obese.

Based on your understanding of the passage, answer any five out of seven questions by choosing the correct options.   **5 × 1 = 5**

1. The products banned by Walt Disney includes
1. candy bars
2. tobacco
3. salads
4. milk products

(a) Only 1   (b) 1 and 3
(c) 1 and 2   (d) 1 and 4

2. Which one of the following was considered a human rights violation by the outraged public?
(a) Banning smoking in public places.
(b) Throwing litter on the road.
(c) Stopping people from drinking comfort drinks.
(d) Using mobile phones while driving.

3. Select the option that suitably completes the dialogue with reference to the passage.

    Joe They shouldn't have banned cold drinks and chips at least. Banning public smoking was already bad enough.

    Sid You can't be serious. ....
(a) Banning smoking was a huge mistake.
(b) They are not really harmful to our bodies.
(c) They are equally harmful to our bodies.
(d) They don't affect us so much so it really was an extreme step.

4. Choose the option that best conveys the message in - 'Limiting food choices is not enough'.
(a) Banning harmful food items is not enough, other steps need to be taken too.
(b) Stopping people from eating altogether is also necessary.
(c) Checking and maintaining proper BMI is also necessary.
(d) Cancelling food choices altogether is the only option.

5. Select the option with the underlined words that can suitably replace 'peddling' (Paragraph 1).
(a) The accused are expected to face charges of embezzlement, bribery and influence <u>advocating wrong actions</u>.
(b) Buyers should also be aware that some sellers are <u>promoting persistently</u> counterfeit MAC products.
(c) It is the sort of climb that you just settle into, get a rhythm, concentrate and keep <u>moving forward</u>.
(d) He took a booth at the craft fair in order to <u>craftly sell</u> his handmade belts.

6. Metaphor is a figure of speech that directly refers to one thing by mentioning another. From the options given below, choose a word that is an example of a metaphor, from the above passage.
(a) Junk
(b) Poison
(c) Fast foods
(d) Trans fats

7. Select the option that lists the actions that are making children fat and prone to diseases.
1. Overuse of mobile and laptops
2. Getting off of their chairs
3. Online gaming
4. Watching television for hours
5. Eating banned foods

(a) 1, 4 and 5   (b) 1, 3 and 4
(c) 2, 3 and 5   (d) 2, 3 and 4

II. Read the passage given below.

1. Tourism, for millennia, has been a perpetual industry. Though initially unorganised and highly chaotic, it retained a place in each nook of history. Present tourism scenario in India is on the rise, with destinations grabbing eyeballs globally and domestically. Being the youngest nation in the world, it's no wonder that the aggregate of 'millennial's' spends more time and money on travel than previous generations. This could be huge for the economy of various states that rely majorly on tourism, if only it were sustainable.

2. Unsustainability prevails throughout the country, in states with higher domestic tourist inflow than foreign. The Dev Bhoomi is a prime example. No matter how popular, Uttarakhand tourism is loop-holed through and through.

3. Approx. 80% of tourists arrive to complete the Char Dham Yatra. Such unchecked tourism puts immense pressure on natural and infrastructure facilities. The extreme shortage of accommodation in correspondence with thriving footfalls has led to the construction of illegal buildings, the majority of which exist on riverbanks.

With an increasing number of tourists coming in through private vehicles to save 'transportation money', pollution levels are rising, increasing temperatures in return. With unlawful construction and pollution on riverbanks, the Ganges could cause direct harm to local species in Rishikesh and Haridwar.

4. Around 10,000 hilly areas are being converted for the construction of roads alone. We know, roads are basic infrastructure, but the Forest Conservation Act requires a project developer to plant trees in a non-forest/degraded forest area equal to or twice the trees it's clearing respectively, to compensate which does not happen.

5. Regardless of what figures say, if we look forward to sustainable tourism being the target market, it leaves little choice to the rest of the hierarchy. Consciously making efforts to be responsible tourists and thinking of how to provide for the local community/environment in a way – tiny or big, could act as a catalyst in obliterating this ruckus due to ignorance. After all, there can only ever be seven Deadly Sins and wanderlust isn't one of them.

Tourist Statistics Year-2018 of Major Tourist Destinations

Sl. No.	Name of Tourist Destination	Year 2018		
		Indian	Foreigner	Total
1.	Dehradun	2453998	30291	2484289
2.	Rishikesh	656074	6044	662118
3.	Mussoorie	2870475	1550	2872025
4.	Pauri	77823	1238	79061
5.	Srinagar	203912	276	204188
6.	Kotdwar (Swargashram, Chilla)	415769	11537	427306
7.	Rudraprayag (without Kedarnath)	273700	1847	275547
8.	Kedarnath	730387	1604	731991
9.	Gopeshwar (Nandprayag, Mundoli, Tharali etc.)	245228	0	245228
10.	Joshimath (Govindghat, Ghangaria)	435537	516	436053

Based on your understanding of the passage, answer any five out of the seven questions by choosing the correct option.　　　　　　　**5 × 1 = 5**

8. The purpose of the passage is to ....

Choose the correct option.

(a) Focus on the drawbacks of tourism

(b) Focus on the profits of tourism

(c) Focus on making tourism a sustainable process

(d) Both (b) and (c)

9. Select the option that is true for the two statements given below.

1. Most of the tourists come to complete the Char Dham Yatra.

2. The Ganges could cause direct harm to local species in Rishikesh and Haridwar.

(a) (1) is the result of (2)

(b) (1) is the reason for (2)

(c) (1) is independent of (2)

(d) (1) contradicts (2)

10. Select the option that gives the correct meaning of the following statement. "There can only ever be seven deadly sins and wanderlust isn't one of them".

(a) One of the sins can be changed but the number can't be changed

(b) Wanderlust is not a sin

(c) Wanderlust is a sin but not a Deadly sin

(d) Both (a) and (c)

11. According to the information given in the above passage, Dev Bhoomi is an example of

(a) The amplification of the number of foreign tourists

(b) The amplification of the number of domestic tourists

(c) The diminishing of the number of domestic tourists

(d) The increase in the number of foreign tourists

12. On the basis of the data given in the passage, which of the following options list the cities with the highest number of visiting tourists?

1. Dehradun
2. Rishikesh
3. Mussoorie
4. Pauri
5. Srinagar

(a) 1,2 and 4
(b) 2,3 and 5
(c) 1 and 3
(d) 1,2 and 3

13. What are ten thousand hilly areas being converted for?

(a) Construction of roads
(b) To develop plant/forest projects
(c) To provide accommodation
(d) Both (a) and (c)

14. This passage suggests that with an increase in the number of tourist population ....

Select the correct option.

(a) Housing problems are increasing
(b) Pollution levels are rising
(c) Population levels are rising
(d) Deforestation is increasing

Section B

Grammar

III. Attempt any five questions from the following seven question. **5 × 1 = 5**

(i) Once upon a time there ...... (live) a man called Damocles.

(ii) He gave me ...... lecture in which he pointed out an error in the book.

(iii) Everyone ...... save the natural resources of the Earth.

(iv) It is time we ...... (act) with determination.

(v) There are ...... tourists who visit the Red Fort in Delhi.

(vi) Change the given sentence into Indirect speech. Sohan said to Shipa, "Bring me a glass of water please."

(vii) Change the given sentence into Direct speech. The officer commanded the troop to move forward.

Writing

IV. You are Devinder / Devika, Secretary of your shcool's Science Club. Write a letter to M/S Scientific Suppliers, Kashmere Gate, Delhi, placing an order for working models of physics principles (3 items - give names) for your club, based on the price list given by the supplier. Invent the necessary details. **2**

Or

Write a letter Mr. Shyam, Manager, ABC Real Estates Inquiring about the purchase of a property in or around Shalimar Bagh Delhi. Include the necessary details such as pricing, budget space, etc. You are Varun / Kavita, resident of C -47 Avenue Park, Delhi.

V. The given graph shows the average number of UK commuters travelling each day by car, bus or train between 1970 and 2020. Write an analytical paragraph based on the graph. **3**

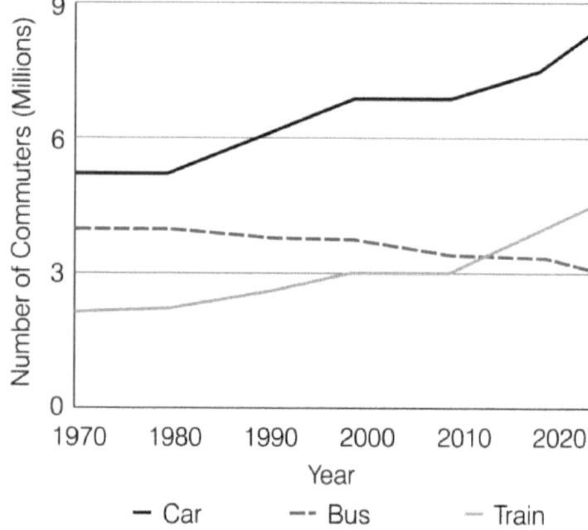

The given graph shows the data collected regarding the sale of different kind of books to understand which category is popular amongst teenagers. Using this data, write an analytical paragraph.

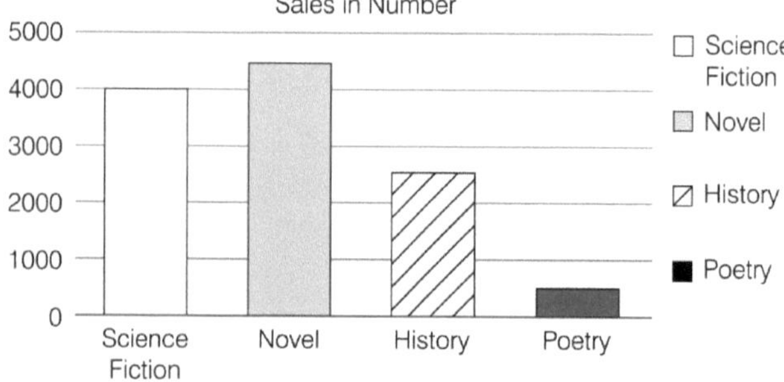

Section C   Literature

VI. Read the following extract and answer the questions that follow.

Valli devoured everything with her eyes. But when she started to look outside, she found her view cut off by a canvas blind that covered the lower part of her window. So she stood up on the seat and peered over the blind. The bus was now going along the bank of a canal.

The road was very narrow. On one side there was the canal, and beyond it, palm trees, grassland, distant mountains and the blue, blue sky. On the other side was a deep ditch and then acres and acres of green fields - green, green, green, as far as the eye could see.   **3 × 1 = 3**

(i) Why did Valli stand on her seat?

(ii) What did Valli devour with her eyes?

(iii) Which word in the passage means the same as 'peeped'?

Or

CHUBUKOV: And that blind hen, yes, that turnip-ghost has the confounded cheek to make a proposal, and so on! What? A proposal!

NATALYA: What proposal?

CHUBUKOV: Why, he came here to propose to you.

NATALYA: To propose? To me? Why didn't you tell me so before?

CHUBUKOV: So he dresses up in evening clothes. The stuffed sausage! The wizen-faced frump!

(i) Who is being talked about in the above extract?

(ii) What kind of proposal is being talked about?

(iii) Who wrote the above lines?

VII. Read the following extract and answer the questions that follow.

"Lutkins? I saw him around here about an hour ago. Hard fellow to catch though - always up to something or other. He's probably trying to start up a poker game in the back of Fritz's shop. I'll tell you, boy - is there any hurry about locating Lutkins"?

"Yes. I want to catch the afternoon train back to the city." I was very important and secret about it.

    3 × 1 = 3

(i) Who is the speaker in the first line of the extract?

(ii) Who was Lutkins?

(iii) Where did the above conversation take place?

Or

New clothes had never been made for Bholi. The old dresses of her sisters were passed on to her. No one cared to mend or wash her clothes. But today she was lucky to receive a clean dress which had shrunk after many washings and no longer fitted Champa. She was even bathed and oil was rubbed into her dry and matted hair. Only then did she begin to believe that she was being taken to a place better than her home!

(i) Why did no one care to mend or wash Bholi's clothes?

(ii) Where was Bholi being taken to?

(iii) What made Bholi believe that she was being taken to a place better than her home?

VIII. Answer the following questions (*Attempt any 2*).

(i) What kind of parents do you think Bholi have?   **3**

(ii) How did everyone in the house used to tease Custard the dragon?   **3**

(iii) Why did Prince Siddhartha leave the palace and become a beggar?   **3**

IX. Answer the following questions.

(i) What question does the poem 'Amanda' raise?   **4**

Or

As adults, one important thing to learn is how to manage our temper. Some of us tend to get angry quickly, while others remain calm. Can you think of three ill effects that result from anger with reference to the play 'The Proposal'?

(ii) A little confession would have changed the life of Matilda. Should we confess our mistakes courageously? Write your opinion.   **4**

Or

Draw the character sketch of the narrator in the story 'The Hack Driver'.

Practice Paper 3*
(Unsolved)

General Instructions

- Time : 2 Hours
- Max. Marks : 40

1. The question paper contains three sections A, B and C.
2. **Section A** Reading section has 14 questions. Attempt a total of 10 questions as per specific instructions for each passage.
3. **Section B** Grammar section has 7 questions. Attempt a total of 5 questions and writing section has 2 questions. Attempt questions as per specific instructions for each.
4. **Section C** Literature section has extract based questions, short answer type questions and long answer type questions. Internal choice is given for individual questions.
5. Marks are mentioned against each question.

As exact Blue-print and Pattern for CBSE Term II exams is not released yet. So the pattern of this paper is designed by the author on the basis of trend of past CBSE Papers. Students are advised not to consider the pattern of this paper as official. It is just for practice purpose.

Section A Reading

I. Read the passage given below.

1. Creamy outlook with soft speech presentation is a prime facial attraction that brings joy on the withering faces with a mixture of sensational touch. A smile with grace is the ultimate boon to mankind, keeping any melancholy at bay. Old age is often miscalculated as a liability with little attention paid to the aged. Their talents and learned potential are buried alive with undue care by an oblivious approach due to their disfigured or deformed physical structure taken over by age. It happens to us all, however hard we may try to delay the process. We grow old. Cosmetic surgery may remove the wrinkles, skin which has sagged may be tightened by means of a facelift and a hairdresser may dye grey hair to a more youthful colour, but we cannot remain young forever.

2. However, what is important is the quality of life. Some people are lucky to be taken care of at home whereas others may have to move to old age residential homes. Most of the elders in old age homes are not very happy as they are confined and feel isolated. But there are some elders who feel comfortable in old age homes for the freedom and friendly atmosphere with other elders who keep their company, enjoying the time with TV, games and gossip. The worst part of ageing is that often the mind becomes less alert. As people grow older, they experience short-term memory loss. Later, some may suffer from dementia, often in the form of Alzheimer's disease. By no means are all elderly people in this category.

3. Many senior citizens are in possession of all their faculties and see retirement as a time of freedom. Not only that, if they have a generous retirement pension, they are likely to be quite well off with money to be spent on a holiday and other luxuries. Because of this, both businesses and government have a new respect for what is known as 'grey power'.

4. It is unfortunate that many people regard old people as geriatrics who have one foot in the grave. Someone should remind them that they too would be old one day! They are honoured with the senior citizen label granted by the authorities with due regard being paid to them by other people. One should always bear in mind the old saying 'tit for tat' which denotes its symbolic regulation of periodical sufferings. The aforesaid misdoings of emotional disparity, done by striding steps, is a curse to mankind.

Based on your understanding of the passage, answer any five out of the seven questions by choosing the correct option.　　　　　**5 × 1 = 5**

1. According to the author, what, from the following, is the greatest lesson being taught by the passage?
(a) Becoming old is a great privilege to be bestowed upon someone
(b) One should always theat old people with the same respect they want themselves to be treated with
(c) Some people are always happy no matter where or how old they are
(d) None of the above

2. Select the option that suitably completes the dialogue with reference to the above passage.

Jenny: Old people are so wierd, with their wrinkled and saggy skin.

Mark: You shouldn't say things like these. ....
(a) They are so lonely, you should pity them
(b) They already live in old age homes, alone
(c) They are more funny than weird
(d) One day will be like them and should respect them.

3. Choose the option that best conveys the meaning of 'tit for tat.'
(a) Treating someone with utmost hatred
(b) Inflicting someone with your injury
(c) Treating someone the some way they treated you
(d) Both (a) and (c)

4. What may cosmetic surgery do for the old people?

Choose one option from the following.
(a) Remove the wrinkled skin
(b) Tighten the saggy skin
(c) Dye grey hair as black
(d) All of the above

5. Select the option with the underlined words that can suitably replace 'confined'. (Paragraph 2).
(a) The doctor <u>openly isolated</u> the patient to his hospital room.
(b) When he was in prison, the inmate was <u>terribly treated</u> in his cell for half of a day.
(c) At least the dog is <u>resting peacefully</u> on the floor.
(d) A conference took place in the <u>uncomfortably restricted</u> room of the hotel

6. Assonance refers to the resemblance of sound in nearby world or syllables.

From the given options, choose a phrase from the above passage that can be an example of assonance.
(a) 'Who have one foot'
(b) 'Old people as geriatrics'
(c) 'Tit for tat'
(d) We grew old

7. Select the option that lists the things that old people do in old age homes.
1. Use a hairdresser to colour their hair
2. Behave friendly with other elders
3. Have cosmetic surgery
4. Watch TV
5. Play games and gossip with each other
(a) 1, 2 and 4　　　　　(b) 1, 2 and 5
(c) 2, 4 and 5　　　　　(d) 3, 4 and 5

II. Read the passage given below.

1. Ask a dying man in a hot desert, and he would somehow enable himself to utter, "I wish I could get some water... ." Without being poetic or philosophic, we must realise that 'water', which is generally taken for granted, might be the most precious commodity in future if we do not mend our ways in the present. There can't be a safe tomorrow if we are not ready to act today. It becomes one of our prime responsibilities to save our precious water supplies. Out of the total water available on the earth, only 3 per cent is fresh water.

   Out of this 3% freshwater, only 1% is available for drinking. In our daily chores we might have observed that we ourselves forget to turn off the tap early in the morning when we go to freshen ourselves up. We, at the moment, do not realise that our carelessness might be one of the reasons for the water crisis for the future generation. 'Many a drop makes an ocean.' Our small efforts can contribute to the conservation of the water in one or the other way. Each one of us has the ability to make a difference.

2. The ground water supply is reducing over time. Due to lack of suitable irrigation water, or the mismanagement of water in India, farmers over-extract water which is thought to be one of the shocking facts that affects the health of the cultivable agricultural lands. It is essential to adopt several water conservation techniques. It is necessary to launch several intensive awareness campaigns regarding the importance

of water and its conservation so that these can make people aware about the wise management of water supply. The unwise use of water is not the only reason for the water crisis; the pollution of water resources is also an important reason for the deterioration of water supplies. So, water should be meticulously harnessed and carefully conserved.

3. Installation of a water meter can help you save water. Growing grass appropriately outside your house or having a lawn can be helpful. Keeping your water supplying taps and showers tightly closed and repairing water leakage can contribute to the conservation of water. Collect water for reuse anytime you are running the water. Simply run it into a bucket, watering cane, or pitcher.

4. Several plans, policies and promises are made by the government, several announcements are made on the electronic media but the problem is still the same because we do not make sincere efforts.

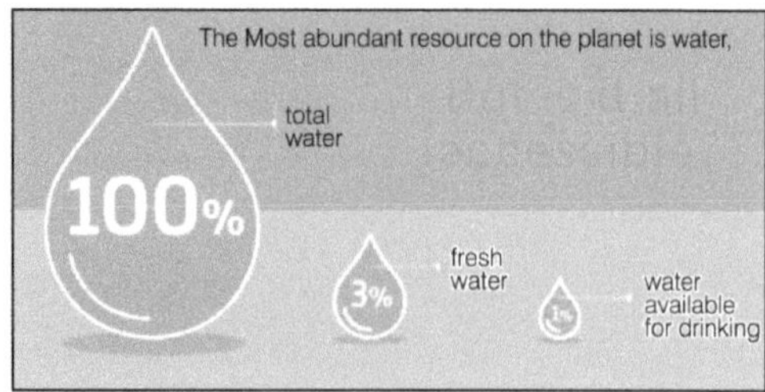

Based on your understanding of the passage, answer any five out of seven questions by choosing the correct option.   5 × 1 = 5

8. The purpose of the passage is to .... Choose the correct option.
(a) focus on the importance and use of water
(b) focus on the lack of water
(c) focus on process of saving water
(d) None of the above

9. Select the option that is true for the statements given below.
1. The groundwater supply is reducing over time.
2. Water should be carefully harnessed and conserved.
(a) (1) is the result of (2)
(b) (2) is the result of (1)
(c) (1) is the reason for (2)
(d) (1) is independent of (2)

10. Select the option that gives the correct meaning of the following statements.
'Many a drop makes on ocean.'
(a) Small efforts can lead to big results
(b) Collect water drops to make an ocean
(c) Collect water to fill the water tanks
(d) Both (b) and (c)

11. According to the passage, …… can help in conserving water.
(a) installation of water taps   (b) having a garden
(c) keeping taps closed   (d) All of these

12. Select the option that lists the reason for water shortage.
1. Less amount of fresh water
2. Repairing of water leakage
3. Mismanagement of water
4. Over-extraction of water
5. Drinking ground water
(a) 1, 4 and 5 (b) 1, 3 and 4 (c) 2, 4 and 5 (d) 2, 3 and 5

13. What percentage of available water is potable?
(a) 3%   (b) 97%   (c) 1%   (d) 0.01%

14. This passage suggests that if we don't save water today, we'll ……………… .
Select the correct option.
(a) have to drink ocean water later
(b) have to drink recycled water later
(c) we'll have no drinkable water later
(d) Both (b) and (c)

Section B
Grammar

III. Attempt any five questions from the following seven questions.   5 × 1 = 5
(i) Mohan said, "we …… go to see the Taj on the moonlit night".
(ii) She said, 'My parents …… (go) to karachi.'
(iii) Childhood is the time when there are …… responsibilities to make life difficult.
(iv) … child finds pleasure in playing in the rain.
(v) Goa …… the smallest state of India.
(vi) Change the given sentence into Indirect speech.
Trisha said, "I will go to fancy restaurant with my friends".
(vii) Change the given sentence into Direct speech.
Mohit advised his friend to be cautious of monkeys on the top of the hill.

Writing

IV. You are Garima / Girish, Manager, Sindhu Enterprises, Ranchi. You need various furniture items for your newly constructed head office. Write a letter to M/S office Equipment Corporation, Ranchi, placing a bulk order for various items of office furniture (minimum), giving necessary details. Ask for discount on bulk purchase and base your order on the suppliers quotation on OEC / 34/17-18.   **2**

Or You are karishma / Mihir of D-47, South Street, Delhi. You saw an advertisement regarding Diwali offers on purchase of new HP Laptops. Write a letter to the Manager of HP World, Kamla Nagar, Delhi to enquire about the offered prices, their terms and conditions, etc.

V. The chart shows the division of household tasks by gender in Great Britain. Write an analytical paragraph describing the chart given below.   **3**

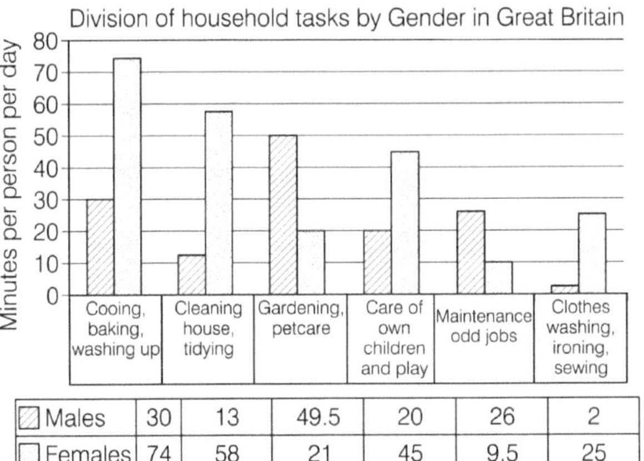

Males	30	13	49.5	20	26	2
Females	74	58	21	45	9.5	25

Or Gautam was alarmed to see the graph that tracked the rising levels of Carbon dioxide in the air of his city, Kanpur. He decided to write a paragraph on the data to show his alarm and painted the present picture in order to caution people against environment pollution. Write the analytical paragraph for Gautam.

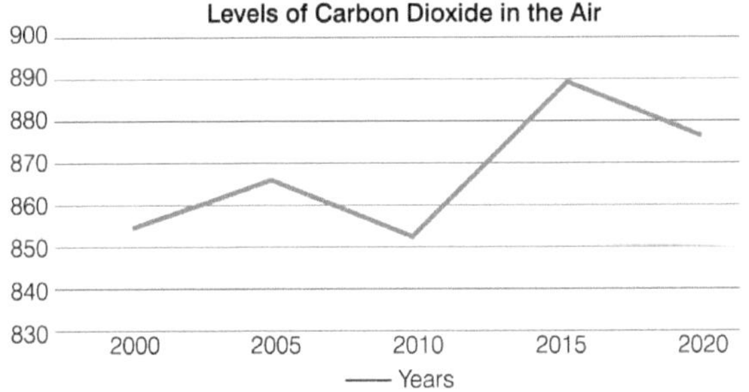

Section C   Literature

VI. Read the following extract and answer the questions that follow.

They do not sweat and whine about their condition,

They do not lie awake in the dark and weep for their sins,

They do not make me sick discussing their duty to God,

Not one is dissatisfied, not one is demented with the mania of owning things,

Not one kneels to another, nor to his kind that lived thousands of years ago,   **3 × 1 = 3**

(i) Which poetic device is used in the first three lines of the extract?

(ii) Who is being referred to as 'they'?

(iii) Which qualities of 'they' are mentioned in the above extract?

Or

Suddenly, suddenly they heard a nasty sound,

And Mustard growled and they all looked around .

Meowch! cried Ink and ooh! cried Belinda,

For there was a pirate, climbing in the winda.

(i) Why did Mustard growl?

(ii) What is the rhyming scheme of the above extract?

(iii) Find a word in the extract which means 'unpleasant'.

VII. Read the following extract and answer the questions that follow.

The day of the ball arrived. Mme Loisel was a great success. She was the prettiest of all - elegant, gracious, smiling and full of joy. All the men noticed her, asked her name, and wanted to be presented. She danced with enthusiasm, intoxicated with pleasure, thinking of nothing but all this admiration, this victory so complete and sweet to her heart.   **3 × 1 = 3**

(i) Why was Mme Loisel a success at the ball?

(ii) What do you understand by the phrase 'intoxicated with pleasure'?

(iii) What does "this victory so complete and sweet to her heart" mean?

Or

"I know Oliver's mother. She's a terror," Bill sighed. "I took a trunk out there for her once, and she almost took my skin off because I didn't treat it like a box of eggs. She's about nine feet tall and four feet thick and quick as a cat, and she sure can talk. I'll bet Oliver heard that somebody's chasing him, and he's gone on there to hide behind his mother's skirts. Well, we'll try her. But you'd better let me do it, boy. You may be great at literature and law, but you haven't had real training in swearing."

(i) Why did the speaker say that Oliver's mother almost took his skin off?

(ii) Which literary device is used in the line "She's about nine feet tall and four feet thick and quick as a cat"?

(iii) What is the tone of the speaker when he says, "I'll bet Oliver heard that somebody's chasing him, and he's gone on there to hide behind his mother's skirts"?

VIII. Answer the following questions. (*Attempt any 2*).

(i) Which project of Ebright won the first prize in the county fair and made him enter the International Science and Engineering Fair?

(ii) How does the author describe 'Coorg'?

(iii) Do you think that Amanda is at fault?

IX. Answer the following questions.

(i) The idea of spirituality and equality are ingrained in animals. Explain.

Or

The story 'Madam Rides the Bus' has a lot of people talking in it. The conductor jokes and laughs with Valli, some passengers try to show their concern for her. Do you think in real life as well, people would react in a similar way when seeing an eight-year old travelling alone in a bus? Support your answers with examples from the text.

(ii) Describe the character of Bholi from the story 'Bholi'.

Or

Everyone in New Mullion was involved in befooling the narrator. Give instances from the story to prove the same.

Printed by Libri Plureos GmbH in Hamburg,
Germany